ATLAS OF NEVER BUILT ARCHITECTURE

ATLAS OF NEVER BUILT ARCHITECTURE

Atlas of Never Built Architecture

Sam Lubell and Greg Goldin

[99]

[20]

[104

ATLAS OF NEVER BUILT ARCHITECTURE

INTRODUCTION
By Sam Lubell and Greg Goldin

In his essay 'The Monuments of Passaic' (1967), the artist Robert Smithson refers to the yet-to-be-built suburban-scape of Passaic, New Jersey, as 'ruins in reverse'. The edifices of this imagined, history-free world, he continues, 'will be the opposite of the romantic ruin, because the buildings don't fall into ruin after they are built but rather rise into ruin before they are built'.

That a building could become *anything* tangible – be it remarkable or despicable, banal or glorious, revolutionary or preposterous – despite not being built is a testament to the fact that buildings are much more than simply concrete, stone, timber and glass. They are foremost a collection of ideas, but also of stories, struggles, cultures and fateful circumstances – materialized, or not, in built form. The built, achieved relatively infrequently, is the tiny shadow cast by a pantheon of ghosts. In exploring the never-built we are engaging in a treasure hunt for the rest of the story: those elusive, often invisible chimeras. A sometimes gruelling search for an alternative reality.

As much the story of failure as it is of triumph, history is littered with countless projects that never made it beyond the drawing board. The first architectural competition, it is said, was a call to build a structure atop the Acropolis in Athens to commemorate the expulsion of the Persian king Xerxes, who had sacked the ancient city in 480 BC. The alternative versions of the Erechtheion are lost, so our concept of Athens – and, perhaps, of classical architecture in its entirety – revolves around a shard selected from a plethora of ideas now eternally buried by the passage of time.

History is written by the victors. Regimes change, architects die and collections are lost, discarded by grieving relatives or shredded by storage companies when overdue bills go unpaid. Or perhaps consumed by fire, as happened with most of the documentation for the thousands of drawings by the pioneering Black architect Paul Revere Williams when his office was torched during the Los Angeles riots of 1992 (luckily, the drawings themselves were later found intact). Erasure is commonplace, sometimes through neglect, sometimes through bad timing, sometimes through malice. Then, too, when something does get built, the unbuilt is often forgotten or, worse, written out of the official record. It is said that Robert Moses, Parks Commissioner and one-time tsar of New York City, had all the drawings of his immediate predecessors destroyed; he did not want any record to exist other than his own. And often, when nothing is built at all – when every proposition remains on paper – the absence begets a totalizing erasure.

Fortunately, over the centuries, drawings, notes, proposals, sketches, paintings, scribbles and other records have been preserved, set aside by hoarders, prescient collectors or alert librarians anxious to keep ephemeral existences alive. Our hunt for these amnesiac riches – in the case of this book, a journey around the world from the first decade of the twentieth century to the present day – began in archives, architecture studios and history books, on websites or any place that contains traces of what could have been. Slowly, both systematically and randomly, we uncovered projects that were on the cusp of realization.

As we unearthed each treasure, shaking off the dust clouds of memory and the inscrutability of faded ink, we were reminded that our reality is far less fixed than we think. Every decision could have resulted in something else. Every tower or bridge or stadium or vacant plot could have been utterly different – or nothing at all. That banal, boxy office building, suited to an industrial park but planted in a key part of downtown, could have been a tower raised on a single, improbable, gravity-defying leg, its presence sparking an architectural upheaval. That city could have boasted a space-age-fuselage monorail, not an ugly, elevated overpass piercing its heart. Another historic medieval town centre could have been levelled beneath a faux-neoclassical assemblage, an organic place made over, Disney-like, into someone's cribbed version of civic space. Likewise, our future could be much less, well, futuristic, than we imagine. It could be where we are living now, amid the less-than-inspired, with the magically inspired consigned to the ash heap of history.

Once we had uncovered the finds we were faced with perhaps the most difficult task of all: distillation and curation. Because the never-built is so common – a sliding scale depending on the visionary nature of an architect or firm – there were thousands upon thousands of projects to choose from. Our 'shortlist' of more than 5,000 was slowly distilled to 1,000, then (a nightmare for this pair of encyclopaedists) mercilessly cut to 350, leaving us with a list whose impact wooed us especially. We're left with a constellation within a galaxy.

Smithson is one of thousands of exceptional names consigned to our chopping block. His proposal for the Dallas Fort Worth Regional Airport included a series of 'earthworks' visible only from the air: circular mounds, squiggling berms, deep craters, angular pathways. It's an inspired concept that we tore from our list because it didn't fit into the category of 'architecture'. And so it went; as we culled, we encountered revelation upon revelation, yet fewer and fewer could fit into the final 'built' book.

The initial surveying complete, we dug into perhaps the most important discovery, at least intellectually: the idea. Some were timeless, others ridiculous, but each, in its own way, was valuable. There were ideas to make cities rational, or to barricade them with freeways. There were ideas for inflatable buildings or underground ones. Ideas persist after buildings die, only to rise again. IM Pei never realized his sculptural chapel for the Inter-American University in Puerto Rico, but its soaring carillon served as a template for the freestanding Joy of Angels Bell Tower that he would design twenty-five years later for the sanctuary of Shinji Shumeikai in Japan. His angular, diagrid-supported BDNI tower in Jakarta, killed by the Asian financial crisis in 1997, would serve as the template for his Bank of China skyscraper in Hong Kong.

Sometimes the idea is the *only* thing: a speculative concept meant as a provocation or a creative release; in the words of the French theorist Michel Ragon, the 'fruit of [the architect's] own initiative'. James Wines, for one, sought to subvert Modernism by shredding the austerity of architectural formalism – 'putting art where you least expect to find it', he said – with such deliberate inversions as Highrise of Homes (1981), a tower composed, as its name suggests, of single-family abodes. The spatial cities of Kenzo Tange, John Johansen (page 66) and Yona Friedman instigated a new approach to urbanism, literally stepping over and rising above the messiness of the urban grid. In the mid-1960s the Polish metaphysical genius Jan Głuszak, known simply as 'Dagarama', drew mega-buildings in crayon and watercolour, 'guardians of life' that could shutter themselves from tsunamis, and 'sunflowers' powered by solar energy, chronicling global warming six decades ahead of reality.

From the beginning of the twentieth century to the early 1970s, such ideas floated on a superstructure of political, social and economic upheaval. Long before the Russian Revolution conferred upon the world Constructivism (as in Vladimir Tatlin's Tower project, c.1920) and supremacism (as in El Lissitzky's proposed Cloud Iron towers for Moscow, 1924), the French architect Tony Garnier cooked up a utopian Socialist city, La Cité Industrielle, inspired by Émile Zola's novel *Travail* (Labour; 1901), in which work is organized around scientific principles, and happiness ensues. Architecture, in a sense, wasn't form following function. It was form following ideology.

Often utopian designs were – somehow – intended for realization, connecting them urgently, if unrealistically, to the poetry, normality and humming chaos of reality. Take Nicolas Schöffer's 347 m (1,138 ft) Tour Lumière Cybernétique (1969; page 156). A fantasia of antennae, hygrometers, thermometers, anemometers, photoelectric cells, microphones and 3,226 colour projectors hanging from a steel-frame structure, the device used three central computers to record, process, regulate and rationalize life in Paris. The tower was a technological marvel, an engineering feat, a madly expressive anarchy, a three-dimensional representation of cyberspace. But it proved anathema. The fumes of the student/worker uprising of May 1968 eclipsed, once and for all, any architectural scheme touted to solve society's ills, particularly a top-down, technocratic proposition redolent with mechanisms for control rather than scaffolds for freedom.

ATLAS OF NEVER BUILT ARCHITECTURE

Architects are forever using philosophy to cloak themselves in, and one can trace this endless succession of 'new' concepts across time and geography, unearthing its connections to, and prescriptions for, the swirling currents of history, narrating the stories of civilization in a novel way. Never-builts from post-colonial sub-Saharan Africa, for instance, tell the tale of newly independent nations importing outsiders to express their national identity. From Côte d'Ivoire to Nigeria, Angola to Zambia, Ghana to Kenya, architects from Scandinavia, the United States, Japan and Israel, and even from the former colonizing powers, have attempted (and in some cases succeeded) to build whole capital cities from scratch, including parliaments, central banks, universities, memorials, arenas, bus stations and markets. Even when the Zairean strongman Mobutu Sese Seko initiated his doctrine of *recours à l'authenticité*, intended to remake the former Belgian colony in the true image of Africa, his chief architect was an Italian modernist. No idea seemed too foreign: Brutalism, Metabolism, Modernism, hyperbolic parabolas. If it occurred outside Africa, it was likely to be reprised within.

Similar stories can be found in the Middle East, where the architectural lingua franca of Europe and the United States was adopted to project a forward-looking image onto nations, such as Iraq, that hoped to gain presence and prestige on the world stage. The greats – Oscar Niemeyer, Le Corbusier, Walter Gropius, Marcel Breuer, Jørn Utzon, Frank Lloyd Wright, Arthur Erickson – were invited to lay out everything from rivieras, corniches, museums, universities and libraries to entire cities.

Amid our untiring excavation for this book we came across another treasure: the designers who dreamed the ideas up. Of course our 'heroes', the usual suspects, are on this list, allowing us to shine new light on the history and progress of their concepts. But inevitably – or, more accurately, concurrently – remarkable architects were doing remarkable work beyond the canon. In Mozambique, Pancho Guedes. In Uruguay, Eladio Dieste. In Sri Lanka, Geoffrey Bawa. In Egypt, Hassan Fathy. Francisco Salamone in Argentina; André Ravéreau in Algeria. In Mexico, Enrique de la Mora y Palomar. In almost every instance, their architecture is rooted in place and in the imagination, and emancipated from the arguments that were concocted to bolster the dominant forms sallying forth from the world's centres of power and wealth. Often, this was hands-on, a product of local traditions and designs absorbed and recombined and given new expression. After all, the past 120 years have brought not just rapid industrialization and the birth of the information age, enmeshing all seven continents in a global network of commerce and instantaneous data, but also, in fits and starts, a swelling resistance keyed to keeping language, custom and inherited knowledge alive. Architecture exists within this tension.

And then we came across the most visceral discovery: the hand of the architect, showcasing incalculable artistic virtuosity, distilling dreams into tangible form. Architects may read and write treatises, and borrow from the philosophers of the day – Jacques Derrida's deconstructivism, for example, fuelled a recent generation of architects – but in drawings (yes, drawings, connected physically to body and spirit, as opposed to computer-aided designs, which enforce their own templates and shape increasingly disconnected visions) they convey the true form of their work. There is nothing quite like encountering, at first hand, a vellum sheet of James Rossant's fine pencil lines: line upon line upon line, creating a grid, emphasizing the scale and geometry of a proposed set of stables for New York's Central Park. Or Marion Mahony Griffin's magisterial watercolour projections of solids and voids in repetitive motifs, after the design by her husband, Walter Burley Griffin, for the Municipal Office in Ahmedabad, India. Or the work of Hungary's Imre Makovecz (page 207), whose unique visions seamlessly merge natural and built forms until the two become indistinguishable. A cathedral melts into the craggy monumentality of a mountain; a youth centre inherits the awe-inspiring skeletal frame inherent to a whale. Architecture was built out of the forms and images flowing from hand to paper.

In this sense, unbuilt works are pure, unadulterated visions. They have escaped the inevitable editing and slashes inflicted by the marketplace or politics, which, sadly, often smudge brilliant imagery into dulled-down reality. That may explain why most architects labour over 'lost' projects, sometimes for decades, while others refuse to make them public, fearful that imperfections will be spotted or that they will become an image 'hung as status-trophy by rising executives', as the poet WH Auden so aptly put it.

Still, drawings do assume lives of their own. Images of unrealized projects can even become more influential than built buildings. Take a snapshot of Heinz and Bodo Rasch's Hanging Houses for Stuttgart, Germany, in 1927 (page 153), and put it side by side with Paul Maymont's Étude Extension de Paris (1962) or Édouard Albert's Hôtels Suspendus of 1964 (which he called 'tour arborescente', 'tree tower'; page 158), and an unmistakable lineage appears. For the Rasch brothers, under the sway of an economy being transformed by the assembly line, mass-produced, industrial-age houses would be suspended from towers. In Maymont's version, decades later, the scattered towers became literal cities in the air, rising above the existing topography on Olympian-scaled masts. Albert had a more modest, one-at-a-time approach, whereby individual, boxy houses, mantled in distinctive geometrically patterned glass, were lofted into airspace, like cargo dangling from a crane. The theme remains the same: capture the space above a city, and build upwards on stilts, pillars and masts.

This brought us at last to the abiding question for each project: why wasn't it built? As we explored that eternal question we uncovered the events and systems, the physical and ideological armature that meant that these ideas were not realistic – the intellectual and logistical soil that instead of allowing them to flourish, led to their collapse.

The reasons buildings materialize are the same reasons they inevitably dematerialize. Economies boom, then bust. The Great Depression of 1929, like a force of nature, tossed aside thousands of remarkable ideas, as did the Great Recession beginning in 2007, which, like a tidal wave, swallowed up the work of apparently untouchable starchitects from Zaha Hadid to Frank Gehry. Wars wipe cities clean, then stop dreams of renewed glory; just think of Albert Speer's 'Germania' or Mussolini's 'New Rome'. Political attitudes are fickle, in dictatorial as well as democratic regimes. Developers' whims force architects aside, as James Cheng, whose towers define Vancouver's skyline, says: 'The invisible hand of the marketplace draws at least three-quarters of downtown Vancouver.' Tragedy strikes; what if Matthew Nowicki had designed the Indian city of Chandigarh (page 307), as he was commissioned to do, instead of dying in a plane crash? And fads come and go; just look at Claude Parent, who went from being the It-boy, with his tilted-plane constructs, to designing nuclear power plants.

And then, far too many gifted visionaries are so prickly, independent or uncompromising – pick your favourite descriptor for unacceptable character traits for an outsider in a collaborative profession – that the better part of their legacy is sheafs of ideas and inspirations labelled 'Never Built'. 'I don't have orders or clients and nobody knows me,' noted Fernando Higueras, a wonderful example of a lonely, brave, cigar-chomping soloist. 'I am aware that my toughest enemy has been me. The life I have and saying what I say has a price which is not having a job. But I am a billionaire in time.'

Ultimately, not building, the Italian master Carlo Scarpa remarks with bitter accuracy, is the only way to ensure peace. Discussing his unbuilt Civic Theatre in Vicenza (page 180), he says, 'It is better to do nothing than to do the theatre; that way everyone will be happy: the city council because it has avoided the criticism that can be directed at those who do something; [...] the opposition because it can say that the administration does nothing, after trumpeting the theatre; those who do not want the theatre, because it will not be there; those who do want it, because they can continue to complain that there is no theatre; and meanwhile dreaming, each on his own, of an ideal theatre, made in his own image and likeness.'

Ah, but what dreams! What ideals! Their spirits, like ours even when they depart our bodies, don't disappear. Somehow they mingle with reality, haunting us, enchanting us, tempting us, urging us on. Perchance to dream, indeed. In the never-built, one finds the afterlife of dreams. We are fortunate to be able to peer into that realm, and ponder all that it can offer. Step inside with us.

North & Central America

ATLAS OF NEVER BUILT ARCHITECTURE

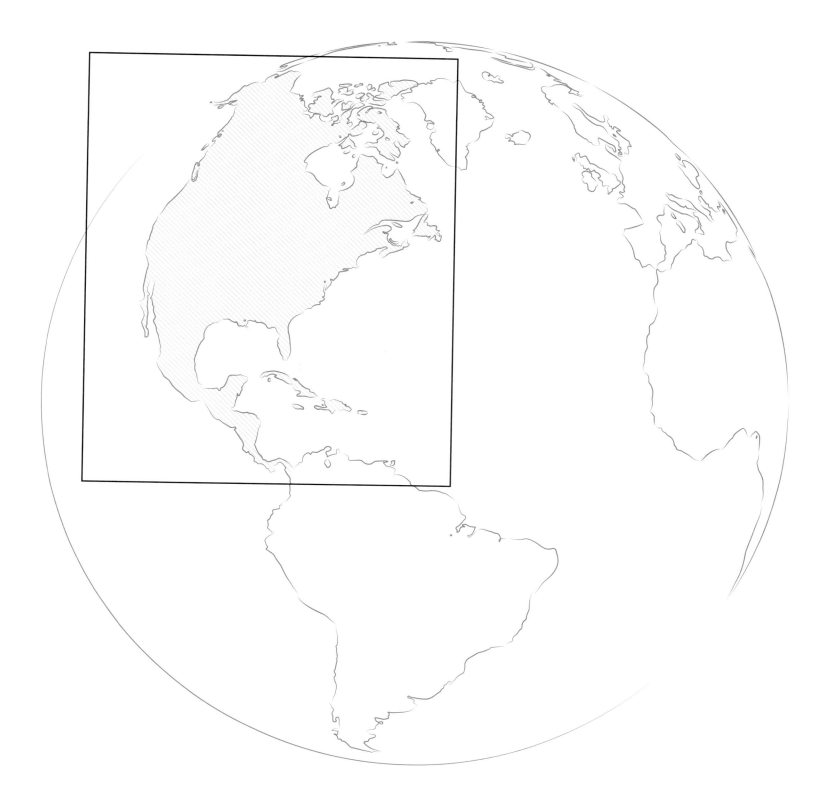

CA [8]

US [72]

MX [10]

CU [5]

DO [1]   PR [1]

SV [1]

MARPOLE-OAKRIDGE COMMUNITY CENTRE
Patkau Architects
Vancouver, British Columbia, (CA), 2010

The Marpole-Oakridge Community Centre, which opened in 1949, was park-filled Vancouver's first, but after seventy years the building was destined for demolition. The city hired

Patkau Architects to ponder what kind of structure ought to occupy a corner of the neighbourhood park, which was surrounded by modest one- and two-storey homes.

Patkau's design flowed from a wish to speak directly to Vancouver's warm – and getting warmer – summers and wet – and getting wetter – winters. The aim was also to build with light. This led to a building with deep overhangs to provide shelter from rain and glare, and to lessen interior heat gain. Glass walls and strategically placed rooflights brought in natural illumination.

Although the two-storey structure was a concrete frame with steel and glulam beams, the undersides of the exterior roof overhangs and the interior walls were made of wood, the supple texture of which would radiate warmth and harmonize with the lush park grounds and tree-lined streets.

It was the building's roofline silhouettes, however, that set it apart. Viewed from the long side, the roof looked a little like a bat fluttering its wings. The sharply climbing walls of the gym, sloping outwards at approximately twenty

degrees, were like the precipice of a ski slope, perhaps inspired by nearby Cypress Mountain. The angular superstructure hung from V-shaped columns of tubular steel, tied together with a wooden version of Mackintosh trusses.

In early 2018 the Patkau plan was still alive, but by November 2019 the city was considering a new community centre with an outdoor pool. Patkau's proposal wasn't even mentioned.

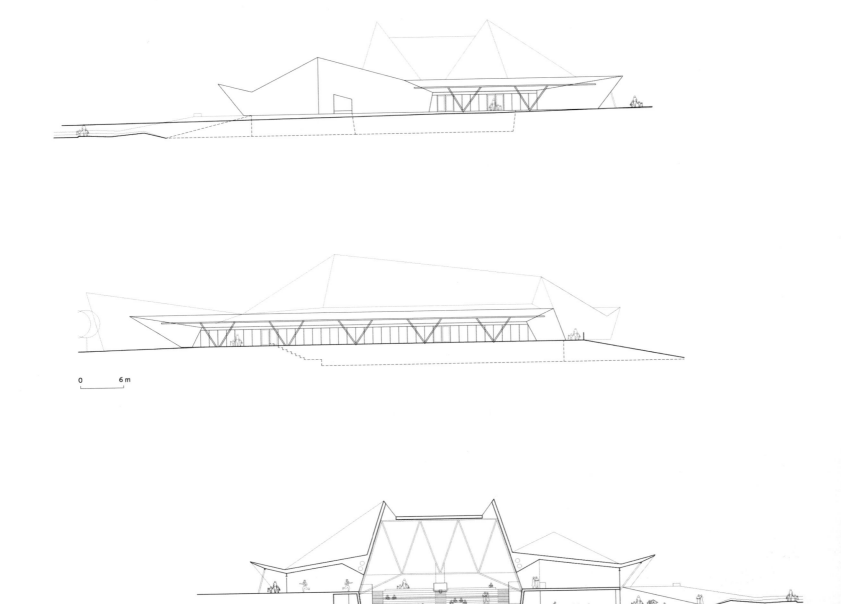

0   6 m

0   6 m

CHINESE ART MUSEUM
AT ROBSON SQUARE
Bing Thom
Vancouver, British Columbia
(CA), 2015

Vancouver has been described as 'an architectural underperformer', its skyline crammed with carbon-copy condos and its narrow residential streets overwhelmed by lot-line-to-lot-line McMansions. Bing Thom was one of a handful of home-grown architects who defied the slide into mediocrity.

Thom's idea for the Chinese Art Museum germinated in the early 2010s, when the Vancouver Art Gallery was thinking of moving out of its neoclassical building of 1911 on Robson Square. For a time, the gallery and the city's concert hall were trying to see how both institutions might be squeezed onto the downtown superblock. Thom, who had been involved in Robson Square's design as a young architect working with Arthur Erickson, had been thinking of burying the art gallery underneath the plaza. When the gallery's plan to move to a new museum, designed by Herzog & de Meuron, gained city approval, he revisited his idea.

Thom's new concept was to bury the Chinese Art Museum. The existing landscaped knolls that occupied the area would be replaced, transformed into undulating eyebrow-shaped rooftops covering a series of glass-fronted lobbies. The arching rooftops were incised with pleated stairs, which could be occupied by anyone wishing to gaze out at the passing scene. The museum itself was spread over several underground levels, conceived in partnership with the Palace Museum at the Forbidden City in Beijing and the Victoria and Albert Museum in London. Thom died in 2016, and a year later Martin Roth, director of the V&A, also passed away. The museum idea was shelved.

CANADA

GOVERNMENT OF CANADA BUILDING
Arthur Erickson
Vancouver, British Columbia, (CA), 1977

Arthur Erickson, one of Canada's triumvirate of great twentieth-century architects, left an indelible stamp on his home town, Vancouver. His mythically scaled Simon Fraser University, his

below-grade civic plaza at Robson Square, and his cast-in-place concrete post-and-beam Anthropology Museum at the University of British Columbia still dominate the city. But there is always one project that an architect wishes never got away, and in Erickson's case, that was his Government of Canada Building.

The site, a block-square surface car park in the heart of Vancouver's central business district, was flanked by the Queen Elizabeth Theatre complex and the Canadian Broadcasting Corporation's bulky building. Erickson proposed

that the immense expanse of office space required for federal bureaucrats be housed in a Zeppelin-like structure set roughly ten floors above the street. His notion was to build a long truss, supported at either end on massive concrete pilings, which would be, in his words, 'externalized as a kind of exoskeleton'. Erickson believed that the metal skein would diminish the size of the tandem buildings, and make them appear lighter, reflecting 'western Canada's traditional antipathy towards distant Ottawa', the nation's capital.

In March 1978 the Greater Vancouver Regional District directors' planning committee gave the building the official nod, permitting Ottawa to increase its size by nearly a third to 83,600 sq. m (900,000 sq. ft). A month later the *Vancouver Sun* reported that the plan was on hold, awaiting 'the day when Ottawa, the masters of delay, will erect the Arthur Erickson-designed building'. It never came.

PARK CENTRE
KPF
Calgary, Alberta (CA), 1981

There's nothing like an oil boom to pump new buildings into the pipeline. In the late 1970s the American cities of Denver and Houston, and Calgary in western Canada, were booming with oil and buildings. In 1979 Calgary's construction frenzy led to more new office space opening there than in New York City and Chicago combined. Cadillac Fairview, Toronto's mega commercial developer, wanted the young New York firm of Kohn Pedersen Fox (KPF) to establish a foothold in 'Cowtown'. KPF had recently completed the American Oil Company tower in Denver, a high-rise 134 m (440 ft) tall with subtle, rounded corners and aluminium bands that gave the skyscraper a soft, satin allure.

A Eugene Kohn handed the design – planned as two fifty-storey towers with a Four Seasons Hotel tucked between them – to his associate Arthur May. May, who had studied with Louis Kahn and had been something of a strict Modernist, was by the early 1980s moving towards postmodernism. His massive office towers hinted at Modernism, being square, with their columns expressed on the exterior. But that's the sum of May's concessions. Park Centre was nakedly postmodern. The towers were an amalgamation of stair-stepped 1920s granite skyscrapers and post-war glass-and-steel monoliths. Shed roofs were appended to the tops of the otherwise spruce-straight structures; a steer's horn-shaped pediment, with a clock in the middle, dangled from a five-storey arch; and a medieval cupola sprouted at the entrance to the hotel.

Kohn fought with May on his 'extreme PoMo', he says, 'but didn't win'. Like all oil booms, the bust of 1984 came with swift finality. Park Centre was dead.

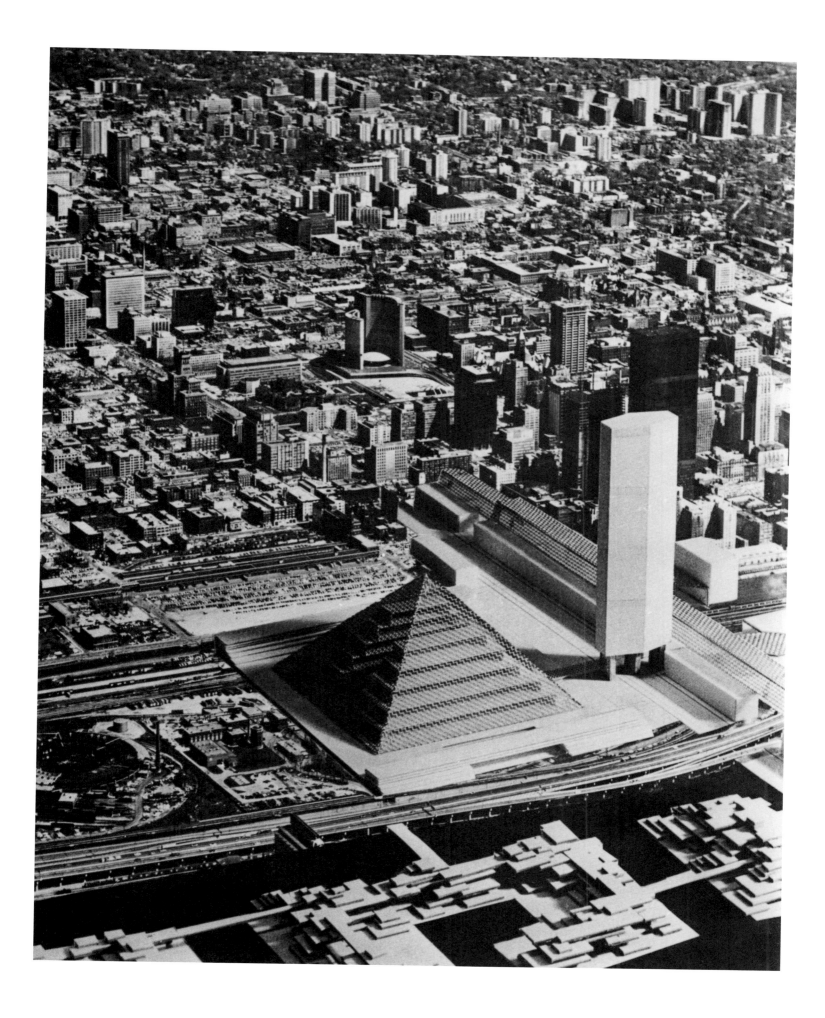

PROJECT TORONTO
Richard Buckminster Fuller & Shoji Sadao
Toronto, Ontario (CA), 1968

Soon after Gerald Gladstone had been commissioned to make three pieces for Expo '67, the Montreal world's fair that put a mirror polish on a technological future, the Toronto sculptor approached Richard Buckminster Fuller, whose geodesic dome had been a huge hit at the Expo, with a tempting offer. Could Fuller imagine buttoned-up Toronto as a completely different, more unrestrained city?

Gladstone's invitation might have remained a cordial correspondence, except that Fuller said 'Yes.' By February 1968 John Bassett, the publisher of the *Toronto Telegram* and president of the television channel CFTO-TV, jumped in to commission Fuller and his partner, Shoji Sadao, to issue a report on Toronto in the twenty-first century. Fuller's first response was the seventy-eight-page 'Project Toronto', detailing his idea that Toronto should build an entirely new waterfront university. He envisioned a 'Crystal Pyramid' 122 m (400 ft) high, shielding two twenty-storey buildings housing shops, galleries and restaurants, a 'Gateway Tower' skyscraper, and an enclosed galleria nearly 1 km (more than half a mile) long, served by a monorail to whisk people to and from the water's edge. But that was not all. Fuller sought to build three floating 'Pro-To-Cities', townships of 3,500–6,500 residents, living in prefabricated houses bobbing on Lake Ontario atop three-sided steel buoys. The floating settlements, complete with supermarkets and schools, could be tugged to different locations at the neighbourhood's whim.

Fuller's price tag was $1 billion. Senior politicians happily met with him, but really only to conciliate the acknowledged genius. The competing newspaper summed it up perfectly: 'The big plan with a small future.' So it was.

CITÉ DES TERRACES/ PROJECT M3
Arthur Erickson, Geoffrey Massey
Montreal, Quebec (CA), 1968

Despite its epic scale, Arthur Erickson and Geoffrey Massey's residential complex for a whopping thirty thousand people atop a Montreal railyard was surprisingly human-centred.

Curved to hug the edges of the site (which was shaped by curving railway tracks and surrounding freeways), the two-building plan left space for a sweeping central park and plaza.

True to its name, the project's hallmark design element consisted of large, inset balconies (terraced on lower levels, vertical above), giving each resident sizeable outdoor space. The developer Marathon Realty, the Canadian Pacific Railway's real-estate arm, agreed to let Erickson test the prevailing orthodoxy of single-use planning, creating a mixed-use 'omnibuilding' or *ensemble*

multifunctional, filled with shopping and recreation carved out by the structures' A-shaped bases. (The architect observed that these active indoor elements were well suited to Montreal's 'bleak winters' and 'urban culture'.)

Erickson and Massey, working in partnership with the local firm David & Boulva, pleaded continuously with Marathon to shrink the overscaled project so as to make it more humane. 'The familiar condominium fortress-tower exhibits little thought for the common welfare,' Erickson remarked. They even hired a sociol-

ogist, who predicted 'social disconnection' for those living too far from the ground. The team also proposed greenery-filled outdoor circulation to soften the complex's impact: 'On good days it would have been marvellous coming down forty floors on those planted, terraced roofs,' Erickson said. But Marathon held firm, and the city eventually rejected the project, largely owing to its overwhelming density.

CENTRE SIMARD
Victor Prus
Lac à l'Eau Claire, Quebec (CA), 1963

The Polish-born Canadian architect Victor Prus, once a researcher for Richard Buckminster Fuller at Princeton University, played a crucial role in the development of modern Quebec province, creating lightweight glass-and-steel stadia, theatres, convention centres and apartments in Montreal, Québec City and beyond. In 1963 he teamed up with the Montreal-based management guru James T McCay and Léon Simard, a scion of one of the province's richest families, to create the International Centre for Advanced Studies in Human Development. Otherwise known as the Centre Simard, it would host research, exhibitions and symposia to help civilization better adapt to the era's astonishing technological change. 'If the human race is to survive it will have to change its way of thinking more in the next twenty-five years than in the last twenty-five thousand,' the philosopher and economist Kenneth Boulding noted in the project's promotional material.

Resembling a basalt-carved hillock, or perhaps a giant porcupine, the centre would occupy a rolling site in Lac à l'Eau Claire, halfway between Montreal and Québec. Filled with libraries, auditoria, exhibition spaces and even a television studio, its domed form consisted of a finely stepped 'weathershield' of plastic hexagonal cones, hovering over a greenery-filled base.

As time wore on, the project, renamed the Integron Centre, was doomed when McCay badly insulted a local official. The team went on to offer the (now patented) concept to several more cities, and even proposed a version to be sited atop Alcatraz Island (pictured above) after the prison was decommissioned. None of the ideas won approval.

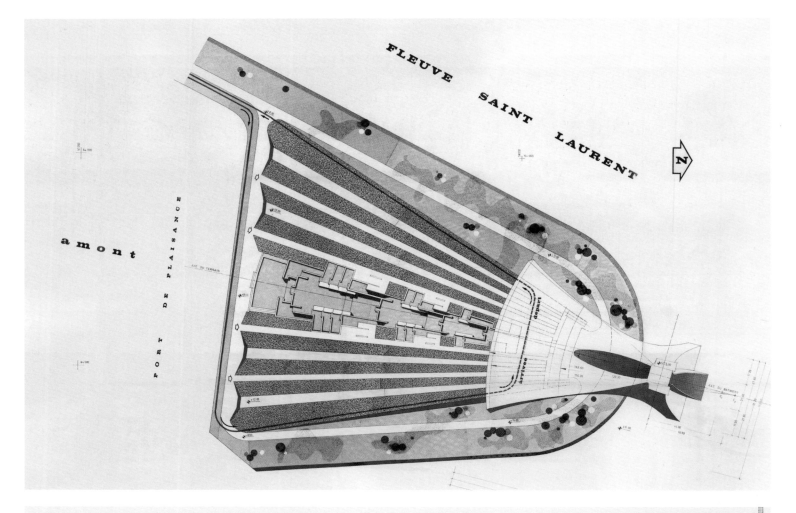

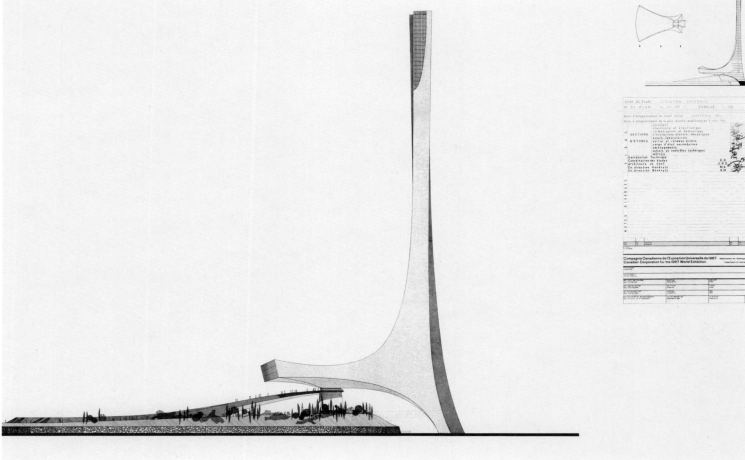

TOUR PARIS-MONTRÉAL
City of Montreal
Montreal (CA), 1967

Far-fetched ideas often beget even more far-fetched fantasies. Take the announcement by Montreal mayor Jean Drapeau on 11 December 1964 that he'd teamed up with Paris to build the Tour Paris-Montréal, a $20 million cantilevered concrete tower that would be the chief attraction for Expo '67.

Drapeau returned from a top-secret mission to Paris toting plans and a model for a tower 325 m (1,066 ft) tall to celebrate the 325th anniversary of the city of Montreal. The leaning pillar looked like 'a giant golf driver', the local paper, *The Gazette*, sniped. Sitting at the tip of Île Ste-Hélène, in the St Lawrence River, it would be taller than the Eiffel Tower, and second only to the Empire State Building in height. From its pinnacle, reached by banks of triple-decker lifts, the view would have extended 80 km (50 miles) in all directions. Expo officials were initially lukewarm about the idea, but Commissioner-General Pierre Dupuy did an about-face, he said, when 'confronted with a work of art which will become one of the best specimens of modern art for the next 30 or 50 years'.

Expo adopted the *Tour*, but the initial cost studies delivered the fatally bad news. The tower couldn't be built for $20 million, so Paris dropped out. Undeterred, Drapeau proposed that the Eiffel Tower be dismantled and shipped to Montreal for Expo. President Charles de Gaulle supposedly gave his blessing, but the French quietly scoffed, offering to lend their monument if Montreal could guarantee to preserve the 18,038 pieces of metal, 2.5 million rivets and 60 tonnes of paint, all of which had to be returned, intact. And that was the end of that idea.

CANADA

PROJECT FOR A COVERED STADIUM
Myron Goldsmith
Squaw Valley, California (US), 1957

Myron Goldsmith never became a household name, even though some of his built work is revered for its taut temperament and clear-headed concision. Goldsmith, who spent almost 30 years at Skidmore, Owings & Merrill, and taught at the Illinois Institute of Technology, built one famous stadium: the Oakland Coliseum, across the bay from San Francisco. It is notable for its circular arena 128 m (420 ft) in diameter, enclosed by a glass wall 21 m (70 ft) tall, behind enormous concrete X-braces.

Goldsmith's Squaw Valley stadium, conceived a decade before the Coliseum, was tightrope restraint by comparison. He had just completed a two-year stint in Rome, studying with Pier Luigi Nervi and, among other things, helping him with a competition entry for a velodrome for the forthcoming 1960 Rome Olympics. Newly arrived at SOM's San Francisco office, Goldsmith conceived a thin-shell concrete skating rink for the Winter Olympics in Squaw Valley, on the banks of the Truckee River. The clear-span arena was redolent of the work of Nervi. The rink was covered by an ultra-thin tortoise shell-shaped lid hung from a pair of concrete arches. Structural ceiling ribs composed a crisp lattice of compressed and relieved arcs, as if the roof were held aloft by bent, flexible tent poles. The roof floated freely above the arena, itself a bowl formed by twin embankments enclosing the rink.

Precisely why Goldsmith's skating rink was rejected by the promoters of the Squaw Valley Olympics is not known. In its place, they built Russell Francis Stechschulte's hip-roofed, cable-supported, ski lodge-inflected arena.

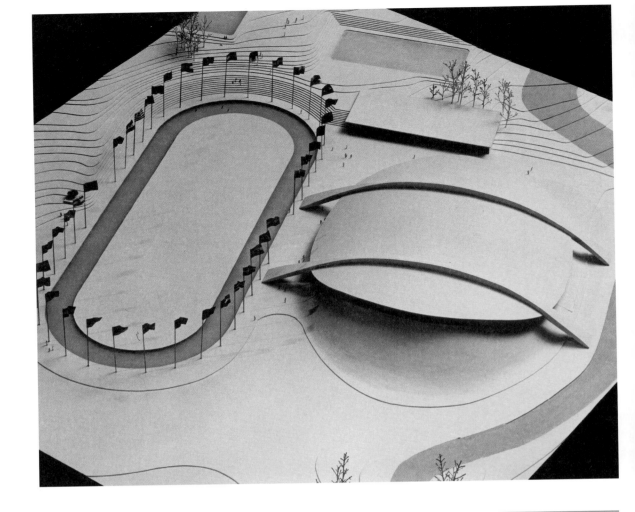

UNITED NATIONS CAPITOL
Vincent Raney
San Francisco, California (US), 1945

As the foundational United Nations Charter was being signed in San Francisco in the summer of 1945, city leaders attempted to leverage the goodwill they'd earned by hosting the meetings in which the global charter was ham-mered out. San Francisco sought to become the 'World Capital', as cities vying for the UN's permanent headquarters hoped to be known. The city's Planning Commission tapped Vincent Raney, an architect who designed petrol stations and cinemas, to sketch the city's official UN concept.

Perched on the slopes of Twin Peaks, Raney's complex would doubtless have been a captivating, if stodgy, symbol of worldwide government. At its centre was a museum capped by a translucent, illuminated globe 47 m (154 ft) in diameter, that turned on its axis. Anchoring the far end was a modern skyscraper, forty or fifty storeys tall and strongly reminiscent of Raymond Hood's Rockefeller Center (1929–40) in New York. At the back of the plaza would be a 10,000-seat assembly hall. A sweeping curved, colonnaded embankment would provide individual buildings for sixty or more nations, and a waterfall would cascade toward hillside mansions for delegates – a nod, it seemed, to Bernard Maybeck's proposal for a 'Cascade at Twin Peaks' (1933).

Raney's plan was almost more than a dream. Delegations from China and Australia favoured San Francisco as somewhere to give world diplomacy a fresh start, a 'city of progress'. The US State Department, however, deemed the city 'more of an outpost than a centre'. All hopes were lost when the United States abstained from voting on the location for the headquarters – which, of course, ended up being New York City.

SAN FRANCISCO STATE STUDENT UNION
Moshe Safdie
San Francisco, California (US), 1967

In 1967 the campus of San Francisco State University was exploding in a fit of protests, strikes, sit-ins, walk-outs and even riots as its students feuded with both the administration and the federal government over minority admissions and a more inclusive curriculum, among other things. Amid this maelstrom, the young architect Moshe Safdie, fresh from the success of his experimental Montreal housing exhibition 'Habitat 67', was invited by the student body to design a new student union containing classrooms, meeting rooms, study areas and dining facilities. (Financing would come from a tax of $10 per student, approved by the student body.) Safdie's mountainous design was as radical as the times, composed of an interlocking array of angled hexagonal precast concrete modules, both landscaped and stepped, creating a continuous network of stairs, landings and entrances to provide access almost anywhere at any time. Inside, hinged and pivoting walls gave students full control over their environment, and cavernous open spaces could accommodate expansive gatherings. 'It's as urban as an apartment house, as western as a pueblo, and as unconventional and uncharacteristic of the establishment as it can be, but it represents the spirit of those who want it,' noted the San Francisco attorney Louis Heilbron, a member of the California State Colleges Board of Trustees and a supporter of the endeavour.

The design was eventually rejected by the board in 1968, setting off still more student protests. Among the trustees who voted against it was the powerful Los Angeles corporate architect Charles Luckman, who called it 'extreme', and questioned the high cost and the fit with the rest of the campus.

'World Trade'

WORLD TRADE CENTER
William Merchant
San Francisco, California
(US), 1951

In 1948 the *San Francisco Chronicle* blasted a front-page headline: '40-Story World Trade Center Urged for Ferry Building Site'. The Ferry Building (1903), with its clock tower that graced the foot of Market Street, seemed the ideal target for demolition. This once thriving transit hub had been languishing ever since the Oakland Bay Bridge converted ferry commuters into car drivers.

William G Merchant, an architect known for his local commercial buildings, was chosen to delineate the '$100,000,000 dream'. He conceived a glassy skyscraper with a three-tier terrace at the top, flanked by two smaller buildings, lined up along the Embarcadero where the Ferry Building stood. A horseshoe of warehouse-like buildings, each enclosing a small plaza, floated on landfill between two old docks. There would be 'Orient', 'Pacifica', 'Europa', 'Pan American' and 'International' courts. The centrepiece was a grand, raised public plaza, facing Yerba Buena Island; in it, a Trylon (the narrow pyramid introduced at the New York World's Fair in 1939) poked up from a round reflecting pool, looking like a sundial to be read from the tower's roof decks.

Four years of plans, copious news coverage and a five-month worldwide tour to increase interest in the project did nothing to forestall the inevitable. Tight-fisted state officials baulked at the price tag, and in 1952 the invincible Ferry Building – which had survived the earthquake of 1906 – was spared and given a $2 million restoration. The World Trade Center, a planned Embarcadero Freeway and the Loma Prieta quake of 1989 could not bring it down. It thrives still, a beloved civic landmark.

NORTH & CENTRAL AMERICA

SANTA MONICA BAY VILLAGE
DMJM
Santa Monica, California (US), 1969

John 'Jack' Morehart, a shrewd real-estate speculator and rancher who admitted he was an 'operator ... not ashamed of making a fast dollar', was a man not entirely lacking in vision, and certainly in possession of a talent for tossing metaphorical Molotov cocktails at the established order. He owned a chunk of Santa Monica Beach shoreline on which, he said, he was going to build a hotel that would be 'unique to these United States'. It was: a 30-storey, 600-room hotel that floated in the Pacific Ocean, about 90 m (295 ft) offshore.

A round tower, entirely sheathed in glass tinted Ray-Ban Wayfarer grey-green, looked like a cylindrical capsule left behind, and forever forgotten, by a race of ancient space invaders. In DMJM's conception, the interior floors – stacked discs hanging off a central core – were glass platters, too. The lower six floors formed an atrium, enclosed, of course, in more glass, this version completely transparent. Visitors would have had a 360-degree panorama of ocean, beach, mountains and city lights. A glass-enclosed bridge with a moving sidewalk would connect the hotel to the beach. The whole thing, defiantly self-contained, pulsed with inscrutable and unobtainable energy, as if it were fed from somewhere deep beneath the waves. Clearly, it came from the hand of DMJM's Anthony Lumsden, a master of aerodynamic curves that feel more like sculptures than buildings occupied by people.

It's not clear whether Morehart genuinely intended to build Lumsden's amphibious cylinder. In the end, owing $281,000 in back taxes, he was forced to shed his property, and the land remained open beach, never to be subject to development again.

SUNSET MOUNTAIN PARK
DMJM
Santa Monica, California (US), 1966

The dream of the Sunset International Petroleum Corporation, Sunset Mountain was a $250 million commercial and residential centre perched atop 850 uninhabited hectares (2,100 acres) in the Santa Monica Mountains, west of Los Angeles. The megaproject consisted of shops, a school, restaurants, offices and a hotel, set at the summit of a steep, craggy hillside. Clinging to the slopes were 4,771 terraced housing units accessible via inclined elevator, stepping downwards as many as 60 storeys and radiating from the commercial centre in all directions. The housing was focused on neighbourhood-like groupings of single-family homes and garden apartments. Seen from above, the project, with its textured, barrel-like structural accumulations and fan shape, was reminiscent of 'Machu Picchu, the Spanish Steps', as the architecture writer John Pastier put it, 'and a 1930s film setting of the City of the Future'.

In addition to DMJM, the project's design team included the landscape architect Peter Walker. In his presentation to the Los Angeles City Planning Commission, Walker stressed that the development, in the hills west of the 405 freeway, was an alternative to the mountain-levelling schemes so common across the region. Sunset Mountain, he said, would 'blend and contour with the natural topography'. Fifty per cent of the area was dedicated to undisturbed open space.

Sunset acquired the massive site in 1964 for $14 million. But the project quickly drew fierce opposition, including busloads of protesters from the Pacific Palisades Property Owners Association. In the end, the protesters triumphed.

LOS ANGELES INTERNATIONAL AIRPORT
Pereira & Luckman
Los Angeles, California (US), 1952

Few never-builts had such potential to remake the image, if not the reality, of a city – the way Jørn Utzon's Sydney Opera House or Frank Gehry's Guggenheim Bilbao did – than the space-age dome that would have been Los Angeles International Airport. Conceived by the powerhouse West Coast firm Pereira & Luckman, which churned out Corporate Modernist buildings faster than California built highways, the idea originated with William Pereira's architecture students at the University of Southern California.

Pereira and his students dreamed up a grand concourse housed under an enormous glass dome. The concept captured the romance of arrival and departure, as the spatial grandeur of such railway stations as the Gare d'Orsay in Paris had half a century earlier – updated with glass and steel, vast expanses of terrazzo, floating terraces and a captivating window into the blue. Hanging from a central column was a circular platform that housed a restaurant, a design (credited to Paul R Williams) that later morphed into the now iconic LAX Theme Building. It was easy to imagine oneself swaggering beneath the dome with an innate feeling of the future having landed – where else than in Los Angeles?

Problems as prosaic as the opinion of city engineers, who said the structure couldn't be built, objections to the cost of air conditioning, and squabbling among the airlines that wanted their own, individual terminals stopped the project cold. Los Angeles airport has never recovered. *Time* magazine declared in 1967 that it 'was brand-new six years ago – and outmoded before the cement on its new runways was dry.'

LOS ANGELES CIVIC CENTER
Lloyd Wright
Los Angeles, California (US), 1925

Lloyd Wright's Civic Center competition entry was meant to guide 'the present and future development of this city to be the greatest of all cities'. It was no small order, but perhaps the fact that he was the son of the man who would be declared the greatest American architect of all time endowed a soupçon of hubris. His failed plan emphasized the ancient symbolism of public buildings sited atop a hill: in this case Bunker Hill (the early site of the city's grandest mansions which became, decades later, a symbol of botched city planning, American-style). The design took the form of an elongated cross, its spine following the existing north-south axis of Grand Avenue (capped today by Frank Gehry's Walt Disney Concert Hall). Flanking a terraced walkway 152 m (499 ft) wide were pairs of buildings that grew in height as they climbed the hill. When seen from afar, the megalith, which Wright called a 'unified, organic structure', evoked an ancient Assyrian temple complex. Up close, the mitred edges and tight vertical lines of shops, offices and government buildings revealed the architect's Art Deco brilliance and bravura. He later called the plan an 'acropolis for the city'. Wright, in common with many of his contemporaries, was obsessed with new modes of transportation. Aeroplanes, helicopters, sub-way trains, lifts and, of course, cars – the last moving in discreetly buried 'speedways' under the broad pedestrian rights of way – suffused his vision. He warned the citizens of Los Angeles: 'We need not wait upon the costly and painful "force of circumstances" to erect a more or less tortured and deformed structure.' In many respects, his prophecy came true for a downtown presently pockmarked with car parks and 'deformed structures'.

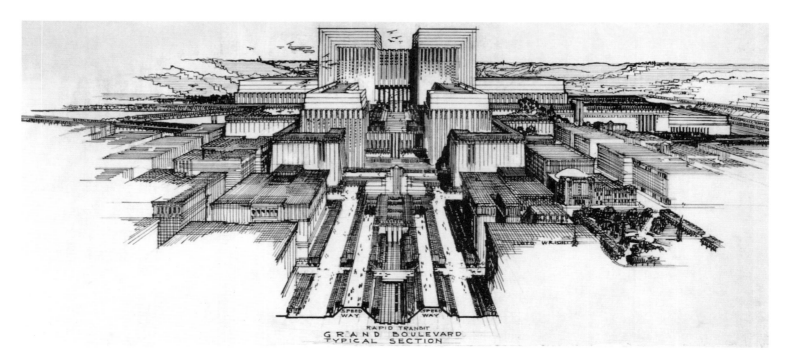

LAUGHLIN PARK
CASAS GRANDES
Irving Gill
Los Angeles, California
(US), 1912

Homer Laughlin, Sr, the Ohio pottery magnate, owned a 13.4 hectare (33 acre) subdivision below Griffith Park, where he had spent twenty years cultivating thousands of exotic trees and specimen shrubs. His son Homer Laughlin, Jr, recruited Irving Gill to design a housing development that would cascade down the hillside. Gill's Casas Grandes were white-concrete-and-glass keeps, composed of buttress-like columns, massive lintels and wide spans of neatly divided windows. Discussing the design in the Los Angeles Evening Herald in August 1913, Gill wrote, 'Throughout this property there will be no artificial ornamentation. What few architectural features are employed will be severely formal and simple in their lines.' Gill wanted to topple historicism, which was then all the rage in Los Angeles. He wrote that 'the straight line, the arch, the cube and the circle' – plain and simple geometry – should be restored as the foundation of architecture. 'We should build our house simple, plain and substantial as a boulder, then leave the ornamentation of it to Nature.' This was modernism before there was Modernism. At Casas Grandes, Gill was as good as his unadorned word.

After Laughlin senior died, however, Gill seems to have been dropped from the project, which was recast as an artistic park containing homes and gardens that would replicate the Italian villas of southern Europe. The curving streets, offering commanding views of the Los Angeles basin, became an exclusive enclave of sixty homes where, among others, Cecil B DeMille and WC Fields once lived.

GRIFFITH PARK NATURE
CENTER
John Lautner
Los Angeles, California
(US), 1972

In September 1972 the Los Angeles Department of Recreation and Parks selected John Lautner to design what would have been his highest-profile commission within the city limits. The Griffith Park Nature Center, near the city's zoo, was surrounded by a sprawling, wooded camping retreat and the 9 hectare (22 acre) Pecan Grove picnic area. The welcome and exhibition outpost measured 1,300 sq. m (14,000 sq. ft) and was set for completion in 1974, its $790,000 price tag covered by state bonds.

Lautner's final plan was a three-pronged building with thin, steel-reinforced-concrete shell 'wings' that cantilevered 12 m (40 ft) from its central core. Sloped glazing along the flanks allowed natural light to pour in. Perched on the hillside, the building looked like a bird spreading its arched concrete-and-glass wings. 'That was his great inspiration: nature. And the way nature designs,' says Helena Arahuete, an associate at Lautner's office from 1971 until the architect's death in 1994. Inside, park offices and an auditorium were clad in Bouquet Canyon stone, an appropriate motif for the site. Exhibition rooms contained a scale model of the park and other nature-inspired presentations. The graphic artist John Follis, who designed the Disney World logo, was to assist with the displays.

Although it was initially funded, the project unravelled during the oil crisis of 1973, which sent construction costs sky-high and kept the county from supporting this inventive scheme. It eventually decided on a prosaic building, which opened in 1981.

METRO 2000
Agustín Hernández Navarro
Carson, California (US), 1994

For filmmakers contemplating a vision of another world, the work of the Mexico City-born architect Agustín Hernández Navarro has been a continual lure. He absorbed the myths and symbols and overpowering scale of Mesoamerican civilizations, fusing them into a unique, unparalleled Brutalist idiom. His Heroico Colegio Militar (Heroic Military Academy; 1976), a neo-Aztec complex on the outskirts of Mexico City, is said to have inspired Ridley Scott for *Blade Runner* (1982), and Paul Verhoeven filmed parts of *Total Recall* (1990) there.

Inspired by Verhoeven's dystopic sci-fi film, a pair of developers made a pilgrimage to Hernández's cantilevered *taller*, commissioning him to design a mall for a toxics-laden former city dump off one of the world's busiest freeways, southeast of downtown Los Angeles. Hernández proposed an enormous oblong of 990,000 sq. m (10.7 million sq. ft), anchored at either extreme by conical towers, with a vast circular plaza 450 m (1,476 ft) in diameter, from which rose the horn of an ibex, in the shape of a glassy, sway-back pyramid. He described his plaza as a 'spherical asteroid' punctured with craters. This astral mall – with a monorail to cover its vast expanse of casinos, hotels, offices, supermarkets, cinemas, gyms and an art gallery – was elevated behind a wall 1.5 km (1 mile) long that looked like straightened metal tubes discarded from an electromagnetic particle accelerator.

Hernández has said, 'Geometry is my religion. I've used every existing geometric form – circles, triangles, squares, rectangles.' Metro 2000 was no exception. The modern-day Tenochtitlán succumbed to the vicissitudes of the stock market, however, its misfortune sealed by an economic downturn.

SAN DIEGO COMMUNITY THEATER
Bertrand Goldberg
San Diego, California (US), 1967

The architect Bertrand Goldberg was no stranger to theatre design, having created such Chicago projects as the Cinestage Theater and the swooping playhouse inside his Marina City complex. But neither approached the ambition of his San Diego Community Theater, a collaboration with the revered artistic director Michael Langham (former drama director at the famed Juilliard School in New York), the University of California San Diego (UCSD) – which was still under construction – and the city's Theater and Arts Foundation.

Hugging a deep, meandering ravine not far from both UCSD and the Pacific Ocean, the shell-like design, shaped by repeating arched flanks and sinuously moulded rooflines supported by pronounced structural ribs, emerged spectacularly from the landscape. 'The earth's surface has been deeply eroded by water for many centuries, and the building shapes are intended to grow out of the terrain,' said Goldberg. It would be 'a kind of organic living form. It moves around, following the land and functions.' Goldberg, enhancing the bond between actor and audience, described the 1,700-seat main auditorium as 'a great space bubble, with no one more than sixty feet [about 18 m] away from the action, and seats at various levels below, above or at stage level.' The main stage was just the beginning. The plan also called for an experimental 550-seat theatre, an open-air Greek theatre, a student theatre, and spaces for workshops, a restaurant, a club and offices.

A full-size mock-up of the auditorium was built inside the abandoned Piccadilly Theater in Chicago. But the Theater and Arts Foundation couldn't raise the funds for the colossal scheme, so the project crumbled like a sandcastle.

SAN DIEGO STADIUM
Charles Luckman,
Felix Candela
San Diego, California
(US), 1963

Charles Luckman will always be remembered for his Madison Square Garden building that, in 1968, replaced New York's Pennsylvania station. At the very moment wrecking balls were slamming into the pink marble columns of the Beaux-Arts railway station, Luckman was hired to build a sports arena in San Diego. He was famously sanguine about his profession: 'I am firm in my belief that architecture is a business and not an art.' Still, when coach Robert Breitbard handed him the sports arena, he turned to Felix Candela, the genius of thin-form concrete shells.

In September 1963 Candela and Luckman were given precisely three weeks to produce an idea for a building. Candela flew in from Mexico and spent five days in Luckman's office, coming up with an inverted conical frustum, a round building with flared walls, topped by a folded-plate hyperbolic roof 45 m (148 ft) high. The $7 million building was dubbed the 'Parabolic Diamond Concept' because its concrete structural skin, in the form of diamond webbing, was attached to a dual bicycle-wheel roof. This roof, akin to two spoked wheels, was composed of radiating tension cables connected to two outer rings, in turn tied to the basket-weave frame. It was incredibly strong yet relatively inexpensive, but even so Breitbard – although sold on the concept – baulked at the cost, and Luckman was dismissed.

Months later, Luckman's San Diego associates informed him that Breitbard and his investors were 'still fumbling around … and have really muffed the whole deal'. In November 1966 an unimpressive oval sports arena, owned by Breitbard, opened exactly where the Luckman-Candela Parabolic Diamond had been meant to go.

VIVA CASINO
Bruce Goff
Las Vegas, Nevada (US), 1961

The Viva Casino, conceived sometime in 1955, would surely have upped the ante in Las Vegas at a time when the Strip consisted of brick boxes bedecked in a pirate's booty of neon. Goff's roughly twenty-two-storey building – sans neon – was like an extruded upside-down tricorn hat, with successive floors increasing in size as they climbed in height. The projecting, cylindrical exterior stairwells at the corners of the hotel looked oddly like the stacked vertebrae of a giant underwater creature, long extinct, left to bake in the desert sun. A trio of Christmas tree umbrellas dotted the far corners of the roof, lonely, ineffectual sombreros ill-poised to protect against the ceaseless solar rays.

But it was the rooftop carousel tent and the oblong, absurdly cantilevered roof deck, surrounded by a gold-encrusted *brise-soleil*, that stole the skyline. Add the 23 m (75 ft) lance jutting straight up from the tent top and the additional white tents anchored in the sand, and the whole thing begins to feel vaguely like the pageant before an imaginary Renaissance joust. It was pure Goff – and prescient.

Goff was coaxed into designing the casino for Hollywood producer Viva Ruth Liles, whose only movie credit was the now lost *Wonder Valley* (1953). Liles spent much of the 1940s and 50s battling her former husband (and her teenage children) in courtrooms in seven states, in a fruitless attempt to latch onto his presumed $11 million in uranium-mining claims. Real or fictive, Liles never got the stake, and Goff's hotel turned out to be a mirage.

XANADU
Martin Stern, Jr
Las Vegas, Nevada, (US) 1975

In 1975 the now-fabled Las Vegas Strip was still relatively underdeveloped, filled with tawdry stores and unremarkable mid-sized hotels and casinos. A 19.6 hectare (48½ acre) site on the southwest corner of Las Vegas Boulevard and Tropicana Avenue was therefore considered a prime opportunity. An investment group called the Xanadu Corporation was keen to take advantage, creating a detailed prospectus for a hotel called Xanadu that included designs by the prolific local architect Martin Stern, Jr, who designed or added to such Las Vegas mainstays as the Riviera, Stardust, Aladdin and original MGM Grand hotels.

Stern sketched an angular, ivory-hued building embracing 1970s futurism and nodding to the vague notion of 'oriental exotic', or 'Shangri-La', the mythical Himalayan paradise chronicled by dreamers ranging from Samuel Taylor Coleridge to James Hilton. A bending wall of rooms, traced in long racing stripes, stepped back from a cavernous open atrium, presaging a number of lofty Vegas spaces. Drawings of the hall depict a circular bar, suspended several storeys high on a slender, stem-like column, as if Shangri-La itself were floating not too far off in the clouds. The team received a Clark County Planning Commission permit in 1976, but soon became bogged down in disagreements with local authorities over such mundane details as who would pay for sewer lines and utilities. Construction never started, and the building permit lapsed. Subsequent attempts to jump-start the project failed, too. The 4,032-room Excalibur opened on the site in 1990, part of a renaissance on the South Strip that included the Mirage (1989), Luxor and the new MGM Grand (both 1993).

COLORADO SPRINGS OPERA HOUSE
Jan Ruhtenberg
Colorado Springs, Colorado (US), 1957

Former Bauhaus student Jan Ruhtenberg, who studied with Ludwig Mies van der Rohe and later worked closely with Philip Johnson (they were rumoured to be lovers), was an architectural Zelig. Among other things, he worked for Wallace Harrison on Nelson Rockefeller's Manhattan apartment; remodelled a home for Helen Resor, the client who first brought Mies to the United States; taught at Columbia for Joseph Hudnut, who would later bring Walter Gropius and Marcel Breuer to Harvard; and helped Herman Miller expand into modern furniture design with his 'World's Fair' line of 1939. As his career progressed, Ruhtenberg took on commissions and teaching assignments in smaller cities, such as Norman, Oklahoma, Indianapolis, Indiana – and Colorado Springs, Colorado.

In Colorado Springs, where he worked successfully for more than a decade, Ruhtenberg proposed (in response to a call by a group of local musicians) what one newspaper described as an 'ultra-modern' opera house set on a ridge on the edge of the city's Mesa neighbourhood. Most of the architect's work embodied the stripped-down glass-and-steel International Style, but the fanning, reinforced-concrete-shell opera house was organic, evoking the city's curving mountains and fractured landscapes. Inside, a system of motor-operated walls could shift the auditorium's seating from 3,000 people to a much more intimate 1,000. An extending wing contained a restaurant, bar and related facilities, while outdoor spaces included gardens and even a swimming pool. While the estimated $1.5 million design won a coveted Progressive Architecture award, it never received financial backing or serious consideration.

PORT HOLIDAY
Smith and Williams
Lake Mead, Nevada
(US), 1963

Whitney Rowland Smith and Wayne R Williams, along with their fellow Southern California architects Armet Davis Newlove, invented the vocabulary of everyday modern architecture in post-war Los Angeles. Their work, known for its combination of 'shelter and openness, restraint and exuberance', dotted the suburbs and small cities growing on the edges of the city from the mid-1940s onwards.

In 1963 J Carlton Adair, a bit-part actor, casino promoter and Las Vegas land speculator who owned swathes of land around Lake Mead, asked Smith and Williams to lend visual panache to his years-long scheme to develop his holdings into a township that he called Port Holiday. Smith and Williams' rendition of Adair's dream had it all: a geodesic dome, an aerial tramway and a Modernist version of a castellated chateau. All was infused with the zippy flair that reflected the optimism of early 1960s plans to turn deserts into oases and convert barren land into multimillion acreage.

Local and state officials endorsed Adair's $320 million plan, which involved an artificial lake with 21 km (13 miles) of shoreline, resort hotels, an eighteen-hole golf course, floating homes and a zoo. Over several years he attracted a series of corporate backers, from Boise Cascade Home & Land Co. to Gulf Oil and General Electric. He overreached himself, however, eventually declaring bankruptcy in 1972, with just $200 in the newly named 'Lake Adair' company's coffers. Adair's vision was eventually given life, albeit lacking the spirit of Modernism. In 1991 a lake was created, known today as Lake Las Vegas, surrounded by Tuscan stucco luxury homes.

ROGERS LACY HOTEL
Frank Lloyd Wright
Dallas, Texas (US), 1946

In 1946 Frank Lloyd Wright and the east Texas oilman Rogers Lacy met in Dallas to make plans for an 826-room hotel occupying a full down-town block near the corner of Ervay and Commerce streets. Wright originally called the project 'Lone Star'. A few months later Lacy made his way to Wright's studio at Taliesin West in Scottsdale, Arizona, to view the initial sketches.
The architect had developed a shimmering forty-seven-storey design, its surface clad in two layers of overlapping triangular panels of translucent glass. (Insulation between the layers would keep the building from overheating.) Inside, the spaces would revolve around a glowing twelve-storey atrium court, wrapped with ground-level lobbies, water gardens, shops, restaurants, bars and cafés, and, above, guest rooms, all linked to the atrium via balconies that Wright called 'sun galleries', instead of along enclosed corridors. The soaring atrium court, bringing a sort of urban theatre inside, set the tone for a plethora of modern hotels, among them John Portman's Hyatt Regency (1967) in Atlanta. 'The plan dramatizes the humdrum life of a hotel, making the usual movements contribute to the interest of the whole and to anyone sitting anywhere in a beautiful spectacle,' said Wright. Rising behind the atrium was a rear tower, a similarly glass-clad structure cantilevering from a diamond-shaped, concrete-clad utility and ventilation shaft.
Frank Lloyd Wright developed more than forty preliminary drawings, but Lacy died unexpectedly on 9 December 1947, before work could move ahead, and the building was cancelled.

MGF CENTER
IM Pei
Midland, Texas (US), 1982

The renowned architectural illustrator Paul Stevenson Oles helped to bring to life many of IM Pei's most crucial buildings – from the Grand Louvre in Paris to the Islamic Museum of Modern Art in Doha, Qatar – before a shovel had even hit the ground. His rendering of Pei's MGF Center in downtown Midland, Texas, heroically captures the thirty-five-storey tower, planned by the local corporation MGF Oil in 1982, when high oil prices were sending company coffers into the stratosphere.
Emerging from the corner of North Big Spring Street and West Illinois Avenue, the building's squared, postmodern base was typical of its time, featuring punched windows, gabled flanks and a capacious glazed entrance lobby. But shooting up from it was a glassy, horizontally striped and chamfered obelisk, an oversized exemplar of Pei's Geometric Modernism, split dramatically in two by tall banks of lifts. The design, led by IM Pei & Partners design principal Harold Fredenburgh, would have dwarfed a town already nicknamed the Tall City (its skyline, although relatively normal, looks much taller from the flat plains of western Texas).
By 1984 the price of oil had plunged, and MGF (along with many Texas oil outfits) filed for Chapter 11 bankruptcy. The party was over. Not that one should feel badly for Pei's firm, which went gangbusters in the region, completing such seminal works as Dallas City Hall (1977), One Dallas Center (1979), Energy Plaza (1983), Fountain Place (1986) and the Morton H. Meyerson Symphony Center in Dallas (1989), and the JP-Morgan Chase Tower (1982; still the tallest building in Texas) in Houston.

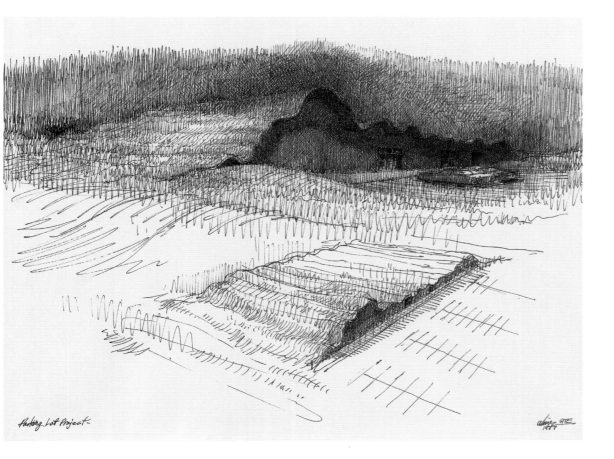

Parking Lot Project

In 1972 the visionary architects James Wines, Alison Sky and their firm SITE (Sculpture in the Environment) were commissioned by Best Products to design a series of stores around the United States. Best's founder, Sydney Lewis, an avid collector of contemporary art, wanted the new facilities to blur the line between art and architecture, challenging the banal archetype that Best had fallen into with the big-box structures also employed by its competitors, such as Walmart, Kmart and Sears.

In 1976 SITE devised one of its most elaborate plans, the Parking Lot Structure, for sites in Houston and Los Angeles. The building's rooftop took the form of a rippling asphalt car park (or 'undulating blanket of pavement', as Wines noted in the firm's monograph *SITE, Inc.* in 1989), painted with parking-space lines and merging with the actual car park along its flanks. 'In a sense this structure implies the elimination of architecture altogether,' Wines wrote. He later added in an interview, 'I wanted the whole parking to ripple and cover the building, turning into its roof ... The idea was to make it look casual. It couldn't be contrived. We wanted it to be completely arbitrary looking, not static. That would have made the building really stand out. You couldn't confuse it with a Walmart or Kmart, that's for sure.' But the idea would prove too expensive, and any hope that it might be revived ended when SITE's partnership with Best ended in 1984. Best would close for good in 1997.

HOUSTON CENTER
William Pereira
Houston, Texas (US), 1970

In 1970 the oil and gas firm Texas Eastern Transmission proposed Houston Center, a mixed-use development on the east side of the downtown area, set to be the largest privately financed construction project in American history. Covering thirty-three city blocks and 30 hectares (74 acres), it would have doubled the size of Houston's central business district with 2.1 million sq. m (23 million sq. ft) of building space. Its chief designer was the Los Angeles architect William Pereira, who had designed the Los Angeles County Museum of Art, San Francisco's Transamerica Pyramid, and the University of California, Irvine. He had also spent time in the film industry (he even won an Academy Award in 1942, for special effects), and his sci-fi visions materialized in the plan's futuristic drawings. Following the urban-planning wisdom of his day, Pereira proposed a multi-level 'platform city', a series of high- and mid-rise offices, hotels, department stores, apartments and entertainment facilities floating above Houston's grid via a network of raised lobbies, glass-clad walkways and bridges, and a tube-like people-moving system. But, this being oil country, the car was still king (Pereira was an avid racing driver, and thus sympathetic), and the development created layer upon layer of parking spaces for 40,000–50,000 cars, not to mention a new system of elevated roads. By the mid-1970s the plan – its ambitions foiled by the country's oil crisis, a sharp economic downturn and skyrocketing inflation – had been scaled down to two rather unimpressive skyscrapers: One and Two Houston Center. It was clear by the end of the decade that the rest of Houston Center would never be implemented.

TEMPLE EMANUEL, OPEN AIR CHAPEL
Herb Greene
Houston, Texas, (US), 1957

With so many mid-century sacred spaces resembling spaceships, you have to wonder if the designers knew something others didn't. A great example is Herb Greene's unbuilt Temple Emanuel chapel, an open, disc-like structure that this acolyte of the organic-architecture masters Bruce Goff and John Lautner conceived when he was working for the Houston-based firm Krakower Architecture.

The circular chapel was designed to give the impression of floating, topped by a greenish roof (on one drawing it appears to be made of copper; in another of translucent glass) hanging from steel trusses, some anchored into the ground and others projecting outwards. Greenery hugged its edges, while flagstones covered the interior walls and floors and spilled beyond the perimeter, connecting it to the earth. The design is a great example of Greene's intuitive response to climate and context. 'I just did things because they were obvious,' he told *The Guardian* in 2022, when he was ninety-two years old. Greene told his great-niece Lila Cohen that he was not positive why the project died, but suspected that it was because of a financial shortfall. Emanuel did eventually build two new chapels in the 1970s and 80s. Its main sanctuary, across the street from Rice University in Houston's Hermann Park neighbourhood, was designed in 1949 by the local firm MacKie and Kamrath. That building's earth-hugging, deep red organic form, with its angled, impressively cantilevered roof, is vividly evocative of the work of Karl Kamrath's mentor, Frank Lloyd Wright. Wright, of course, was also the mentor of Goff and Lautner.

CEMETARY CHAPEL FOR TEMPLE EMANUEL, HOUSTON,

PLAN
SCALE $\frac{1}{8}$"=1'-0"

DRIVE

WALK

SECTION I-I

AN OPEN AIR SHELTER THAT CAN BE ENCLOSED WITH GLASS
HERB GREENE, CONSULTING ARCHITECT

SELENE MONUMENT TO MAN'S CONQUEST OF THE MOON
Wang Da-hong
Houston, Texas (US), 1969

Throughout the 1960s and 70s the architect Wang Da-hong proposed the 'Selene Monument to Man's Conquest of the Moon', commemorating the *Apollo 11* mission's lunar landing in 1969. The project, which was named after the Greek goddess of the moon, consisted of two white stelae, reaching towards the heavens, wrapping a memorial hall.

Inspired since he was a teenager by humankind's quest for the moon (he even wrote a sci-fi novel, *Phantasmagoria*), Da-hong had begun the scheme in the mid-1960s, convinced that humanity would soon conquer the lunar surface. But his proposal, planned for a site in suburban Houston near NASA's Mission Control base, was not just about the United States, or space. It was also a way for Da-hong to pay tribute to Chinese culture. The twin stelae, for instance, represented the Chinese concept of yin and yang, while the sparsely lit memorial hall was designed to evoke Chinese mysticism.

By the mid-1970s the monument had also become about honouring the United States Bicentennial, and the Committee for the Selene Program lobbied support and gathered donations. Construction was set to begin on 4 July 1976, but soon internal squabbles over design and implementation bogged it down. Multiple complex factors, including the resignation of the committee's chairman, sounded its death knell but Da-hong continued promoting the monument – arguably his most beloved project – privately until the 1990s.

REPUBLICBANK AND TEXAS THEATER
Michael Graves
San Antonio, Texas (US), 1982

For six weeks in 1982, it seemed as if Michael Graves might get his next big commission. The Portland Building, across from City Hall in Portland, Oregon, had established the architect and firmly implanted postmodernism – whether loved or hated – in the public mind. Graves, perhaps to his everlasting regret, was lured into a pitched battle between San Antonio preservationists and the powerhouse RepublicBank, which wanted to demolish the Texas Theater, an ornate movie palace constructed in 1927. RepublicBank had already hired the city's preeminent firm, Ford Powell & Carson, to design a 92,900 sq. m (1 million sq. ft), $125 million office and retail complex overlooking the San Antonio River. But the San Antonio Conservation Society went to court and persuaded the bank to delay demolition of the theatre for sixty days, during which time the Society could come up with a way to save the landmark. Graves's firm, which was denounced by his putative rival, O'Neil Ford, as 'carpet-bagging eastern architects', got $125,000, and offered a clutch of four towers standing shoulder to shoulder in an 'L', embracing the old theatre. The tower facades, an abstracted Beaux-Arts vision, were made of coloured bands of native limestone and glazed terracotta. Ascending from the columnar bases – with pediments that mimicked the belfries of adobe churches – the boxy buildings were surmounted by vaguely Mesopotamian-looking pyramids. RepublicBank waited exactly one week before rejecting the proposal. Two towers from Ford Powell & Carson's design were completed, and the theatre facade was preserved as the entrance to shops and a plaza café. Graves later described his tower designs as 'the most vulgar things [sic] we've done'.

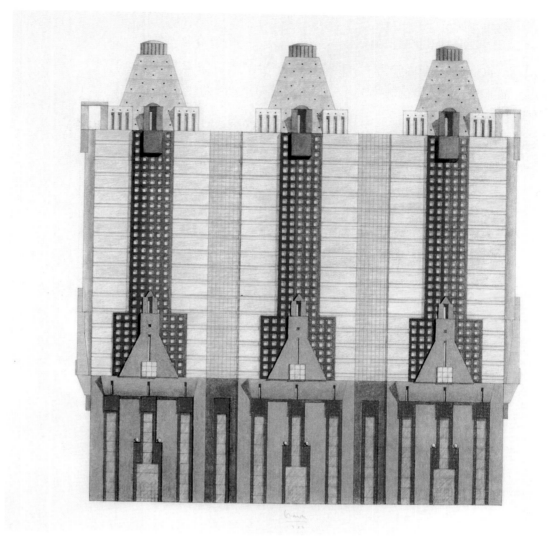

HORIZON HILL CENTER
Arquitectonica
San Antonio, Texas (US), 1982

Arquitectonica, then a young Miami firm, arrived in San Antonio on the tailwind of its acclaimed, and much publicized, Atlantis condos in Biscayne Bay. The Atlantis, newly opened in 1982, was a slender, twenty-storey slab washed in Caribbean sea-blue, with a cube 11 m (36 ft) long cut out of the centre, forming a transparent 'sky deck', outfitted for maximum vertiginous effect with a narrow, red open-sided helical staircase. The firm of self-styled radicals was breaking ranks with modernism and postmodernism, grafting a Pop art colour palette onto high-tech materials. It was redefining the Miami skyline, and its work was immortalized in the opening credits of the huge television hit *Miami Vice* (1984–9).

The San Antonio developer Efraim Abramoff wanted to import the thrill. Arquitectonica sketched four mirrored glass towers, forty-six storeys high, with a connecting bridge at the top and a fire engine-red swaddle fastening the foot. The massive triple arch was as flat as a billboard, as hard-edged as an Ellsworth Kelly painting, and as minimal as a solid-state circuit board. As with its Miami predecessor – and largely based on early Russian Constructivist ideas – the arches were voids, simply three towers subtracted, leaving four behind. At the base Arquitectonica abandoned the seemingly pedantic for the supposedly whimsical, drawing a blue running track shaped like a paperclip, a mini pyramid modelled on that at Giza, and leafy Canary Island palms (which don't grow in Texas).

Texas Monthly summed up the colossus: 'It is more like a practical joke that has fallen flat.' The massive arch would have been the tallest building in San Antonio, but a glut of office space and collapsing oil prices meant it never materialized.

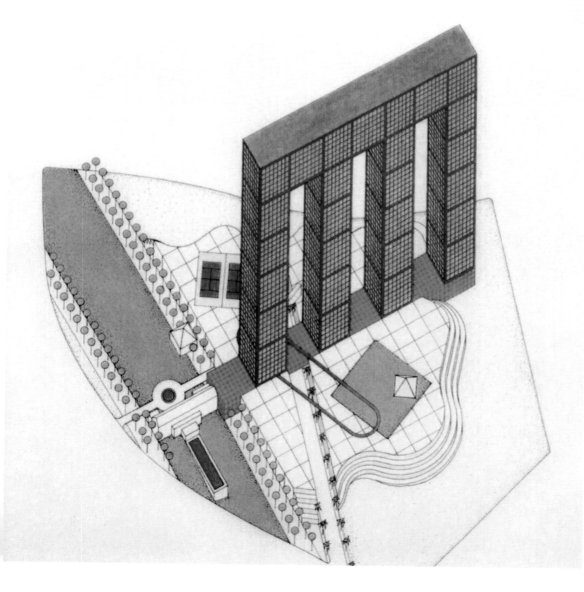

FARGO-MOORHEAD
CULTURAL CENTER BRIDGE
Michael Graves
Fargo, North Dakota and
Moorhead, Minnesota
(US), 1978

A superb symbol of Michael Graves' vision to steer architecture away from the austere functionalism of Modernism was the Fargo-Moorhead Cultural Center Bridge, a pastiche of colour, form and historical references intended as a rethinking of the idea of a bridge altogether. Devised to celebrate the centennials of Fargo, North Dakota, and Moorhead, Minnesota, in 1975, the project was planned to replace a vehicular bridge spanning the Red River, connecting the two small cities.

The new bridge contained an art museum on one side and a concert hall, cultural interpretation centre and public radio station on the other. The architect's vision, which the critic Ada Louise Huxtable called 'probably one of the most beautiful architectural drawings of recent times', was also a symbol of Graves' immense skill as a draughtsman. (Indeed, his drawings generally eclipse the quality of his built work.) The project's union of infrastructure and architecture gave the architect unique opportunities to incorporate, and manipulate, playful classical allusions, such as columns, arches, keystones and wedges. Some columns, for instance, held up nothing at all. His varied, textured colour palette energetically incorporated the terracotta hues of the land and the blues of water and sky. In a referendum held in November 1978, some 53 per cent of Fargo's voters opposed funding the project. The city of Moorhead continued to work with the architect on the interpretation centre, but that too failed to move forward. Today just a blank, utilitarian bridge stands on the site.

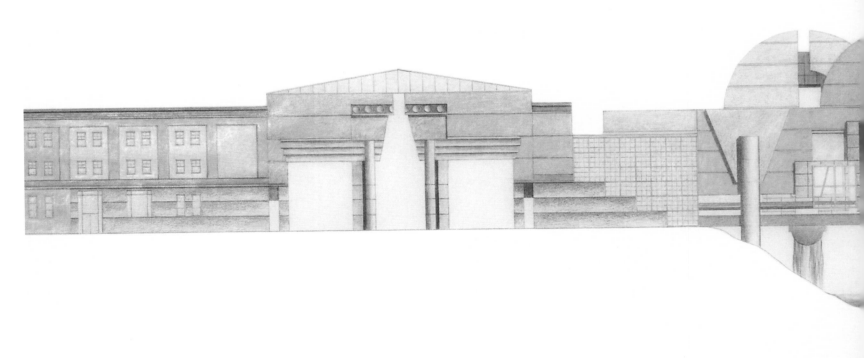

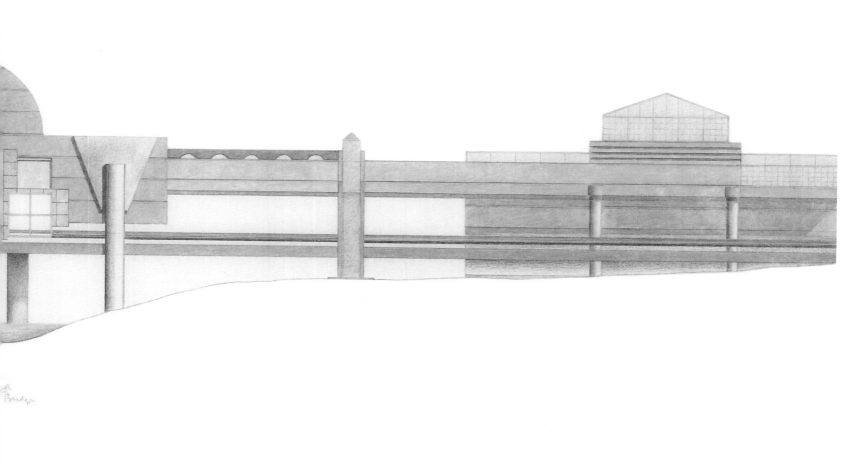

KANSAS CITY OFFICE BUILDING
Louis Kahn
Kansas City, Missouri (US), 1966

Louis Kahn reached the apex of the architecture profession, designing celebrated government complexes, research facilities, museums, churches and homes. But he never got to design an office tower.

In 1966 the Kansas City developer Altgar Enterprises asked Kahn to design a twenty-four-storey skyscraper filling an entire block near the corner of 11th and Walnut streets. It would contain offices as well as street-level shops, an upper-level clubhouse and a heliport on the roof. Kahn's sculptural design consisted of squared, poured-concrete corner columns (two per corner) supporting a multi-storey, arched truss structure above ('like a building within a building', as he put it), from which the bulk of the structure's floorplates would be suspended via steel cables. Kahn mocked most lightweight tower designs of the time as 'tin-can construction'. With the truss as its de facto base, he proposed – working with his long-term colleague the structural engineer August E Komendant – that the tower be built from the top down. The project progressed over the course of eight years and evolved over that time, including changing site, an alteration that led the architect to create a new plaza, layered with urban amenities.

The client was never able to secure funding for Kahn's challenging design. Instead, it awarded the commission to the corporate firm Skidmore, Owings & Merrill, without notifying Kahn. The architect remarked that the episode exemplified 'what is wrong with our profession: no ethics'.

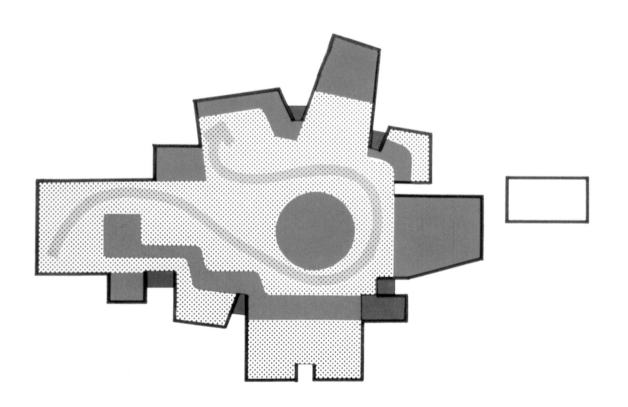

EXPERIMENTAL THEATER, WASHINGTON UNIVERSITY
Hans Hollein
St Louis, Missouri (US), 1963

Shortly before Hans Hollein's 1966 design for a candle shop on a fashionable street in Vienna won him international recognition – and the $25,000 RS Reynolds Memorial Award for Architectural Achievement – he had arrived at American University (AU) in St Louis, Missouri, with little other than a portfolio of drawings. Joseph Passonneau, dean of the school of architecture at AU, had set out to transform what he called a 'street-car college' into one of the nation's pre-eminent schools, inviting Hollein, Fumihiko Maki, Frei Otto and Aldo van Eyck, among others, to teach there.

How Hollein's commission for the Experimental Theater originated and why it remained on paper eludes explanation, but in it he demonstrated his prescient interest in designing forms that defied either type or structure. He drew a linear building – a continuous, open, elongated space – which, he wrote in his notes, 'avoids the excessive centring of pure arena theatres'. The stage was unconditioned, the seats movable, the spectators and actors 'completely intertwined'. The exposed concrete structure, which faced a quadrangle surrounded by Collegiate Gothic buildings, was bursting with massive trapezoids telescoping above the ground floor. It was honeycombed with staircases and penetrated by earthworks, making it completely permeable. The exterior doubled as an outdoor theatre, playground and climbing wall. 'It is a building that generates activities, invites uses, provokes discovery,' Hollein said.

Bruce Goff's legacy lies mostly in the houses he built for ordinary Midwesterners: carpenters, schoolteachers, farmers, small-town store owners. His unexpected, unpredictable, outlandish buildings – curved and torqued, splashed with Kool-Aid colours, and made with everyday things like anthracite coal and chips of Coke-bottle-green waste glass – constituted as profound an exploration of idiosyncratic unconformity as the unruffled flatlands of Kansas and Oklahoma ever produced. Goff, who was both a composer and an architect until he left writing music behind, said of his work that 'each project is a unique story never to be repeated in any way.'

From his offices and home in Bartlesville's Price Tower, a commission he'd steered to his mentor and friend Frank Lloyd Wright (and the master's only realized skyscraper), Goff came up with the Circle Tower Apartments, also known as the 'Texas Towers'. The design was lifted from his Circle Center Development, a Bartlesville shopping centre that included two cylindrical residential towers. The Circle Apartments were free of columns and beams, with circular floors supported by a central silo and suspended at the perimeter by tensioned steel cables. The slab floors, blank as the Oklahoma prairie, could be reconfigured for any use with movable partitions. The skin was made of adjustable louvres that would be infinitely variable, changing at the whim of each tenant. Goff thought the simplified structure would cost about a third less than a conventional tower, and, owing to its flexibility, would never become obsolete.

TENSILE STADIUM
Richard Bradshaw; Welton Becket & Associates
New Orleans, Louisiana (US), 1964

It was foreseeable that Welton Becket, a titan of Corporate Modernism, would turn to Richard Bradshaw to collaborate on a stadium for the New Orleans Saints football team. Bradshaw had been instrumental in the design and engineering of the Theme Building (1961) at Los Angeles International Airport, which when completed had put an all-but-indelible 'future' stamp on the city then suffering from impostor complex. Becket wanted to lure New Orleans with a whiff of the new, and Bradshaw came up with a hyperboloid whose pinched waist was formed by a girdle of cables. The covered, multipurpose, air-conditioned stadium was meant to seat 50,000, and was equally suited to a Beatles concert or a presidential nomination convention.

The roof was hung from twenty-four pylons, secured to the ground by a thicket of guy wires. A cat's cradle of 192 cables strung between a ring near the top of the pylons and a compression ring around the arena permitted a clear-span structure 183 m (600 ft) in diameter. The building looked as if it had been drawn using a Spirograph; the only thing missing from the roulette curves was colour.

Although part of the architectural vocabulary since 1896, when the Russian engineer-architect Vladimir Shukhov built the first hyperboloid tower, the Bradshaw–Becket design was prescient: Frei Otto would use tensile-structure tents at Expo '67 in Montreal and the 1972 Munich Olympics, and hyperboloid forms have since proliferated. Still, Becket's early 1960s gambit failed to win a design contract. A few years later New Orleans commissioned Curtis and Davis Architects to build the Superdome, which opened in 1975. A purely hyperboloid stadium remains a pipe dream.

NEW ORLEANS NATIONAL JAZZ CENTER
Morphosis
New Orleans, Louisiana (US), 2006

When Hurricane Katrina made landfall in New Orleans on 29 August 2005, the 225 km/h (140 mph) winds and torrential floods swamped the city and scrubbed away more than 100,000 homes – 62 per cent of the area's housing stock. The elderly, the poor and African American people were hardest hit as the lid was blown off the city's shameful inequality. But for the city's elite, the hurricane was less disaster than opportunity, providing a chance to remake the city's civic centre.

The New Orleans National Jazz Center was the linchpin of the plan. Laurence Geller, whose firm owned the Katrina-damaged Hyatt Hotel adjacent to the site, hired the Pritzker Prize-winner Thom Mayne, of Morphosis, to give New Orleans a 'global view. His designs are dramatic, not trite,' the property investor said. Sitting at the corner of Poydras Street and Loyola Avenue, the Jazz Center was like a giant armoured whale shark, rearing to take a bite out of the street. With a skin of bent and folded silver mesh, which formed a shed over the main performance hall, the building peeled open, revealing its glass-enclosed underside and interior plaza.

If this was jazz, though, it was hard-bop, not Dixieland. And pure Mayne: a solitary landmark that overwhelmed its surroundings, intent on shredding the local cultural and political heritage it so vehemently rejected. Still, the Jazz Center fulfilled Geller's hope for an icon that would give New Orleans a fresh face. The city didn't come up with the money, however, leading Mayne to remark that 'the outsiders are more interested in your town than the insiders.'

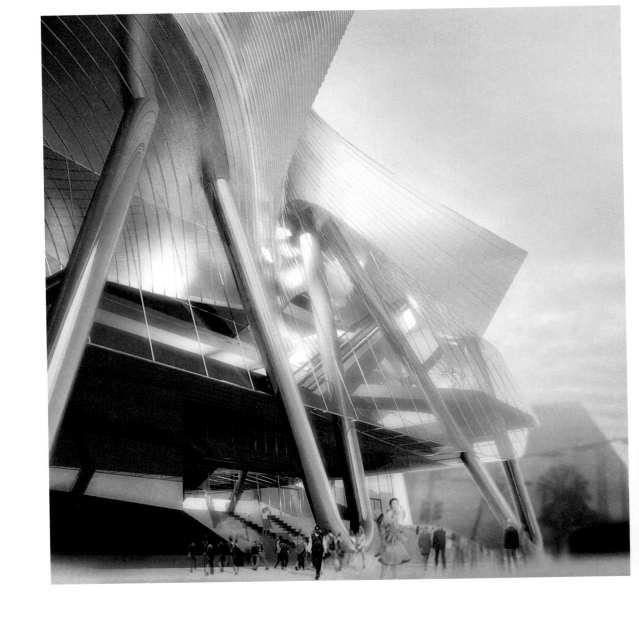

NORTH & CENTRAL AMERICA

PIAZZA D'ITALIA PHASE II
Charles Moore
New Orleans, Louisiana
(US), 1984

A monument to New Orleans' sizeable Italian community, Charles Moore's Piazza d'Italia is one of the icons of the Postmodern movement. Located just south of Poydras Street (the main artery of the city's Central Business District), the fantastical space is a jubilant blend of styles, shapes, allusions and colours, including semicircular colonnades, protruding arches, varied classical orders, neon and metallic surfaces, and strange satyric busts spitting water into a shallow, circular fountain.

A few years after the piazza's splashy opening, Moore began producing drawings for Phase II, in which the city would entice developers to fund an adjacent commercial development, including a hotel, a casino and an office building. That vision took the piazza's aggressive eclecticism even further. In addition to Italianate pediments and arches, the caricatured historical references now included Victorian glasshouses, Egyptian squared arches and streamlined porthole windows. The architectural writer Drexel Turner called it a 'complex, quasi-operatic facade'.

But the idea was a victim of bad timing. The oil bust and recession of the mid-1980s, the piazza's surprising lack of popularity, and funds still owed from the construction of Phase I made it unappealing to buyers, and only one developer made a bid, which was rejected. The plan quietly faded away. While preservationists worried it might destroy the piazza, the Loews New Orleans Hotel, which opened in a former office building on the site in 2004, was ordered to contribute $1 million towards restoring the decaying gathering spot, which it duly did – although sadly it did little to attract new visitors to the space.

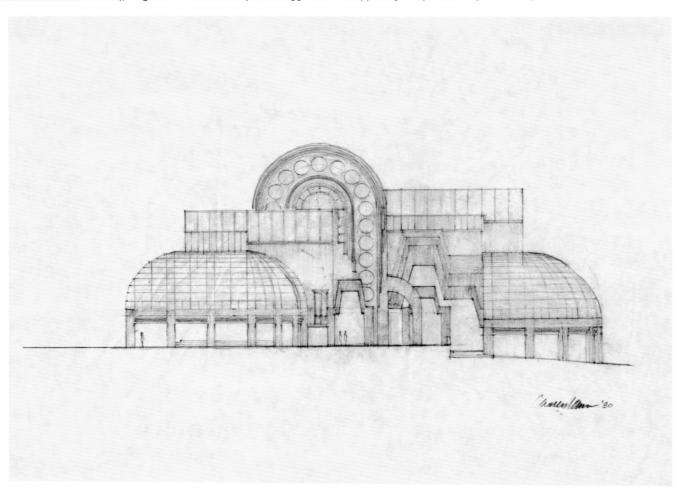

TOURIST TOWER
Robert Rasche
Milwaukee, Wisconsin
(US), 1964

About a decade after the opening of Disneyland, and two years after the Seattle Space Needle began welcoming visitors, the Milwaukee architect Robert Rasche proposed for his city a cylindrical tower that would in effect combine the two. His 267 m (876 ft) tall Tourist Tower dominating the Brew City's skyline, was a serious proposal, and Milwaukee sold him the site, on Wells Street, about a block from City Hall, at a majorly discounted price – about $11,000.

A thin central core was fitted with seven stacked 'exhibition areas', including a revolving beer garden and an artificial stream for fishing, with external metal latticework supporting the weight of each floor. Glass lifts would rocket through the core to the observatory in two minutes. The project's backers, according to the journalist Matthew Prigge, claimed the building would draw a million people to the city each year.

In 1965 Rasche, tinkering with the concept in order to attract funding, proposed a new edifice standing 305 m (1,000 ft) tall and rechristened the 'Diamond Tower', thanks to its sleek, diamond-patterned facade. The bulk of its entertainment programme – including a 'jungle safari', revolving 'rotorama theatre', porpoise show, 'dancing waters' beer hall and shooting gallery – was inside a bulky three-storey base. At the top, revolving restaurants and a flying saucer ride would keep guests entertained. Ground broke in 1966, but Rasche had failed to secure enough financing. The site remained a hole in the ground until his death in 1979, when the city reacquired it and filled it in. It is now a car park.

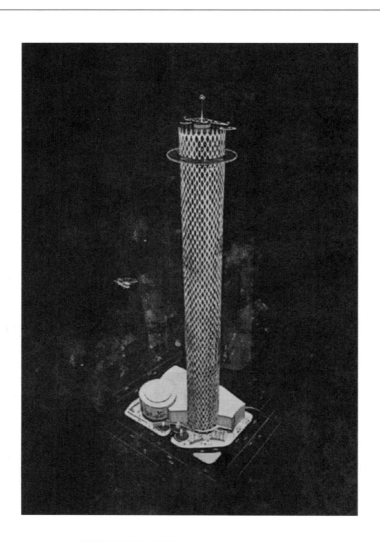

CONVENTION CENTER
Ludwig Mies van der Rohe
Chicago, Illinois (US), 1953

As early as 1927, Robert R McCormick, the publisher of the *Chicago Tribune* and a prominent isolationist who would oppose America's entry into World War II, was lobbying for a lakeside convention centre in the city he dominated.

Plans came and went. Ludwig Mies van der Rohe's proposal, first made in 1953, was the best, but was destined never to be.

Supported by the South Side Planning Board – an unsanctioned group of academics and civic leaders hoping to transform what the *New York Times* architecture critic Ada Louise Huxtable called the largest slum in North America – Mies offered a structural *coup de maître* that would have been the world's biggest convention centre. A huge hall 213 m (699 ft) square, the centre was 30 m (98 ft) high and sat beneath a continuous web of steel trusses. There would be no interior columns in a vast room that could hold 50,000 people. The aluminium exterior cladding was an abstract bas-relief of alternating pyramids and triangles, mimicking the steel structure to which it was affixed.

Chicago's political authorities rejected the plan, saying that it would take too long to evict the 3,000 residents of the area and acquire the land. In 1958 ground was broken for a $35 million facility designed by Alfred P Shaw, and named after McCormick. It burned to the ground in 1967, and was replaced in 1971 by a dark steel-and-glass structure by Mies's former colleague Gene R Summers.

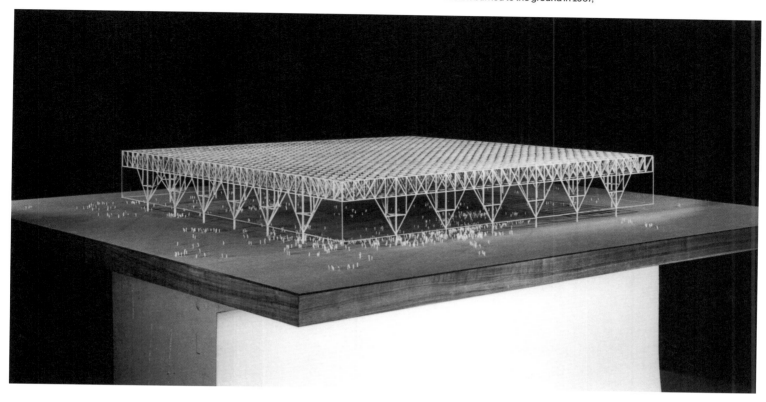

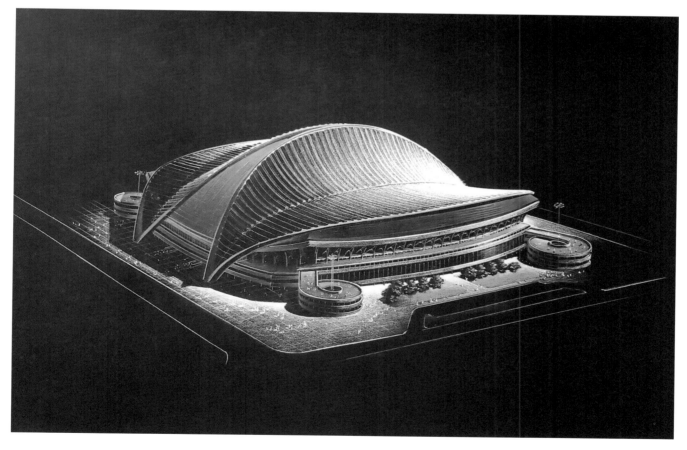

CHICAGO CONVERTIBLE STADIUM
Charles Deaton
Chicago, Illinois (US), 1986

The Colorado architect Charles Deaton is best known for his 'Sleeper House', the clam-shaped mountainside structure featured in Woody Allen's sci-fi comedy *Sleeper* (1973). Deaton was one of the most creative thinkers of his time, dreaming up ideas both inspired by nature and of 'why didn't I think of that?' utility. Perhaps his greatest obsession was stadia, particularly reconfigurable ones. He designed Kansas City's Truman Sports Complex, including the beloved Arrowhead and Kauffman stadia, but his plan to top both with a half-moon-shaped roof rolling from one side to the other on tracks never got the green light.

In 1986 the Chicago developers Daniel Shannon and Robert Wislow, who had secured a stadium site in the city's South Loop neighbourhood, hired Deaton, who designed a conch-shaped facility for the Chicago White Sox and Bears that could morph from a 50,000-seat venue for baseball to an 80,000-seat spot for football. Movable stand segments, rolling and pivoting on tracks, could be reconfigured to change the shape of the field from a diamond to an oval, avoiding the awkward compositions common in multi-sport complexes. The same year Deaton filed for (and later received) a patent for his 'multi-purpose stadium system'. 'Most spectators want a football stadium to look like a football stadium and a baseball stadium to look like a baseball stadium,' the filing noted. 'Convertible stadiums now in use look like a make-shift compromise.' While the White Sox agreed to go ahead with the $255 million endeavour, the Bears couldn't be convinced to share a home or leave their current stadium, Soldier Field, and so the project was doomed.

MILE-HIGH TOWER
Frank Lloyd Wright
Chicago, Illinois (US), 1956

Despite his aversion to density – and to congested cities in general – Frank Lloyd Wright devised one of the most audacious skyscraper schemes in history. In 1956, at the age of eighty-nine, he unveiled his design for 'The Illinois', or Mile-High Tower, at a press-filled reception at the Sherman House Hotel in Chicago. The presentation board itself was more than 7.6 m (25 ft) tall, depicting an extremely thin three-sided structure that steadily tapered and eroded as it rose, like a fractured stone.

Housing 100,000 occupants (as well as 76 tandem-cab lifts and parking for 15,000 cars), the 528-storey mixed-use tower was intended as a vertical city, freeing space around it by eliminating the need to build tall nearby. (This was a key element of Wright's never-realized Broadacre City, with its generously spaced towers.) The plan drew on the architect's 'tap-root' experiments, employing a deeply embedded steel-reinforced-concrete core, from which individual floors were cantilevered via steel supports, like the branches of a tree. He devised tap-root towers in several cities, but the only successes were the Price Tower in Bartlesville, Oklahoma, and the Johnson Wax Tower in Racine, Wisconsin. Needless to say, the Mile-High never came to fruition. Wright, who died three years after unveiling the proposal, never found a client or a site for the concept. Yet the plan has had a lasting influence. Just look at the tallest building in the world, the Burj Khalifa in Dubai, a tripod tower that could be its fraternal twin.

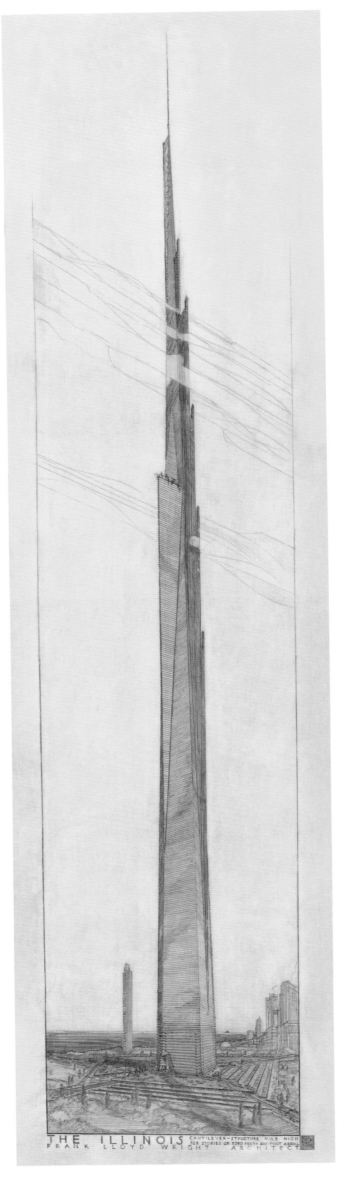

NORTH & CENTRAL AMERICA

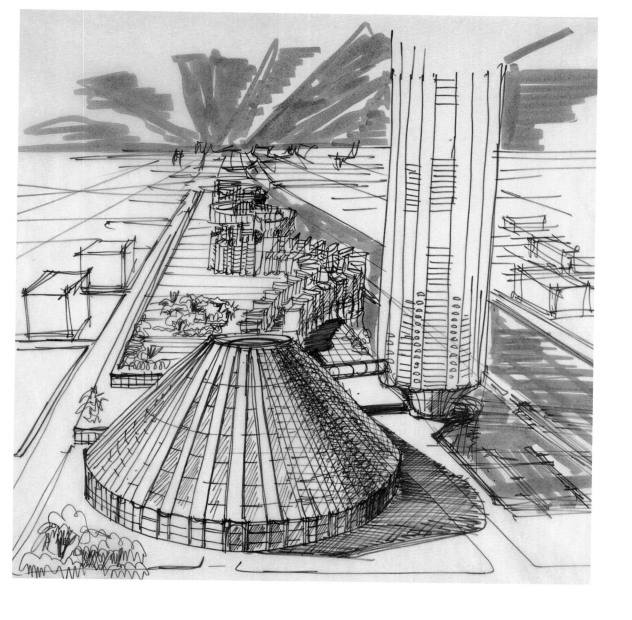

RIVER CITY
Bertrand Goldberg
Chicago, Illinois (US), 1972

Walk along the Chicago River and your eye is certain to stop, slightly stunned, at Marina City (1967), a five-building 'city within a city' highlighted by two cylindrical towers sixty-five storeys high, their scalloped balconies resembling strange concrete flower petals. But Bertrand Goldberg, a former student of Ludwig Mies van der Rohe who migrated towards a far more organic form of Modernism, had his sights set on something altogether more ambitious. In 1972 he proposed plans in South Loop for River City, a complex of dozens of similarly cylindrical seventy-two-storey towers (the plans show as many as thirty buildings), growing out of sunken bases and linked via skybridges into sets of three, or 'triads'. In later variations smaller structures followed a snake-shaped path for about 0.8 km (1/2 mile) down the riverside.

Goldberg developed several iterations, but each time he took the city-within-a-city concept much more literally, slotting in residences, offices, schools, shopping centres (called 'shopping spirals'), theatres, hotels and a festival market, among other components. Goldberg had first discussed the idea in 1968 with Harris Ward, CEO of the energy utility Commonwealth Edison, who was thrilled by the concept of devising a new type of urbanity. But Ward died of cancer in 1974, and was replaced by Tom Ayres, who instead hired Skidmore, Owings & Merrill to design Printers Row, a more conventional development.

Goldberg's plan wasn't dead, however. He worked with the Chesapeake and Ohio Railroad, which owned the railway land along the river, and later the developer Dan Epstein, stopping only when the single S-shaped apartment block he had designed, also called River City, went up in 1986.

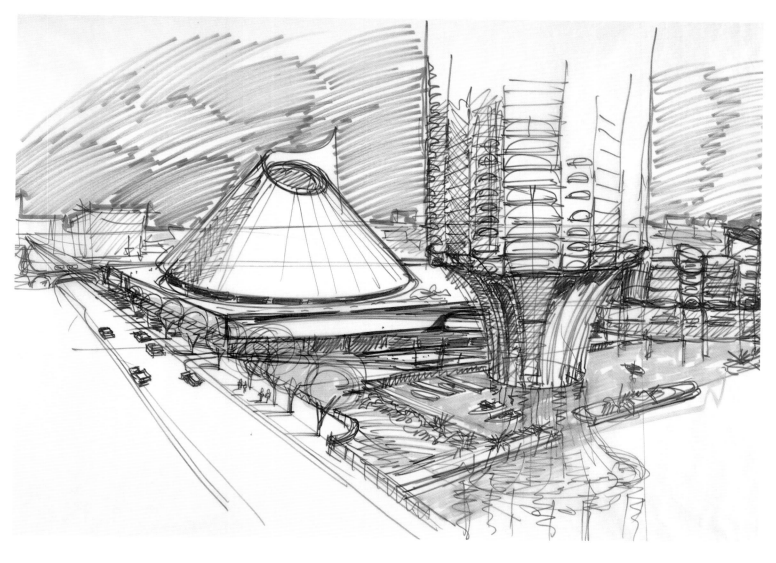

MONAGHAN FARM TOWER
Gunnar Birkerts
Ann Arbor, Michigan
(US), 1987

Located on a 121 hectare (299 acre) site just outside Ann Arbor, Michigan, Domino's Farms Office Park is a complex 0.8 km (1/2 mile) long designed in 1985 by the Detroit-based architect Gunnar Birkerts. The project was the vision of Domino's Pizza founder, Tom Monaghan – one of the greatest collectors of Frank Lloyd Wright artefacts in the world – who asked Birkerts to create a company headquarters that would pay homage to Wright's prairie style, with a low, copper-clad roof, deep overhangs, red walls and thick planting. The pencil-thin facility – now multi-tenanted and landmarked – still houses a chapel, a petting farm, and a museum containing much of Monaghan's Wright collection.

But the highlight of the complex – a sort of campanile to Birkerts's building – was never to be. Nicknamed the 'Leaning Tower of Pizza', the thirty-storey structure was inclined to the east by at least 15 degrees. 'Vertical is neutral and I've been working with the vertical all my life,' said Birkerts, who drew initial sketches for the project while on a trip to Italy. The drawings reveal a textured, light brown edifice with a roof that projects out and up, like the sharp prow of a ship. Thin structural columns support the off-centre behemoth, with thin grids of windows providing illumination.

Local planning problems stymied its progress, however, and any hope of completion died when Monaghan sold Domino's in 1998. 'I thought I'd have a tower,' he told a local reporter in Ann Arbor. 'The tower was the main thing when I started this.' Today a 15 m (49 ft) scale model of the design stands on the site of the proposed building.

NORTH & CENTRAL AMERICA

HOMESTYLE CENTER
Paul Rudolph; George Nelson; Eliot Noyes; Ralph Rapson; Richard Buckminster Fuller
Grand Rapids, Michigan, (US), 1956

What do Paul Rudolph, George Nelson, Eliot Noyes, Ralph Rapson and Richard Buckminster Fuller all have in common? They all participated in an effort spearheaded by the Detroit corporate lawyer Jason L Honigman to create experimental residences for the Homestyle Center, a so-called outdoor museum of houses on a site near Grand Rapids, Michigan.

In 1954 Honigman, vice-president of the Market Realty Company, partnered with the local architect Arleigh 'Bud' Hitchcock to form the Home Research Foundation, which laid out plans for fifty abodes set in a ring around a lake. The advanced designs proposed by many of the country's leading architects might well have propelled the United States' home-building business into new realms of ambition and innovation. Rudolph's steel-frame home opened completely to the elements, but with the push of a button its plastic walls could descend for protection. Nelson's home on stilts consisted of identical bubble-topped prefabricated concrete cubes that could be assembled in any way the owner wanted. Noyes created a domed concrete house on four piers, while Fuller, unsurprisingly, incorporated geodesic domes. Frank Lloyd Wright was invited to participate, but would join only if he could be in charge. The project was highlighted on NBC's *Today Show* and garnered plenty of press, but unable to secure private or municipal financial backing for even its first set of homes, the foundation closed its doors in 1957. The lake around which the homes were to be built is now part of the Frederik Meijer Gardens & Sculpture Park.

LOT NUMBER	ARCHITECTS' HOMES
1	R. BUCKMINSTER FULLER Raleigh, No. Carolina
2	ALDEN DOW Midland, Michigan
3	CLIFFORD WRIGHT Detroit, Michigan
4	JOHN B. DINWIDDIE New Orleans, La.
11	PAUL RUDOLPH Cambridge, Mass.
12	ELIOT F. NOYES New Canaan, Conn.
13	ROBERT A. LITTLE Cleveland, Ohio
14	GEORGE NELSON New York, N. Y.
22	HARWELL H. HARRIS Fort Worth, Texas
23	KAZUMI ADACHI Los Angeles, California
24	RALPH RAPSON Minneapolis, Minnesota
25	PAINTER, WEEKS & McCARTY Knoxville, Tennessee
26	ZEMA & BUMGARDNER Seattle, Washington
27	WURSTER, BERNARDI & EMMONS San Francisco, California
28	JONES & EMMONS Los Angeles, California
29	RURAL REHABILITATION
30	URBAN REHABILITATION
31	IMPORT HOME
32	ROYAL BARRY WILLS Boston, Massachusetts
33	COMPONENT HOME
34	PREFABRICATED HOME
35	BUILDER HOME
36-37	UNIVERSITY OF ILLINOIS Urbana, Illinois

home research foundation, inc.

PLOT PLAN - ORIGINAL 25 HOMES AND SERVICE BUILDINGS

AREA	SERVICE BUILDINGS
A	RELIEF STATION
B	GROUND MAINTENANCE & SERVICE BUILDINGS
C	CHILDREN'S SUPERVISED PLAY AREA
D	ADMINISTRATION BUILDING
E	OUTDOOR PATIO
F	EXECUTIVE OFFICES, RESTAURANT & AUDITORIUM
G	MAIN ENTRANCE

KERN BLOCK TOWER
Glen Howard Small
Detroit, Michigan (US), 1966

The road to the redevelopment of downtown Detroit – a city whose name has become synonymous with urban decline – once led through Monument Valley, Arizona, some 3,050 km (1,900 miles) to the southwest. Circuitous, unlikely, *rus in urbe*? All of the above.

In 1966 Glen Howard Small was working for Charles Blessing in Detroit's planning department. Blessing, Small said, 'was a romantic, and loved Monument Valley'. Small's job was to sketch a new civic centre for 2 hectares (5 acres) of mud – a 'dismal swamp', the *Detroit Free Press* called it – a pentagon-shaped patch that had been flattened by urban renewal. His resuscitation took cues from the 300-m (1,000-ft) high sandstone buttes of his beloved valley. He drew two pairs of pencil-thin, cedar-straight towers, bookending a cluster of stair-stepped stacks of glass cubes mounted on a grid-frame system, allowing them to be swapped at will. These inclining pieces rotated off axis, creating a vast baroque, conical atrium, criss-crossed with lifts and terraces connecting shops, travel agencies, nightclubs and restaurants, flanked by a hotel and apartments. Small was channelling John Portman's atrium hotels a decade before Portman channelled them himself. The interior space had the life of a railway station or an opera-house lobby.

Detroit magazine featured the design on its cover on 8 January 1967, asking 'What Might We Do, What Can We Do, On Our Big Block?' 'Nothing' was the answer. From 1966 to 1999, the block at the literal crossroads of Detroit – filled in and laid in concrete – was a park in name only, devoid of trees, fountains, monuments and people.

INDIANA TOWER
César Pelli
Indianapolis, Indiana
(US), 1981

In the early 1980s the Midwestern city of Indianapolis was looking for a monument to rival St Louis's Gateway Arch and Seattle's Space Needle. The Argentina-born architect César Pelli, who later gained world fame with such buildings as the Petronas Towers in Kuala Lumpur, was brought in to design the 'Indiana Tower'. He envisioned an obelisk-like spire 228 m (748 ft) tall, made of concrete and limestone, with a walkway 2.8 km (1¾ miles) long spiralling to the top, from where visitors could peer 65 km (40 miles) across Indiana farmland. Along the walkway, the story of the state would be etched into the limestone stairwell.

Pelli claimed, 'Like the Eiffel Tower in Europe, it will be the thing you must see. It will be known as well in Moscow as it is in Singapore.' Others disagreed, warning that there was nothing to see in Indiana even with a bird's-eye view. Pelli's faceted $15 million tower, which would have been the centrepiece of the city's White River State Park, was curiously understated, its only detailing the dully repetitive spiral of arched windows piercing the exterior. Critics condemned it mercilessly, comparing it to a gigantic corn cob or an oil derrick. Raymond Ogle, then president of the Indianapolis chapter of the Indiana Society of Architects, chimed in: 'It's just unbecoming.' He quoted the aphorism, 'If you're going to make it bad, don't make it big.' Undaunted, Pelli said, 'I cannot make everybody like everything.'

The state declined to pay for the tower, and no private developer stepped up. By November 1984 the project was on hold, destined to become a charcoal-and-graphite memory.

GARY TOURIST CENTER
Bertrand Goldberg
Gary, Indiana (US), 1990

Gary, Indiana's claim to fame is being the birthplace of Michael Jackson and his family. But the small, scrappy city on Lake Michigan – essentially a suburb of Chicago – might have had a close second hallmark if Bertrand Goldberg's lakeside tourist and recreation centre had received the green light.

In about 1989 Goldberg and Gary's mayor Thomas V Barnes began sketching out a vision to transform the town's decrepit, fading industrial waterfront (much of it owned by US Steel, which was eager to get the land and its property taxes off their books) into a thriving marina for more than 1,200 boats, along with a series of artificial islands. Some of Goldberg's ebullient drawings contained golf courses and swimming pools, while the lively marina consisted of a string of kernel-shaped pods hovering on stilts over boat launches. Other renderings fore-

grounded the plan's money-making engines: a convention centre, hundreds of homes, and four or five casinos. These buildings, with powerful klieg lights shining up from their roofs, resembled otherworldly castles, pyramids, domes, tents and parachutes.

With Gary bleeding residents and jobs at an alarming rate, the plans were quite popular. But while residents approved a referendum supporting pro-gambling legislation for Gary in 1989, the state legislature blocked the effort several times, and the project faded away.

By 1995 the state had approved riverboat gambling in Gary for two entities only: Trump Casino and Barden's Majestic Star, both of which had opened by 1996.

PROGRESSIVE
CORPORATION TOWER
Frank Gehry
Cleveland, Ohio (US), 1987

Jammed into the United States' collective psyche thanks to its advertisements featuring fictional salespeople, such as the always perky 'Flo', Progressive Corporation is headquartered in Mayfield, Ohio, a tiny suburb northeast of Cleveland. But if its chairman Peter B Lewis had had his way in the 1980s, its base would be in a Frank Gehry-designed skyscraper in the centre of Cleveland.

In 1986 Lewis asked Gehry to design a tower nearly 260 m (853 ft) tall overlooking Lake Erie from the northeastern corner of the city's Daniel Burnham-designed Mall (1903). Perched atop concrete platforms laid over the railway tracks (and portions of the Shoreway freeway) separating the Mall from the lake, the project would help to connect Cleveland's downtown core to its waterfront. In addition to 93,000 sq. m (1 million sq. ft) of office space, the tower included an art museum, a 'creativity centre', a research centre and a health club. Gehry proposed two connected vertical structures, one clad in stone and the other in shiny metal. Each side partially deformed while adding unorthodox elements, such as metallic grids and a crown resembling an oversized newspaper. Further plans for the development included an adjacent high-rise hotel, a 30 m (98 ft) walkway from the Mall to the lakefront by Donald Judd, and sculptures by Richard Serra and Claes Oldenburg.

The proposal – Gehry's last major urban waterfront scheme before the Guggenheim Bilbao – did not gain the support of civic leaders, and Progressive's board voted to nix it. Lewis and Gehry, who also failed to build Lewis's house, finally collaborated in 2002 with the opening of Case Western Reserve's Peter B Lewis Building in Cleveland, home of the university's Weatherhead School of Management.

AIR FORCE MUSEUM
Roche Dinkeloo
Dayton, Ohio (US), 1963

When the Air Force Museum Foundation first approached Kevin Roche, then a partner in Eero Saarinen's office, to build a new museum at Wright-Patterson Air Force Base near Dayton, they wanted a monument to the Age of Aircraft.

The structure had to be so large that it would make a ten-engine B-36 jet – the largest mass-produced aircraft ever built, with the longest wingspan of any combat aircraft – appear like a scale model.

Roche, working after Saarinen's death in 1961, designed a soaring, wedge-shaped roof covering 3.2 hectares (8 acres), made of a lattice of cables covered with a steel deck suspended from steel pylons at the four corners. The enormous tarpaulin stretched over the entire floor, floating 36 m (118 ft) above, without any interior supports, an unobstructed span of 244 m (801 ft) at its longest. The pylons were buried in huge earth mounds, tying the building to the flat site. Roche said at the time, 'It's as if you roofed over three-and-a-half city blocks at the 12-storey level.' A walled walkway, descending to a rotunda, effectively kept the huge hangar out of sight, so that the building was revealed only when the visitor emerged onto a runway outside. There, the planes sat on progressively elevated platforms, always silhouetted against the open sky at the far end of the structure.

At the time the project was unveiled, an awed spectator looked at Roche's model and said, 'It'll never get off the ground.' It never did.

BOSTON CENTER PLAN
Walter Gropius,
Martin Wagner
Boston, Massachusetts (US), 1944

Joseph Hudnut, first dean of the Harvard University Graduate School of Design, lured former Bauhaus director Walter Gropius, Gropius's protégé Marcel Breuer and the legendary Berlin planner Martin Wagner to his school following their exile from Nazi Germany. In 1942 Gropius and Wagner taught a seminar, 'The New Boston Center', in which students reimagined the core of the struggling city. From this seed grew the duo's entry into the Boston Contest, a competition held in 1944 with the aim of overhauling the city entirely, from political organization to city planning, sponsored by the Boston Society of Architects, local universities, the mayor of Boston and the Governor of Massachusetts, among others. The purse for the three winners was just $5,000, but the true 'prize' would be influence. Juror Elisabeth May Herlihy of the Boston City Planning Board, promised that her organization would help to implement the winning plans.

The entry Gropius and Wagner submitted was both radical and brutal, calling for the large-scale demolition of the centre's outdated buildings and streets, to be replaced with a mega-scaled core suited to the modern age. The new centre (pictured above in an artist's impression from a 1944 issue of *Popular Science*) would take the form of an arc-shaped megastructure lined with slabs and towers of all functions – from hotels and housing to bus and helicopter terminals – spaced around green courtyards and parks, fed by highways, and sited above myriad underground car parks.

Gropius and Wagner did not prevail, but the three victors would fail as well. All had suggested a degree of metropolitan-level planning that the communities around Boston were unwilling to accept.

1976 WORLD EXPO
Jan Wampler
Boston, Massachusetts
(US), 1967

The United States, planning to celebrate the bicentenary of its founding, was keen to host a World Expo in 1976. Preparing extensive bids were three cities that had played a pivotal role in the country's history: Philadelphia, PA, Washington, DC, and Boston, MA. Of that group, the most surprising proposal presented to the White House's American Revolution Bicentennial Commission came from Boston, a notoriously provincial city that suggested an $800 million megastructure projecting far into the harbour. Leading the design was the visionary architect, poet and Massachusetts Institute of Technology professor Jan Wampler, whose scheme, backed by the Boston Redevelopment Authority and New England dairy millionaire Gilbert Hood, was positioned not as a Disney-like carnival or 'festival in a park', but as an 'all-out attack' on the nation's problems of housing, sprawl and inequality, serving city residents long after the fair and becoming a prototype for the expansion of other coastal cities. Floating, multi-level latticed-steel platforms containing event venues, housing and more than 142 hectares (351 acres) of open space and public amenities – including a large water plaza and a transparent dome 152 m (499 ft) in diameter for recreation – would extend from Columbia Point in the city's Dorchester neighbourhood to Thompson Island, about 1.6 km (1 mile) east.

But Wempler couldn't even rally enough support in his own city, where many were wary of – among other things – the plan's cost and its potential impact on the harbour. After the city council rejected the plan unanimously on 9 September 1969, the Bicentennial Commission chose Philadelphia. The Philadelphia plan fell apart, too, and in the end, no city hosted a World Expo in 1976.

KENT SCHOOL, GIRLS' CHAPEL
Marcel Breuer
Kent, Connecticut
(US), 1967

Founded in 1906 by the Episcopal Reverend Frederick Herbert Sill, the Kent School is one of the northeastern United States' most prestigious blue-blood boarding academies. But it has always had a progressive streak (at least compared to its sister schools), and in 1960 the institution took the then radical step of establishing a girls' school about 6.5 km (4 miles) from its original campus.

In 1967 Kent commissioned an equally radical architect, the Modernist master Marcel Breuer, to design a chapel for the new school. Embracing Kent's innovative spirit, the edifice would be a revolutionary take on traditional church design, embodying – as the headmaster, Sidney N Towle, wrote in a letter to Breuer – 'the new theological insights, and the most suitable contemporary materials and engineering techniques'. Perched on a stone base, its heavy, canted concrete walls popped out in places, carving out niched windows, doors and space for the organ. Inside, a diamond-shaped sanctuary featured a circular central altar surrounded by banks of pews on both the ground floor and in the balcony. Intersecting diagonal beams spanned the ceiling, creating decorative coffers and mysteriously glowing light wells. A separate concrete campanile, punctured by square cutouts for both bells and bell-ringers, took the form of a twisting hyperbolic paraboloid.

The muscular concrete designs of both church and campanile bear a striking resemblance to Breuer's breathtaking St John's Abbey Church in Collegeville, Minnesota, completed in 1961. But the school administration decided not to build the girls' chapel, preferring, as they put it, to 'spend the money on people not buildings'.

NEW HAVEN GOVERNMENT CENTER
Paul Rudolph
New Haven, Connecticut (US), 1968

Led largely by Richard Lee, who was mayor of this Connecticut city for eight terms, mid-century urban renewal was not kind to New Haven. It resulted in the demolition of expansive stretches of the Colonial-era city, including almost 2,200 businesses and numerous homes. But when it all began, it was viewed as a model for reforming the blighted American metropolis. Robert Weaver, secretary of housing and urban development under President Lyndon B Johnson, said, 'New Haven is coming close to our dreams of a slumless city,' while the labor secretary W. Willard Wirtz called it 'the greatest success story in the history of the world'.
The planned centrepiece of New Haven's resurrection-by-Modernism was to be its new Government Center, designed by the star architect Paul Rudolph, then dean of architecture at Yale (he had famously designed the school's Brutalist-style Art and Architecture Building, 1958–63). The complex, on the edge of the New Haven Green park in the centre of town, would include a new city hall, library, plaza and police station, among other elements. Bookending the city's High Victorian Gothic City Hall and County Courthouse, its exposed concrete-and-glass wings bridged meandering street-level plazas. The lofty interiors would meander in a similarly urban fashion, topped by cement bridges and long rooflights.
Rudolph worked on the gargantuan endeavour for more than a decade, trying especially hard to remain sensitive to a growing preservation movement (hence the salvaging of the existing buildings). But the project's cost – and slashed city budgets – finally brought it down in the early 1980s.

NEW HAVEN RAILROAD STATION
Minoru Yamasaki
New Haven, Connecticut (US), 1955

For a brief twenty-one months, the New Haven Railroad had at its helm the pugnacious Patrick B McGinnis. McGinnis had gained control through a hostile proxy fight in 1954, when the railways were haemorrhaging money and passengers to aeroplanes and cars. He hoped to stem the bleeding by changing the perception – and perhaps even the reality – of the failing company's image. First he hired the brilliant graphic designer Herbert Matter, who created a truly modern logo, a slab-serif stacked 'NH', that would outlast the railway. Next, he commissioned Minoru Yamasaki to design an entirely new railway station in the line's namesake city in Connecticut.
The plan was to construct a quartet of buildings on the far side of the tracks and demolish the Beaux-Arts station from 1920, by Cass Gilbert (who also designed the Woolworth Building in New York City, 1908–13, and the US Supreme Court in Washington, DC, 1935). There would be a low-lying L-shaped building with a fan-folded roof, a twenty-storey black steel-and-glass hotel with Matter's 'NH' stamped on the sides of the rooftop lift shaft, and a *shoji*-like restaurant pavilion on stilts above a reflecting pool. But it was Yamasaki's depot that gave the ensemble the necessary sense of modernity and movement. The transparent building had thirteen parabolic arches skinned in heat-absorbing glass. For all those straight lines, Yamasaki proposed a curve as his most eloquent answer.
McGinnis was ousted in 1956, and later spent time in prison for bilking another railway company. The New Haven Railroad itself declared bankruptcy in 1961.

ARCH OF FREEDOM
Wallace Harrison
Albany, New York (US), 1963

With its expansive raised podium, bombastic edifices and thousands of tonnes of white marble, Wallace Harrison's 40 hectare (99 acre) Empire State Plaza in Albany, New York, is one of the grander civic complexes on the planet. Harrison, the architect of choice for New York State's governor/would-be pharaoh Nelson Rockefeller, specialized in such Brasília-like work, having led the development of both the United Nations headquarters and the Lincoln Center. But the Empire State scheme, intended to transform the state capital into what Rockefeller called 'the most beautiful and efficient capital city anywhere in the world', could have been even more titanic. When first unveiled in 1963, it was to be highlighted by a chunky parabolic arch 102 m (335 ft) tall, anchoring the south end of the site and wedged between the planned New York State Library and the New York State Museum. The raised base of the arch contained a 1,500-seat amphitheatre as well as a 'shrine' containing an early draft of Lincoln's Emancipation Proclamation.

By the time ground was broken in 1965, however, the arch was gone, killed off by cost and logistics: both museum and library wanted more space, and something had to give. Ironically, this grand arch died the same year that Eero Saarinen's Gateway Arch in St Louis was built. Now the two facilities occupy Harrison's neo-Palladian building on the site, the New York State Museum Library & Archives, replacing the arch with a beacon not to freedom but to history, culture and bureaucracy.

SYRACUSE CITY HALL
Paul Rudolph
Syracuse, New York
(US), 1964

Syracuse, New York – once a thriving manufacturing centre served by the Erie Canal – has a grand City Hall to prove it: Charles Erastus Colton's rough limestone, Romanesque Revival pile from 1892. In 1963 the city, engaging in an aggressive campaign of urban renewal and hoping to gain space for its cramped municipal offices, proposed plans for a new iteration down the street, at a cost of $5.5 million, designed by the skyrocketing architect Paul Rudolph.

The centrepiece of the $35 million Community Plaza, the U-shaped Brutalist complex wrapped around an octagonal amphitheatre and a paved porch for public gatherings, and stepped up in angled tiers along each flank to provide rooftop gathering spaces. A glassy, tubular structure bridged the open far side, preserving views across the city. The hulking complex was connected via ramps and walkways to the plaza (as was IM Pei's future Everson Museum, which still stands), inviting citizens inside literally and figuratively.

The plan, which was criticized by some as bunker-like and over-scaled, and lauded by others as a symbol of a modern, efficient Syracuse, was delayed by associate architect Ketcham, Miller & Arnold, which toiled for several years on the complex construction drawings. By the late 1960s the city had begun to feel the pain of industrial decline, and by 1970 it was reporting untenable deficits, squashing the dream of this radical building. The site now contains a prison, the hideous Onondaga County Justice Center (1992). The naysayers who warned that Rudolph's design would resemble a prison finally got what they had feared, only much worse.

SKY MOUND
Nancy Holt
Kearny, New Jersey
(US), 1984

Nancy Holt was a key member of the Earth, Land and Conceptual art movements. She was recruited by New Jersey's Hackensack Meadowland Development Commission to transform a highly visible landfill site of 23 hectares (57 acres), 30 m (98 ft) high, containing roughly 10 million tonnes of garbage. Holt saw the wasteland – on the New Jersey Turnpike just 6.5 km (4 miles) from the fume-belching Holland Tunnel – as 'a place where sky and ground meet, where you can track the Sun, Moon and stars with the naked eye, and where you have 360-degree panoramic views of Manhattan, Newark, the Pulaski Skyway, networks of highways and train tracks, old steel turn-bridges, and here and there decaying remnants of the Industrial Revolution'.

Holt's earthwork was conceived as a sculpted observatory. The flat-topped pyramid would rise to a height of 33.5 m (110 ft) and be criss-crossed by gravel paths leading to smaller mounds aligning with the sun, moon and major stars on the solstices and key astronomical dates. A portion of the methane gas produced by the decaying rubbish would be piped to hillocks outfitted with methane jets that would be ignited in periodic starburst flares. These sunspots were designed to be visible from planes taking off from and landing at nearby Newark Airport.

All that was built, however, was a pond that, Holt hoped, would bring migratory birds and wildlife to the grassy knolls, and drain surface water from the mounded heights. Work ceased in 1991, never to resume.

KEY PLAN FOR ELLIS ISLAND
Frank Lloyd Wright
New York, New York
(US), 1959

After Ellis Island was decommissioned as an immigration processing site in 1954, the US General Services Administration (GSA) opened the site to bids from developers. The highest offer, of $2.1 million, came from the New York-based Damon Doudt Corporation, for a 'completely self-contained city of the future', designed in early 1959 by none other than the architectural master Frank Lloyd Wright. Wright's 'Key Project' was named after its site's historical role as a 'key to a land of freedom and opportunity', as the architect put it. According to a promotional poster, it was the last commission Wright – who died in early April that year – ever accepted.

The Jules Verne-esque plan was resolutely futuristic. A circular podium was placed on top of the island, and above that a 500-room luxury hotel and apartment towers for 7,500 residents rose like stacked plates and candlesticks around a central court, while glassy, domed theatres, hospitals, churches, schools, a library and a sports arena were set in a terraced park at the perimeter of the site. Embedded into this landscape, an 'agora' (inspired by the central public space of ancient Greek cities) contained shops, banks, restaurants and nightclubs. Below this was a yacht basin for 450 boats. Most structures would be supported by gold-hued steel cables, working like suspension bridges. The car-free complex, filled with moving walkways, would be adorned by fountains and landscaping, meant to 'look like a jewel, suspended over the water and surrounded by it, free of congestion and noise'.

In the end, all proposals for Ellis Island were rejected by the GSA, and the site was declared a national monument in 1965. A museum opened there in 1990.

APARTMENT COMPLEX FOR NEW YORK
Frei Otto
New York, New York
(US), 1959

Renowned for his billowing, lightweight tensile structures, among them the stadium for the 1972 Munich Olympics and the German Pavilion at the Montreal World Expo in 1967, the architect and engineer Frei Otto constantly rethought the rigid expectations of architecture. In 1959 he dreamed up a manifesto for a series of apartment buildings near New York's Central Park that would alter the city's box-like model drastically. Their key component was a central steel spine, or mast, dug deep into the city's famed bedrock. This sturdy core would allow floors to cantilever or 'grow' outwards in virtually any formation, like the branches of a tree. 'While there would inevitably be structural and economic limitations, they would not entail the need to adhere to any particular form,' wrote the architect.

Otto's sketches depict endless configurations of platforms, living spaces and balconies, radically opening the city's 'tight-fitting', internalized living model, opening all sides to views, and incorporating the advantages of the quickly growing suburbs: greenery, patios, extra space. 'I can imagine apartments that don't feel cramped or crowded, apartments that suit their inhabitants, that are adaptable,' he wrote. The central mast contained the building's support systems; lifts, electricity, water and mechanicals, while horizontal podiums of shops and galleries blocked street noise and united several towers, creating de facto communities.

The idea, Otto argued, would help to stem the exodus to the suburbs: 'There are hundreds of thousands of people here, and they won't be pushed aside. They want to live their lives here for as long as the city exists.' The architect never got to the stage of a concrete proposal, but he remained very serious about building adaptable, affordable buildings in city centres.

HOLOCAUST MEMORIAL
Erich Mendelsohn,
Ivan Meštrović
New York, New York
(US), 1949

Warsaw Ghetto Memorial Plaza, a circular space at the south end of one of Riverside Park's promenades, at 83rd street, takes its name from the granite plaque at its centre, honouring those who bravely led the Warsaw ghetto uprising, as well as the millions more Jewish victims of Nazi brutality. One of the first Holocaust monuments in the United States, the plaque was dedicated on 19 October 1947 by Mayor William O'Dwyer. This modest tribute was meant to be the cornerstone for a much larger monument. Several artists and architects, including Jo Davidson and Percival Goodman, proposed schemes for the site, only to have them rejected by the city. The most successful was the architect Erich Mendelsohn – one of the pioneers of both Streamline Moderne architecture and Modernism – who had fled Germany in 1933. In 1949 Mendelsohn, who had been actively designing synagogues around the United States, joined an invited competition for the memorial, and in 1951 the New York City Art Commission unanimously backed his design, which was a collaboration with the Croatian sculptor Ivan Meštrović. The monument consisted of two monumental black granite tablets, 24.5 m (80 ft) tall and inscribed with the Ten Commandments, set atop a wall 8 m (26 ft) tall bearing a central inscription. Alongside the plaza a wall 30 m (98 ft) long contained a bas-relief depicting humankind's struggle to fulfil the Commandments, along with a large carving of Moses. Opposite was an open meeting area edged with curving stands, overlooking the Hudson River. When Mendelsohn died in 1953 fundraising efforts for the memorial stalled, and the project was soon abandoned.

LEAPFROG CITY
John Johansen
New York, New York
(US), 1968

The architectural dreamer John Johansen was serious about a plan that would have created a new neighbourhood above the tenements of East Harlem, and perhaps altered the insidious process of urban renewal. He developed 'Leapfrog City' for a struggling area known as East Harlem Triangle, bounded by 125th Street, Park Avenue and the Harlem River.

Inspired by over-scaled industrial facilities and rail viaducts, Leapfrog employed a prefabricated superstructure of ten- to twelve-storey steel towers to create housing above existing buildings. Towers linked by trusses contained steel wings that extended in two to four directions at various levels. 'For the first time, the planner and architect may be liberated from the straight-jacket of horizontal zoning and horizontal or two-dimensional definitions of ownership, and deal with a truly three-dimensional concept accommodating freely disposed and changing elements of urban life,' wrote Johansen. The system of 'sites over sites' would allow families to just 'move upstairs', saving the city millions of dollars in relocation costs. In his feasibility study, the architect stressed that the system could be established 'in any neighborhood to any extent, at any time and in any configuration without destroying that neighborhood'. He sketched a similar plan extending down Park Avenue, and one more for a university.

Johansen made forays to the local chamber of commerce, local banks, the US Department of Housing and Development, and the Community Association of East Harlem. (The last expressed interest.) But his effort was never able to attract the financial or political backing it needed.

third phase: Complete newly balanced neighborhood.

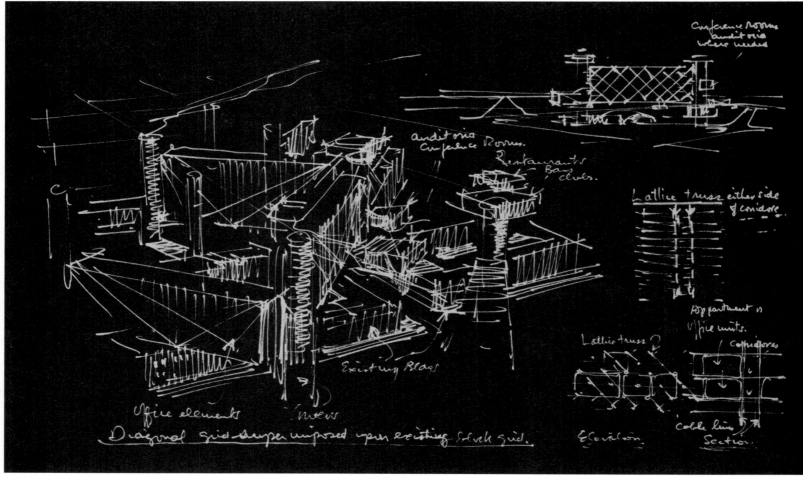

FINANCE PLACE
Henry Cobb
New York, New York
(US), 1963

In the post-war years no figure – other than the legendary power broker Robert Moses – commanded real estate with more raw bravura than William Zeckendorf. Any deal involving Zeckendorf – from his Manhattan airport to his leveraging of the land where the United Nations headquarters was built – was assured to be a humdinger.

In 1961 Zeckendorf acquired the Beaux-Arts Singer Tower (1908), briefly the tallest building in the world. His idea was to attract the New York Stock Exchange, which had outgrown its building on Wall Street, to a replacement tower on the Singer's site. His 'Wall Street Maneuver', as he called it, was embodied in Henry Cobb's 'beautifully tapered Mayan temple'. The forty-five-storey tower, a few blocks north of Wall Street, was huge, containing three-quarters as much space as the Empire State Building. The walls sloped inwards from the trading-floor base 82 m (269 ft) wide to a width of just 27 m (89 ft) at the top. Cobb, who was part of IM Pei's firm, devised an ingenious tensile steel structure that permitted the floors to hang from rooftop trusses, allowing the enormous trading floor to be entirely free of columns.

Zeckendorf claimed he had the backing of the Stock Exchange, but it never materialized. Admitting that his was 'a lost cause', he sold to US Steel, which in 1973 opened Skidmore, Owings & Merrill's inscrutable US Steel tower – the apotheosis of corporate capitalism's effort to appear outside history and impervious to change. Ironically, Zuccotti Park, the result of a trade-off that gave US Steel more height and greater floor space, became the focus of the Occupy Wall Street movement thirty-eight years later.

HYPERBOLOID
IM Pei
New York, New York
(US), 1954

In the 1950s, as struggling railways across the United States began to sell their holdings to make up for severe revenue losses, Robert Young, newly elected chairman of the ailing New York Central Railroad, looked for ways to develop the valuable land where Grand Central Terminal sat, at 42nd Street and Park Avenue. According to Young, the railway was losing $24 million a year operating the station, which had opened on 2 February 1913. Not exploiting the air rights above the building, he said, was as foolish as owning 'a stretch of farmland worth $100 billion and never putting a plough to it'.

Young teamed up with the property magnate William Zeckendorf, whose in-house architect, IM Pei, proposed the Hyperboloid, a 456 m tall (1,496 ft) office tower and transit hub to replace the station. The 109-storey, $100 million edifice would have been the world's tallest – and most costly – structure, besting the Empire State Building by more than 61 m (200 ft). The hourglass shape sharply reduced wind forces and required far less structural steel. Zeckendorf described the plan as more valuable than the existing 'second-rate Beaux-Arts Building. The main hall is to me not really a great space. One look and you've seen it all. Great spaces should be infinitely varied, constantly changing.'

Young, besieged by the railway's plummeting profits and by a Senate investigation of the industry's decline, committed suicide in January 1958, halting any hope for the structure. The attempt to replace Grand Central station sparked the modern preservation movement, and the terminal received city landmark status in 1967, preserving the beloved icon forever.

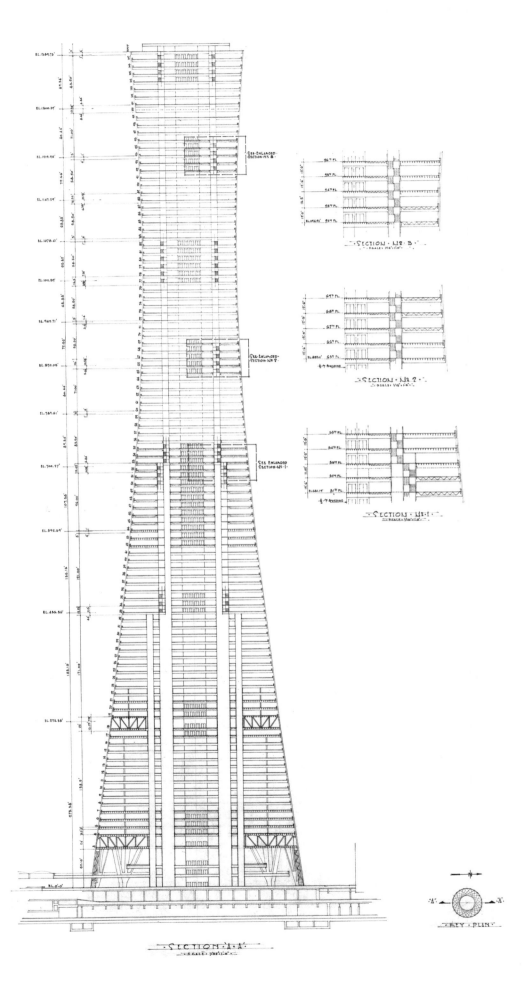

POINT PARK CIVIC CENTER
Frank Lloyd Wright
Pittsburgh, Pennsylvania
(US), 1947

Year after year Pittsburgh, the capital of America's massive steel industry, had let pollution and hulking industrial structures mar its urban landscape, including the exceptional natural point where its two rivers, the Allegheny and Monongahela, meet (now Point State Park). In 1947 the department-store magnate Edgar J Kaufmann, who about a decade earlier had commissioned Frank Lloyd Wright to design his nearby home, Fallingwater, enlisted Wright to propose a sparkling new city centrepiece on this natural focal point. (Kaufmann was a board member of the Allegheny Conference on Community Development, which was studying the site.) Wright prepared preliminary drawings for the Point Park Civic Centre, highlighted by a fifteen-level circular ramped concrete structure containing convention facilities, galleries, a planetarium, a sports arena, forums, music halls and car parks. The ramp – similar to that of his Guggenheim Museum in New York and a handful of his other visions, both built and unbuilt – measured 304 m (997 ft) in diameter, was 7.2 km (4½ miles) long in total, and cantilevered from the core structure on struts of prestressed steel. Connected to the far banks of each river via stunning cable-stayed suspension bridges, the complex was edged and topped with lush greenery, punctuated by an exotic central fountain, and abutted triangular extensions at the river's edge.

The grand plan was just too impractical and expensive, and indeed Wright admitted that 'these plans may be way ahead of their time.' According to the architect's biographer Bruce Brooks Pfeiffer, however, the powers that be in Pittsburgh rejected the scheme largely out of anti-Semitism directed at Kaufmann, whom they had no interest in involving in civic projects.

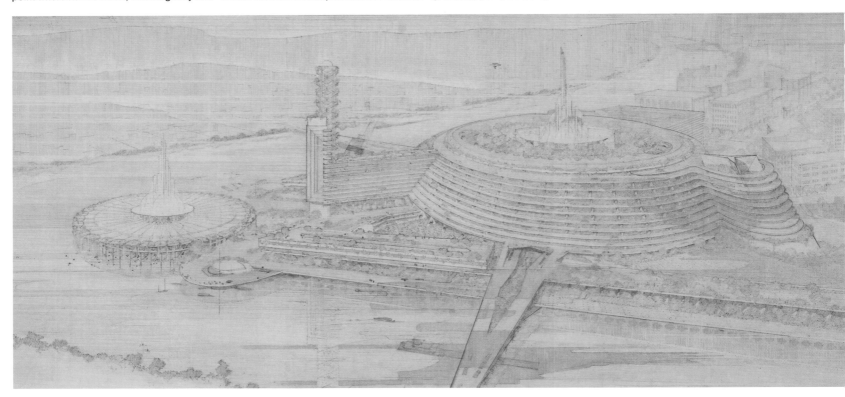

CIVIC CENTER FOR PHILADELPHIA
Louis Kahn
Philadelphia, Pennsylvania
(US), 1957

Louis Kahn, whose office was in the centre of Philadelphia, was well aware of the destructive impact of cars and highways on historic urban cores. He once compared a city centre unprotected from vehicles to 'Carcassonne without walls'. So, in his proposed Civic Center for Philadelphia – one of several urban-scale proposals he devised while a professor at the University of Pennsylvania – he employed a sort of architectural defence system, stretching over five cruciform blocks on Market Street between City Hall and Independence Hall, keeping cars along the edges. Cylindrical concrete buildings, wrapped by hotels and offices, with parking garages (holding 1,500 cars each, topped by raised plazas) at their cores, were the first line of protection. Peripheral elevated expressways that Kahn called 'viaducts', shaped with arched walls, were another. In the centre, which the historicism-loving architect called the 'Forum' after the central space of ancient Roman cities, ordered streets and a concentration of commercial, cultural and civic functions were punctuated by monumental structures, which, Kahn argued, couldn't be 'manufactured' like products or 'chewed apart by developers'. These included his tetrahedral space-frame city hall (developed with his long-time colleague Anne Tyng), a 'lampshade'-covered arena and a truncated pyramid. Snubbing conventional planning wisdom, all foregrounded humans, with streetside activity, walkability and green space.

Kahn developed the concept when Philadelphia's planning commission, led by Edmund Bacon, began studying the area for redevelopment. Despite his persistent efforts, none of Kahn's planning ideas for Philadelphia came to fruition. It didn't help that Bacon pigeonholed him and his 'utopian fantasies' as ignorant of the complexities of planning.

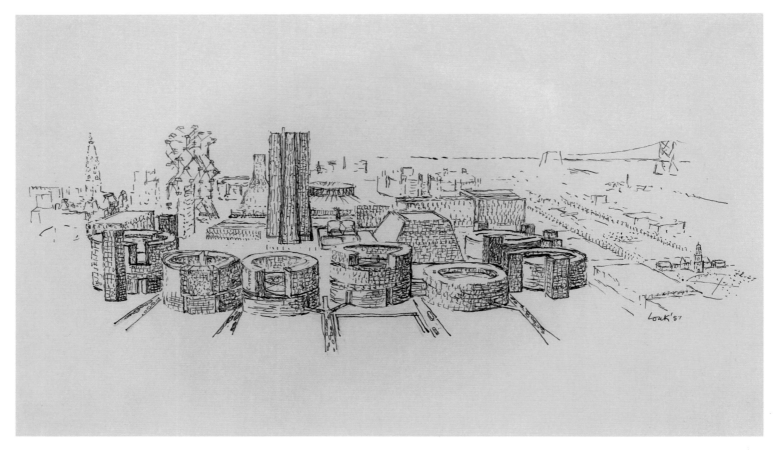

BUCKS COUNTY ELEMENTARY SCHOOL
Anne Tyng
Bucks County, Pennsylvania (US), 1949

The architect Anne Tyng will forever be tied to her colleague and mentor Louis Kahn, who, while married, secretly fathered children with both her and another of his employees, Harriet Pattison.

But Tyng's talent deserves to be recognized on its own merits, particularly her ability to fuse complex, repetitive geometries into lightweight, malleable and robust architecture. One of the most potent examples of her approach is a proposed elementary school in Bucks County, Pennsylvania, a bucolic area known for its quaint towns and plentiful historic sites.

Tyng worked on the project from 1949 until 1951, and published it in the journal of the Philadelphia chapter of the American Institute of Architects in 1952. For the school's structural roof

Tyng – who was also an acolyte of Richard Buckminster Fuller – exceeded her idol, expanding his concept of a single layer of interconnected triangular trusses so that it stepped down into two and even three layers. Tyng 'grew the geometry', as she put it, building the school's three space-frame canopies into integral structural forms that could support themselves and protect the spaces below, touching down via their pyramidal trunks.

The highly resolved, prefabricated system was a precursor to several notable space-frame

structures, among them those of the 'high tech' architects Norman Foster, Richard Rogers, IM Pei and Nicholas Grimshaw. But Tyng is rarely cited in such conversations. The year she exhibited this project, she was rejected for a Fulbright Scholarship to study with the Italian engineer Pier Luigi Nervi. The school, which represented the epitome of Tyng's concept of 'inhabiting geometry', was always a speculative proposition and thus was never built.

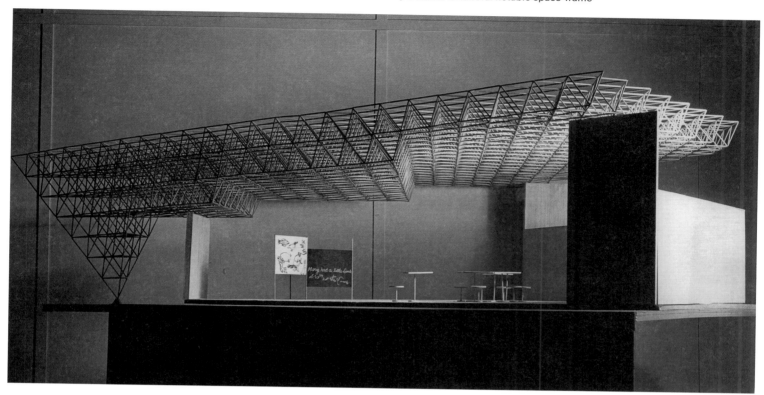

MIKVEH ISRAEL SYNAGOGUE
Louis Kahn
Philadelphia, Pennsylvania (US), 1963

Amid a fever of post-war synagogue construction in the United States, in 1961 Louis Kahn was hired by Philadelphia's Mikveh Israel, one of the oldest Jewish congregations in the country

(calling itself the 'Synagogue of the American Revolution'), to design a new temple near Independence Mall, in the historic centre of the city. Kahn, who liked to divide his buildings into 'a society of rooms', separated the structure into three volumes: for study, prayer and community (the last a museum of Jewish history.) The centrepiece was the octagonal sanctuary, a monumental space topped by a convex concrete ceiling and surrounded by layered concrete walls and cylindrical 'window rooms' or 'light towers', which provided seating and ushered

diffused light into the space. The ark was to the east, between two light towers, with seating stepping to north and south. From outside, the turret-like light towers and high walls made the synagogue look like an ancient castle. Mikveh Israel, though, did not share Kahn's passion for spatial division – or indeed much else.

After more than a decade of tense deliberations, and no fewer than ten proposed schemes, the building committee demanded that Kahn, among other things, drastically reduce the cost of the project and unify his plans into a single

space. The architect would not oblige, and on 19 December 1972 the committee voted unanimously to fire him. The next year it hired Harbeson, Hough, Livingston & Larson (H2L2). That firm's far less ambitious scheme at 44 North 4th Street opened on 4 July 1976.

WASHINGTON CHANNEL BRIDGE
Chloethiel Woodard Smith
Washington, DC (US), 1966

One of many overlooked women architects of the mid-twentieth century was Chloethiel Woodard Smith, whose single-family homes and residential and commercial masterplans had a profound impact on the evolution of Washington, DC. While Smith was a shrewd businessperson (Woodard Smith & Associates was at one point the largest female-owned architecture firm in the country), she never stopped proposing unflinching solutions to the challenges of the age.

In 1966, hoping to inject life into the struggling Southwest Washington DC Urban Renewal District, she and the National Parks Service proposed the $5 million Washington Channel Bridge, or 'World Bridge', a development inspired by the famous Ponte Vecchio in Florence and containing more than 100 shops, galleries and restaurants, spanning the 266 m (874 ft) wide Washington Channel and connecting the Maine Avenue waterfront with East Potomac Park. Supported on five concrete 'islands' with massed piles delving into the riverbed, the meandering pedestrian structure, following the outline of its irregular straddling boxes, incorporated broad plazas, two- and three-storey buildings, lookouts, boat berths and even mini trains.

The National Park Service pushed the plan, but the necessary private funds never materialized.

A similar fate met successive visions for the site. In 1968 Kevin Roche proposed a 'Ponte Vecchio' connected to his doomed glass-topped National Aquarium. And, just two years later, Wilbur Smith Associates proposed a pedestrian bridge with a two-level parking garage atop its east end. That, too, failed to gain financing. The area, although now significantly revitalized, never got its pedestrian bridge, and is still marred by a thunderous jumble of automobiles.

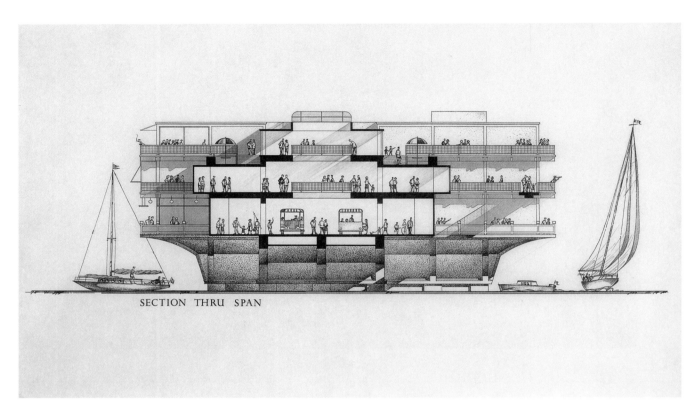

SECTION THRU SPAN

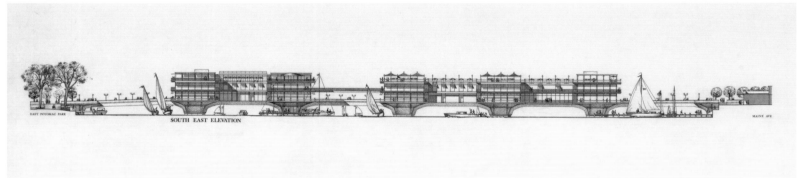

SOUTH EAST ELEVATION

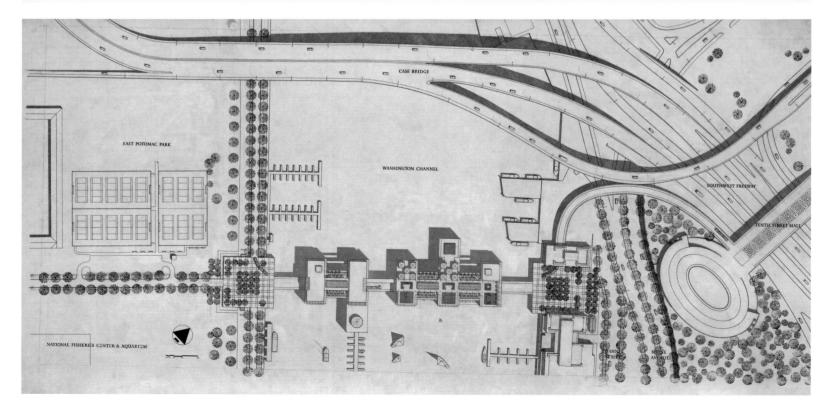

TREE HOUSE
Haigh Jamgochian
Richmond, Virginia
(US), 1962

Before he died in 2019, the visionary architect Haigh Jamgochian developed a reputation in his home town of Richmond, Virginia, as a renegade, creating buildings with unorthodox shapes (flying saucers, doughnuts, crescents) and equally weird skins (his Markel Building of 1965, covered in crinkled and dented aluminium, is said to have been inspired by a foil-wrapped baked potato). 'He does what he wants and it's kind of crazy,' Vincent Brooks, senior archivist at the Library of Virginia, told Richmond's *Style Weekly* in 2006. 'But he's never given up and he's never compromised.'

In 1962 the Central Richmond Association published images of the architect's 'tree house', an apartment building proposed for the corner of Franklin and Foushee streets. The fifteen-storey structure cantilevered its angular units more than 15 m (49 ft) from both sides of its pre-stressed concrete core, allowing maximum exposure to light and views, not to mention a dynamic profile. To fit into the area's strict zoning regulations, the units tapered dramatically, from 6.7 m (22 ft) to 2.4 m (8 ft) wide.

The plan was praised by the Editorial Board of the *Richmond News Leader*, which said, 'it may be just the thing for an ailing neighbourhood.' But the city council eventually rejected the project, which didn't fit into its strait-laced conception for the area. Local officials also threw out the architect's ideas for a rotating hotel complex, a 'floating building', a spiralling 'Communications Executive Center', and more. 'I couldn't get anyone to listen and the city was going nowhere,' said Jamgochian, who called modern skyscrapers 'merely large boxes with cubicles packed inside'.

GEORGIA WORLD CONGRESS
John Portman
Atlanta, Georgia
(US), 1971

John Portman rose to fame with the Hyatt Regency Hotel (1967) in his native city of Atlanta. He'd turned a hotel inside out, creating a soaring atrium where rooms and hallways normally would be, and employed glass-enclosed elevators that raced skywards to the umbrella canopy of his circular Parasol Lounge. It was an instant landmark, and established Portman as a flamboyant futurist, bucking the corporate mould, a populist purveyor of trippy, oddly naturalistic fantasies crafted within the confines of an unconventional tower. His signature soaring atria had the vertical thrust of a Titan missile and the visual excitement of a Baroque interior, made infinitely more vast by modern building techniques.

In 1970 the state's General Assembly dished out $175,000 to study where in Atlanta the Georgia World Congress should go. Portman, donning his developer's hat, promoted his Civic Center landholding as the key to reviving the downtown's sagging west side. He conceived a massive, tiered, inward-facing cube – he loved plain, geometric forms – illuminated by an entirely glass roof. The centrepiece was an amphitheatre formed by a pair of kissing, satellite-shaped parabolas balanced on a single concrete column, hovering above a reflecting pool.

Portman lost his bid after he condemned the site selection committee, saying 'any damn fool can see that the Civic Center site was best.' Angry officials blackballed him, instead tapping another Atlanta firm, Thompson, Ventulett, Stainback, to proceed with a glassy box elsewhere that was the largest convention centre to be built in the United States and which today sprawls over 325,160 sq. m (3.5 million sq. ft).

ATLANTA SYMPHONY CENTER
Santiago Calatrava
Atlanta, Georgia (US), 2005

In February 2005, two years after Los Angeles opened Frank Gehry's shiny new Walt Disney Concert Hall, the city of Atlanta – not to be outdone – unveiled plans for its own gleaming starchitect-designed musical venue: Santiago Calatrava's $300 million Atlanta Symphony Center. At the corner of Peachtree and 14th streets, near Richard Meier's High Museum of Art, the 26,000 sq. m (280,000 sq. ft) behemoth would include various venues (among them a main hall, a studio hall, a rehearsal hall and a learning centre) as well as a large public plaza, embedded with landscaping and seats for outdoor concerts. 'The Atlanta Symphony Orchestra has been a truly visionary client,' Calatrava told the *Atlanta Business Chronicle*, adding that his would be a 'building in which people can recognize the singularity of their city and state and take pride in them'. Gehry's so-called Bilbao Effect, in which glitzy, sculptural civic structures were being imported to bring attention and visitors to their cities, was in full swing.
Like many of Calatrava's constructions, this one took inspiration from natural forms, with its shell-like curves and wing-like protrusions. Rising from behind the structure were two 'bent leaves' of latticed steel, which swooped over the building, landing in a gentle curve on the other side. The plan also seemed to draw inspiration from an earlier Calatrava building: his Auditorio de Tenerife, completed in 2003, which is a dead ringer for the design, albeit with wings of concrete and tile, not steel. The Atlanta version was felled by the global financial crisis of 2008, forcing the orchestra to remain in the long-outdated Atlanta Symphony Hall of 1968.

TALLAHASSEE CIVIC CENTER
Walter Gropius
Tallahassee, Florida (US), 1956

Sometimes never-built ideas refuse to die. Take Walter Gropius's civic centre for Florida's capital city, Tallahassee. In the mid-1950s the population of the city, like that of much of the Sunshine State, was exploding. Calls arose for a new 'civic block' of government buildings on the edge of the downtown area, including a city hall and civic auditorium. Tallahassee's Civic Center Committee, chaired by car dealer Fred Drake, Jr, chose as its architect a name that was almost unknown in the city: Walter Gropius (then dean of architecture at the Harvard Graduate School of Design) and his Cambridge, Massachusetts-based firm The Architects Collaborative (TAC).
Displays of the $4 million plan, which was to be underwritten by a 10 per cent utility tax and about $800,000 in federal urban-renewal funds, were installed at prominent locations in the city, while meetings were held between Gropius and the requisite civic groups. The centrepiece of the project was the auditorium, a sizeable, bifurcated structure with a floating, patterned block facade and a thin, multi-vaulted roof hanging from a bow-shaped steel suspension structure. (The building was an almost identical twin to the unbuilt competition entry of 1932 by Gropius's contemporary Le Corbusier for the Palace of the Soviets in Moscow.)
In November 1956, wary of Gropius's radical design – not to mention the tax boost – local voters turned it down. But the vision hadn't died, at least not yet. In 1958 virtually the same building (without the suspension structure) appeared in renderings as the auditorium for Gropius and TAC's new campus for the University of Baghdad – the firm's largest commission ever. The campus went ahead, but extreme political turbulence scuttled many of its projects, including Gropius's ill-fated auditorium.

JACKSONVILLE CENTER OFFICE TOWER DEVELOPMENT
Venturi Scott Brown
Jacksonville, Florida (US), 1985

As many American cities in the mid-1980s were, Jacksonville was looking to revitalize its decaying downtown. The Jacksonville Downtown Development Authority was cautious about the prospects of what it dubbed the 'Billion Dollar Decade'. Jacksonville (named after Andrew Jackson, the first military governor of the Florida Territory and seventh President of the United States) is on St Johns River, on the Atlantic Coast in northeastern Florida. The boosters proclaimed in their 'Jacksonville Downtown Profile' bulletin of 1985 that 'the City is very carefully planning commercial, cultural and recreational development along this waterfront.'

The linchpin of the redevelopment enterprise was Jacksonville Landing, a marketplace of touristy small shops and restaurants that opened in 1987 to the fanfare of a drum-and-bugle corps and the dedication of a 1,270 kg (2,800 lb) bronze statue of the city's namesake astride his rearing horse. Venturi Scott Brown's contribution was to be two large office towers, a third smaller one and an outdoor arcade that would form a pedestrian promenade linking the Landing, the waterfront and the lobbies of the towers. The taller, paired towers were awash with bands of blue, from lapis to azure to ice, becoming an orangey-yellow that picked out an Art Deco sunburst crown, reminiscent of New York's Chrysler Building.

Why the project never got beyond a set of concept sketches is not known, but it is apparent that the towers, at least, were a fitting – if literal – emblem for the 'sunshine state'. Even on paper, they remain so.

E.P.C.O.T.
Walt Disney
Orlando, Florida (US), 1966

When we hear E.P.C.O.T., most of us envision an amusement park in Orlando where national-themed exhibits cluster around a golf-ball-shaped orb called Spaceship Earth. But Walt Disney had originally planned E.P.C.O.T. (the Experimental Prototype Community of Tomorrow) as a visionary city of 20,000 people, a car-free urban template that could fix the ills of American cities. In a promotional film in 1966, he unveiled his plan, sketched out (and animated) by his top designers. Located south of the theme park, connected to it via mass transit, it was to be what Disney called 'by far the most important part of our Florida project; the heart of everything we'll be doing in Disney World'.

The radially planned community, connected by a dizzying array of monorails and people movers, fanned out from a core of offices, shops, restaurants (many themed for different countries), hotels and cultural facilities, and extended to high-density housing, a green belt for recreation, and finally low-density neighbourhoods. Diverging from the country's decaying urban centres, the core would be protected from the elements by a clear dome. Cars and lorries would travel underneath, so that traffic lights weren't required and pedestrians would be insulated from traffic noise, pollution and accidents.

Calling his plan 'a living blueprint of the future', Disney intended to lean on American industry to provide the latest technology. 'E.P.C.O.T. will always be a showcase to the world for the ingenuity and imagination of American free enterprise,' he noted. But he died just two months after creating his pitch video, and the Disney Company's board of directors thought the city was too risky a bet to pursue.

NIGHT WORLD
Bertrand Goldberg
Orlando, Florida (US), 1979

Bertrand Goldberg famously said, long before computer-aided design came to dominate architects' desks, 'for the first time in the history of the world we can build whatever we can think.' That was his mantra, and it led him to explore the limits of concrete curves and structures posted on or hanging from masts of all kinds.

Goldberg's Night World was a fantasy playground near the Walt Disney World Resort – the Disneyland Anaheim, California doppelgänger that had opened in 1971. The idea was to capture the crowds leaving Disney World at closing time and give them somewhere to continue the party. Four domes would house a cabaret, cinema, theatre, television studio and exhibitions. A vast tent, modelled on Frei Otto's lightweight structures, stretched around the domes, covering portions of the lagoon above which the complex stood. The tent's sharp points and

multiplicity of round canopies made it look self-propagating, lending a feeling of galactic exploration to the project, as if it were a preliminary design for colonizing space.
But Goldberg's Automobile Spiral was the true showstopper. The monolithic concrete structure contained a double-helix driveway supported from a central mast by steel cables. The ramp was meant to be a perpetual auto show where cars would be on display, like a concours d'élégance, but could also be driven, like a dealership. It was easy to imagine the midnight

encounters that would have come as cars passed one another, going up and down and around, under the night sky.

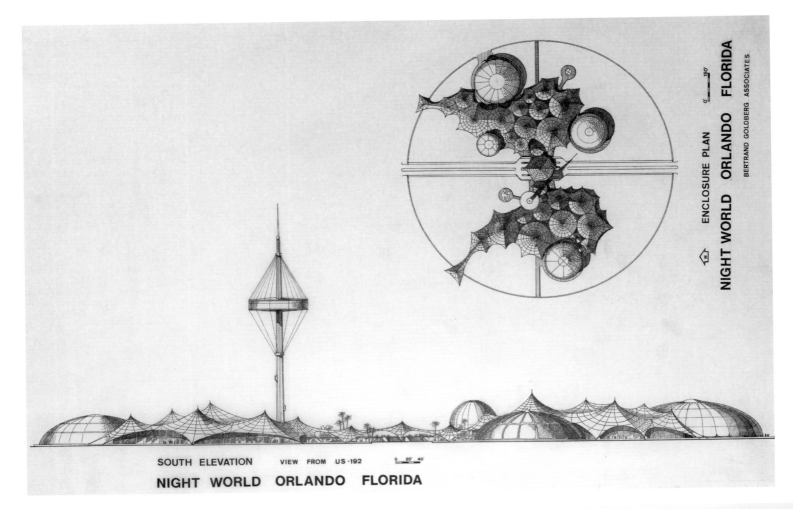

SOUTH ELEVATION   VIEW FROM US-192   0   20' 40'
NIGHT WORLD ORLANDO FLORIDA

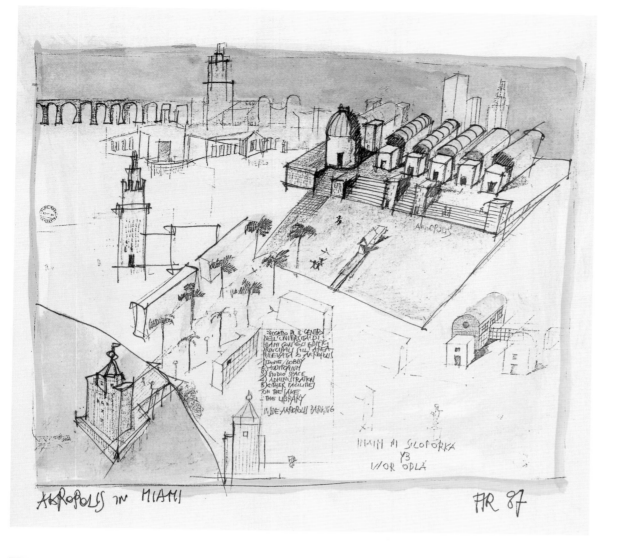

UNIVERSITY OF MIAMI SCHOOL OF ARCHITECTURE
Aldo Rossi
Miami, Florida (US), 1986

Taking one look at the University of Miami, Aldo Rossi diagnosed its debility: 'the absence of a centre… capable of constituting a clear, precise reference'. With Thomas Jefferson's University of Virginia as not-quite-literal lodestone, he drew a new complex that created that focus. Along a central axis Rossi devised an acropolis raised high on a massive plinth, linked by a long avenue of palm trees to a library built on a platform in an existing lake. Atop his earth-work rampart stood a huge pantheon, transplanted via the University of Virginia's rotunda; beside it stood a sequence of five parallel, identical structures that looked as if they had been extruded through an ironworks die. Rossi planned to clad the front and rear of these buildings in brick, while the sides were to have large windows or be completely constructed of glass. The arched roofs were copper or steel. At the opposite end, the library – a reprise of Rossi's Teatro del Mondo for the Venice Biennale in 1980 – stood like a moated castle guarding the halls of knowledge. In at least one version of this rhetorical, affected construct, Rossi added a clock tower. The eleven-storey library tower contained three double- and triple-height rooms meant specifically to 'physically illustrate the basics of architecture': a dome room with a conical clerestory piercing the roofline; a round room; and a cubic lobby'. Construction began in 1991, but according to Aldo's biographer Diane Ghirardo, 'financial difficulties halted the project, and after Rossi's death, the university turned to Léon Krier to design new facilities.'

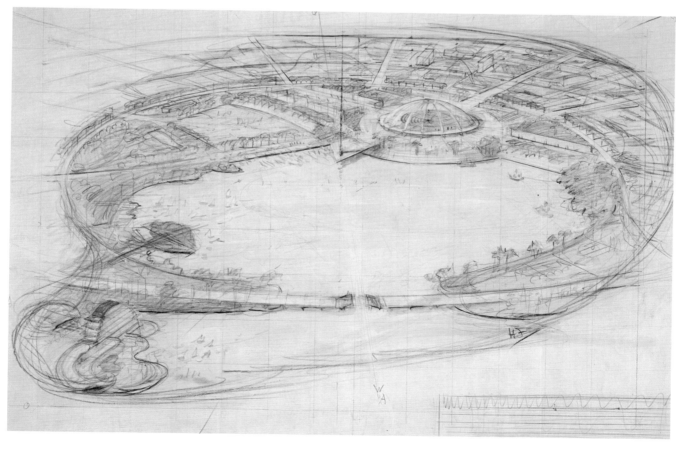

INTERAMA
Robert Fitch Smith et al.
Miami, Florida (US), 1956

For decades, from the Truman era to the Nixon presidency, the city of Miami promoted Interama, a world's fair for its Biscayne Bay lagoon that was a melange of United Nations, Pan-American fairgrounds and cultural exchange intended to advance the unity of North, Central and South America and ensure Miami's place as 'Gateway of the Americas'. A who's-who of architects – including Louis Kahn, Marcel Breuer, Paul Rudolph, Pietro Belluschi, Edward Durell Stone, Josep Lluís Sert, Minoru Yamasaki and Harry Weese – laid out plans that amounted to an exquisite mountain of abandoned drawings. Robert Fitch Smith's early scheme with its half-dome Hemisphere Hanging Gardens and Spire, as drawn by Hugh Ferriss (pictured above) evoked the globalism of the New York World's Fair of 1939, but by 1956 the globe had dematerialized into three arches nearly identical to Eero Saarinen's design for the St Louis Gateway arch. When $35 million in federal funds evaporated, the project appeared dead, only to be revived by the Cuban Revolution which kick-started another decade and a half of proposals asserting US hegemony over Latin America under cover of JFK's 'Alliance for Progress.' The architects translated this into a series of buildings that borrowed, often incorrectly, from the ruins of pre-Columbian Mesoamerica. Their buildings echoed the Aztec ball courts of Tenochtitlán, the Mayan pyramids of Tikal and the Zapotec fortress mounds of Monte Albán. Only Minoru Yamasaki's three-legged Freedom Tower broke rank, emphasising modernism over Latin-inflected motifs.

By 1967 Interama was millions in debt, and it was finally shuttered in 1975. In 1983 the artists Christo and Jeanne-Claude wrapped a clutch of Biscayne Bay islands in bright pink canvas, at last turning the Interama site into the international destination its promoters had envisioned.

INSTITUTO TECNOLÓGICO Y DE ESTUDIOS SUPERIORES DE MONTERREY
Enrique de la Mora y Palomar
Monterrey (MX), 1945

Along with his collaborator Félix Candela, with whom he produced numerous important works, Enrique de la Mora y Palomar was regarded as a key structural expressionist in Mexico. At the age of thirty-three he designed the Iglesia la Purísima Concepción (1940) in Monterrey, and its poured-in-place, thin-shell concrete parabolic volumes, expressed as a cross, quickly became the symbol of Mexican modernity. 'El pelón' (the bald), as de la Mora was affectionately called, was recruited five years later to hammer out a masterplan for Monterrey's university. The Instituto Tecnológico y de Estudios Superiores was modelled on the Massachusetts Institute of Technology: a private university intended to train Mexico's elite engineers. The plot of land given to the project was a scrub-brush plain on the outskirts of the city, at the base of the Cerro de la Silla mountain. De la Mora laid out a relatively classical campus on an east–west axis, a self-contained city surrounded by flat, dry-land farms. This didn't deter him, however, from conceiving a centrepiece library that pushed the limits of concrete. This time, he twisted the arcing shapes into an oval, which he propped up with spidery L-shaped legs holding a canopy above the entrance to the building.

The plan was ultimately dropped, and replaced with a rectangular prism, neatly squared up and shielded from the sun by curved lattices. But de la Mora was undeterred, and continued to build his thin-form structures.

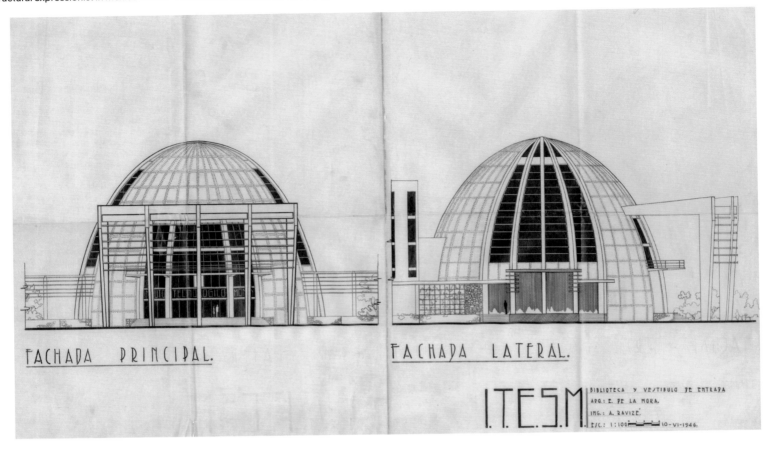

HOTEL URBAN DEVELOPMENT
Teodoro González de León
Barra de Navidad (MX), 1958

The work of the Mexican architect Teodoro González de León has been described as Brutalism meets an abstract reinterpretation of Mesoamerican architecture: poetry in concrete. On returning from France, where he'd studied with Le Corbusier, he was commissioned to draw up an urbanization plan for Barra de Navidad, a city designed from scratch in a remote spot on the coast of the state of Jalisco. The brainchild of Agustín Yáñez, the novelist who had been appointed governor of this impoverished state, Barra was intended to convert 'the virgin, beautiful, and marvellous bay', as Yáñez described it, into a tourist and housing development. This was colossal architecture, in the manner of Corbusier, as social gesture: turn a poor region into a prosperous, progressive home for the region's inhabitants. González de León proposed concrete and more concrete, configured as cones, cubes, rectangles and paraboloids, for offices, schools, churches, markets and clinics, on one side of a plaza. On the other he set gardens, shops, restaurants, nurseries, theatres, casinos, a car park, a bus terminal, a club and a jetty for cruise ships. Completing the vision were a slab hotel – an upright suitcase in the sand – and an apartment building, thin and narrow as a lolly stick, running along the bay.

Yáñez's dream of a modern Jalisco coast collapsed when his term as governor ended, in 1959. The following year he published his third novel, *La tierra pródiga* (The Lavish Land), recounting his effort to modernize his home state. González de León later gained a global reputation, but this corner of Jalisco remains a tiny fishing village to this day.

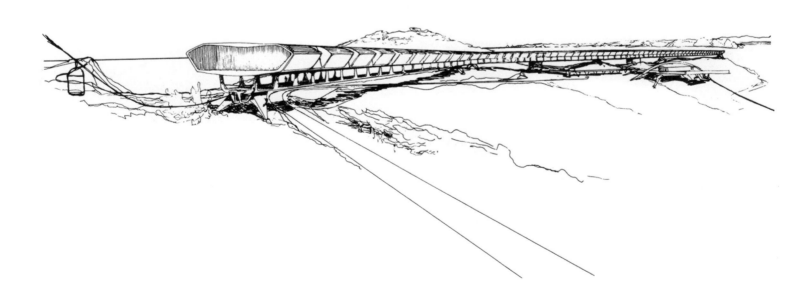

JVC ENTERTAINMENT AND COMMERCIAL CENTER
Coop Himmelb(l)au
Guadalajara, Jalisco
(MX), 1998

Embodying the turn-of-the-millennium obsession with international 'starchitects' and their potent impact on urban transformation was the JVC Center, a $500 million business and convention complex on a dusty site of 304 hectares (751 acres) about an hour's drive north of Guadalajara, Mexico. The dream of Omnilife supplements magnate Jorge Vergara, the development would contain flashy, sculptural buildings from the likes of Jean Nouvel, Daniel Libeskind, Zaha Hadid, Thom Mayne, Toyo Ito, Philip Johnson (who was then ninety-five), Tod Williams Billie Tsien Architects, Carme Pinós, Jean-Marie Massaud, Teodoro González de León, Enrique Norten, and the radical Austrian enfants terribles Coop Himmelb(l)au. (Frank Gehry declined to join.) Coop envisioned a massive entertainment and commercial centre that they dubbed the 'Marketplace of the Future', merging tech R&D offices with cinemas, restaurants, bars, clubs, shops, a fitness and pool area, and a 'Space of Knowledge', an animated exhibition area outlining recent tech innovations. This 'urban landscape' was broken down into varied blocks revolving around a fractured central plaza, partially dug into the ground. Square cinema buildings contrasted with jagged metallic structures, extending underground, topped by a twisted roof, allowing filtered sunlight to reach the plaza, which was edged by a complex series of stairs and serpentine ramps.

The project, already held up by environmental concerns, was dealt a death blow by the Great Recession, the equalizer in an era of frenzy, speculation and ego. The only piece to emerge from the rubble was Massaud's Omnilife Stadium (2010; now the Akron Stadium), its dramatic levitating roof and grassy, mound-like base evoking what could have been.

MEXICO

MUSIC HALL Y CENTRO DE ESPECTÁCULOS
Tatiana Bilbao Estudio
Irapuato (MX), 2009

Mexico City-born Tatiana Bilbao has achieved global prominence by producing work that has no signature identity. Her designs are not so much eclectic as distinctive, and individual. Half a decade after she established her own firm, the municipality of Irapuato, in Central Mexico, commissioned her to develop a combined music hall and sports venue. The building would do double, triple and even quadruple duty, as do many similar 'centres' in regional cities across Mexico. One night there could be a boxing match, another a cockfight, another a chamber-music concert, another a ranchera dance. Irapuato nestles against the Cerro de Arandas in the fertile Bajío Valley, and is famous for its rich strawberry crop. The city is surrounded by fields, and it was in one expanse of furrows, to the north, that the INFORUM, as it was called, would erect Bilbao's building. Her proposal was a limestone-white circular five-storey structure, shaped like a flattened turban, its bands wound around the central hall. The circular walkways were platforms for restaurants, bars and terraces, open to vistas of countryside and hills. The hall itself was a forum with steep, high rings of seats, designed so that no audience member would be further than 23 m (75 ft) from the stage.

In an interview in 2011, Bilbao said, 'We finished the executive project and I believe that construction will begin in 2012, with the next administration. It depends on the municipality. If the municipality does not promote it, it is not achieved.' Her prognosis proved sadly accurate.

CORPORATIVO CUAUTITLÁN
Pedro Ramírez Vázquez
Cuautitlán Izcalli (MX), 1973

By the early 1970s, Pedro Ramírez Vázquez was Mexico's unstoppable architect. In Cuautitlán Izcalli he was given the job of creating from scratch a municipal palace (the 'Corporativo Cuautitlán'). The job flowed, it seems, from his position on the official commission charged with creating the entirely new city roughly 38 km (24 miles) north of the nation's capital. Cuautitlán was planned as a stand-alone city and intended to be an efficient example of modernity, divided between industrial, residential and green spaces. At the core would be Ramírez Vázquez's municipal headquarters. Sited on a prominent hill, it consisted of a huge, square three-storey concourse enclosing a piazza. From the middle emerged a thirty-six-storey tower, topped by a pyramidal cupola. The tower was unprecedented in its form; the upper eleven floors sloped away from the massive column, with each successive floor plate protruding further, creating a sequence of awnings and recessed ledges. The imagery was unmistakable: the building was a massive tree. In Náhuatl, 'Cuautitlán Izcalli' means 'your house among the trees'. Ramírez Vázquez had given the city's name its three-dimensional simulacrum, cast in glass and concrete and surrounded by reflecting pools. According to some accounts, there were to be monumental statues at the entrance and exit of the complex, and the letters 'CI' were to embrace the lanes of the Mexico-Querétaro Highway, which connected the town to Mexico City.

The structure never got underway, however. After the Mexico City earthquake of 1985, the plan evaporated as people flooded in to Cuautitlán Izcalli, fleeing the threat of future earthquakes.

NORTH & CENTRAL AMERICA

CONFEDERATION OF MEXICAN WORKERS
Juan O'Gorman
Mexico City (MX), 1934

Juan O'Gorman was arguably Mexico's first and, for a time, foremost modern architect. In the early 1930s he had become a devotee of Le Corbusier, committed to functionalism: a building's use was its aesthetic. 'Antiquity does not provide us with the necessary services for our present life: on the contrary, it hinders us at every moment,' O'Gorman said.

The homes O'Gorman designed for his father and for the artist Diego Rivera – simple poured-concrete cubes, large expanses of glass, walls painted blue, yellow, red and brown, cantilevered projections and concrete spiral stairways without banisters – launched his career. He went to work for the reform government of Lázaro Cárdenas, building twenty-eight functionalist concrete-and-glass public schools on a budget that would previously have been spent on one. His headquarters building for the Confederation of Mexican Workers seems to extend his functionalist ideal, with skinny pilotis, ribbon windows and unadorned exterior walls. But the adjacent auditorium, its armadillo shape held by concrete straps, is no carbon-copy of Le Corbusier's Villa Savoye or Swiss Pavilion. It hints at renunciation, which O'Gorman would commit four years later. Functionalism, he said then, was a capitalist scam to extract 'maximum revenue with minimum investment …

[It] is mechanically rational and humanly illogical, since man is not a machine.'

O'Gorman then adopted an organic approach to architecture, and returned to painting and making murals, both with abiding genius. His library at the National Autonomous University of Mexico in 1956 renewed his global fame, yet he called the building 'a *gringa* dressed up as a *poblana*'. Sadly, he descended into depression and committed suicide, hanging himself from a tree in the garden of his first functionalist home.

MONORAIL SYSTEM
Mario Pani
Mexico City (MX), 1965

A founding father of Mexican Modernism, Mario Pani – an ardent disciple of Le Corbusier – adhered to a holistic approach of 'architectural urbanism', in which every element of the city would be consciously designed. He was indeed able to create large urban swathes in Mexico, perhaps most famously Ciudad Satélite (Satellite City), an early suburb of Mexico City filled with modern houses, apartment slabs and superblocks of schools, shops and offices, which he saw as the first of a network of similar new cities around the capital. (Mexico City, Pani noted, was hopelessly congested and had long since exhausted its natural and man-made resources.) While cars were to play a major role in such new developments, Pani also envisioned a network of elevated trains or monorails, which he regarded as faster and more economical than such mass transit solutions as subways, while also helping to form an axis for future development. The stations, too, would serve as symbols in the sky, angular, futuristic beacons of a new type of living. Pani collaborated with the German manufacturer Alweg, best known at the time for developing monorails for Disneyland and the Seattle Century 21 Exposition, to develop the system's streamlined vehicles, which would glide atop elegant concrete pylons.

Mexico City inaugurated its mass transportation network in 1969, but it neither employed monorails nor extended to Ciudad Satélite. Subsequent 'satellite' cities, meanwhile, suffered from a dire lack of planning, resulting in chaotic, ad hoc suburban development that continues to this day.

SOCIAL PALACE
Fernanda Canales
Mexico City (MX), 2017

In the early 2000s the Mexican government ramped up a more than $100 billion effort to provide credits to developers to create affordable dwellings for millions of people. Owing to poor planning and a lack of services and infrastructure, many of these sprawling peripheral developments became landmarks of neglect, violence and abandonment. According to some estimates, there are now more than 5 million abandoned single-family homes in the country's suburbs and exurbs.

In 2017 Mexico's INFONAVIT (Instituto del Fondo Nacional de la Vivienda para los Trabajadores; Institute of the National Housing Fund for Workers) commissioned the architect Fernanda Canales to create an alternative for the sprawling slums outside Mexico City. Inspired by such spatial visionaries as Yona Friedman and Cedric Price, Canales proposed what she called 'Social Palace', a system of new structures on top of abandoned houses providing much needed flexibility and a wider offering of programming. A basic prefabricated module could be attached via a steel scaffolding system to existing homes, providing collective services, public spaces, schools and transportation infrastructure, and growing and changing with the needs of the community. 'You have the foundations and the structures. Then you occupy the rooftops and re-densify the very horizontal neighbourhoods,' said Canales.

In December 2018 the national government changed, as did the leadership of INFONAVIT, and the plan was abandoned. Since then, Canales says, the government has aggressively auctioned the houses for resale, a system that has done little to combat the situation. 'If houses are not linked to education, culture, health and work,' she maintains, 'they're not houses. They're abandoned spaces.'

PROJECT FOR THE SENATE OF THE REPUBLIC
Agustín Hernández Navarro
Mexico City (MX), 2003

Near the turn of the millennium, Mexico finally went about constructing a new home for its senate, whose members had for decades been scattered in offices around the city. This was a problem more than 100 years in the making. Emilio Dondé's sumptuous Beaux-Arts legislative hall from 1897 was begun but never completed owing to a lack of funding. (Its abandoned structure, including a crowning dome, was eventually employed to construct the city's Monument to the Revolution.)

In 2003 the federal government launched a competition for the Senate, located along the city's central spine, Avenida Paseo de la Reforma. The winning entry by Muñoz Arquitectos featured a curving agglomeration of structures that, now built, feels like a watered-down United Nations Headquarters. A far more ambitious proposal came from the Mexican architect Agustín Hernández Navarro, who was legendary for his sculptural, nature-inspired work. His monumental scheme, meant to reinforce the concept of a prodigious, future-looking body, was also embedded with symbols of the country's past. 'Dualities are part of life, and I would hope that is reflected in my work,' he once said. Folded concrete plates supported by steel trusses created a truncated pyramid, alluding to the country's prodigious ruins. The building was fronted by an angular, beak-like canopy emblazoned with the country's coat of arms, a Mexican eagle perched on a prickly-pear cactus, devouring a rattlesnake. Inside, a carved entryway led to a staggered, multi-storey chamber, topped by a transparent dome, with layered seating for spectators.

IGLESIA ECUMÉNICA DE CANCÚN
Pedro Ramírez Vázquez
Cancún (MX), 1975

It is impossible to think of Mexican Modernism without repeating the name Pedro Ramírez Vázquez. The concrete canopy of his Museo Nacional de Antropología (National Museum of Anthropology) in Mexico City, held aloft on a slender column doubling as an impluvium, alone captures his nerve-racking bravura. In Tijuana, then considered the farthest corner of Mexico, he built 'La Bola', an utterly unadorned sphere of concrete and stone that is unabashedly modern yet somehow feels eternal. He was an architect who didn't tiptoe.

The Iglesia Ecuménica de Cancún (Ecumenical Church of Cancún) speaks to this philosophy. At the time the church was proposed, in 1975, Cancún was being transformed from a small fishing settlement into a beach playground for international tourists. Ramírez Vázquez sketched a dagger apparently pointed at the blocky hotels rising from the now-famous sand-bar. His tilted ochre pyramid seems to be reaching for the blue firmament, the sense of skyward movement emphasized by the lightning-bolt pattern he etched into the concrete. The steep angle of the church wall, pierced by stained-glass windows at plaza level and by a cruciform clerestory near the pinnacle, mimics the rake of the Mayan temples of the Yucatán Peninsula.

Strangely, almost at the same time as he was designing the unbuilt Iglesia Ecuménica, Ramírez Vazquez donated plans for another church – the Parroquia de Cristo Rey, a modest, palm-frond-roofed building, which was realized elsewhere in Cancún. Seen next to the Ecuménica, Parroquia seems to have been torn from another architect's sketchbook. Did Cancún's diocese recoil from the decidedly unorthodox form? We may never know.

BAY OF PIGS MONUMENT
Fábio Penteado
Playa Girón (CU), 1962

It is hard to imagine how much the United States' defeat on the beach at Playa Girón, 160 km (100 miles) southeast of Havana, cemented Fidel Castro as a national hero and the *caudillo* of global anticolonialism. Yet, one year later, when it came to the monument to the Cuban victory at the fateful beach, the Brazilian architect Fábio Penteado dispensed with any overtly political or even remotely historical allusion.

The international call for designs – which garnered 274 entries from 35 countries – sought a monument, a square for 30,000 people, and a museum to display the weapons seized from the ill-fated invaders. Penteado simply buried the captured tanks and guns in an underground vault, and left the beach essentially intact – except for his starburst of concrete beams, some measuring 90 m (295 ft) long, which shot outwards like shards of light from an invisible prism. The composition of massive, weighty spars extending – seemingly impossibly – beyond the tottering point was a poem to human ingenuity and the drive to best the laws of physics. It was thus a metaphor for revolution. The Japanese architecture journal *Kokusai Kentiku* described the monument as 'the cry of victory of a crowd, suddenly frozen in space'. Penteado said, 'From afar it is landscape. Up close a monument. The square is the people.' Although a Polish team won the competition with a Brutalist reprise of the actual invasion, Castro preferred Penteado's concept. He invited Penteado to further the plan, but the military coup of 1964 in Brazil stopped the avowedly leftist Penteado – who once said that architecture 'always served little kings and false gods' – from leaving his native country.

EDIFICIO LIBERTAD
Martín Domínguez Esteban
Havana (CU), 1959

Unlike other Spanish architects, such as Josep Lluís Sert or Felix Candela, who also fled Francisco Franco's fascist victory in the Civil War, Martín Domínguez Esteban was exiled into relative obscurity. He emigrated to Cuba, where he worked for more than thirty years, only to be exiled a second time, by Fidel Castro – whom Domínguez had hoped would be a patron, not an antagonist – and fell further into obscurity. Domínguez first gained prominence for his Zarzuela racetrack (1935) in Madrid, and in Havana, in 1956, his thirty-nine-storey egg-box concrete FOCSA building became the tallest in the western hemisphere. The year of the Cuban Revolution, he unofficially won the competition to build the Edificio Libertad. His fifty-storey high-rise, designed in collaboration with Ernesto Gómez Sampera, was H-shaped, with offset floors and alternating bands of six- and eight-storey sections, of varying width. The building, which rose from the shoreline of eastern Havana, had a precise rhythm and the energy of a tuning fork. Domínguez's son, also Martín, said: 'The jury of architects was going to give [it] first prize … But when they showed the project to Fidel, he said it was unacceptable, and that this Galician was not going to build again in Cuba.' Domínguez – who was in fact born in San Sebastían, in the Basque region of Spain – fled Cuba. He ended up teaching at Cornell University in Ithaca, New York, where the Martín Domínguez Award for Distinguished Teaching was named in his honour.

BANCO NACIONAL
Mario Romañach
Havana (CU), 1958

Mario Romañach was one of Cuba's rebellious architecture students who in 1944 rejected the curriculum, which was shackled to principles of the classical orders. Modernism, especially the form-and-function teachings of Walter Gropius, was their new syllabus. Romañach is credited with helping to transform Cuban architecture – although he was not a strict adherent to the relentless rationalization and linear order. The year before he fled Cuba, in 1959, in the wake of Fidel Castro's revolution, Romañach produced two versions of the Banco Nacional, facing the Caribbean across Havana's waterfront esplanade, the Malecón. The first was a slender twenty-four-storey tower with thin columns descending from the parapet to the ground; the building was held aloft on a central core and the picket of columns, creating a covered plaza four storeys high. Two rectangular buildings projected from this void, the smaller one wrapped in a metal screen, the larger one an entrance pavilion with a veranda formed – like the plaza from which it emerged – from its upper storey, cantilevered and supported on a row of columns. The second version was no less dramatic. A pair of short, stout, square buildings, hoisted on massive concrete pillars at each corner, had waffle-pattern cast-concrete floor plates and movable vertical metal screens to filter sunlight and, perhaps, guard against tropical storms. Neither of Romañach's designs was accepted by the bank, and Nicolás Quintana, a fellow Modernist, succeeded him, drawing his own concrete tower. In late 1959 Che Guevara assumed control of the National Bank and halted high-rise construction. The project was debarred, and the architects who had worked on it soon in exile.

PALACIO DE LAS PALMAS
Josep Lluís Sert,
Mario Romañach
Havana (CU), 1957

In July 1957 Cuba's dictator, Fulgencio Batista, unveiled a model of a new presidential palace, the 'Palace of the Palms', which was to be situated strategically on the bluffs overlooking Old Havana, on a wide piece of land sandwiched by the historic fortresses of El Morro and La Cabaña. Josep Lluís Sert (a Catalan architect in exile from fascist Spain) and the Cuban Mario Romañach had been hand-picked by Batista to produce a four-storey building that would house the government's executive offices, salons for official ceremonies, and a private residence for the president and his family.

The $8 million palace was three-sided, framing a large public square – with one side left open to the cooling trade winds of the Caribbean – and built around numerous patios, large and small. Sert was inspired by these courtyards, described by the Cuban essayist and architect Eugenio Batista as 'an indispensable element of our architecture', and which Sert saw as the true source of civic life. The dominant feature of the palace, however, was the huge, hovering roof, which projected the monumental building onto the Havana skyline.

Sert and Romañach recruited another Spanish exile, Felix Candela, to engineer thin-form concrete 'parasols', arched shells balanced on octagonal columns recalling the size and shape of royal palm trees – the symbol of Cuba – with an umbrella of concrete fronds deflecting sun and rain from the enormous structure. But at 3 am on 1 January 1959, in the wake of Fidel Castro's victory, Batista fled into his own exile, and the palace project was soon scuttled by the revolutionary government.

BACARDI RUM HEADQUARTERS
Ludwig Mies van der Rohe
Santiago de Cuba (CU), 1957

Bacardi Rum originated in Santiago de Cuba, once a fortified city from which the Spanish commanded the northern Caribbean, and, more than 300 years later, the place where the distiller produced its first batch of the fermented sugar-cane alcohol. Prohibition in the United States enriched the firm, which promoted nearby Cuba as a tropical heaven and a cocktail-culture haven. By the 1950s, Bacardi's president, José 'Pepin' Bosch, wanted to build a new headquarters in Santiago. His inspiration was Ludwig Mies van der Rohe's Crown Hall (1956), a simple building of penetrating clarity at the Illinois Institute of Technology in Chicago. Bosch hired the German-born American architect to give him an 'ideal office … where there were no partitions, where everybody … could see each other'. Mies realized that flush glass edges like those of Crown Hall could never shield the unrelenting Caribbean sunshine. In his Bacardi design he accordingly brought the flat roof out 9 m (29 ft) from the glass perimeter, on pairs of slender columns, allowing the single space, 39.5 m (130 ft) square, to float beneath a ceiling 5.5 m (18 ft) high. Instead of steel, which would rust practically overnight in the salty air, concrete formed the chief structural material. Concrete beams, running from side to side and front to back, supported the roof, which thickened at the centre. The building was elevated on a podium, making the glass walls appear virtually weightless between two layers of hefty concrete.

Bacardi's Cuban holdings were seized when Fidel Castro came to power in 1959. The project was abandoned, but the design became the template for two more buildings by Mies: the Neue Nationalgalerie in Berlin (1968) and Bacardi's global headquarters in Bermuda (1972).

COLUMBUS MEMORIAL LIGHTHOUSE
Konstantin Melnikov
Santo Domingo (DO), 1928

In March 1929 an international jury of three assembled in Madrid to review 2,500 drawings submitted by 455 architects from 48 countries in a global competition to build a Columbus Memorial Lighthouse on 1,012 hectares (2,500 acres) of empty land on the shore of the Ozama River, in the east of the colonial city of Santo Domingo. The jury of Raymond Hood, representing North America, Eliel Saarinen, representing Europe, and Horacio Acosta y Lara, representing Latin America, promptly cleared out the few Modernist and Expressionist concepts while – oddly – excluding every architect from south of the Rio Grande who had deigned to sketch a plan.

Of all the submissions, the Russian architect Konstantin Melnikov's, in retrospect, would seem to have ticked all the jurors' boxes. It had two opposable cones, balanced on their tips, held in the grip of 'powerful flyaway wings', wrapped in a helix that twisted seven times around the structure, forming a 'musical scale', Melnikov wrote. The upper cone collected rainwater, funnelling it into a turbine below and causing the monument to rotate slowly on its axis. The upper section, too, would spin in the wind, 'leaving each time a new impression on the inhabitants of San Domingo', as Melnikov noted in his handwritten explanation.

The winner, Joseph Lea Gleave's cross-shaped entry – an unmistakable paean to the glory of Christianity and therefore seemingly anathema to a Latin America rediscovering its Indigenous roots – was sidelined by a military coup in the Dominican Republic. It languished for six decades before being resurrected, built (somewhat according to plan) and inaugurated on 6 October 1992, for the 500th anniversary of Columbus's presumed first landing in the New World.

INTER-AMERICAN UNIVERSITY CHAPEL
IM Pei
San Germán (PR), 1961

Shortly after starting his own practice, the young architect IM Pei entered a competition to design a chapel for the Inter-American University, a private Christian institution in Puerto Rico. Located on a hilltop site in San Germán, at the southwestern corner of the island, Pei's proposed building was wrapped in a hood of folded concrete planes, like origami, a jewel or perhaps a strange insect. It opened to the elements on all sides and framed views of both the surrounding forests and the Caribbean Sea, while offering protection from strong sunlight and tropical rains. A narrow light slot in the roof admitted a slice of sky and beams of filtered daylight. The structure perched, as if about to take flight, atop a wide stone plaza jutting over a steep promontory.

Pei never shied away from borrowing from his unbuilt work, and the chapel's sculptural X-shaped carillon would to some extent inspire his Joy of Angels Bell Tower at the sanctuary of Shinji Shumeikai near Kyoto, Japan (which he designed twenty-five years later), a slender concrete structure 60 m (197 ft) tall that flares out dramatically at its apex. The project is also reminiscent of Walter Netsch and Harold Wagoner's daringly pleated US Air Force Academy Cadet Chapel in Colorado, completed the next year.

Pei did not win the competition, and the chapel, an octagonal building with a shooting spire designed by Ramírez and Ramírez de Arellano architects, opened in 1967. It was dedicated to university trustee (and pastor of Park Avenue Presbyterian Church in New York) Paul A Wolfe, who oversaw its fundraising campaign.

CATHEDRAL DE SAN SALVADOR
Oscar Nitzchke
San Salvador (SV), 1953

Recognized for his graceful drawings as much as for his buildings, the Swiss architect Oscar Nitzchke collaborated with a who's who of architects, including Le Corbusier, Auguste Perret and Wallace Harrison (with whom he oversaw the design of the United Nations Headquarters in New York in 1951). He also befriended numerous artists, among them Pablo Picasso, Fernand Léger, Alexander Calder and Man Ray.

In 1953 Nitzchke was invited to enter the second iteration of a competition to design the new Metropolitan Cathedral of the Divine Saviour of the World for San Salvador, El Salvador. (The previous structure had been destroyed by fire in 1951.) Framed with reinforced concrete to protect against earthquakes, the building's folding walls would be formed from coloured strips of metal-framed glass, set at 45 degrees to the columns, with small, concentric circular chapels at the base. In the drawing, the cathedral appears light as air, its shell-like concrete vaults alternating in rhythm with the bends of the walls. The lacy glazing enabled by the elegant concrete skeleton would flood the airy space with coloured light.

Nitzchke was bested in the contest by the German church design specialist Dominikus Böhm, whose audacious entry was crowned with a conical dome 60 m (197 ft) high surrounded by a ring of ten round, domed chapels. That plan, too, was doomed, when Böhm died in 1955. It would be years before a new cathedral – quite similar to the one lost to fire – was completed.

South America

VE [4]

CO [1]

PE [2]

BR [7]

UY [1]

AR [5]

PETROLEUM MUSEUM
Jorge Rigamonti
Cabimas (VE), 1984

Cabimas is the city on the shore of Maracaibo Lake, near the Gulf of Venezuela, where the famous blowout ('El Reventón') of 1922 at the Barroso II oil well marked the beginning of large-scale oil extraction in Venezuela.

The architect Jorge Rigamonti, who was concerned about the ripple effects of oil production both economically and environmentally, saw in the Petroleum Museum a way to compress into a structure the history, culture and hidden meaning of petroleum extraction as a way of life. His building was conceived as a set of independent shapes, drawn from the mechanical elements used in the oil industry: circles and squares and their three-dimensional equivalents, cylinders and cubes. The core of the museum, containing exhibition spaces, was of reinforced concrete, the thick walls insulating visitors from the constant, humid heat of the Caribbean littoral. Corridors, stairways and halls were lightweight aluminium structures, surrounded by a water 'mirror', intended to make it seem as if the building had percolated up from the ground, the way oil once did on the site. Rigamonti fitted a three-dimensional tubular framework, in a chequerboard pattern, as an exoskeletal facade. A concrete cylinder, standing in for an oil derrick, was at the centre of the museum. The symmetrical volume took on the appearance of a refinery, without the flare-offs and constant belching of smoke, but its slim vertical posts also referred to 'Palafitos', the Indigenous stilt dwellings that once occupied the waters of Lake Maracaibo. The government of President Luis Herrera Campins commissioned the project, and the drawings were shovel-ready. His term ended in 1984, however; his successor wasn't interested, and axed it.

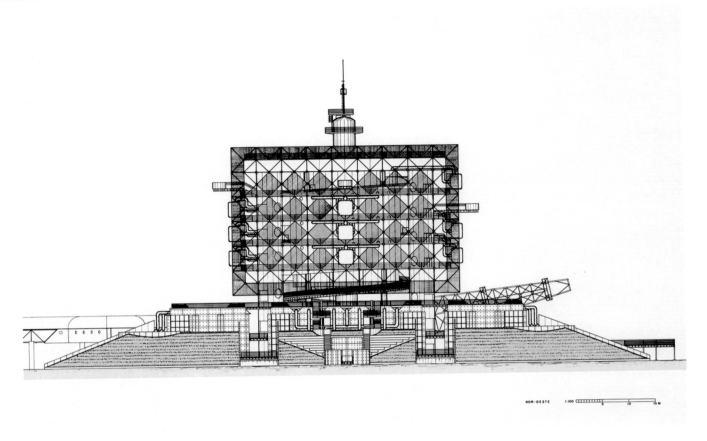

RECREATIONAL APARTMENTS
Marcel Breuer
Tanaguarena (VE), 1958

Bauhaus student and teacher Marcel Breuer is known for his serious, methodical approach to architecture, but he was never afraid to produce uninhibited, sculptural designs. A prime example is this twenty-two-storey cooperative apartment complex in Tanaguarena, a beach town just north of Caracas, Venezuela (the country had been developing a reputation as a home for unorthodox architecture, drawing many of Modernism's brightest stars).
Breuer and his longstanding associate Herbert Beckhard collaborated with the exuberant and prolific Venezuelan architect Julio Volante on the undertaking: a serpentine, twenty-storey building raised on piloti, overlooking the ocean on one side and mountains on the other. The long edifice was intended to house 600 families. Its S-shape kept it shaded, created a rhythmic profile, exposed as many rooms as possible to ocean views and softened its impact. North-facing ocean rooms had colourful projecting balconies, while the south face was shielded by screened exterior walkways. The apartments were warmed by wood and stone and divided by brightly coloured, flexible barriers. Equally expressive recreational facilities, gathered around a large pool, included cabanas with barrel-vaulted roofs and a beach club topped by thin-shell hyperbolic paraboloids supported by central columns, like inverted umbrellas.
The dictatorship of Marcos Pérez Jiménez toppled the same year as the proposal, and the resulting economic crisis (and the new administration's lack of interest in kickbacks from developers) forced the project's promoters to abandon it. Breuer's only other Venezuela project, the 'El Recreo' urban centre in Caracas, consisting of four office towers set in a pedestrian plaza, also failed to move forward.

MUSEUM OF MODERN ART, CARACAS
Oscar Niemeyer
Caracas (VE), 1955

In the 1950s, with Venezuela's oil industry ramping up at unprecedented levels, Caracas experienced dizzying growth, led by large public works and petro-conglomerate-led developments. One of the city's flagship urbanization plans was Colinas de Bello Monte (CBM), along the southeastern edge of the city, which proposed ambitious vertical expansion up Caracas's outer hillsides. Hoping for a press-friendly centrepiece for the project, CBM's president, Inocente Palacios – the owner of one of the largest collections of modern art in the country – proposed building the Caracas Museum of Modern Art atop a cliff 970 m (3,182 ft) above sea level. Palacios first discussed the project with Ludwig Mies van der Rohe, who declined, citing time conflicts. By 1955 Palacios had reached an agreement with Oscar Niemeyer, who within weeks had proposed a heroic five-storey inverted pyramid supported by inclined concrete ribs and lightweight steel girders, transferring loads to a heavy concrete foundation. Perched over the city, the scheme would attract maximum attention, said Niemeyer, and be 'bold and pure in the landscape'. Inside, large open spaces and small window openings created a sense of serene monumentality and spatial surprise. A glass ceiling, protected by aluminium *brise-soleils*, would admit ethereal natural light to every level.
But the museum was doomed by myriad factors. By 1958 Venezuela's president, the dictator Marcos Pérez Jiménez, had been ousted, and the new democratic government had little interest in pursuing his monumental ambitions. An economic crisis paralysed construction in the country, while experts started to question the geological stability of the museum's site. Some have theorized that the ill-fated plan inspired the Canadian Pavilion at Expo '67 by Rod Robbie in collaboration with others – another dramatic inverted pyramid, albeit in glass.

CATEDRAL DE CIUDAD GUAYANA
Oswaldo Molina
Ciudad Guayana (VE), 1981

The cathedral for Ciudad Guayana, at the confluence of the Orinoco and Caroní rivers, dates from the early 1960s, when the old town of San Félix was united with the new town of Puerto Ordaz to form a planned industrial city designed by Massachusetts Institute of Technology and Harvard University. The cathedral was slated for high ground with views of the spectacular Llovizna waterfall on the Caroní River.
Oswaldo Molina made several designs for the building. In one, he perched his truncated half-cone cathedral on a large square intended to allow open-air liturgical celebrations in a semi-circle subtracted from the spherical structure. A massive central column supports a space frame tied to the radiating concrete fins enclosing the nave. In another version, the space frame disappears, replaced by a flue resembling the mouth of a volcano. A raised walkway in the shape of a question mark traces a path around a sunken plaza, giving the impression that the cathedral is the nose of a rocket ready to launch. This was no accident since Molina wanted to ensure that his building would be visible from all over the city.
The cathedral's sponsors, the College of Architects of Venezuela and the industry-supported Venezuelan Corporation of Guayana hoped it would trigger low-density development in the surrounding area. It did, creating a neighbourhood that from the air looked like the cul-de-sac suburbs of Phoenix, Arizona – not surprisingly, very Americanized. Molina's cathedral, on the other hand, never sprang to life, but was fatally snagged in bureaucratic bickering. In 1985 Pope John Paul II dedicated a different site for a different cathedral, which remains only partially constructed.

URBANIZACIÓN ALTOS DEL RÍO
Rogelio Salmona
Cali (CO), 1979

Rogelio Salmona, regarded as the greatest Colombian architect of the twentieth century and the first Latin-American architect to win the Alvar Aalto Medal, was a master in brick. He was born in Paris to Jewish parents, and his family fled to Bogotá before Hitler's rise to power, but when right-wing violence erupted in Colombia, he returned to Paris, where he spent time working with Le Corbusier. When he finally returned to his adopted country in 1957, he had abandoned his mentor's views, drawing inspiration instead from the rhythmic, handmade Islamic brickwork of Granada, Spain, and the Moroccan, Tunisian and Algerian mosques that he had visited. His Torres del Parque, built next to Bogotá's bullring, are monumental, sweeping essays in red brick that distil the essence of his work; they resonate with majestic, timeless silence, like the surrounding mountains that inspired them.

For Urbanización Altos del Río, Salmona staggered twelve multifamily cooperative houses on a steep hillside, imitating the lie of the land. With tall chimneys rising above the parapet-like buildings, and large, high windows glistening like glass fragments in a matrix of brick, the complex rises from the landscape like an artificial forest. The homes are entered from U-shaped courtyards that slice between paired structures, emphasizing the slender boundary between public and private, and forcing residents to wander past one another in shared spaces. Salmona worked tirelessly for years on ideas for cooperative housing, refining as well his concept for hillside dwellings, many unbuilt. 'Good architecture becomes ruins,' he said. 'Bad architecture disappears.' Sometimes good architecture disappears, too, never leaving the architect's desk.

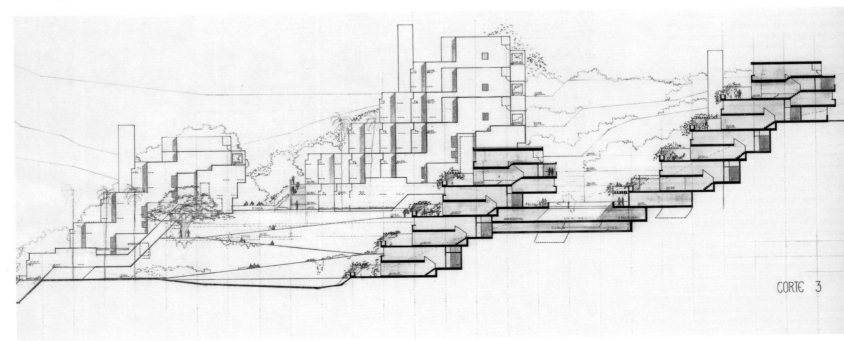

CORTE 3

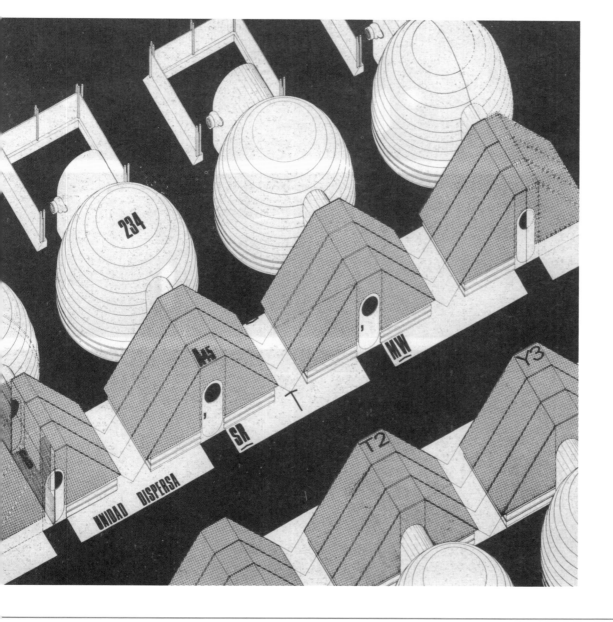

EMERGENCY SOCIAL UNITS
Antonio Fernández Alba
Lima (PE), 1968

Working in an age of experiment and social upheaval, the Spanish architect Antonio Fernández Alba realized projects of a scope and scale that most architects can only dream of. In the late 1960s he teamed up with a group of noted colleagues, including Juan Daniel Fullaondo (not to mention industrial designers, graphic artists, engineers and health professionals), for the design of the Emergency Social Units (Unidades Sociales de Emergencia), prefabricated structures of plastic, tubular metal, canvas and other lightweight materials, intended to allow first aid and provide housing during natural disasters. The overarching approach incorporated craft, industry and technology in equal parts to develop prototypes. To maximize efficiency, hard-shelled units would be constructed industrial-style and delivered ready-made for easy construction. Once in place, most would be laid out in carefully planned repetition, stacked via lightweight tubular-steel armatures, revolving around essential service modules, from bathrooms and generators to schools. Unlike the prison-style emergency housing of Alba's time – and today – units would receive as much natural light and air as possible, and many had their own small terraces, giving individuals both privacy and respite.

The units were intended to be customized to their surroundings. In Lima, for instance, a hillside settlement housing fifty families would hug the natural slopes at the periphery of the city, creating terraces edged with vegetation to shade and beautify the area and ensure stable soil. But the entire project was eventually, as Alba put it, 'amputated', proved unfeasible by the realities of politics, production standards and economics.

MACHU PICCHU HOTEL
Miguel Rodrigo Mazuré
Machu Picchu (PE), 1969

The Peruvian architect Miguel Rodrigo Mazuré was a master of discreet Modernist houses as well as monumental, structurally expressive, large-scale buildings. His Brutalist Ministry of Fisheries (1972), made of interlocking volumes clad in bare concrete panels, is regarded as the best building to have been completed in Peru during that decade.

The slightly earlier Machu Picchu Hotel hovered over the Andes like a condor god frozen in concrete. The winged structure, Mazuré said, was composed to 'allow the visitor to experience the heights of the landscape … from multiple angles'. To experience vertigo too, perhaps, since one might begin to feel giddy while peering down through the sloping windows on the undersides of the cantilevered hotel 'tubes', as Mazuré called them, or gazing from the rooftop deck, propped on enormous concrete piers more than 30 m (98 ft) above the slopes. Mazuré's concept – part science-fiction fantasy, part computer-age rigorousness – would seem to have conceded little to the ruins of the mid-fifteenth-century Inca citadel; nothing of Machu Picchu's carved white-granite temples and houses was present in the design. Yet the hotel was meant not just as a tourist attraction in and of itself, an object whose presence was as unabashed as it was unaccountably alien. In fact, following the *coup d'état* of 1968, monumental concrete structures were seen as reflections of Peru's pre-Hispanic past, as up-to-date equivalents to the huge mud-and-stone buildings of the Inca civilization, so deeply embedded in the country's consciousness. Nationalism is the stock-in-trade of military regimes, but why Mazuré's tourist hotel wasn't among its built representations is now lost to time.

BELO HORIZONTE CATHEDRAL
Clemens Holzmeister
Belo Horizonte (BR), 1942

Clemens Holzmeister received a personal invitation from the archbishop of Belo Horizonte to conceive a new cathedral for this hilly city in southeastern Brazil. The Austrian architect, who throughout his career would design more than sixty-five churches, wanted to build the largest possible cathedral using modern materials. His plan for this one was indirectly inspired by Hagia Sophia, the vast domed basilica in Istanbul, where he had been living.

On a rise of land Holzmeister drew a circular cathedral 70 m (230 ft) in diameter, captured beneath an enormous cupola 150 m (492 ft) high, mimicking the papal tiara – the crown worn by popes since the eighth century. The round structure gave parishioners unobstructed views of an elevated altar, which sat beneath an interior dome 50 m (164 ft) high; stained-glass windows, piercing the dome, as well as a skylight at its pinnacle, allowed light to flood onto the altar. At a height of 25 m (82 ft) above the altar, a ring supported by gigantic angels formed a gallery for the organ and the choir. Holzmeister's huge white reinforced-concrete crown would be as visible to the surrounding city as that of Hagia Sophia was. The three tiers of arches – the first glassed in, the second alternately open and hung with bells, the third entirely open and reaching 116 m (381 ft) – culminated in a cap made of concrete spandrels.

Holzmeister sent the diocese ninety-four drawings of his idea. But, as in so many other cases, money was in short supply, in inverse proportion to the grandeur of the proposition.

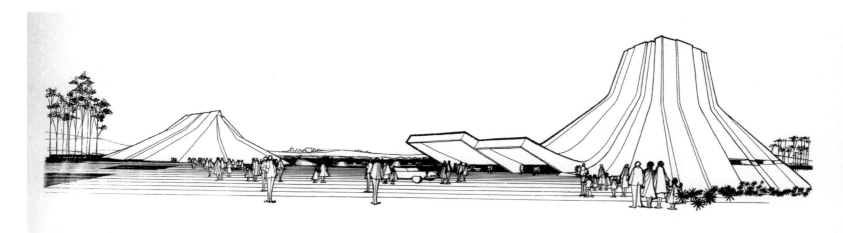

TEATRO DE OPERA
Fábio Penteado
Campinas (BR), 1966

With the Teatro de Opera at Campinas, the southeastern Brazilian city whose history is linked to coffee, cotton and sugar cane, Fábio Penteado had a Brechtian objective: to erase the rigid formality and class snobbery inherent in the experience of theatre-going. He ripped up the competition brief (for a 1,500-seat theatre in the city's most important urban park) and reconfigured it as an essay in theatre as public space – theatre whose architecture and landscape would spontaneously suggest to a passer-by a sense of ownership, of belonging. Theatre and citizen were to be reunited, as they had been in the Renaissance.

Penteado did this with three poetic structures. The centrepiece opera looked like a volcano, constructed from enormous leaning concrete slabs forming a cinder cone. The smaller comedy theatre looked like a circus tent. The open-air theatre, on an artificial island in the Taquaral lagoon, bobbed like a raft in the water. It wasn't just the suggestion of these familiar natural or plebian forms that would break down the stolid, intimidating facade – physical and psychological – of theatre. Penteado made an opera house whose stage itself was a kind of town square, with the audience entering from all sides and the singers performing in the middle, crossing paths. The banks of the lagoon formed an amphitheatre, and an underground service tunnel (where the stage equipment, scenic arts and workshops would be located) was the public passageway between theatres. Penteado lost the competition, but later the city built his Centro de Convivência Cultural de Campinas (1976), an outdoor theatre that became the kind of plaza-theatre he had wanted.

POLYTHEAMA
THEATRE RENOVATION
Lina Bo Bardi
Jundiaí (BR), 1986

In 1985 André Benassi, mayor of Jundiaí, a city just north of São Paulo, invited Lina Bo Bardi to renovate the Polytheama ('many spectacles') Theatre of 1911. Once one of the region's most illustrious gathering spaces, hosting theatre, political meetings, balls and even circuses, the eclectic building had been abandoned for more than two decades, prompting the city to purchase it. Bo Bardi led the renovation of its facade and interior, but her unbuilt additions would have made the project truly radical.

Known for eliminating boundaries between inside and out (see her own spectacular glass house in São Paulo), Bo Bardi proposed creating novel connections to the outside world in a building type that is often cloistered. By obtaining the surrounding plot she proposed creating an outdoor lobby, featuring a lush, somewhat mystical garden filled with winding paths and colourful vegetation. A glazed wall at the rear of the stage allowed natural light to pour in and provided views of the city, while pipe-shaped, lightweight concrete corridors, connected to the building via large portholes, would provide direct access to the upper galleries of the auditorium. A new 'cave' dug under the theatre housed a restaurant and bar with independent access.

'Theatre is my way of participating in politics,' said Bo Bardi, who spent much of her career working on production designs. But Benassi was voted out in 1988, shortly after construction began, and by the time he was re-elected in 1993 Bo Bardi had died and the remaining plans were abandoned.

MUSEUM OF THE
SEASHORE
Lina Bo Bardi
São Vicente (BR), 1951

Completed in 1968 on the bustling Avenida Paulista, Lina Bo Bardi's São Paulo Museum of Art is one of the city's great architectural landmarks: a rectangular prism of glass suspended from bright red concrete brackets, floating over a large plaza. But in 1951, long before completing that masterpiece, Bo Bardi – always interested in the ways in which structural engineering could unlock her designs – attempted to build in the nearby seaside city of São Vicente what would become a sort of trial run, simply called Museum of the Seashore.

São Vicente's mayor, Charles Dantas Forbes, invited Bo Bardi and her husband, the curator and collector Pietro Maria Bardi, to collaborate on the concept. Elevated over the sand of Itararé beach, hanging from red reinforced-concrete beams, the museum's moderate elevation sheltered the art from humidity and created a shaded space underneath without blocking views of the Atlantic Ocean. Walls were clad in white marble, and the seafront facade was left open via slab-to-slab glass panels. The building's suspended frame helped to keep internal spaces open for maximum flexibility, divided only by movable walls.

Although the project had Forbes' support, funding could never be secured. (Some hypothesize that the mayor simply used the concept to help him get re-elected.) The design informed – and was also informed by – Bo Bardi's own home, the famed Glass House in São Paulo: an elevated glass prism completed around the same time. And, of course, it was a seminal step on the road to her museum in the same city, a close cousin, albeit nowhere near the beach.

MUSEUM OF CONTEMPORARY ART OF THE UNIVERSITY OF SÃO PAULO
Paulo Mendes da Rocha
São Paulo (BR), 1975

The Brazilian architect Paulo Mendes da Rocha was a master of prestressed concrete, making it bend and float as if it were paper, often unlocking surprising possibilities. One of the major missed opportunities of his career was a commission to design a new facility for the Museum of Contemporary Art of the University of São Paulo (MAC/USP), on the central campus, Cidade Universitária. (The museum, founded in 1963, houses one of the greatest collections of modern art in Latin America. Its home at the time was the third floor of Oscar Niemeyer's Ciccillo Matarazzo Pavilion in Ibirapuera Park, about 5 km/3 miles southeast of Cidade Universitária.)

Mendes da Rocha's collaboration with the powerful architect and planner Jorge Wilheim took the form of an inverted trapezoidal concrete mass floating over its site, supported by a largely hidden system of stilt-like central columns and skeletal transverse roof beams. Mendes da Rocha placed a sculpture garden under the building, and inserted within its structural armature a series of suspended exhibition floors, connected by a system of ramps offset by half levels, creating a labyrinthine spatial complexity accentuated by the play of natural light.

Work began in 1976, but late that year landslides during the digging of the foundations prompted a change in the construction approach that drove up the cost. This and the advent of a new museum director, Wolfgang Pfeiffer – who was more interested in conserving the museum's existing spaces – doomed the undertaking. In 2010 the museum moved within Ibirapuera Park, into a retrofitted version of Niemeyer's 1950s Agriculture Pavilion.

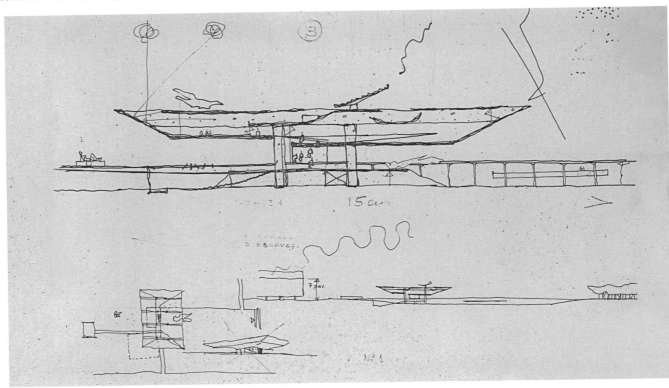

PALÁCIO DO GOVERNO
Flávio de Carvalho
São Paulo (BR), 1927

Flávio de Carvalho was a wealthy Brazilian, educated in France and England, who was both an engineer and an artist, devoted to confounding bourgeois propriety. He often donned women's clothes in the name of performance art, and his architecture was no less provocative – Le Corbusier called him a 'romantic revolutionary'.

Carvalho's competition entry for a new government palace in São Paulo was romantic, revolutionary and more: the reinforced-concrete building was a symmetrical pile of cubes and rectangles stacked around a vaulted, railway tunnel-like entrance. He declared that it was 'the first piece of modern architecture in Brazil'. Seemingly devoutly modern, it looked like an up-to-date fortress, as conceived by Genghis Khan or a twelfth-century Crusader. Immured behind its thick walls were banks of lifts of differing sizes and lengths running at various speeds; ornate terraces displaying specimen plants; aviaries; and private apartments for the nation's president.

Much of this was of little consequence to Carvalho, however. He intended the building as a political statement, a bulwark against the political turmoil that had engulfed Brazil in the 1920s. He accessorized the 'bellicose character of this palace', as the newspaper *Diario Nacional* described it, with 'a complete plan for defence against attacks by land and air', employing permanent searchlights, a battery of rapid-fire anti-aircraft cannon, a landing strip for high-speed fighter planes, a hangar for the squadron, catapults, cranes, radio transmitters and receivers, and a power station. Carvalho's building was a compilation of militaristic means to crush the opposition – any opposition. His proposal was rejected, and he later implied that it was just another ironic gesture.

APART HOTEL
Carlos Bratke
São Paulo (BR), 1983

The draughting-board imagination is rarely inherited. Eliel and Eero Saarinen are the oft-cited exception, and outside Brazil, few know Oswaldo Bratke and his son Carlos Bratke. Oswaldo was a figurehead of Brazilian Modernism, a contemporary of Oscar Niemeyer and Vilanova Artigas. Both Bratkes were brilliant draughtsmen, working in pen and pencil, but Carlos rebelled against his father's generation of 'pure crystal boxes', as the Brazilian architect Hugo Segawa described them.

Carlos helped to define a new generation of São Paulo corporate skyscrapers, using exposed concrete, prefabrication and irregular planes to shatter the 'glazed canon'. During his peak years, from the 1970s to the 1990s, his office buildings proliferated; in Cidade Monções alone, the southwestern neighbourhood of São Paulo today occupied by many multinational corporations, more than sixty sprang up – hence the neighbourhood being dubbed 'Bratkelândia'. Bratke said he wanted to make his buildings 'dance'. The Apart Hotel, a contraction (of sorts) of apartment and hotel, took inspiration from Paul Rudolph's hanging components for his unbuilt Trailer Apartment Tower (1959), but with the twist of having a tower by the American architect Minoru Yamasaki spring from the middle of its zigzag residential pyramidal base. Massive, slanted pillars allowed the homes on the lower floors to hang freely, and there were palapas, sheds and Quonset huts dangling like lights from a Christmas tree. A golden thirty-two-storey extruded cube resided above, apparently balancing on the tip of the pyramid below. The site, at the intersection of Rua Dr Mário Ferraz and Rua Prof. Artur Ramos, is now occupied by high-rise buildings, but Bratke's scheme has remained on paper.

JOSÉ BATLLE MONUMENT
Jorge Oteiza
Montevideo (UY), 1957

In 1956 the government of Uruguay launched a competition to erect a monument overlooking Montevideo Bay and honouring José Batlle y Ordóñez, the late nineteenth and early twentieth-century president who is largely considered to be the father of democracy in the country. (The event marked the centenary of Ordóñez's birth.) Competing with finalists from Argentina and Italy were the Spanish sculptor Jorge Oteiza and architect Roberto Puig, who proposed a cubist edifice merging 'statue and temple', housing Batlle's library and drawing the public in. Their entry, supported by a structural steel skeleton and topped by a continuous series of skylights, took the form of a floating horizontal prism 54 m (177 ft) long, resting on six metal pillars that raised it 4.5 m (nearly 15 ft) above a hill in what is now Parque Rodó. Its form, with thin concrete walls, evoked the sacred through sublime contrasts of void and solid, dark and light. A long, narrow arm served as a protective wall, floating under the suspended structure. Inside, pristine, symmetrical spaces included the library, an auditorium and a majestic foyer containing a generous double staircase.

While the Italian team (including the architect Mario Romano and the sculptor Cesare Poli) received the most votes, Oteiza and Puig filed a formal protest, citing several irregularities. After lengthy back and forth, the national commission overseeing the monument declared the competition void. While it didn't say why, obvious reasons included an economic recession and the fact that the National Party (also known as the White Party) had just come to power, and was far less interested in executing a project instigated by its rival Colorado Party.

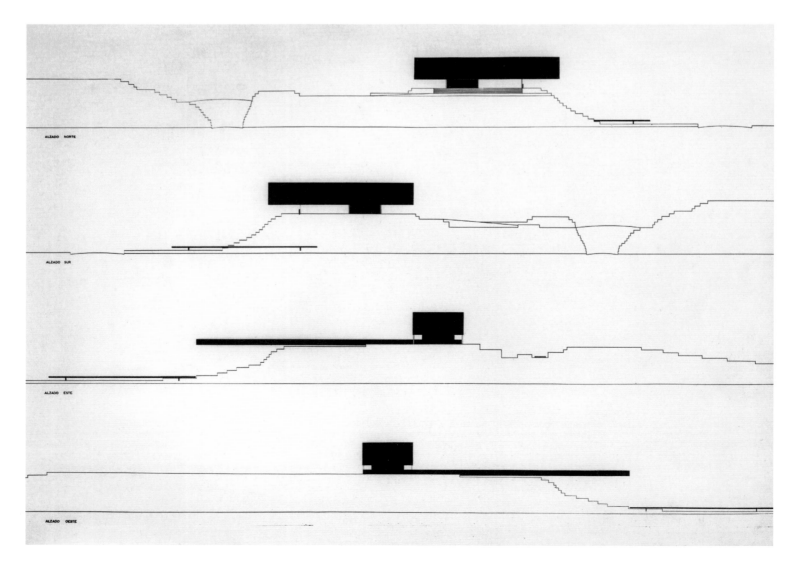

SOUTH AMERICA

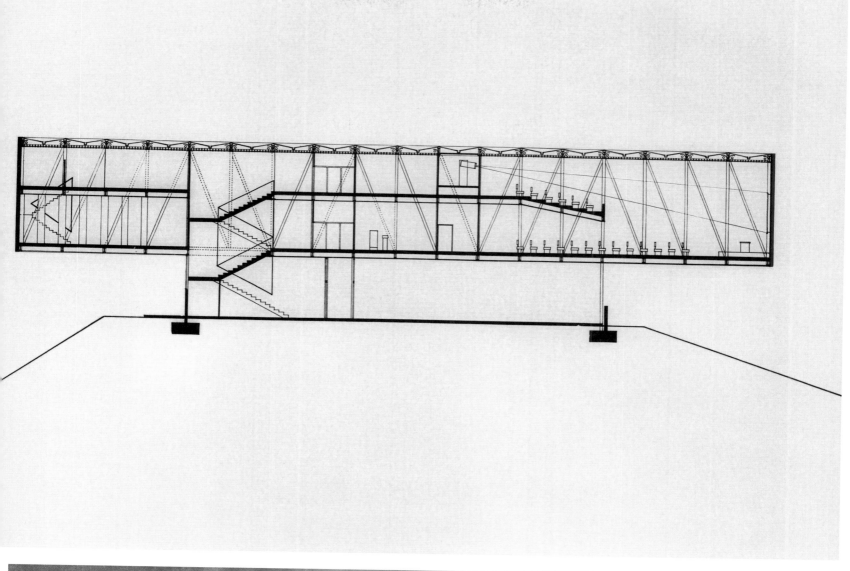

SUSPENDED OFFICE BUILDING
Amancio Williams
Buenos Aires (AR), 1946

In 1938 the twenty-five-year-old Amancio Williams determined that engineering and aviation, his chief pursuits, were not his true calling. He declared that he'd 'led a foolish life' in 'decadent' Buenos Aires, leading him 'to completely break with this society that surrounded me'. Architecture would be his field, 'because I found human aspects in it: social, technical, economic, political, plastic ... all this with great artistic possibilities'. Eight years later, in an impassioned letter to Le Corbusier – whose name and works had never been mentioned during Williams's academic training – he explained that his small workshop was dedicated to 'spatial solutions resolved with the greatest purity'.

Williams would one day be hailed among Argentina's most brilliant architects, although the vast majority of his works were never built. He conceived a new airport, a modular umbrella column that could support vast loads while collecting rainwater, a doughnut-shaped theatre for sound, and a city for Antarctica. His Suspended Office Building was a riposte to North American skyscrapers, whose forests of load-bearing columns prevented clear floor plates. The building consisted of three slabs, like huge granite-hewn altars, of eight floors each, and a fourth slab of four floors, all suspended from a skeleton of concrete and tensioned cables. Between the blocks were through-and-through voids. The entire structure, 115 m (377 ft) high, hovered 18 m (59 ft) above ground, forming an open plaza underneath.

Williams believed that his concrete-and-cable building could provide work for metallurgical factories in the wake of World War II. He suggested Berlin as a site, but in some drawings the structure is clearly placed in belle époque Buenos Aires. He never found a taker for the concept.

ALTAR DE LA PATRIA
José López Rega
Buenos Aires (AR), 1974

Just days after the death of the Argentine dictator Juan Perón, the country's lawmakers passed an act demanding the erection of a monumental mausoleum containing the remains of Perón, his legendary second wife, Eva, and several more national leaders. According to the dictum, passed on 8 July 1974, the Altar of the Fatherland – at 60 m (197 ft), taller than Rio's famed Christ the Redeemer – would become the centrepiece of a massive plaza on Avenida Figueroa Alcorta, near where the Plaza Naciones Unidas sits today. Its frontispiece would be engraved with the phrase 'United in glory, we watch over the destinies of the homeland.'

Launched by the notorious government minister José López Rega (nicknamed 'El Brujo', 'The Warlock'), the marble-clad project exhibited stretched Roman arches, stained-glass windows, a blocky pediment and a strangely small central dome, making it an awkward approximation of so many Fascist claims to sacred legitimacy. (And, as with so many Fascist monuments, the name of the architect was suppressed, so as not to siphon away glory.)

While the monument's foundation stone was laid on 23 November 1974, its failure was a symptom of what had long become an inept state. Workers on the site met with endless impediments, not the least of which was the solid concrete base of another failed monument: Eva Perón's Monument to the Shirtless (1952), which, at 137 m (449 ft) in height, was to be the 'tallest monument in the world'. The Altar project slowed to a crawl, and was officially abandoned when a coup overthrew Perón's widow and successor, Isabel Perón, in 1976.

MUSEO DE LA CIENCIA Y LA TECNOLOGÍA AGROPECUARIA
Clorindo Testa
Castelar (AR), 2006

Near the end of his long career, the celebrated Argentine architect Clorindo Testa was hired by Instituto Nacional de Tecnología y Agropecuaria (INTA) to build a museum for the display of old agricultural machinery in the city of Castelar, on the rural pampas west of Buenos Aires.

The ultra-flat site of 2 hectares (5 acres) was once part of a cattle ranch, but a remnant of forest provided Testa with a natural backdrop for the thirteen freestanding, 'loose' buildings he designed. The architect described them as 'typical Pampas construction'. He laid out six metal sheds with sheet-metal roofs, a pair of roundhouses, a small hotel for researchers, and a 1,000-seat auditorium, strung along an arcade that he called the 'connector'. At one point the connector, which was otherwise arrow-straight, caved in on itself, making way for an indigenous *ombú*, the massive evergreen tree with multiple trunks that is the national tree of Argentina. Unlike the galleries, the round buildings were of painted brick and the auditorium a concrete structure with an inclined roof of varying pitch in a sawtooth pattern; the jagged shape gave the interior spatial movement and improved the acoustics. As with the other buildings, the auditorium spoke directly to the outdoors; the backdrop to the stage was made of sliding doors that opened to expose the forest and connected directly to a small amphitheatre. Shot through with colour – reds, blues, yellows, greens, pinks – INTA was, like all of Testa's prolific output, dynamism in the service of a singular, idiosyncratic, yet uniquely localized idea. It was scuttled when new management took over the Institute.

PALACIO DE LOS 16 BLASONES
Francisco Salamone
Buenos Aires (AR), 1952

The biography of Francisco Salamone reads like a pulp novel. When he was four, his family emigrated from Leonforte, Sicily, to Rio de Janeiro. He became an engineer and architect and reputedly through political connections in the 1930s emerged as a Promethean master of public buildings in the Pampas, only to end up in self-imposed exile in Uruguay, under a cloud of accusations of fraud. He lived the rest of his life out of favour, an architect with a massive portfolio and no clients.

Remarkably, over just four years, from 1936 to 1940, Salamone designed and built more than seventy public buildings – town halls, slaughterhouses, cemeteries and squares – with enormous, expressive, Brancusi-like facades, scattered across the 300,000 sq. km (116,000 sq. miles) of the province of Buenos Aires. His avalanche of concrete monumentality – bent, folded, sculpted – set against the flat void of the grasslands landed in these small towns of 1,000 inhabitants like asteroids hurled from a future century.

Salamone's Palacio de los 16 Blasones (Palace of 16 Coats of Arms) may be his most outlandish unbuilt project: a sixty-storey skyscraper, named after what were then the sixteen provinces of Argentina, for the corner of Avenida de Mayo and Avenida 9 de Julio (which is said to be the widest avenue in the world). It was a wedge layered with scalloped, Art Deco walls, topped by a beacon projecting a beam that could be seen 213 km (132 miles) away in Montevideo. Ezequiel Hilbert, Salamone's film chronicler, says Salamone tried to convince President Juan Perón and his government to build the apartment tower, but, as with so much about Salamone, there the story fades to dust.

BUENOS AIRES
AUDITORIUM
Alberto Varas
Buenos Aires (AR), 1972

Even before the coup of 1976, Argentina had embraced the spirit of early 1970s radicalism. So in 1972, when the city of Buenos Aires held a competition for a new municipal auditorium on the sizeable site of its recently demolished

national penitentiary, a traditional concert hall was out of the question.

The winning bid, from a multi-headed team led by the prolific Modernist architect Alberto Varas (at the time, still in his twenties), was fittingly sci-fi and egalitarian. Consisting of three partially sunken polyhedral domes connected by glass-and-steel-clad foyers and bridges, it included halls for 3,000, 1,800 and 500 spectators respectively. A case study for the increasingly popular concept of 'open architecture', its exposed structure and mechanical systems

would incorporate new elements as the facility evolved, like adding pieces to an Erector Set. Green space meandered through it, and large geometric plazas would facilitate public outdoor gathering. There were no 'privileged' spaces: views, experiences and public services would be equally effective in every zone. Sinking the buildings into the earth, meanwhile, minimized disruption to the neighbourhood and provided extra sound insulation.

The coup put a stop to any plans of the previous regime, particularly ones as progressive as this.

The land, in the city's Palermo neighbourhood, was abandoned until the early 1980s, when the city transformed it into Parque Las Heras, a popular park named after the nineteenth-century war hero General Juan Gregorio de Las Heras.

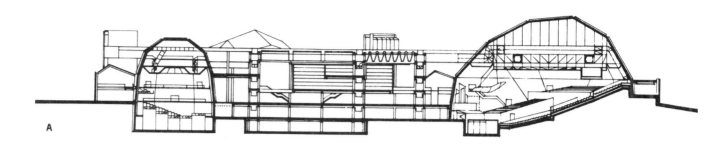

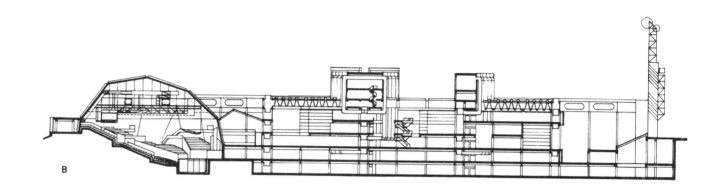

Europe West

FI [1]

SE [1]

NO [1]

DK [4]

IE [1]

GB [16]

NL [9]

DE [20]

BE [3]

AT [5]

FR [12]

CH [3]

MO [1]

IT [18]

AD [1]

ES [7]

PT [1]

ATLAS OF NEVER BUILT ARCHITECTURE

HATLEHOL CHURCH
Cornelius Vöge
Ålesund (NO), 2015

For more than forty years, the parishioners of Hatlehol had been collecting funds to build a new church. This hamlet of 8,000 residents in Ålesund, on the west coast of Norway, sits in a landscape of unrivalled beauty, surrounded by fjords, woods and craggy mountains. Here, nature is more than a backdrop; it is a raw presence.

The young Danish architects Nanna Vöge and Dan Cornelius won an international competition, besting 123 other entrants, with their church, which they described as a 'meeting between mountains, water and light'. The site is rocky, among larch, birch and pine trees, open on one side to a cemetery; there are views to the surrounding mountains to the north, and a narrow stream flows along the western edge. Rain and a lack of sunlight are persistent. Cornelius Vöge made an abstract set of concrete mountains, like shards that might have tumbled from the peaks and landed on the natural plateau. The bell tower, baptistry and presbytery stick up and are canted away from the central nave, standing above the treetops, as visible as an old Norse stave church would have been with its tall wooden towers. Inside, the roof traces the undersides of these forms, as if someone had excavated a space within the pile of massive stones.

The conglomerated pieces, knitted together as a single building, became a kind of bonsai mountain range, a symbolic meeting of heaven and Earth, the physical and the spiritual. But tiny Hatlehol never raised enough money, and the project was put on hold – permanently.

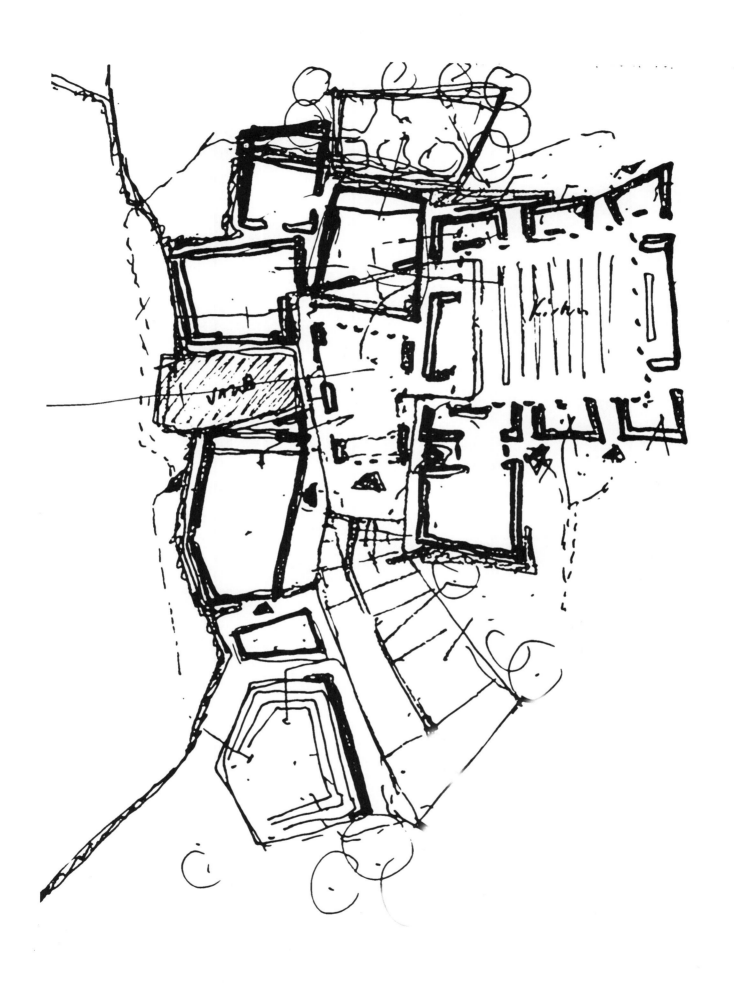

NORWAY

BROMMA AIRPORT
Gunnar Asplund
Stockholm (SE), 1934

When, in 1934, the Stockholm authorities invited four well-known Swedish architects to establish the first commercial airport at Bromma, 7 km (4 miles) west of the capital, the city was among dozens in the years between the two world wars to hold a competition to accommodate the boom in civilian aviation.

Gunnar Asplund's air station was a floor-to-ceiling ribbon of glass sandwiched between two thin layers of concrete, extending from the hillside and overlooking the runways. The slender structure had a clear span of 50 m (164 ft), allowing aircraft to taxi beneath the 8-m (26-ft) high terminal, while waiting passengers absorbed the thrill of take-off and landing with a spectacular view of the airstrips radiating over the flats below them. At the far end, just above the ground-level apron – where travellers embarked and disembarked – was the control tower. A narrow operations building occupied the heights, anchoring the end of the terminal, where cars could drop off or pick up passengers. With its rounded tip and tapering profile, and the feeling that it grew spontaneously from the raised embankment, Asplund's lofty terminal seemed a likeness of winged flight itself; certainly, he had imbibed the idea of a new industrial form.

One of Asplund's colleagues described his entry as 'artistically brilliant but over-emphasized, falsely rational, costly and hardly appropriate', and the experts agreed, awarding the job to the Modernist architect Paul Hedqvist, whose proposal was simpler and more precise. Yet Asplund's elegant solution of physically making the terminal the jetway anticipated by decades the nub of airport design today.

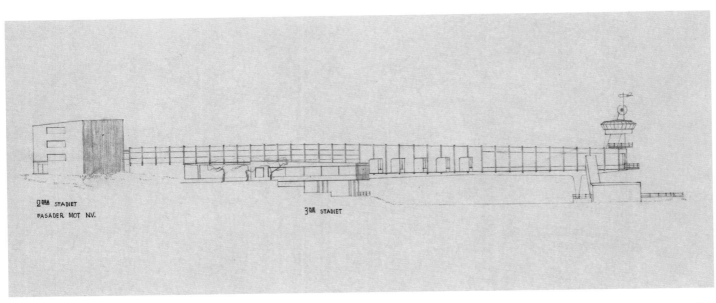

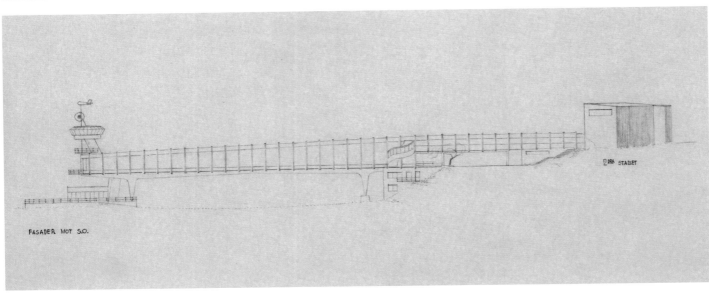

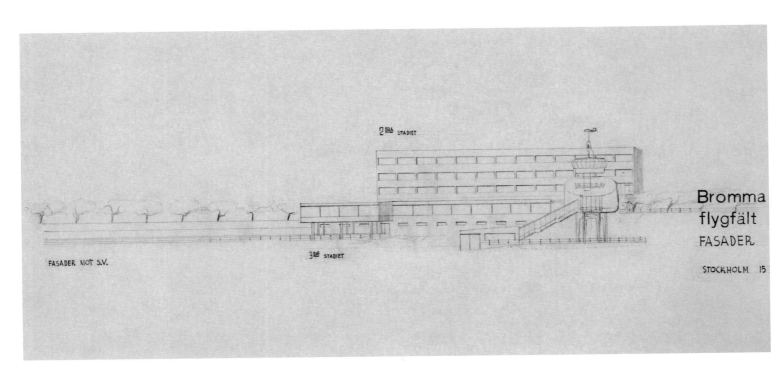

KALEVALATALO
Eliel Saarinen
Helsinki (FI), 1921

The Kalevalaseura, a centre for Finnish cultural studies, was founded in 1911 by Matias Äyräpää (the father of Finnish dentistry), the artists Alpo Sailo and Akseli Gallen-Kallela, and Eemil Nestor Setälä (author of Finland's declaration of independence). A decade later, the organization commissioned Eliel Saarinen to create for it a building that would embody an abiding sense of Finnish nationalism (Kalevala is the Finnish national epic poem and Kalevalatalo means 'Kavela House'). Saarinen produced a forty-page booklet describing his ambition: 'The lofty goal of the Kalevalaseura is specifically to shed light on the culture of the Finnish people … based not so much on historical sources as on the people's own language and ancestors – both spiritual and material.'

A private landowner donated a rocky promontory in the Munkkiniemi neighbourhood, overlooking the shore 5 km (3 miles) from the centre of Helsinki. Saarinen's huge building, surrounding a courtyard, contained a museum, a library, an amphitheatre, a lecture hall, workshops and galleries for artists, a reading room, a ballroom, apartments for researchers and, towering over everything, a sixteen-sided Pantheon 80 m (262 ft) high. Beneath its floor, Saarinen wrote, 'deep inside the rock, would be the silent tombs of our great men who are enjoying their last rest … its vaults decorated with frescoes of the great Masters and statues along the walls'.

The backers of the Kalevalatalo ran out of money, and the muralist Gallen-Kallela pulled out, condemning the design as having 'progressed too far into the sign of antiquity'. That ended it, although the idea remained on the group's agenda until 1970, when a hotel was constructed on the site, around which a residential neighbourhood has grown up.

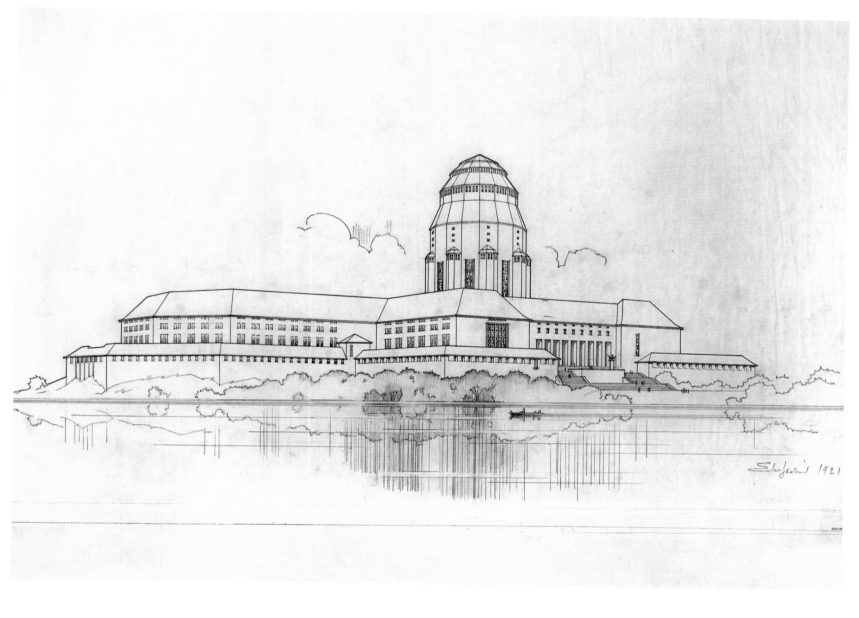

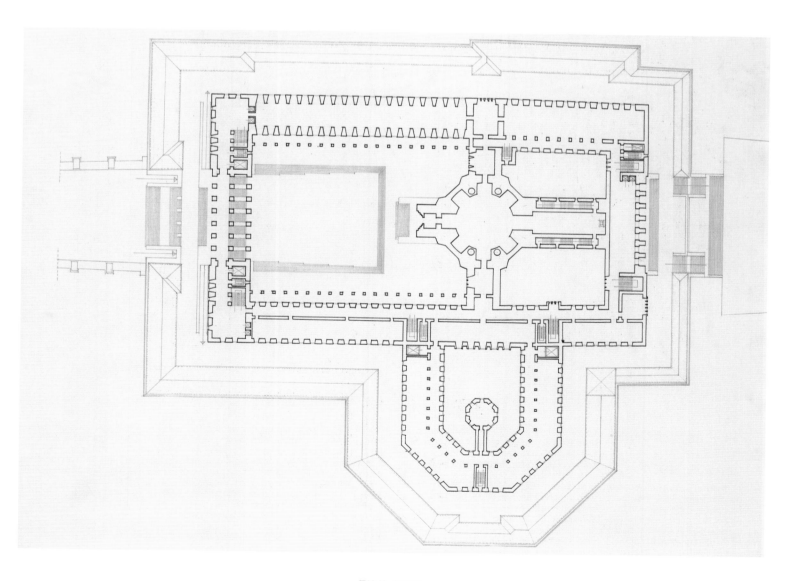

FINLAND

COPENHAGEN GATE, GATE L & GATE M
Steven Holl
Copenhagen (DK), 2007

In 1990 the New York architect Steven Holl proposed that a cluster of pencil-thin, super-tall skyscrapers be moored in the Hudson River at 72nd Street. These unbuilt structures, the Parallax Towers, as he called them, were linked by skybridges, carving a new urban space out of thin air. The idea appeared in a number of Holl's later works, most notably his mixed-use Linked Hybrid complex, which opened in Beijing in 2009.

Holl's design for the harbour entrance in Copenhagen involved a pair of towers from which two bridges extended over the water, at a height of 65 m (213 ft). The Gate L building, on the Langelinie side, had the silhouette of a ship's prow, its four trapezoidal stacks facing the Øresund strait with an enduring, implacable regard. Gate M, the Marmormolen tower, kinked along the quay, animated as much by the city as by the docks. The cable-stay bridges sprouted from the buildings like twigs, a vertiginous walkway across the water. The torqued geometry of the site prevented the buildings from squaring up to each other; accordingly, the bridges angled outwards, rather than meeting to form a straight line. This gave them the breathless aura of trapeze artists hoping to latch hands.

Both towers had glass curtain walls with a veil of photovoltaic panels, while wind turbines on top of the bridges provided electricity to light the public spaces. Seawater heated and cooled the structures, and operable windows allowed fresh air in. City officials had high hopes for the landmark gateway, but the project never recovered from the financial crisis of 2008.

PROJECT FOR LANGELINIE
Jørn Utzon
Copenhagen (DK), 1954

For all its beauty, Copenhagen has precious few vertical landmarks, particularly along the water's edge. Jørn Utzon set out to change that dramatically with his competition entry for the Langelinie Pavilion, a new facility on a strip of waterfront best known for its bronze statue of Hans Christian Andersen's Little Mermaid. Before the competition, a pavilion had stood on the site from 1885 as a restaurant and club, then from 1902 another building (destroyed by the Nazis during World War II) that housed the royal Danish yacht club.

In his design Utzon channelled his fascination with organic forms, such as mushrooms and shells, and with East Asian structures, among them pagodas. He envisioned a terraced, multi-floor restaurant, closely connected to the water. From this base would extend a tall tower – visible from everywhere in the city – consisting of ten disc-like floors of varying circumferences connected by a central tower housing stairs and lifts. Glass curtain walls would protect visitors and provide uninterrupted views. In his writings, Utzon notes that the design also had a nautical inspiration: 'After a visit to the top of the rigging on a bark, I was aware that it had to be a tower in which I got above the five-storey city's roofs and could see the wonderful towers of Copenhagen.'

The winning design for the competition, by Eva and Nils Koppel, has nothing in common with Utzon's plan. The low, rigid, International Style pavilion, which opened in 1958, is deferential and quiet; anything but spectacular. It functions as a wedding and conference venue that most visitors walk right past on their way to commune with the Little Mermaid.

ET SINDSSYGEHOSPITAL
Ib Lunding
Copenhagen (DK), 1930

The Danish architect Ib Lunding was a jewellery maker, furniture designer, the developer of an urban tram system, and municipal architect for Copenhagen for forty years. He is known to the cognoscenti for his exquisite water towers and his Champagne Building, a quirky functionalist apartment complex with a stream of differently sized round windows rising like bubbles in a champagne flute.

Lunding designed his Sindssygehospital (Psychiatric Hospital) five years after leaving architecture school. He made dozens of drawings and renderings, and wrote a seventy-one-page book explaining his conviction that such a hospital should be the very opposite of idyllic and monotonous. It should be 'vivid … strong … impactful', he wrote, to give patients 'impulses towards a mental activity that can compete with [their] pathological thought complexes'. He chose the edge of a rugged plateau, ravaged by storms, with views of the sea and horizon framed by the gnarled limbs of windblown trees. Fourteen narrow, single-storey wings stretched out, like bent arms, from the long, tapering spine of the building; each designed to treat a specific condition. From panopticon to cosy is how Lunding described the arrangements. The low-slung hospital ran parallel to the ocean, and was detailed with extruded windows beneath metal 'eyebrows'.

Lunding said, 'Ideally, the main building should express itself in its design for the brave struggle of men against powers they do not understand.' The church (pictured) that was part of the complex advanced the same idea through a mass of overpoweringly enormous, thoroughly modern stelae posed above the ocean. The hospital won a competition (lost to history), but was never commissioned.

OFFICE BUILDING FOR DANISH STATE RAILWAYS
Anton Rosen
Copenhagen (DK), 1924

When other Danish architects were imbibing old Danish architecture, steeped in a romantic historicism, Anton Rosen was looking to the Chicagoan Louis Sullivan for inspiration. One could see in Rosen's architecture some decorative elements of Denmark, but these were like illustrative scales appended to rigorously stripped-down buildings. Between 1922 and 1926 Rosen designed a trio of unrealized skyscrapers, beginning with his entry to the competition for the Chicago Tribune Tower (in fact, his drawings were never entered; they were apparently held up at customs) and ending with that for a massive tower standing over two low-slung buildings then under construction next to the site for the League of Nations in Geneva, Switzerland.

The second proposal, an office tower for the Danish state railways, extended from the existing Central Station, which opened in 1911, its steeply pitched gabled slate roof and brick and granite archways all in keeping with the prevailing romanticism. Rosen's twenty-one-storey pillar would have permanently altered the impression of the city to newly arriving train travellers and commuters riding Copenhagen's urban transit. Its facade was a continuous vertical glass surface of windows separated by skinny mullions and pencil-thin vertical columns, a light fixture suspended from a scaffold of four reinforced-concrete standards.

Rosen conceded a little to prevailing sentiment, adding Art Nouveau grilles in one version of the building, and in another, putting the Danish Crown Regalia – the triple-tier symbol of the Danish monarchy – at the top of each window array. But the state-owned railway rejected his forward-looking office tower, leaving the long glass shed and reception hall in solitary reminiscence.

CENTRE OF CONTEMPORARY IRISH CULTURE
Níall McLaughlin Architects
Kenmare (IE), 2009

When Frank Gehry's Guggenheim Bilbao opened in 1997, its striking success dramatically shifted the calculus for cities hoping to attract tourists, investors and acclaim. In just a few years metropolises of all sizes scrambled to build their own architectural magnets, including Kenmare, an Irish village of just over 2,000 people along the Ring of Kerry, County Kerry's stunning coastline drive showcasing rugged, emerald landscapes and jaw-dropping cliffs. In 2009 the town unveiled plans for a €12.5 million centre for Irish culture on a site overlooking Kenmare Bay. The designer would be Níall McLaughlin Architects, and the practice outlined a 2,053 sq. m (22,100 sq. ft) structure 21 m (69 ft) tall, composed of a series of angular, glazed geometries, stacked against one another. Clearly inspired by the region's shifting hillsides and jagged sandstone and slate boulders, it opened to a barely touched terrain, descending to the water. 'The building can be read as a microcosm of the whole landscape,' the firm explained. Inside were seven galleries, with a viewing tower on top.

According to the local businessman John Brennan, chair of the project's steering committee, the team had raised €11 million from public and private sources (townspeople had bought museum windowpanes, roof slates and even parking spaces), but was hitting a wall. Their great hope was the Irish-American businessman Chuck Feeney, who was already interested in converting the nearby estate of Dromquinna Manor into 'a kind of residential Davos'. The board offered to name the museum in Feeney's honour, but not long afterwards he lost interest in the Manor and in the museum. The project died shortly after that.

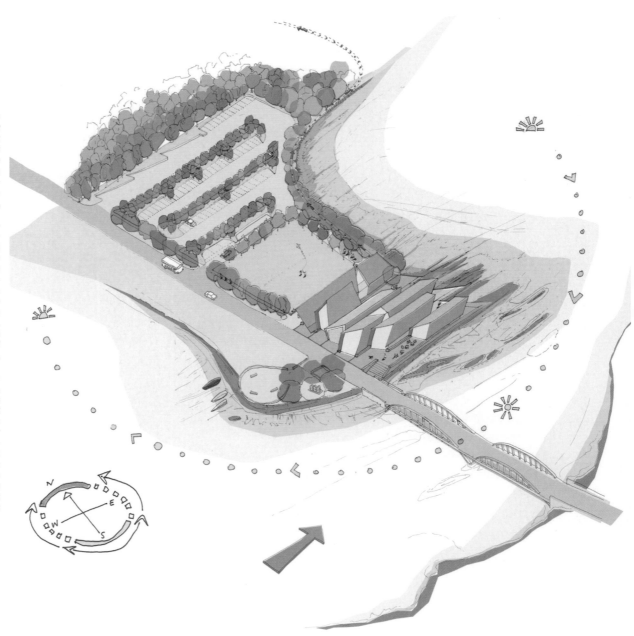

DEPARTMENT OF ZOOLOGY
Chamberlin, Powell & Bon
Oxford, England (GB), 1961

While the University of Oxford is rightly celebrated for its exceptional historic architecture, it is also replete with modern designs from such top-tier designers as Arne Jacobsen, James Stirling, Leslie Martin, Dixon Jones and Alison and Peter Smithson. One mid-twentieth-century firm that struck out in the city was Chamberlin,

Powell & Bon, a dominant force in London that designed, among other transformative projects, the Barbican Estate.

In 1961 the practice submitted plans for a 9,300 sq. m (100,000 sq. ft) zoology complex on about 0.4 hectares (1 acre) of the University Parks, a large park northeast of the city centre. It was signalled by a twenty-eight-storey tower 79 m (259 ft) tall, its angled flanks giving it a curious East Asian flavour. The project received approval from the university in February 1962. 'It will be a real disaster if this plan, which is of the greatest

significance to the university and is perhaps the last chance to make architectural sense of part of the science area, is defeated,' Walter Fraser Oakeshott, Rector of Lincoln College at the time, told the *Birmingham Daily Post*. Detractors objected vociferously to the loss of parkland, but they had other complaints too: 'It would be folly to ruin for posterity the skyline of Oxford and to destroy the whole atmosphere of the parks for the sake of this ingenious and perverse monstrosity,' commented the historian Robert Norman William Blake of Christ Church. By June

the university had reversed its course, rejecting the proposal by 275 votes to 122.

Martin's Zoology and Experimental Psychology facility, called the Tinbergen Building, eventually rose in 1971, consisting of squat precast-concrete buildings connected by bridges; it was knocked down in 2020, after asbestos-containing materials were found.

NEW PITT RIVERS MUSEUM
Pier Luigi Nervi
Oxford, England (GB), 1966

Housed in an expansive, delightfully quirky cast-iron Victorian cabinet of curiosities designed in 1884 by the Dublin architect Thomas Newenham Deane, Oxford's Pitt Rivers Museum is one of the most beloved institutions in England. It contains more than 500,000 archaeological and ethnological objects, from Benin bronzes to a gold torc from Scotland. In 1966 the University of Oxford commissioned the Italian engineer Pier Luigi Nervi, along with the London architectural firm Powell & Moya, to prepare preliminary drawings for a new facility uniting the university's expansive archaeological and anthropological activities, from varied academic departments to the collections of the Pitt Rivers, Balfour Library, Institute of Archaeology and much more.

Spearheaded by the ambitious new museum curator Bernard Fagg, the proposed structure took the form of a concrete-and-glass rotunda 92 m (300 ft) in diameter, providing 28,400 sq. m (305,700 sq. ft) of interior space over four storeys (two above ground, two below). In the centre, a giant glass dome covered a tropical and sub-tropical plant house known as the 'Climatron', while radiating circular galleries allowed collections to be arranged both geographically (by circumference) and temporally (radially).

Soon after the plans became public, however, things went awry. Nearby residents erupted in protest, other university departments complained about being short-changed, and fundraising targets began to fail. Ultimately Oxford City Council rejected the plan, which involved demolishing sixteen homes (including several old Victorian houses) along Banbury and Bradmore roads. Peter Spokes, vice-chairman of the Oxford Planning Committee, called it a 'preposterous overloading' of a residential area.

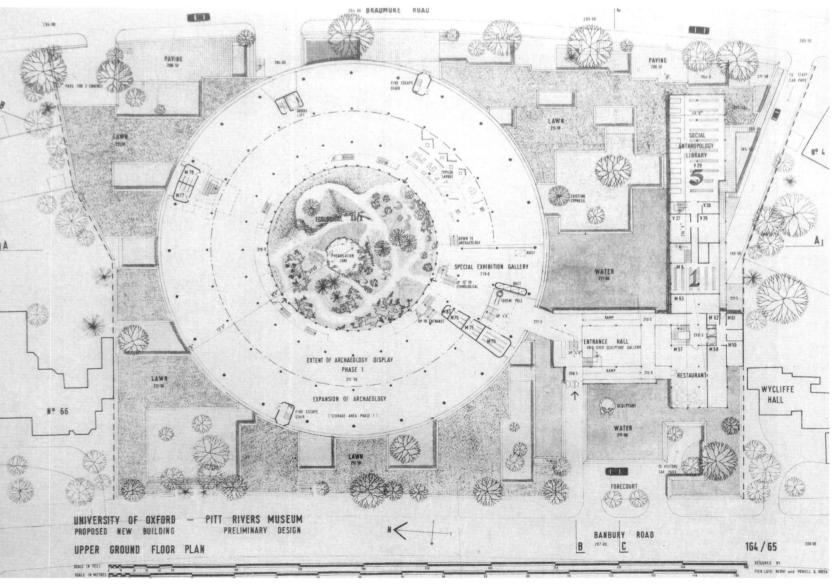

UNIVERSITY OF OXFORD — PITT RIVERS MUSEUM
PROPOSED NEW BUILDING   PRELIMINARY DESIGN

UPPER GROUND FLOOR PLAN

164/65

MANSION HOUSE SQUARE
Ludwig Mies van der Rohe
London, England (GB), 1962

Richard Rogers called Ludwig Mies van der Rohe's Mansion House Square 'the culmination of a master architect's life work'. King Charles III (then Prince of Wales) denounced it as 'a giant glass stump better suited to downtown Chicago'. Either way, Mies's Seagram Building lookalike was blocked not because it was too tall or because its corporate Modernist sangfroid was falling out of vogue by the time the architect died, in 1969. Instead, the bronze-clad and amber-glass tower – commissioned in 1962 by Lord Peter Palumbo, who had gone to Chicago to meet his architectural hero – fell victim to a backlash against the 1980s political turmoil unleashed by Prime Minister Margaret Thatcher's neoconservative government.

The nineteen-storey office building – which Mies had lovingly detailed, down to its door handles and ashtrays – was sited in the core of the City of London, surrounded by Edwin Lutyens' neoclassical Midland Bank, Christopher Wren's Baroque church of St Stephen Walbrook, John Soane's Bank of England, and the Lord Mayor's official residence, the Mansion House. The site was strategic, so Mies set the building back from the street, creating a large public plaza across from the city's seat of power. In the 1960s, this seemed fitting. But by the 1980s, after two decades of acrimonious planning reviews, the mood had shifted. Not only had postmodernist historicism gained favour, but also the notion of Mansion House Square becoming another venue for civil disobedience and rioting riled conservatives, who quashed the proposition.

Palumbo got his revenge, in a way. He instead built on the site No. 1 Poultry, a pink, postmodern pastiche by James Stirling, which was promptly dismissed by King Charles III as 'a 1930s wireless set'.

LONDON CENTRE FOR MUSIC
Diller Scofidio + Renfro
London, England (GB), 2017

Opened in 1982, London's Barbican Centre – equally loved and hated for its coarse concrete, hovering fountains and fortress-like walls – is one of the largest performing arts centres in Europe. Hoping to flee its ageing home at the Barbican Hall, the London Symphony Orchestra in 2017 launched a plan to build a ground-up facility on the site of the Museum of London's new home at nearby Smithfield Market, which at the time of writing was scheduled to open in 2026.

In stepped Diller Scofidio + Renfro, whose competition entry beat those of Norman Foster, Frank Gehry, Renzo Piano, Amanda Levete, Snøhetta and several others. Shifting the Barbican's notoriously inward-facing campus outwards, the £288 million torquing glass pyramid, edged with visible switchback ramps, stacked a floating concert hall above an unfolding, light-filled, multi-level foyer containing cafés, informal performance areas and learning spaces for the Guildhall School of Music & Drama. In the sweeping auditorium, wrap-around seating situated all audience members close to the stage, while a clerestory public gallery gave views of the performances below, not to mention the rest of the city. The car-dominated zone next to the site became a layered pedestrian plaza. But with the City of London Corporation (owner of the Barbican) offering to chip in only about £6.8 million of the full cost, and the COVID-19 pandemic decimating philanthropic giving, funding fell well short. The corporation instead decided to employ the funds to upgrade the entire Barbican Centre. 'New times need new solutions,' explained the Barbican's managing director, Sir Nicholas Kenyon.

ROYAL FESTIVAL HALL
Sir Misha Black
London, England (GB), 1950

Designed in 1951 by Robert Matthew, Leslie Martin and the London County Council Architects Department, the hulking Royal Festival Hall is a solid but not particularly pulse-quickening fixture on London's South Bank, created for the Festival of Britain, the United Kingdom's grand showcase of technological prowess launched just a few years after the end of World War II. A leading player in that event was the architect, teacher and industrial designer Sir Misha Black, who created many of its exhibits and designed its sleek Regatta Restaurant.

In 1946, just before he was appointed a coordinating architect of the show, Black proposed – on the site where the Festival Hall now stands – an oval ramp topped by a curved megastructure containing several cultural buildings, which would 'rise in terraces to the sky platform fifteen hundred feet [nearly 460 m] above London', as he put it. Clad in a variety of bending glass walls and crowned by a saucer-topped spire, the structure resembled a spaceship, an ocean liner or, as one website put it in 2022, 'a vast nuclear submarine rising from the Thames'.

While the proposal (drawn by Black's colleague Hilton Wright and published in *The Ambassador* magazine) was sketched for the South Bank, it could, Black noted, be 'positioned equally well in Hyde Park or Regent's Park'. Surely if the project had been even partially realized – and Black's vision of a gigantic cultural centre had won out over a single concert hall – he would be remembered for much more than his current claim to fame: the iconic black-and-red-on-white design of London's street-name signs.

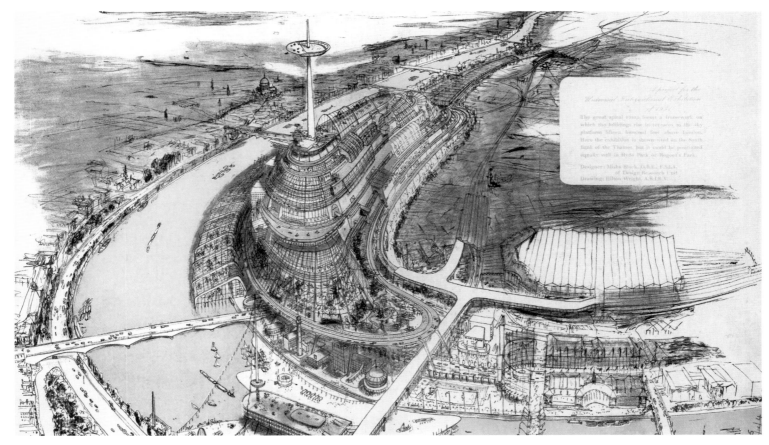

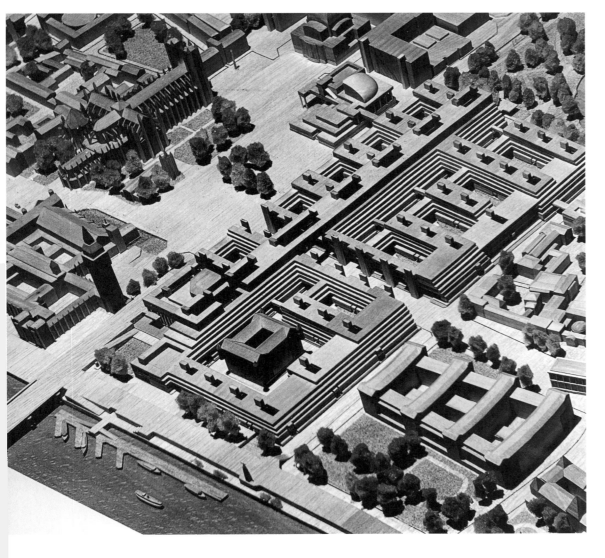

PLAN FOR WHITEHALL
Sir Leslie Martin
London, England (GB), 1965

Sir Leslie Martin's makeover of Whitehall, regarded then and now as 'the heart of the capital', would have created a traffic-free domain of low-rise ziggurat office blocks built around a sequence of courtyards and interior galleries. The massive plan contemplated the demolition of most of the government's Victorian buildings – including Sir George Gilbert Scott's Foreign Office and Treasury – while the entire north side of Parliament Square would be lined with the new stair-stepped offices.

Martin's proposal was bold in its breadth and compass, and his drawings produced a classic epitaph in the *Architect's Journal*: 'Ziggurats for Bureaucrats'. The north-facing cascading forms, which would be made of different materials, among them glass and zinc, were designed to combat the dreary conditions Martin and his colleagues had encountered while touring the offices occupied by the government's clerical staff. Martin inverted the stair-steps for the new buildings along Parliament Street, creating a shaded pedestrian way and adding terraces, which were intended to be used as viewing platforms when processions passed through. The plan was, essentially, schematic, intended not so much as a detailed architectural concept as a way of organizing new government offices and providing humane working conditions in a pedestrian-friendly, campus-like setting.

While the Foreign Office complained bitterly about not waiting indefinitely for a modern replacement building, government ministers chipped away at Martin's plan, first parcelling out assignments to other architects, then silencing him by ignoring him without ever formally firing him. Martin was left adrift. Ironically, the government dithering – and budgetary woes – saved the Foreign Office building, which reopened as a symbol of national pride after a £100 million restoration in the 1980s.

CRYSTAL PALACE SCULPTURE PARK
WilkinsonEyre
London, England (GB), 2003

No building did more to confirm the ascendancy of the British Empire as the unrivalled industrial power of the nineteenth century than Joseph Paxton's Crystal Palace. The original, an almost fully glazed building on an iron frame, was built in Hyde Park, London, for the Great Exhibition in 1851, then re-erected on Sydenham Hill in the southeast of the city, only to collapse into a heap of molten glass and iron in a disastrous fire in 1936.

The London-based architectural practice WilkinsonEyre, best known for its bridges, was asked by the Crystal Palace Campaign, a group run by local residents, to design something to counter a proposal to build a multiplex cinema in the park. The Crystal Palace redux, although smaller than the original, occupied the same space as the transept of the palace, and was just as high. The 150 m long (492 ft) oblong was elevated on eight stilts, placing it above the highest tree-lined ridge in London and making the giant illuminated creature visible far and wide.

While the legs (and the interior mezzanines) were made of steel, the bubble enclosure was to be constructed entirely of laminated glass ribs sheathed in a glass skin embedded with photovoltaic cells. Within, the 'sculpture garden,' would feature modern works. The building would have behaved like a giant sensor, automatically adjusting lighting and heating depending on weather and sunlight. The longest escalator in the world would have brought visitors into the belly of the new space, while a garden flourished below. Chris Wilkinson said it was 'very much my interpretation of what Paxton would do now'.

LONDON CENTRAL MOSQUE
Rifat Chadirji
London, England (GB), 1969

In 1969 Rifat Chadirji, later known as the father of modern Iraqi architecture, entered a competition to design a new mosque and Islamic cultural centre for the edge of Regent's Park, in London. He did not win, but his design helped to crack open the architectural firmament, then still dominated by the International Style. Working from Baghdad, Chadirji had already begun his journey away from strict glass-and-steel Modernism towards an idea of regionalism. He believed that architecture should be 'a true synthesis of the technically progressive and the conservationist'. So, while he embraced such materials as concrete, he infused his work with the language of Iraq and, more deeply, the Islamic world. But he was in no way a historicist. The London Central Mosque refers to the four-iwan mosques of Iran and Iraq, in which a four-sided vaulted space opens on one side to a courtyard, but in Chadirji's version, the prayer hall, courtyard and complex of buildings – a bookshop, and apartments for the imam and caretaker – are irregular octagons. Four long walls and four short walls enclose the spaces. Light enters the *masjid* (literally, the place of prostration) through floor-to-ceiling windows screened by an array of stagger-stepped, unadorned arches. The form is used throughout the series of buildings. The exterior walls, too, distil Islamic geometry – which typically employed elaborate interlaced patterns – to standing vertical lines of concrete that seem to undulate from the surface of the buildings. Chadirji's mosque was regional and romantic in character, as he put it, 'yet simultaneously modern, part of the current international avant-garde style'. It was lumped by the *Architects' Journal* into the category of 'disappointing entries ... none really convince and few excite.'

VICTORIA AND ALBERT MUSEUM EXTENSION
Daniel Libeskind
London, England (GB), 1996

Some never-builts, such as Daniel Libeskind's extension to the storied Victoria and Albert Museum in London, languish on life support for years until they finally peter out. Libeskind won a competition to design the project in 1996, defeating such local favourites as Norman Foster and Zaha Hadid for a site wedged between Henry Cole's baroque pile of 1860 and Aston Webb's dome from 1909. Studio Libeskind described its exuberant scheme as 'an upward spiral of intersecting planes, creating a jagged vortex'. Covered in patterned tiles, the folded building's off-kilter edges would become increasingly translucent as the structure rose. While the plan gained the support of English Heritage and the Royal Borough of Kensington and Chelsea, criticism wasn't hard to find. According to *The Guardian*, one observer likened the design to the 'Guggenheim in Bilbao turned on its side and then beaten senseless with a hammer'. When New Labour came to power in 1997 its leaders promised free admission to major London museums, undoing a key source of revenue. Subsequent efforts to secure financial support for the project from various lottery funds were turned down one by one, and private financing fell well short. Despite Libeskind's work to scale down his vision, the V&A finally gave up in September 2004, just as the nearby Barbican Art Gallery was feting the architect with an exhibition of his work.

In 2017 the museum opened a more affordable, largely underground extension by the London-based practice AL_A. 'I think in a sense the demise of the Libeskind project marked the end of the age of the building as icon and all the hubris that went with that,' remarked AL_A's founder, Amanda Levete.

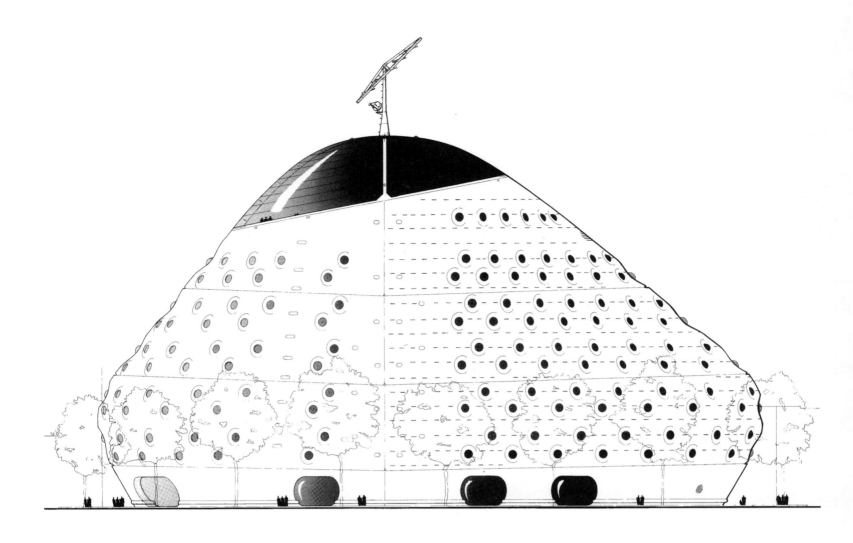

GRAND HOTEL TRAFALGAR SQUARE REPLACEMENT
Future Systems
London, England (GB), 1985

London's Grand Hotel, a Victorian building of Bath stone on the southeast corner of Trafalgar Square could have become a pyramid-shaped blob resembling a humidifier. Built in 1879, the original edifice – its curving, colonnaded mass lunging towards Nelson's Column – was by 1984 beset with structural problems, including decaying stone and severe subsidence. The hotel announced an architectural competition for its replacement.

The most talked-about entry was by Future Systems, led by the futurist Czech architect Jan Kaplický. Their proposal, aptly enough called 'The Blob', was a tapering form clad in white ceramic tiles, supported by an internally stiffened skin dotted with deeply inset circular windows. The odd shape was in fact quite practical, designed to maximize ground-level and floorplate area within the envelope permitted by the planners, as well as allowing as much sun exposure as possible for a hemmed-in site. Atop the humidifier/spaceship/Hershey's Kiss was a deep truss-supported roof deck. According to Kaplický, the design – easily the least contextual building in the competition – was too far ahead of its time. 'It's extraordinary how we started to create plasticity some time ago, and at that time people didn't have a clue what it meant,' he told *Icon* magazine some years later.

The competition-winning design, by London practice Sidell Gibson, could not have been more different. The firm demolished the hotel and replaced its facade with a virtual facsimile. But the frontage of what is now called the Grand Building is a stage set of sorts; inside, the tall, glassy, modern interior atrium, airy and filled with shops though it is, could stand in for a corporate hotel anywhere.

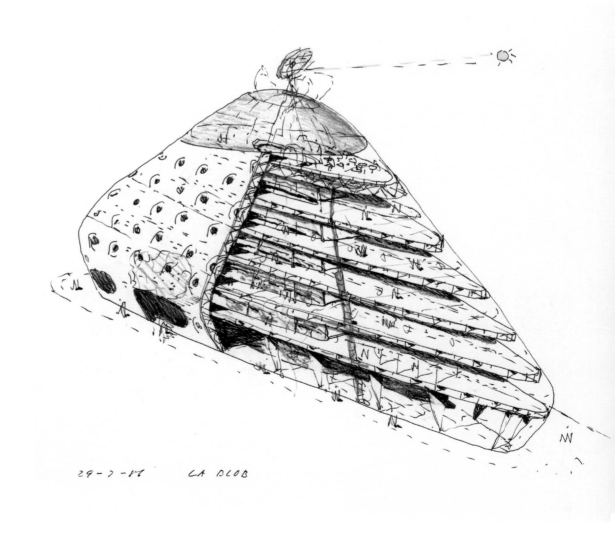

29-7-86   LA BLOB

THREE CHELSEA STUDIOS
Charles Rennie Mackintosh
London, England (GB), 1920

Work dried up for Charles Rennie Mackintosh – one of the most talented, imaginative and versatile designers ever to work in Scotland – after he left his home in Glasgow in 1914, in his mid-forties, for England, where he and his equally talented wife, Margaret MacDonald, lived until 1923. One of Mackintosh's few commissions during this time came from fellow artists Harold Squire, Francis Derwent Wood and Arthur Cadogan Blunt, as well as a group called the Arts League of Service, to design the so-called Chelsea studios: three-layered, side-by-side buildings on Glebe Place in Chelsea, London.

As usual, Mackintosh conceived of designs that were far ahead of their age. The block looked nothing like its Georgian and neo-Tudor neighbours, and could pass for a 1980s folly from the likes of Charles Moore or Robert Venturi. For Wood, Mackintosh designed a gabled structure, its ground-floor studio and workshop lit by an outsized expanse of gridded windows. For Squire he imagined a rectangular block with a vertical window, fronted by a unique triangular gateway. For the Arts League, an idealistic organization established after World War I to 'Bring the Arts into Everyday Life', he sketched a tall, narrow building, bound by its tight site, with four studio flats stacked on top of one another, all with large windows. The high cost of the proposal (not to mention the Arts League's closure owing to lack of funds) prevented the realization of all but a modified version of Squire's studio.

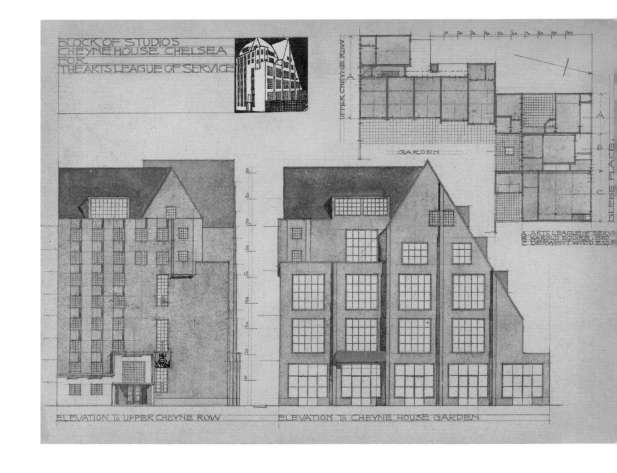

BARBICAN CENTRE PYRAMIDAL CONSERVATORY
Chamberlin, Powell & Bon
London, England (GB), 1956

Built on a London site devastated by bombing during World War II, the Barbican Centre was designed not only to replace valuable lost housing, offices, schools, and recreational and cultural spaces, but also to make a statement about a revived United Kingdom's modern vision for the future. Queen Elizabeth II herself called it 'one of the wonders of the modern world'. The hulking, 2.8 hectare (7 acre) hammered-concrete development-as-neighbourhood, designed by architectural practice Chamberlin, Powell & Bon, underwent numerous iterations before the plans were finalized. The list of scrapped ideas is long, including cladding buildings in white marble, extending the complex's raised walkways to the rest of the city, installing beer gardens, and even parking landmarks, such as Christopher Wren's Temple Bar, on the site.

Perhaps the most dramatic visual shift was the removal of a plan to have the complex's lush conservatory – which is now wedged stealthily between the Barbican's library and cinema – take the form of a mammoth pyramid in the centre of the lake between Speed House and Andrewes House, effectively making it the centrepiece of the Barbican's public spaces. The firm's plan from 1955 called for a stepped pyramid with a swimming pool, squash court: and an exhibition hall. By 1956 the idea ha evolved into a garden topped with a glass pyr amid, supported by thin steel trusses, reachable from ground level and via raised bridges.

By the time construction had started in 197 the pyramid was long gone, but the glasshouse went ahead. Now containing more than 2,00 species of plant and tree, it is London's second largest conservatory, after that at Kew.

NATIONAL GALLERY EXTENSION
Ahrends, Burton and Koralek
London, England (GB), 1982

William Wilkins' neoclassical Georgian facade of the National Gallery had watched over Trafalgar Square for nearly two centuries, but by 1958 the gallery was desperate for more space. An empty plot next door, the remnant of a World War II bomb site, was purchased, and plans laid for an expansion – which resulted in the parcel becoming a car park for decades.

At last, in 1982, Peter Ahrends, Richard Burton and Paul Koralek of ABK Architects won a competition for a new gallery – with the strange caveat, imposed by Prime Minister Margaret Thatcher, that the extension be paid for by a private development squeezed onto the tight plot. It was a 'questionable arrangement', as Ahrends later said. His design began as a reflection on the circular geometry of Nelson's Column, drawing a hemispheric facade that carved out a semicircular plaza that he called an 'antechamber to Trafalgar Square'.

The interior space, however, was more gallery than commercial offices, and was rejected. Ahrends returned with revised sketches, which retained the curving court but inserted a tripartite, stair-stepped, glass-and-stone office tower 28 m (92 ft) tall into the plaza. A skeletal scaffold of steel tubing embraced the tower, extending above the trio of glassed-in offices, allowing banners and pendants to fly.

In what would become an infamous speech on the occasion of the 150th anniversary of the Royal Institute of British Architects, King Charles, then Prince of Wales, effectively killed the project, saying it was 'a kind of vast municipal fire station complete with the sort of tower that contains the siren ... What is proposed is like a monstrous carbuncle on the face of a much-loved and elegant friend.'

BBC MUSIC CENTRE
Foreign Office Architects
London, England (GB), 2003

Located about 6.5 km (4 miles) west of central London, at White City, BBC Television Centre was one of the most advanced production hubs in the world when it opened in 1960. But by the end of the twentieth century it had become tired and obsolete. As part of an ambitious makeover, the broadcasting corporation chose (via competition) Foreign Office Architects, an edgy firm led by the then husband-and-wife team of Farshid Moussavi and Alejandro Zaera-Polo to design the so-called BBC Music Box.

The scheme was intended to contain studios and performance spaces for the BBC Symphony Orchestra, the BBC Symphony Chorus, the BBC Concert Orchestra and the BBC Singers, as well as office space for a revamped BBC White City Campus. Actually resembling a music box (albeit an ultra-modern one), the white, tightly curved structure focused on visibility, its large glass facades – triple-glazed to insulate sound and temperature – allowing the public to watch performances from the street, and its ribbon-like folded surfaces serving as screens for the broadcasting of graphics and images. The ribbons differentiated the project's varied programme, dividing the two major studios and delineating the office spaces above. On top of the building, the meandering folds carved out shaded rooftop viewing decks, while at street level shops led to a new public plaza for everyday gathering and large-scale events.

In 2008 the BBC cancelled the project, choosing instead to develop new facilities in various parts of London. The corporation ceased broadcasting from Television Centre in 2013.

UNITED KINGDOM

LONDON BRIDGE CITY
Philip Johnson, John Burgee
London, England (GB), 1989

Norman Foster's London City Hall – a bulbous, slumping glass almost-sphere edging the south bank of the River Thames, next to Tower Bridge – has been compared to an onion, a helmet and a misshapen egg, but its most popular moniker originated with former Mayor of London Ken Livingstone, who called it the Glass Testicle. In 2020 the Greater London Authority announced that it would be vacating the structure altogether.

Back in the late 1980s, the site came close to becoming something very different: the second phase of London Bridge City, a glassy development of office, retail and residential spaces controlled by the St Martins Property Group (itself owned by Kuwait's Sovereign Wealth Fund). The final iteration of the 111,500 sq. m (1.2 million sq. ft) project was designed by the historicist architect John Simpson, who proposed a downsized version of Venice, complete with its own Piazza San Marco and campanile (no canals, though). But the original plan had been created by Philip Johnson and John Burgee, who sketched a glass-clad, neo-Jacobean homage to the Houses of Parliament and Tower Bridge, complete with crenellated towers and Hogwarts-esque low-rises.

While the design was approved by the London Docklands Development Corporation, Nicholas Ridley, Secretary of State for the Environment at the time, forced it to undergo a public inquiry. This process forced St Martins to propose the Simpson design, and another alternative by the London firm Twigg Brown. Only Simpson's plan won approval. But the architect balked at a plan to drape his facades over conventional offices, while the recession of the late 1980s and early 90s killed the vision for good.

ARTIFICIAL ISLAND FOR ENGLISH CHANNEL CROSSING
EuroRoute
English Channel, 1985

Dreams of building bridges or digging tunnels to connect England and France had been around since about 1802. Napoleon III had his plan in 1865, as did Winston Churchill in 1936.

An actual tunnel, however, didn't open until 1994, its inauguration presided over by Queen Elizabeth II and French President François Mitterrand. Yet even that twin-bore railway passage was far from inevitable. In fact, it was among four contenders for making a fixed-link crossing – that is to say, something other than by sea or air.

The best proposal came from EuroRoute, a group that included the French train manufacturer Alstom, British Steel and Barclays Bank. The consortium had lined up nearly £7.2 billion in funding for a combination railway and motorway, made up of a pair of dramatic cable-stay bridges connected to a tunnel 21 km (13 miles) long. Each bridge, spanning 8.5 km (just over 5 miles) and standing 50 m (164 ft) above the water, touched down on an artificial island via a corkscrew spiral that then descended beneath the sea to the mouth of the tunnel. Cars would have left the tunnel along an identical spiral, swooping on to the bridge deck en route to landfall. Drivers would also have been able take an island break to fuel up, grab coffee, do some duty-free shopping, hire a boat from a marina or check into a hotel for some shut-eye.

Polls at the time showed that motorists preferred to drive their own cars rather than put them onto trains. But the EuroRoute proposal was three times the cost of Eurotunnel. It was deemed too expensive, and lost the bid.

NEW GRONINGEN UNIVERSITY LIBRARY
Herman Hertzberger
Groningen (NL), 1975

Along with such colleagues as Aldo van Eyck, the Dutch architect Herman Hertzberger was a leader of the Dutch Structuralist movement, developing fractalized buildings that fused architecture and sculpture. But probably his best-known unbuilt project was quite different: his proposed reuse of the neo-Gothic church of St Martinus (1895) to create the new Groningen University Library.

By the early 1970s it had become clear that the existing library – scattered among old, cramped buildings around campus – was no longer functioning properly. In 1975 the city council elected to tear down the church (technically a cathedral, which the Catholic diocese had closed in 1970), on the city's centrally located Broerstraat, to clear the way for a new library. The church had been designed by the legendary Dutch architect Pierre Cuypers, creator of Amsterdam Central Station and the Rijksmuseum, among many landmarks. Many people fought to rescue it through obtaining landmark status for it, but instead Hertzberger proposed the library conversion. In doing so he was far ahead of his time, in an era when the term 'adaptive reuse' didn't exist and the idea was very unusual for a church. The scheme incorporated the cathedral's long, multi-storey nave as a reading room, with stacks and more intimate reading zones built into its surrounding spaces, while gaining new square footage via several connected barrel-vaulted additions and a large new space under Broerstraat itself.

The university and the city considered Hertzberger's proposal both financially and technically unfeasible. In 1982 the church was demolished to make way for the new library, designed by the architect Piet Tauber. Construction of that rather awkward hybrid of historical and modern was completed in 1987.

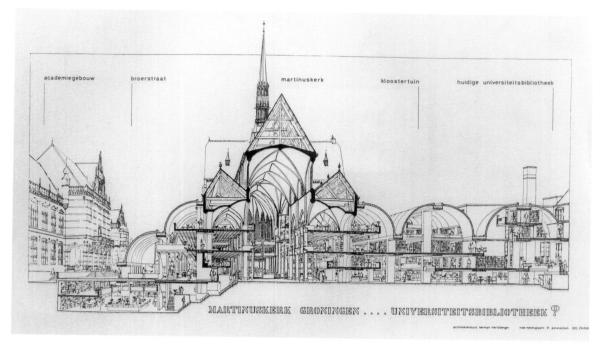

ROYAL ACADEMY OF VISUAL ARTS
Bernard Bijvoet, Johannes Duiker
Amsterdam (NL), 1917

In 1917 the Dutch government organized a competition to design a new home for the Royal Academy of Visual Arts, which had long outgrown its building of 1875. The new structure would be at the end of a monumental axis in Plan Zuid (Plan South), a new development zone to the south of the city. This being an art school, the jury had high expectations, as the brief made clear: 'It will therefore have to be designed in such a way that both in its totality and in its detail it will, as far as possible, deserve to be called a work of art.' The modern-leaning jury furthermore warned against using too many 'decorative elements'.

After two rounds of voting, the first prize was awarded in 1919 to design VI, by Bernard Bijvoet and Johannes Duiker, students at the Delft School of Architecture who were closely linked to De Stijl, a group known for its simplified, abstracted compositions of form and colour. (Second prize went to the much more established Expressionist architect Michel de Klerk.) Bijvoet and Duiker's proposal consisted of a rectangular building with two planted inner courtyards. On the structure's yellow and green surfaces, the team employed only geometric representation – no figurative art. The building itself would become abstract art, through a dynamic tension of hovering vertical and horizontal planes of varying sizes, employed on virtually every surface, from walls to ceilings to windows to furnishings.

The design was never realized, however. The struggling government, crippled by the recent war (despite having remained neutral), was never able to secure funding.

AMSTERDAM CENTRAL STATION
Karel Jacobus (Dick) Greiner
Amsterdam (NL), 1947

Dick Greiner's proposal to remake Amsterdam Central Station was aimed at reversing history. Until 1880 the IJ waterfront – the great bay on which Amsterdam sits – was wide open, with unobstructed views; but artificial islands were added for the station building. Greiner said, 'The Central Station closes off the city completely from the IJ, and that is and will always be a thorn in the crown for Amsterdam.' He proposed to 'lift this closure' with a new, elevated station divided into two wings connected by a span raised between 8–9 m (26–30 ft) above a newly enlarged plaza, facing the water.

In effect, Greiner was creating a huge window on to the bay. His drawings depict the dramatic, restored view as ships roll into the frame of the raised station, which sits on slender pilotis. The enormous clock perfectly centred on the grid-wall becomes the only label necessary to identify the building as a railway terminus.

In 1953 Greiner's plan was widely published, with his additional idea of digging pedestrian and cyclist tunnels under the IJ, connecting the station to boat moorings, up to then reached only by ferry. Writing to Greiner, the editors of *Bouwkundig Weekblad* (Architectural Weekly) bemoaned, 'It's not that the plan can't be made, but the costs will be so fantastic that our little Dutch community can't afford it, however much they might want to.' Greiner himself described the station as 'a wish that will never be fulfilled. The Dutch Railways … will never let go of this place.' His prophecy was right; they never did.

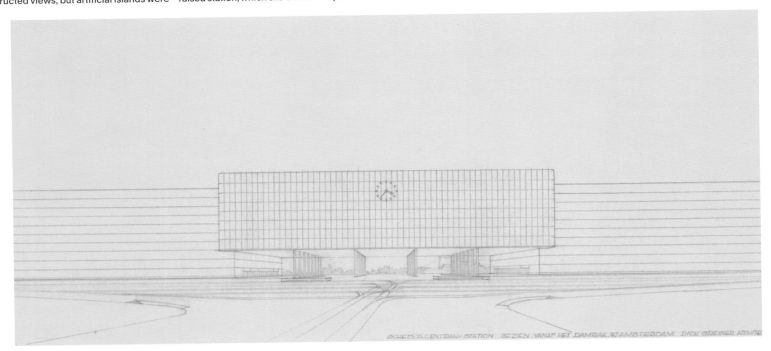

SILOO O
NL Architects
Amsterdam (NL), 2011

After losing the city-run competition in 2009 to adapt two decommissioned sewage silos on the disused industrial island of Zeeburgereiland, Amsterdam, NL Architects was approached by a private developer to create 'a world-class venue for climbing and mountaineering' instead. The makeover would be for a third silo that had not been included in the competition.

Flat though the country is, climbing has become the national sport of the Netherlands. The original silo was 21 m (69 ft) tall. NL decided to double its height, then wrap it in an artificial lithosphere of triangular fieldstones, resting edge to edge to form prism-like peaks and valleys at the circumference of the cylinder. The climbing surface on the south wall was generated by deforming the regularly patterned skin of the north wall, which was also punctured with eight rows of triangular windows. At the base, the architect peeled away the steel cladding of the original silo, adding an entrance to an interior climbing wall and cave.

Outside, a small knoll became the landing pad for kids corkscrewing through a tubular Plexiglass slide, while a hill would be built as an overlook for climbers and their admirers to watch as people scaled the south side of the massive cylinder. Roughly at the midway point, balconies jutted from the silo, like wide, flat hips, their undersides, presumably, meant to satisfy the more daring mountaineers. The artificial scarps, like crags of sheer rock, described an infinite number of tricky routes via overhangs, couloirs and slabs to the roof 40 m (131 ft) above. At the time of writing, none of the silo projects had gone ahead.

PIER ZANDVOORT
Hendrik Wijdeveld
Zandvoort (NL), 1961

One of the Netherlands' great provocateurs, the architect, set designer and graphic designer Hendrik Wijdeveld began employing new ideas, materials and techniques to reshape architecture as early as the 1910s, from theatres dug deep into the earth to housing towers spaced far apart to fight sprawl, over-densification and stratified social hierarchies simultaneously. He showcased many of his ideas as editor of the magazine *Wendingen* (Dutch for 'upheaval' or 'twists'), founded in 1918.

Wijdeveld's final major proposal was for a pier in Zandvoort, the crowning glory of his vision for a sprawling, tower-dotted, 'cityless' city between Amsterdam and Zandvoort, a coastal resort to the west. The megastructure, he said, would elevate typical beach entertainment to a kind of 'total theatre', merging nature and culture through unique activities and vantage points. Visitors, approaching the structure via a radial road from Amsterdam, could take in an aquarium, shell museum, cinema and theatre, or explore the ocean via low platforms (also used for fishing) or a tall lookout tower. Wijdeveld's architectural and infrastructural forms, evoking the sea, resembled large shells, with spiralling ramps (also inspired by the work of his friend Frank Lloyd Wright), grooved and domed roofs, sea-mushroom-like columns and sea-themed frescos.

In common with many of Wijdeveld's city-scale proposals, the pier was a utopian vision. ('Anything is possible, except realizing your dreams,' he once quipped.) But the ideas put forward in it had a major impact on Dutch architecture and on the development of cities in the country, which, more than most places, still manages to balance adroitly open space and urbanization, nature and culture.

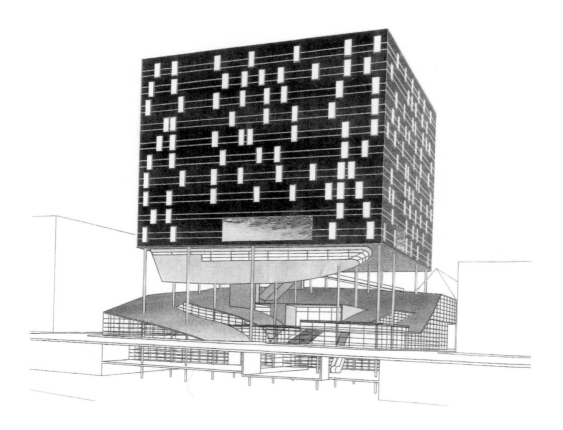

HILTON HOTEL
OMA
The Hague (NL), 1990

Grote Marktstraat (Main Market Street) was created in the 1920s by bulldozing the streets and slums that once led to The Hague's central, outdoor market plaza. In 1990 the street was still dotted with department stores, famously De Bijenkorf, an Expressionist masterpiece in brick, stone, glass and copper.

OMA's Hilton Hotel was disruptive yet somehow suited the spirit of Grote Marktstraat. Outwardly, it was a dark thirteen-storey cube, with windows punched out like the perforations of a player-piano scroll; inwardly it was a sequence of continuous surfaces, pitched at varying trajectories – some utterly useless, other than to provoke tension and drama. Koolhaas labelled the sloping floors a 'social magic carpet'. A chunk of the hotel tower was sliced open, and a podium inserted into the void, supported by V-shaped columns. Cars would enter from one side street, drive through the building, emerge under the overhang of the hotel, then swoop back into the building along the down ramp, emerging onto the opposing side street. The boomerang-shaped ramp formed the ceiling for a ballroom below. An escalator, with just three switchbacks covering ten floors, rose through an oval core, taking visitors to the tenth-floor restaurant, whose slab floor was bent and curved like a leaf. Under pressure from city officials to incorporate the facade of the existing building on the site, and prodded by Hilton to 'make an alternative design that is sober and profitable', OMA bowed out. The 'social magic carpet' later found its way into the practice's Seattle Central Library (2004), a small taste of revenge.

WORLD HARBOUR CENTRE
Jean Nouvel
Rotterdam (NL), 1989

Looking at the drawing for Jean Nouvel's World Harbour Centre in Rotterdam, one could be forgiven for mistaking the work for a Russian Constructivist proposition from about 1921. Aptly called 'The Tail of the Whale', the colossal black object was commissioned by the Port of Rotterdam, which wanted to draw tourists to land's end, at the North Sea.

Maasvlakte, the vast, griddle-flat area of the port created in the 1960s by reclaiming land from the sea, itself lacks all scale. Ships 250 m (820 ft) long and 30 m (100 ft) tall, steel containers stacked 20 m (65 ft) high, cranes with booms capable of hoisting objects 55 m (180 ft) into the air: gigantism undermines any sense of proportion. Little wonder, then, that Nouvel sketched a fantasy, something that looked unknowable and deeply other, standing in an ocean of outsized objects whose redundancy triggers sheer boredom.

The harbour centre actually had two distinct parts. An exhibition hall was to be built of discarded containers, 'a bit rusty, stacked up', Nouvel said. One would enter through hangar doors, the kind that run on steel trolleys, then pass through to the end of the dock, to a platform at the edge of the water. That's where the 'tail' of the whale was to be, a hollow steel sculpture as tall as a crane. From a crow's nest high up inside the whale fins, one would have a bird's-eye panorama of the port and the North Sea. In 2021, with no whale in sight, the port commissioned another architect to build a landmark for the port.

BLIJDORP HOUSING
JJP Oud
Rotterdam (NL), 1931

As a young architect, Jacobus Johannes Pieter Oud joined the painters Piet Mondrian and Theo van Doesburg to found the group of avant-garde artists known as De Stijl (The Style). Their preoccupation with geometry and colour helped to catapult Oud to the forefront of his profession, yet he always remained something of an enigma. He left De Stijl, converted to the white, rational cubes of Le Corbusier's Modernist asceticism, and was soon celebrated by the New York Museum of Modern Art's architectural gatekeeper Philip Johnson as one of the greatest architects of his day, but was later booted from the ranks for adding ornamentation to his post-war buildings.

In 1931, as Municipal Housing Architect for Rotterdam, Oud was working on the last of his pre-war government housing projects. The design called for 306 homes in the form of nine long, four-storey apartment buildings, each layer defined by ribbon windows running the length of the block. The ground-floor apartments had private gardens, in defiance of the prevailing philosophy of the Nieuwe Bouwen (New Building) movement, which adhered to egalitarian principles of worker housing. Still, communal gardens acted as streets between the buildings, and the wide spaces, generous windows and through-and-through apartments fulfilled the desire for housing that escaped the dreary conditions of working-class slums. Oud had introduced a new building type: the apartment complex. Seemingly mass-produced, these were light, airy and spacious.

Ironically, however, Oud's Blijdorp proposal wasn't mass-produced enough. It used too much land in return for too few apartments, was deemed too costly for worker housing, and so was never realized.

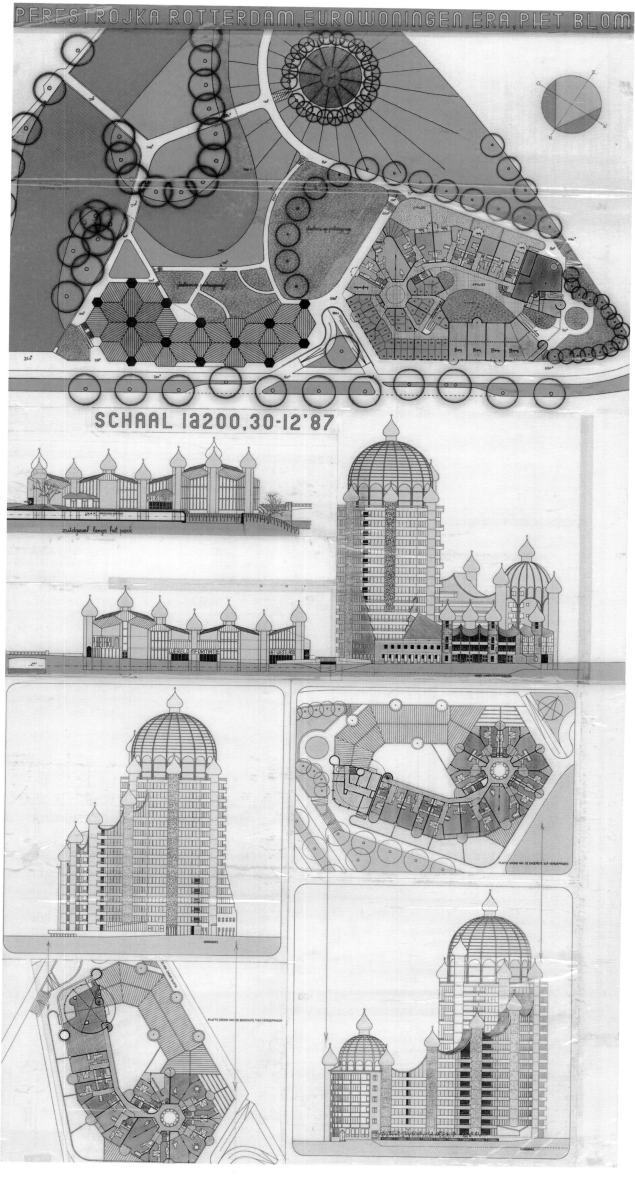

PERESTROIKA PROJECT
Piet Blom
Rotterdam (NL), 1986

The Dutch architect Piet Blom cultivated his reputation as a maverick, offering lively, provocative alternatives to the monotonous repetition of post-war Dutch architecture. Anyone who has toured Rotterdam is sure to have noticed his most prominent work: the 'Cube Houses', an abstract forest of three-storey, cube-shaped homes in the city centre, tilted 45 degrees and raised on concrete pillars above pedestrian plazas.

About 1 km (just over 1/2 mile) north of this site, Blom proposed on a triangle of land in the unremarkable, disconnected area of Pompenburg a development that he cheekily called 'Perestroika', a reference to the 1980s reform movement in the Soviet Union. Influenced by the historic churches and palaces of Russia, the somewhat cartoonish conglomeration of buildings curled into one corner of its site, leaving ample room for tree- and water-filled public space – like a palace garden, as Blom put it. The plot would be facilitated by burying the jumbled transit connections, and its centrepiece was a cylindrical high-rise, topped by a round, steepled dome, its circumference dotted with bright (and somewhat phallic) onion domes. Smaller buildings, connected by curved and zigzagging rooflines, culminated in another ornate cylinder. 'This is about creating attention to restore urban connections,' said Blom, who proposed installing an architecture museum and 'world documentation centre' at the base of the residential structures.

Blom was unable to secure approval or funding for the Perestroika Project. However, he brought its vivid language of curling forms and evocative domes to his 'Russian Palace', a house he designed in 1993 in Amersfoort for the young Russian concert pianist Yennah Prusha and her husband.

NEW CEMETERY
Renaat Braem,
Octave de Koninckx
Deurne (BE), 1961

Like most visionaries, the Belgian architect Renaat Braem was all too familiar with failed proposals and regularly complained about uninspired bureaucrats and backward-looking citizens. One focus of his struggles was Deurne, a suburb of Antwerp, where he worked for a time as a planner. 'Most of my designs for Deurne were messed up in one way or another because the clients had no idea of the obligation to have a large design completed in a grand manner,' he wrote.

With fellow architect and planner Octave de Koninckx, Braem proposed a new cemetery for the town that boasted an astonishingly grand entrance: an H-shaped, parabolic archway extended with enormously tall, pointed columns. Directly behind this sat a cone-shaped, skylit auditorium, surrounded by an elliptical colonnade, like "the course of atoms around the nucleus". Flanking the colonnade at oblique angles were two service pavilions containing offices, storage, bathrooms, and the cemetery's mortuary.

Braem likened a walk through the structure to passing both through brush (the arch) and tall trees (the columns). But the municipality rejected the entrance and left the rest of his plan to its municipal garden team. 'They trivialized the whole in an annoying way,' the architect noted. Despite his griping, in 1958 Braem built his own house in Deurne, a serene cubist masterpiece in brick that is one of two architect's house museums in the country. (The other is Victor Horta's, in Saint-Gilles, Brussels.) He was also able to create one of his best large-scale projects in Deurne: the masterplan for the Arenawijk housing project, celebrated for its blend of organic Brutalism and seamless connection to landscape.

Still, Deurne continues to plague Braem. Arenawijk's centrepiece, its sleek ten-storey towers, would never come to fruition, while at the time of writing the complex was threatened with partial demolition.

FREE UNIVERSITY OF BRUSSELS, ORIGINAL RECTORATE
Renaat Braem
Brussels (BE), 1978

Braem, celebrated for his unique organic Brutalist style, was particularly interested in learning. He wrote articles, founded design magazines, and consistently promoted design education and apprenticeships. One of his most famed projects is the rectorate for the Free University of Brussels, an institution created in 1971 as a place of academic independence from Church and State. His thin, elliptical building, reflecting the course of the planets around the sun (and, by extension, a heliocentric world view and the search for ultimate truth), has become a monument to Belgian Modernism.

Braem's original plan, however, was altogether different: a compilation of three circular towers, their floors receding as they rose, connected by a central meeting space and circulation core. The circle, Braem argued, is infinite, with neither beginning nor end, and therefore a fitting symbol of learning. Hovering over a pond (which also served as a drainage basin), like spaceships about to set off in quest of further knowledge, the complex 'had the appearance of a Temple of Sciences', he wrote in his book *Het lelijkste land ter wereld* (The Ugliest Country in the World, 1968).

But while the school administration was at first 'very much in favour' of the design, as Braem put it, Brussels' director general of urban planning, Pol Hendrick, advised against it as a 'dangerous and expensive experiment'. The rector of the university agreed, much to Braem's dismay, who wrote: 'It was very painful for me to see a well-known culture bearer drag the importance of construction culture through the mud.'

NOTRE-DAME BASILICA
Henry Lacoste, Michel Claes
Beauraing (BE), 1943

A pioneer of reinforced-concrete architecture and a passionate student of bygone civilizations, Henry Lacoste created fantastically unique buildings – particularly churches, monuments and exhibition buildings – between the two world wars. After studying at the École des Beaux-Arts he led surveys, excavations and the rebuilding of ancient sites and villages in such places as Greece and Syria, and during World War II he drew up urban plans for war-ravaged Belgian cities and towns.

In 1943 Lacoste and the architect Michel Claes designed a remarkable basilica in Beauraing. This tiny village in southeastern Belgium had become a pilgrimage site after the Virgin Mary was said to have appeared to five children about a decade earlier. The building was part of the two men's vision to transform the tiny town, which now received thousands of visitors a day, with such elements as a new town square, an assembly hall, a market, a school, hotels, a railway station and an enlarged convent. As with most of Lacoste's work, the triangular basilica was a modern reinterpretation of the ancient. Partnered with a spiralling campanile, it drew on the turrets, spires and arches of the Romanesque and Gothic, the monumental scale and shape of the ancient world's pyramids, temples and ziggurats, and the simplicity, advanced materials and structural ambition of modernity.

The scheme was far too ambitious for the tiny town, but Claes went on to design a far more modest stone chapel there in 1954. A marble statue, *Our Lady with the Golden Heart*, stands nearby, on the spot where Mary is said to have materialized. Pilgrims still visit to this day.

ALSTERZENTRUM HAMBURG
Hans Konwiarz
Hamburg (DE), 1965

Neue Heimat, a union-owned German construction and housing company headquartered in Hamburg, provided innovative, but not radical, German worker housing for much of the twentieth century. Among its many talented in-house architects was Hans Konwiarz, who laboured in relative anonymity until he had the chance to apply his expertise to the company's epic-scaled proposal for 'Alsterzentrum', an urban renewal project in Hamburg's St Georg neighbourhood, just east of the city's main railway station.

The scheme would have replaced virtually all the quarter's ageing buildings with a terraced megastructure containing housing, restaurants, theatres and virtually every other function the area offered at the time. Only a few buildings along the edge of the district would be preserved, cowering in the shadow of the behemoth. Rather than Neue Heimat's typical square blocks, Konwiarz's drawings depict a rounded progression of five organic towers, grooved with integrated balconies, connected at the base via a raised platform and rising like stalagmites. Tucked into the curving megastructure would be a grid of smaller rectangular and circular edifices.

The plan, which was intended simply to demonstrate the possibilities of the area (Neue Heimat intended to host an architectural competition) was – as such plans usually are – taken literally, appearing in publications, exhibitions and TV shows. After gaining initial public support, by the end of the 1960s it was starting to face stiff opposition, particularly among local citizens' associations, which demanded to be included in the planning process. The city opted instead for a more gradual revitalization of the area, relegating Konwiarz's vision (along with its impressive architectural model) to the Neue Heimat archives.

AMERIKA-GEDENKBIBLIOTHEK
Steven Holl
Berlin (DE), 1988

From the time of its inception in 1951, Berlin's Amerika-Gedenkbibliothek (American Memorial Library) was Cold War propaganda designed during a tug-of-war over the zeitgeist of post-war West Berlin. On one side was

Hans Scharoun's proposal for an Expressionist building with a seven-storey-high billboard of sixteen neon circles rising above the glass-walled slab. Scharoun's lights, which would be visible from the dim streets of East Berlin, beamed a message that life in the West was *heiter* (sunny and cheerful). Fritz Bornemann and Willy Kreuer's curved, International Style ice-cube-tray concrete facade, which was completed in 1954, reflected the view that sobriety, not exuberance, embodied the West's message.

Forty-five years later the building was again snared in Cold War politics after Steven Holl won the competition to add 14,000 sq. m (150,000 sq. ft) to it. In keeping with the library's commitment to open stacks, he proposed to wrap the Modernist building in a 'browsing circuit', consisting of a soaring rectangular reading room, a slender glassy walkway elevated on steel legs, a Zeppelin-shaped lantern passageway, and an observation tower to take in the views of Blücherplatz and the Church of the Holy Cross. Wolfgang Nagel, the German senator in charge

of public works, summarily rejected the design, saying, 'Holl's architecture ... subordinates what was already there.' The old symbol should remain, Nagel insisted, forcing the jury to award the $95 million project to the young New York architect Karen Van Lengen, whose cantilevered prow structure floating above a concrete base seemed less intrusive. After the Berlin Wall came down in November 1989, the city went deeply into debt, and the project was abandoned in 1992.

FRIEDRICHSTRASSE SKYSCRAPER
Ludwig Mies van der Rohe
Berlin (DE), 1921

The German architect Ludwig Mies van der Rohe, the most celebrated practitioner of the minimalist International Style, would not build a glass-and-steel skyscraper until the Seagram Building in 1958. But he had envisioned such a structure for decades. In 1921 he entered a municipal architectural competition for Berlin's first skyscraper, intended for a triangular site bounded by the Spree River, Friedrichstrasse railway station and Friedrichstrasse itself, the city's busiest shopping thoroughfare.

Submitted under the name 'Honeycomb', the crystalline edifice soared above the centre of Berlin, its corners thrusting upwards like aeroplane wings or levitating glaciers. Mies had previously designed only smaller buildings made of heavy materials, such as brick and stone. Here, massive sheets of plate glass hung like curtains from the edges of the floor slabs, accentuating the building's uninterrupted verticality and revealing its internal structure: a sort of open, honest framework that Mies described as an architecture of 'skin and bones'. 'Only in the course of their construction do skyscrapers show their bold, structural character, and then the impression made by their soaring skeletal frames is overwhelming,' he wrote. Now that initial impression would remain pure. Faceted surfaces reflected the light like jewels, while the dark, heavy facades of neighbouring buildings appeared as lifeless background characters. 'It had the quality of transfixing one,' noted the architect John Hejduk of the plan. 'Everything else just dropped away.'

The winning proposal, by Alfons Baecker, Julius Brahm and Rudolf Kastelleiner, was a conventional winged block wrapping around a central courtyard. But none of the entries would be built, and only Mies's design – far ahead of its era – has stayed relevant, still prompting discussion and debate.

TOTAL THEATRE FOR ERWIN PISCATOR
Walter Gropius
Berlin (DE), 1927

The Bauhaus founder and director Walter Gropius tended a school that would become an epicentre of experiment not just in architecture and the visual arts, but also in theatre and ballet. His students and teachers designed startlingly unorthodox theatres, sets and even costumes, drawing on the Bauhaus's mission of collaboration and artistic unity.

Near the end of his time as director, Gropius took on an assignment for the German director Erwin Piscator, who was famed for creating 'Epic Theatre' – unorthodox productions that mixed media, frenetically moved sets, and boldly mingled actors and audiences. For Gropius, the 'Total Theatre' would help to erode the bourgeois class segregation of traditional theatre while shedding the stale tropes of typical performing arts production. Not only would the theatre 'draw the spectator into the drama', he wrote, but also it would be 'capable of shaking the spectator out of his lethargy, of surprising and assaulting him and obliging him to take a real interest in the play'.

First, Gropius removed the proscenium, eliminating a major barrier between players and audience. To achieve 'convertibility, flexibility and anonymity', he planned an open, oval auditorium joined by a three-part stage fitted with turntables, platforms and scaffolding, which could be rotated, raised, pivoted and slid, creating endless configurations. The auditorium could be rotated, as well, varying perspective, while several screens allowed film projections on stage, in the audience and elsewhere, setting the audience 'inside' the film, as he put it. Germany's economic collapse of 1927 doomed the project, but it inspired theatre designers and producers around the world to break the theatrical mould.

CITY EDGE
Daniel Libeskind
Berlin (DE), 1987

A tradition of international architecture expositions stretching back to the late 19th century has helped to cement Berlin as a land of urban experimentation. The most celebrated was Interbau (1957), where such masters as Le Corbusier, Walter Gropius, Alvar Aalto, Arne Jacobsen and Oscar Niemeyer designed the Modernist neighbourhood of Hansaviertel on a bombed-out site in West Berlin. In 1984, before the fall of the Berlin Wall, West Berlin and the Federal Republic of Germany hoped to capture similar magic with the International Building Exhibition (IBA), a $1.2 billion programme to create housing for 30,000 people in derelict areas of West Berlin. With guidelines set by the Berlin architect and planner Josef Paul Kleihues, IBA attracted such stars as Gottfried Böhm, Mario Botta, Peter Eisenman, John Hejduk, Arata Isozaki, Charles Moore, Aldo Rossi and James Stirling. *Time* magazine called it 'the most ambitious showcase of world architecture in this generation'.

Hundreds of buildings went up, but the best remembered is one that failed. In 1987 Daniel Libeskind won a competition within the IBA framework for City Edge, a residential development for a beleaguered area edging Tiergarten park. Embracing Berlin's chaos and complexity, the building/monument consisted of an angled structure 450 m (1,476 ft) long, straddling the fractured site, displaying – through energetic artworks, projections and colliding landforms – the city's harsh scars of war and unrest. Raised on 75 million cu. m (2,649 million cu. ft) of debris, the Deconstructivist masterpiece was a clear rejection of the heavy, historicist 'Berlin of Stone'. But when the Berlin Wall fell, just two years later, the concept was suddenly rendered outdated, and the project was abandoned.

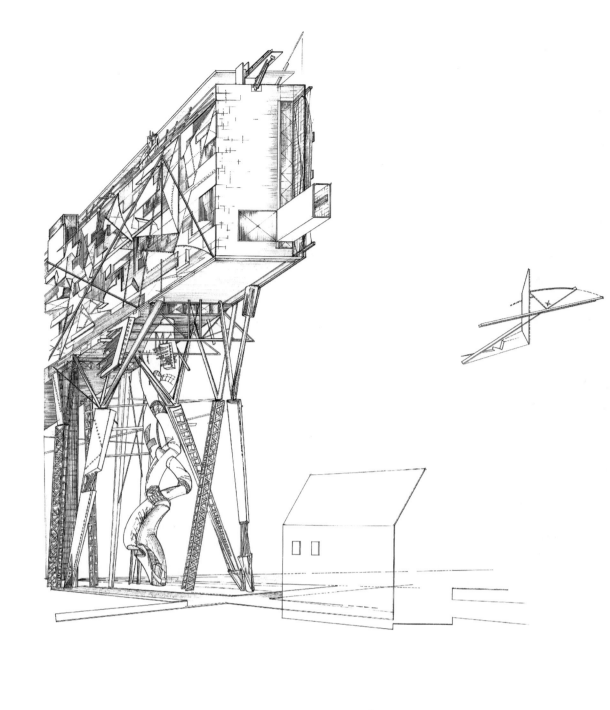

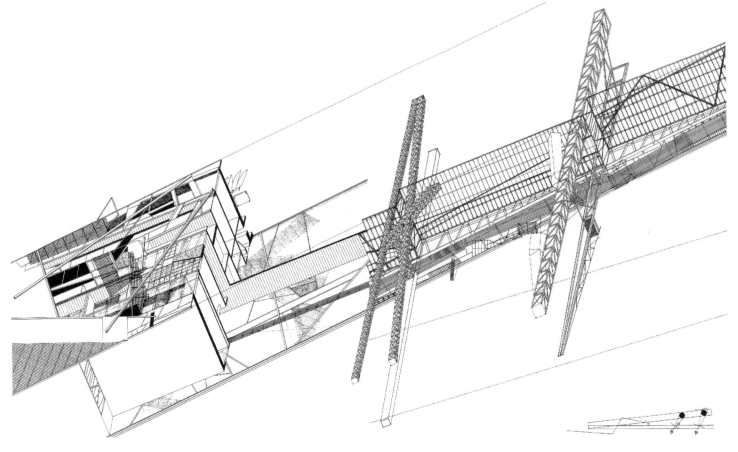

GERMANY

REICHSHAUS BUILDING AT KÖNIGSPLATZ
Otto Kohtz
Berlin (DE), 1920

A leading proponent of the league of high-rise cities, Otto Kohtz was obsessed with converting Berlin from a low-rise metropolis into a city of towers. His most daring plan was to build a massive home for government bureaucrats – the Reichshaus – across the plaza from the seat of government.

For nearly a decade, Kohtz produced version after version, beginning with a decidedly square box, then a staggered box, next a pyramid, and finally a set of ziggurats: three-layer, five-layer, twisted and scooped-out layers, no layers and, finally, eight layers. He chose the Greek cross – a square, central mass with four arms of equal length – as his form, with a soaring plaza, again laid out as a cross, occupying the interior void, the walls of which were staggered, like the exterior, as they climbed upwards. The base of the structure's arms measured 130 by 130 m (427 by 427 ft), its height fifty storeys. The concrete building would have been made of stacks of identical units, in a way similar to the idea of modular construction today. Although the design seems somewhat schematic, Kohtz drew sheet after sheet of exterior claddings. Some shimmered like polished steel; others quivered like striated quartz slabs; others were solid like granite. He also sketched murals with Zeppelins, aeroplanes and bridges, seeming to lend an air of life not tied down, of possibility, following the long nightmare of World War I and the bloody revolution of 1920.

Economic unease, high unemployment and hyperinflation eclipsed the ambitious idea. But Kohtz remained optimistic: 'May these sheets of the tower house idea recruit new friends,' he said.

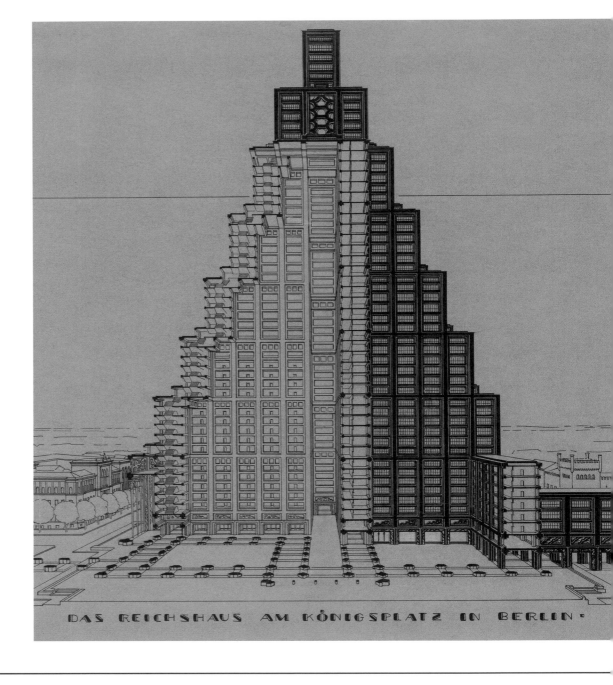

DAS REICHSHAUS AM KÖNIGSPLATZ IN BERLIN·

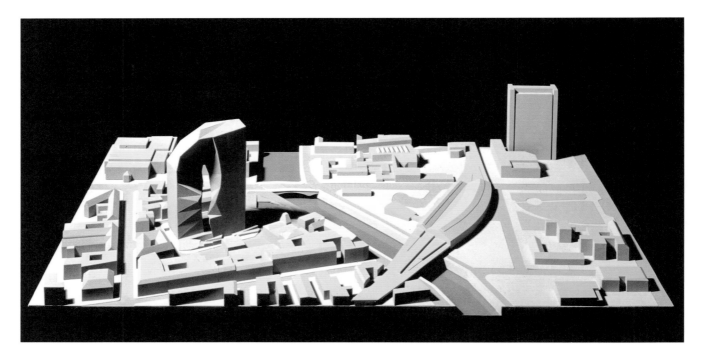

MAX REINHARDT HAUS
Peter Eisenman
Berlin (DE), 1992

The Max Reinhardt Haus was intended to be a memorial to the Berlin theatre impresario whose scenic and directorial innovations influenced generations of directors and dramatists. Backed by the Frankfurt developer and art patron Dieter Bock, the thirty-four-storey scheme would have been the iconoclastic architect Peter Eisenman's first high-rise.

Conceiving the design shortly after the fall of the Berlin Wall, Eisenman sketched a Möbius-strip building, its sides and top nearly forming a continuous band with neither beginning nor end. It was proposed for a prime corner in the former East Berlin, a site that had once been home to the legendary Grosses Schauspielhaus, the Jewish theatre designed by Hans Poelzig, which Reinhardt owned before fleeing the Nazis in 1933. Eisenman's Möbius rose from one location and, after twisting and arching through space to a height of 128 m (420 ft), landed a few metres away.

Wrapped in a geometric blanket of mauve, teal and cobalt glass, the building was awkward and ponderous, like two sloths trying to embrace. The price tag was estimated at $200 million. Of the multifaceted structure, Eisenman declared, 'The building … needs to fold into itself – but also open itself out to – an infinite, always fragmentary, and constantly changing array of metropolitan references and relationships.' There were two obstacles to the scheme: Reinhardt's son, who supported Eisenman's design, needed the German authorities to restore ownership of the parcel of land, which the Nazis had confiscated; and the tower was nearly four times Berlin's height restriction at the time, of 22 m (72 ft). The hurdles proved insurmountable.

HOCHSCHULSTADT
UNIVERSITY BERLIN
Otto Kohtz
Berlin (DE), 1937

In December 1937 Albert Speer, Adolf Hitler's chief architect for the Third Reich, presented a thirty-four-page booklet announcing a 'public ideas competition for University City'. The Hochschulstadt was meant to be the first stage in the plan to rebuild Berlin as a world capital, called 'Germania', filled with wide boulevards and monumental architecture, aspiring to become a new Rome. Seven hundred architects from around the world entered the competition, which aimed to combine all Berlin's universities into a new 'Reich University of Berlin'. Situated near the Olympic Stadium, by the Grunewald forest, the university was meant to become the western gate to the city.

Otto Kohtz, who had established himself as a lifelong advocate of the vertical in architecture, designed a cluster of four linked high-rises, 250 m (820 ft) tall. An enormous forecourt plaza anchored by a pair of square rostra holding aloft the German Eagle – one of the symbols of the Nazi regime – was lined by tombstone-like buildings with repetitive, flat-topped rectangular forms that emphasized the verticality of Kohtz's towers. The towers were depicted as thin fins projecting skywards, and the composition looked something like a purified edition of Raymond Hood's Art Deco Rockefeller Center (1933) in New York.

The competition offered prize money of 100,000 Reichsmarks, but a winner was never announced. As World War II got underway, the Reich couldn't afford the Hochschulstadt; all resources were diverted to the war effort. After the war Kohtz repositioned his university design as a high-rise city set in a huge reflecting pool – without the Nazi symbols.

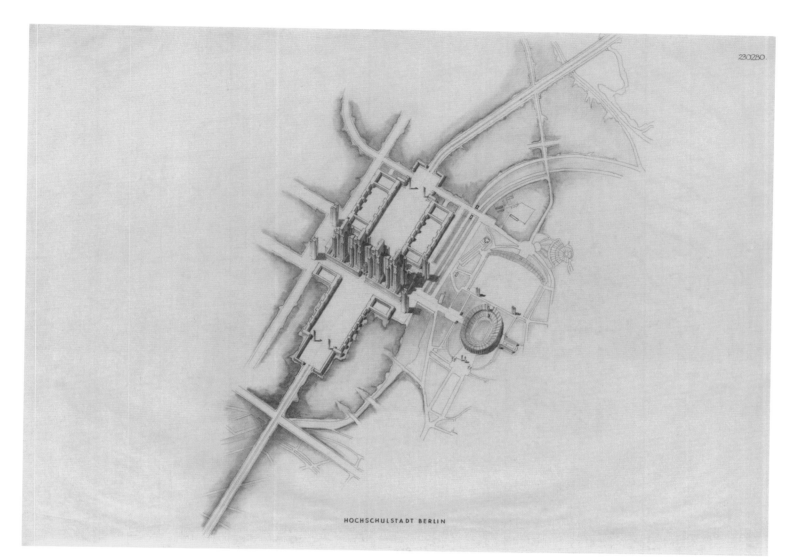

HOCHSCHULSTADT BERLIN

STERNKIRCHE
Otto Bartning
Berlin (DE), 1922

After World War I, Otto Bartning joined a vanguard of Modernist architects and drafted the craft and workshop principles that Walter Gropius would later use to found the Bauhaus in Weimar. In the 1920s Bartning's work, which was an amalgamation of Expressionism and the emerging Modernism, ranged from hospitals to residential housing blocks. But it was his Protestant churches that proved to be his muse. His Stahlkirche (Steel Church) in Cologne, completed over just four months in 1928, distilled his architectural ambition of using steel and glass to 'reveal the essential eternity of the Christian ideal in purely modern terms'.

A few years beforehand, Bartning had released the prototype Sternkirche (Star Church), a seven-pointed star with a broken-ribbed roof made of layered arches. He placed the pulpit in the centre of a sunken floor, surrounded by stepped seating for the congregation. The pinnacle was a glazed crystal 'in which the sevenfold shattered light finds itself', Bartning wrote later, referring to the invisible mystery of God. The roof girders, surprisingly, were supported on thin, slightly curved pillars that converged into Gothic arches. Lips formed by the roof eaves were filled with coloured glass. The beams and pillars were wooden – consciously organic and traditional – but using plank truss technology, 'wood construction of the most modern, technically well-trained' form, Bartning wrote. Elsewhere, he proposed reinforced steel and iron. Conservatives in the Protestant Church rejected this thoroughly modern concept. In the end, however, Bartning's ideas for the Sternkirche prevailed as the model for the 'emergency churches' that were built quickly after World War II.

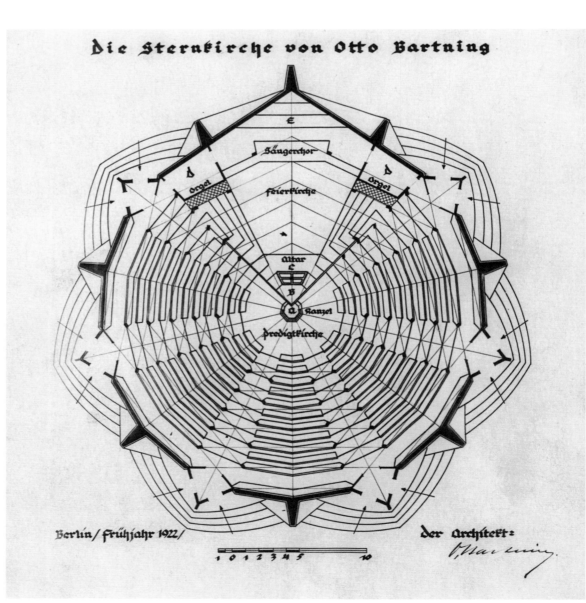

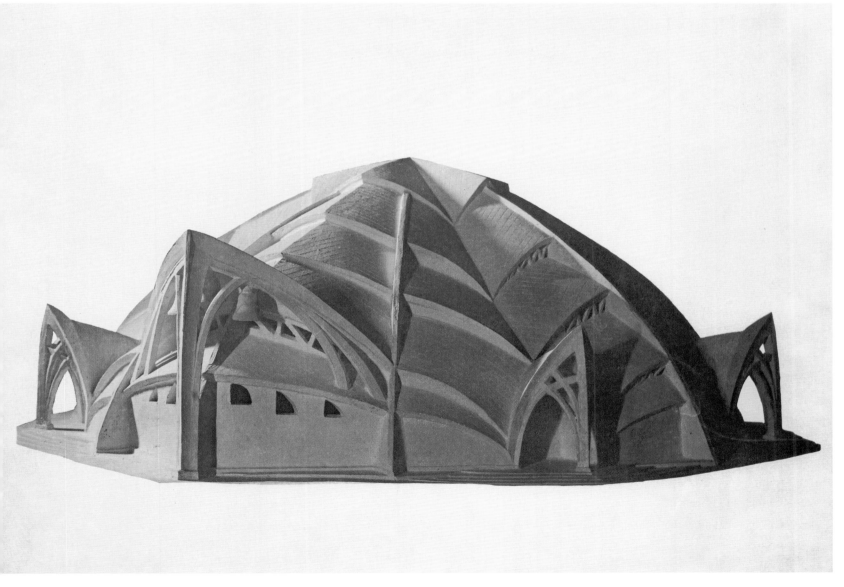

HOUSE OF HOUSES
Josef Küpper
Cologne (DE), 1964

For generations, such architects as IM Pei (The Helix, 1949), Moshe Safdie (Habitat '67, 1967) and James Wines (Highrise of Homes, 1981) have laboured to provide the comfort and privacy of the single-family home within the density and excitement of the city. One fascinating scheme lost to history was dreamed up by the Cologne architect Josef Küpper, who in 1964 proposed what he called the 'House of Houses', a 25-storey, cylindrical tower 100 m (328 ft) high embedded with steel support platforms into which could be slid varied, staggered housing modules, all connected via radial accessways. Shopping and playing facilities were on the roof. Küpper shopped his idea far and wide, and according to the publicity agency Keystone Press (which hired a young model to showcase his architectural model), he was 'already in touch with towns from various countries which show interest in his new house-house'. In 1970 Küpper received a patent in the United States for 'Detached Building Units on Plural Support Platforms', further outlining lateral 'uprights', which not only supported each home, but also ensured that no two residences had walls in common. 'The desire of the inhabitant for a completely detached home is fulfilled, without involving an undue demand on building ground,' noted the patent. With 20 homes per floor, the building could house 250 families. Despite his various patents, however, Küpper was never able to secure a developer or other source of funding for his idea.

STATE THEATRE
Hans Scharoun
Kassel (DE), 1952

Rebuilding Germany after World War II was a mission that evoked a strange mix of social amnesia and nostalgia. Hans Scharoun's theatre in Kassel became the most notorious victim of the desire to forget yet not exactly move ahead. He had won the competition to replace the Wilhelmine theatre, which had been given to the city by Kaiser Wilhelm II in 1909 but had been largely destroyed in a huge air raid in October 1943. The new theatre didn't look like a theatre, and the project sparked instant controversy. It was applauded by architects but despised by local residents, and knives were drawn. Scharoun's plan – condemned as 'hypermodern' and a work of 'architectural disharmony' by critics – had dispensed with the old hierarchy of a low auditorium backed by a tall fly tower. He presented a building whose silhouette curved gently from high to low, with asymmetrical, stepped roofs gingerly receding into each other, never yielding a central view of the theatre. In doing so, he also opened the view to the surrounding mountainous landscape, deliberately connecting the theatre to nature. It was as if Scharoun had deconstructed the very idea of a theatre and the progression that led one from the privacy of home to the threshold of suspended belief.
Work got underway on Scharoun's building, but was halted allegedly because old ramparts were uncovered, which would make the project too costly. While it idled, officials secretly hired the architect Paul Bode to proceed with his more conventional design. Bode's theatre, which opened in 1959 at three times the cost of Scharoun's, was later dismissed by locals as the 'Materials Testing Office'.

KUGELHAUS PROJECT MESSEHOTEL
Peter Birkenholz
Leipzig (DE), 1928

In the vast galaxy of built buildings, it was not until 1928 that a total sphere was constructed. The theoretical orbs by the French revolutionary architects Étienne-Louis Boullée and Claude-Nicolas Ledoux – the Cenotaph for Sir Isaac Newton (1784) and the Spherical House (c.1789), respectively – were extremely influential, as were the spherical visions of the Soviet Constructivists. Still, the Munich professor of architecture Peter Birkenholz's Kugelhaus (ball or sphere house) at the annual Dresden industrial exhibition 'The Technical City', became the world's first spherical building.

The sphere, resting on a central column, was 24 m (nearly 80 ft) in diameter and made of a steel scaffold with a skin of aluminium sheets. There were five levels, and a passenger lift rose through an atrium-like opening to the top-floor restaurant, which was the only enclosed space. The Dresden Kugelhaus was, for Birkenholz, an overture. He planned to reprise the idea over and over again in a variety of settings, from simple garden houses to entire cities and, as he suggested, in the form of a multi-sphere hotel in Leipzig.

Birkenholz, who had originally studied engineering, never tired of underlining the advantages of spherical construction. Such buildings, he said, permitted maximum space with a minimum surface area, and could be prefabricated and set down just about anywhere. Decades after its debut, Birkenholz was still seeking takers for his spherical idea, the latest, in 1954, a garage for 1,000 cars in parking-space-starved Dresden. In 1938 the Nazis condemned the original Kugelhaus as 'un-German' and 'degenerate art to be destroyed', but the era of spheres finally arrived in the twenty-first century.

GERMAN HYGIENE MUSEUM
Wassili Luckhardt
Dresden (DE), 1920

Erected in 1930 on the western edge of Dresden's Großen Garten, the architect Wilhelm Kreis's Deutsches Hygiene-Museum is a classic of restrained, monumental functionalism. With its blank, staggered forms, central colonnade and bilateral wings, the behemoth evokes a stripped-down Greek temple. But had the museum gone ahead in the early days of the Weimar Republic, as originally intended, its design would have been remarkably different. At that point the museum's founder, Karl August Lingner, manufacturer of the mouthwash Odol, held a competition that drew 192 entries, including those by such radical architects as Hans Scharoun, Hans Poelzig and the Luckhardt brothers, Hans and Wassili.

The Luckhardts – Expressionist designers who made major contributions to the urban fabric of 1920s Berlin – each submitted their own plan. While not a hit with the competition jury, Wassili's struck a chord in the architecture community. The wide building, with its slightly curved wings, featured a base evoking a grouping of chiselled rock buildings above which rose five serrated, crystalline peaks, their jagged, sculpturally modelled volumes evoking stalactites, mountains, starbursts or perhaps orange juicers. Based in the earth, but rising towards the sky, the plan was a rebuke of cold Modernism in favour of a bright architectural utopia, far removed from the country's mounting challenges.

For all its openness to the competition, however, Dresden remained a conservative city, never committed to the avant-garde. Furthermore, the museum's large endowment was almost completely lost owing to the devastating inflation Germany suffered in 1922 and 1923, and the contest was scrapped. Kreis was chosen by the museum's board – without a competition – in 1926.

DARMSTADT SCHOOL
Hans Scharoun
Darmstadt (DE), 1951

Best known for his tent-like Berlin Philharmonie (1963), Hans Scharoun is widely considered Germany's premier post-war architect. But his career reached all the way back to the 1920s, making his approach a unique hybrid of vivid Expressionism and radical, technically advanced Modernism.

In 1951 Scharoun was invited by the city of Darmstadt, then in West Germany, to participate in a conference entitled 'Man and Space', for which architects were asked to produce projects for various public buildings. Scharoun's proposed elementary school – setting the tone for his unbridled later work and bristling at the factory-like order of many mid-twentieth-century learning facilities – became a sensation in the German architectural world. United by a fractured, spine-like corridor, the facility contained three contrasting classroom buildings, designed for advancing age ranges. The 'lower' school provided spatial protection through domestic-inspired spaces and was designed to encourage learning through play via simple design, shared social zones, and maximum exposure to sunlight. The middle school promoted discipline and focus, while the spaces for the oldest group encouraged social responsibility and easy access to the outside. Common facilities included a gym, auditorium and multi-storey administration building. Students would advance through unstructured 'neighbourhoods' by means of varied outdoor spaces, including open courtyards, fan-shaped terraces, gardens and pools.

Scharoun saw the building as both a guide and a symbol for child development. Pupils would start as unstructured 'heaps', learning to associate themselves within both structured groups and unstructured spaces through self-determination and an emerging critical consciousness. The conference was intended to showcase ideas, and this one remained just that, albeit one that had a profound impact over subsequent years.

MUSEUM OF CONTEMPORARY ART
Gottfried Böhm
Stuttgart (DE), 1990

The architect James Stirling's colourful and serpentine Neue Staatsgalerie – a quirky, beloved monument of postmodernism – helped to culturally reinvigorate this manufacturing and financial centre when it opened in 1984. Just a few years later, the Pritzker Prize-winning German architect Gottfried Böhm entered a competition for a contemporary art museum diagonally opposite, that would have served as a gateway to the downtown area, completed the city's so-called cultural mile, and stood as a fitting pairing with Stirling's edifice.

Claiming as little green space as possible, the cylindrical, vertically orientated structure was inspired by the city's many industrial and infrastructural edifices, from oil tanks and steel furnaces to the old railway station's outsized tower. Clad in a grid of glass panels, the building was focused on a soaring central atrium, around which emerged haphazardly organized playful details, including a funnel-shaped crown, scaffold-like cylindrical exterior stairs, cantilevered floors, and several outdoor balconies for the display of sculpture.

According to the art historian Wolfgang Pehnt, the jury was 'afraid' of the building's dominant presence on the cityscape, while museum officials couldn't figure out how to make its polygonal exhibition galleries work. Arata Isozaki (a good friend of Stirling) took first place in the competition with a gridded cube flanked by large geometric forms that matched Stirling's PoMo spirit. But nobody would really win. The project's champion, Lothar Späth, minister-president of the state of Baden-Württemberg, was investigated on corruption charges and had to step down. After he left, the project – already a target of criticism owing to its siting in a popular park – collapsed.

EUROPE WEST

HANGING HOUSES
Heinz and Bodo Rasch
Stuttgart (DE), 1927

At about the same time that Richard Buckminster Fuller proposed his Dymaxion House – a structure suspended by cables from a central mast – Heinz and Bodo Rasch devised their Hänghauser (Hanging Houses). Worlds apart in type and geography, their objectives were largely identical: to adapt the efficiencies of modern manufacturing to mass-produce housing. In theory, homes would be cheaper by the dozen; lightweight, transportable shells could be assembled on-site by less skilled workers. In their early twenties at the time, the Rasch brothers conceived of social housing – as opposed to Fuller's freestanding individual homes – in a burst of energetic propositions for 'real utopias' (Bodo, for instance, explored inflatable pneumatic cells decades before the radical architects of the 1960s got onto the

idea). The hanging houses consisted of two rows of masts with cables suspending towers arrayed in a zigzag along a long, straight spine of glass passages. The roof of the corridor became a magnificent promenade. Below, the ground was free and clear.

The brothers promoted their dream – suspended houses, swimming pools, stadia – in books and magazines they wrote and edited. They became well known in artistic and architectural circles, mixing with everyone from Ludwig Mies van der Rohe to Otto Dix and Kurt Schwitters. But the

suspended houses failed to attract investors, and the brothers' collaboration imploded as they bickered over copyright, ownership of their joint work and, reputedly, falling in love with the same woman. They challenged Mies for swiping their design of the tubular cantilever chair, and for decades battled Fuller over the original conception of suspended construction. It seems they were destined never to get a lucky break.

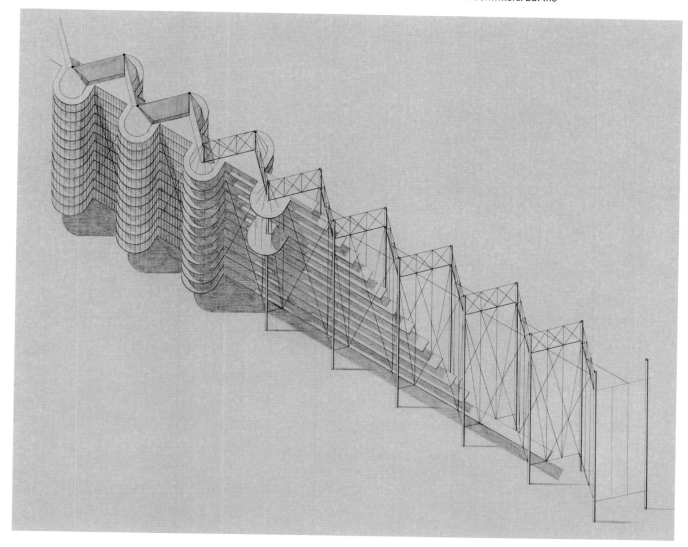

ULM MEDICAL ACADEMY
Frei Otto
Ulm (DE), 1965

In 1965 the newly founded university at Ulm, the birthplace of the celebrated physicist Albert Einstein) enlisted Frei Otto to design temporary buildings for the medical school, which would open in 1967 with another architect at the helm.

Otto had been investigating how to achieve more with less – to construct greater spans of extreme lightness and extreme strength using less material – since his early youth, when he spent his time inventing and building model aeroplanes. After World War II, while in the United States on a student exchange, he happened to see a model of Matthew Nowicki's Dorton Arena (1952) for Raleigh, North Carolina, the first large structure to have a roof suspended on tensioned cables. The saddle-shaped curved roof so wowed Otto that he wrote his doctoral

thesis on the new construction technique and later established his Institute for Development of Lightweight Constructions in Berlin.

Over the ensuing decades Otto challenged monumentality and permanence in architecture with visions of light, ephemeral tensile structures. The Ulm Medical Academy was the third idea for the temporary structures at Ulm. He proposed a linear tent-like ensemble 355 m (1,165 ft) long, 82 m (270 ft) wide and 55 m (180 ft) high. Suspended between the catenary curves of the wire ropes, hung from nine masts,

were terraces of patients' rooms, operating theatres and research facilities.

Otto said of his projects that their 'realization will be temporary enough not to be in man's way'. It was a radical proposition, then or now, and although the university declined to proceed, the idea led to his plastic-sheathed Alps-shaped Olympic Stadium in Munich in 1972. Worldwide recognition as a revolutionary architect and engineer followed.

MUNICH RAILWAY STATION
Albert Speer
Munich (DE), 1937

With the Third Reich ascendant, Adolf Hitler's chief architect, Albert Speer, went to work supervising the physical manifestation of a future Fascist civilization. His and his subordinates' oversized city plans filled with oversized buildings not only satisfied Hitler's oversized ego, but also projected intimidating power and awe-inducing timelessness, and helped to complete what Hitler called 'a grandiose makeover of our way of thinking and feeling'. Speer's 'Germania' scheme for Berlin is by far his most documented, but equally overwhelming is his plan for Munich, the birthplace of Nazism and the 'City of the Movement'.

Whereas Berlin, which Hitler envisioned as 'the most colossal city on earth', would be the Reich's government capital, Munich would be the 'city of art', a centre of culture with a long, wide east–west axis adorned with an opera house (nine times the size of La Scala in Milan, drafted by Hitler himself), theatres, museums, swimming pools, ballrooms and skyscrapers. At the centre of the axis was a gargantuan railway station, drafted by Munich city architect Hermann Giesler, with a dome 270 m (886 ft) wide supported by a massive steel skeleton. The station, edged by Roman-style columns, would dwarf St Peter's in Rome (as illustrated by this image which puts the plans, at centre, alongside other structures for scale). Next to it stood the 'victory monument to the party', its central column 214 m (702 ft) tall and about 25 m (82 ft) in diameter, topped by an eagle with a wingspan of 33 m (108 ft). While it's questionable if Speer and Giesler could have realized their impossibly grand plans, the Nazis' defeat and Hitler's suicide doomed them for good.

PLATZ DER TECHNIK
AND PLATZ DER KUNST
Peter Birkenholz
Munich (DE), 1941

Famed for his exceptionally modern spherical building, the Kugelhaus (1928) in Dresden, the German designer and engineer Peter Birkenholz spent the early 1940s envisioning monumental urban plans for the Nazis. In Munich, he sketched two new squares that, as did most of the Third Reich's visions for the metropolis, completely ignored the existing urban fabric, placing gestures of control and intimidation above all other considerations.

To mark Platz der Technik (Technology Square), adjacent to the Deutsches Museum (1925), a science centre on an island in the Isar River, Birkenholz employed another geometric strategy: a massive cone-shaped structure that would dwarf every building in the city, serving as an exaggerated expression of power. Surrounding streets and apartments would be demolished, and the plaza would extend north towards the city centre. Inside the industrial-inspired cone (its function not yet specified), wide ramps, rather than stairs, would connect the levels. Joined to it via a long north–south axis would be the Platz der Kunst (Art Square), an even larger plaza flanking the Haus der Kunst (1937), a Nazi-designed historicist temple to German art, civilization and propaganda. Surrounded on three sides by monumental, vaguely Roman buildings, and by myriad oversized sculptures atop large pillars, the sweeping square would focus on an obelisk 120 m (394 ft) high, topped with a viewing platform. Munich was severely bombed barely three years after Birkenholz's plans were submitted. By 1945 the Nazis had surrendered to the Allied forces, erasing any chance that these staggering emblems of a heinous era would be built.

SIEMENS AG HEADQUARTERS
James Stirling
Munich (DE), 1970

James Stirling gave birth to a new architectural language in 1959 with his Engineering Building for Leicester University, in the English Midlands, whose fractured palette of brick, glass and concrete was a hand grenade tossed at the emptiness of Corporate Modernism. By 1970, when he was invited to enter the competition for the Siemens AG Headquarters in Munich, he was a postmodernist, equally loved and reviled, widely regarded as one of the best architects of his day.

Siemens, Europe's largest industrial manufacturer, had acquired a huge farmland site in Perlach, on the edge of Munich. For this site Stirling devised a city – of sorts – for 10,000 people. Ten drumhead steel-and-glass office cylinders, with rotating sunscreens, were aligned in complete symmetry along a wide street lined with colonnades and served by a travelator. The towers sat atop identical rows of frustums, great concrete truncated pyramids that formed a plateau above the surrounding land. The whole was monumental, axial, geometric and classical, yet the imagery evoked industrial smokestacks and power-plant cooling towers.

Stirling had asked his chief designer, Léon Krier, 'What's the image?', but Siemens wasn't interested in the symbolism, no matter the references. By 1971 the Rotterdam architectural practice Van den Broek & Bakema (now Broekbakema) was building the research centre and offices. The buildings were arrayed on a diagonal to maximise the available acreage, and were tagged according to the areas of research: yellow for the growing field of communications, red for technical pursuits, blue for heating, ventilation and air conditioning. Still, Stirling's unrealized imagery has had an almost eternally glowing afterlife whereas Broekbakema's mega-complex has led a trudging, listless existence.

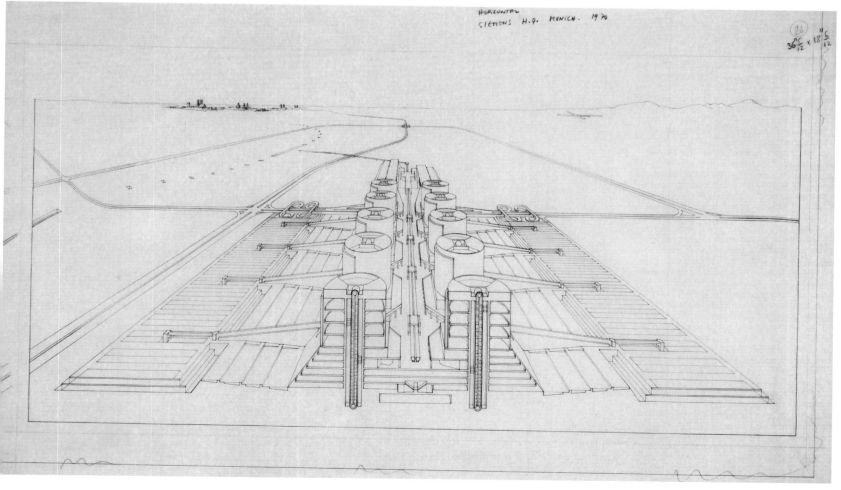

TOUR EUROPÉENNE
Will Alsop, Jean Nouvel,
Massimiliano Fuksas,
Otto Steidle
Hérouville-Saint-Clair
(FR), 1988

Will Alsop, Jean Nouvel, Massimiliano Fuksas and Otto Steidle were still just baby 'starchitects' from England, France, Italy and Germany when they collectively won the commission in 1987 to build the Tour Européenne (also known as the Tour Geindre), a tower 100 m (328 ft) tall containing residences, a hotel, offices and shops. The project, to be engineered by Arup, was the brainchild of François Geindre, the mayor of Hérouville-Saint-Clair, a newish, rather faceless Normandy town near Caen. Geindre, a seasoned bureaucrat, knew that bringing in world-class names from around Europe could attract international investors to the town – a precursor to Frank Gehry's 'Guggenheim effect' in Bilbao. Each architect worked on a piece of the project, so that the building was by nature a kit-of-parts Frankenstein's monster. Alsop designed the ground-level shopping centre, a glassy, armadillo-shaped structure perched on stilts and supported by repeating steel ribs that bridged the adjacent road, while Nouvel designed the hotel tower above the large podium and Fuksas and Steidle designed the tower's fragmented base, beneath the podium, which contained offices and residences. Other elements, supported by steel columns and embedded concrete cores atop a lofted steely podium, resembled space capsules, oil derricks and launch pads. Such diverse components, as well as the building's many uses, were a way to bring a sense of urbanity to a rather monotonous suburban condition. The vision dragged on until 2001, when Geindre finally threw in the towel. But in 2009 the town's new mayor, Rodolphe Thomas, brought the plan out of its slumber, launching an ill-fated competition for another generation of (doomed) starchitects that never went anywhere.

TOUR LUMIÈRE
CYBERNÉTIQUE
Nicolas Schöffer
Paris (FR), 1969

La Défense, the cluster of modern buildings raised atop a superblock on the western edge of Paris, has for almost a century served as a testing ground for global architects' visions of the future. Of these perhaps no idea was as futuristic as the artist Nicolas Schöffer's 347 m (1,138 ft) Tour Lumière Cybernétique (Cybernetic Light Tower).

Schöffer (who has been honoured with a namesake museum in his native Kalocsa, Hungary) was one of the leading lights of the cybernetic art movement, in which electronics, information, feedback and communication superseded aesthetic, social and other concerns. His tower would deliver feedback in spades. Every form of communication conceivable at the time – loudspeakers, flashing lights, coloured lights, spotlights, smoke signals, moving rods, rotating mirrors and more than 5,000 projectors – was supported by a series of open steel frames, relaying myriad conditions in the city and beyond, including traffic, weather, news and even citizens' movements. Schöffer described it as 'an intense living flame, constantly transformed and transformable'. He praised its ability to 'democratize' information, which, he posited, was otherwise limited to those in control of government and production. With its endless notifications, it was essentially a skyscraper-sized smartphone.

But while Schöffer did get to build something similar in Liège, Belgium, in 1961 – a sculpture 52 m (171 ft) tall – the mammoth Paris project was never to be. By the early 1970s the magical possibilities of cybernetics were seen as insidious menaces, enabling the wanton invasion of privacy and limitation of personal freedom. (Sound familiar?) Momentum for the project crashed, and Schöffer couldn't find a backer.

PARIS SOUS LA SEINE
Paul Maymont
Paris (FR), 1962

The inspiration for Paris sous la Seine (Paris beneath the Seine) was Montreal's 33 km (20 mile) network of pedestrian tunnels and underground malls, which today constitutes a subterranean city of 2,200 shops and restaurants, ten major hotels, museums and theatres, connected to sixty office buildings overhead. Paul Maymont was among a group of French architects in the 1960s known as 'spatial urbanists', who cranked out futuristic visions of linear cities, massive changeable, floating and hovering housing blocks, and cities beneath the city. The work was less about buildings than about moving people through space.

Maymont's problem in Paris was that there was no space left below the city; it had long been thoroughly punctured with subways, sewers, cellars, wells, quarries and catacombs. The only fresh turf lay beneath the Seine, which he planned to temporarily dam, dredge and divert, adding a megastructure 60 m (197 ft) high. Fourteen levels held hospitals, universities, post offices and fire stations, all swept underground to free space above. A motorway, seven lanes in each direction, diverted traffic from the city streets, and a 500,000-space car park sat under the plaza of Notre-Dame. Maymont's grand view was that the soils beneath the Seine could become one extended linear city.

In the late 1960s the spatial urbanists were met by an increasingly hostile public, wary of architectural schemes that proposed to solve all society's problems in a single stroke. The uprising in May 1968 eclipsed, once and for all, these top-down, technocratic propositions. Perhaps Paris's Périphérique motorway is the only lasting side effect of these visionary works, which were, in the words of the French theorist Michel Ragon, 'fruit of [the architect's] own initiative'.

CENTRE POMPIDOU
André Bruyère
Paris (FR), 1969

The architect André Bruyère could be described as a sensualist, rebelling against the Modernists' rationalist ethos. His entry for the international competition in 1969 for the Centre Pompidou, to replace the historic Les Halles marketplace in the heart of Paris, was L'Oeuf – the egg. It was a self-conscious radical protest. Bruyère said, 'It is impertinent in its simplicity; it has no precedent. Time, instead of being linear, like the straight streets and vertical skyscrapers, will become oval, in tune with the egg.' This was more than an attack on the straight lines and right angles of urban grids; it echoed the rallying cry of the Situationists in Paris in 1968, when Gaullist France was brought to a halt. The building itself would become a 'situation', and change the way people acted.

Roughly 105 m (344 ft) tall, this hymn to a nearly impossible engineering feat stood on three legs, and was covered in thousands of 2 m (6½ ft) scales of alabaster, glass or concrete. It was in constant flux both inside and out. A monorail entered the egg and circled through the structure along a sinuous, floating ribbon. The foyer was an enclosed globe, like a yolk.

Bruyère said of his egg: 'I propose … some other impressions: the respite, a surprise, humour, contestation and the discovery that between the hard geometries comes the sweetness of a volume, curves in all directions changing, in contrast to these facades where the angle always falls right from the sky, always similar. So, the egg.' But he lost the competition to Richard Rogers and Renzo Piano.

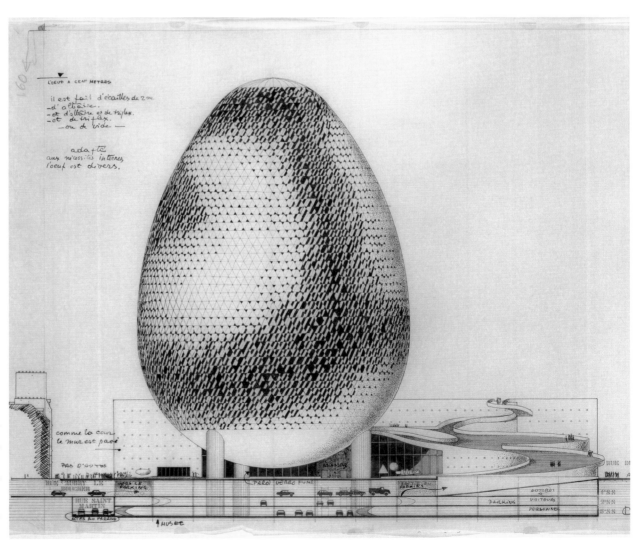

HÔTELS SUSPENDUS
Édouard Albert
Paris (FR), 1964

The mid-century French architect Édouard Albert specialized in radical approaches and materials, from three-dimensional urbanism (in which buildings take shape above and below the ground plane) and prefabrication, to construction using steel tubes, prestressed concrete and fibreglass. His Croulebarbe Tower in Paris, also known as the Tour Albert (1960; near Place d'Italie), supported by external, concrete-filled steel tubes interspersed with horizontal blocks of concrete, was the first skyscraper in the city.

Another residential building proposed by Albert, a little east of the Eiffel Tower on Place de la Résistance, combined virtually all these innovations. The Hôtels Suspendus (Suspended Residences) – sometimes referred to as the Tour Arborescent (Tree Tower) – was 120 m (394 ft) tall, its vegetal components a modern extension of the tree-filled avenues and riverbanks nearby. Suspended from cylindrical concrete cores was a sequence of tubular steel frames – vertical, horizontal and diagonal – that in turn supported a branch-like progression of twenty-two cube-shaped apartments (of three levels apiece), each with its own roof garden, and clad in glass etched with colourful geometric forms. The vibrant building's lively play of solid and void represented a radical turn from the blocky, repetitive masses of the day's towers, carving out unique, playfully varied living experiences.

Albert hoped his 'big plant' would enliven the lifeless forms around it, but he could never find a developer to back it. The triangular site is now home to the Bulgarian Embassy and a branch of LCL bank.

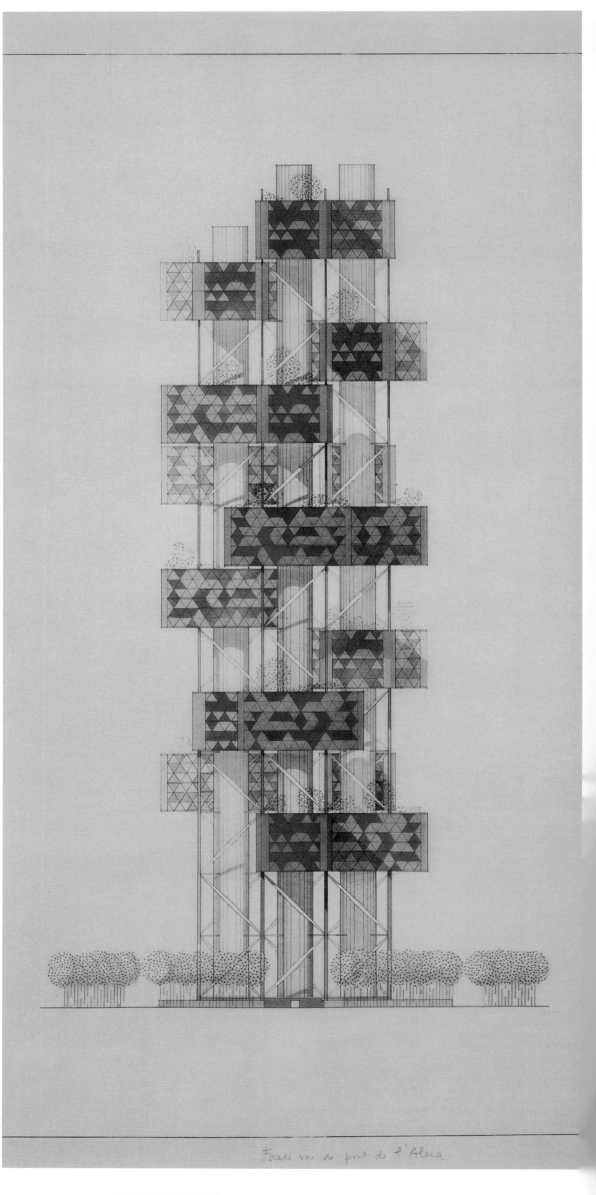

Façade vue du pont d'Alma

The Paris architect and landscape designer André Lurçat (brother of the famed modern textile artist Jean Lurçat) played a pivotal role both in the success of Modernism in France and in the country's rebuilding after World War II. Among other commendations, he was a founding member (with Le Corbusier) of the influential Congrès Internationaux d'Architecture Moderne (International Congresses of Modern Architecture; CIAM) in 1928.

In 1932 Lurçat proposed an airport for small aircraft atop Île aux Cygnes (Swan Island), a narrow, peaceful artificial island on the western side of the city, a little downriver of the Eiffel Tower. (The Allée des Cygnes, a tree-lined path extending through its centre, is one of the city's great hidden oases.) Called Aéroparis, Lurçat's scheme – typically grandiose at a time when technology-obsessed Modernists were rethinking cities – received the tacit backing of Léon Riotor, president of the city's Municipal Aeronautics Commission. The double-level structure, mounted on piles bored into both the island and its surrounding riverbed, was 11 m (36 ft) wide and 890 m (2,920 ft) long. Its top level contained a long runway, while below that lay passenger services and aircraft storage, accessible via giant freight elevators. Existing bridges across the Seine would pierce the structure laterally. But the plan was not tenable. The runway was already too short for most passenger aircraft of the time, and local residents and unions protested against the destruction of the island's trees, and the noise, light and health hazards of having an airport in the neighbourhood.

LA PETITE CATHÉDRALE
Ricardo Bofill
Cergy-Pontoise (FR), 1971

Faced with unprecedented mid-century growth in and around Paris, local leaders created what became known as 'Nouvelle Villes', several new towns at the periphery of the metropolitan region. Cergy-Pontoise, about 35 km (22 miles) northwest of Paris, was established in 1972. To end the yet-to-be pop-up city a much-needed identity, the Barcelona-based architect Ricardo Bofill stepped in, master of the 'cultural symbolic', aligning new architecture with the great monuments of the past. Bofill built several such structures in France, including Les Espaces d'Abraxas in Noisy-le-Grand. Its oversized references to classical palaces, colonnades, amphitheatres and forums not only gave the area a distinct identity – for better or worse – but also were intended to provide monumental architecture (once the reserve of the ruling elite) for the middle and working classes.

For Cergy-Pontoise, the Catalan master proposed a grand covered shopping street called the Petite Cathedrale – 300 m (984 ft) long, 70 m (230 ft) high and 20–60 m (66–197 ft) wide – which took the appearance and form of a great Gothic cathedral, complete with cavernous entrance, nave, transept, apse, and flanking chapels and cloisters. Clustered around the street were stacked cubic forms filled with apartments, offices, schools, shops, theatres, recreation facilities and green space. The mixed-use megastructure was never to be;

Bofill couldn't convince local leaders to execute his grandiose vision. Yet in 1985 the persuasive architect secured Cergy-Pontoise's backing for Belvedere Saint Christophe, a neoclassical semicircle of apartments for 190 families, facing a tall central tower. It opened the following year.

AVENUE OF TOWER-HOUSES
Auguste Perret
Paris (FR), 1922

From the time of Napoleon III, Georges-Eugène Haussmann's perfectly straight Parisian boulevards, with their arcades of seven-storey cream-colored limestone buildings, had withstood the march of skyscraping modernity. But in 1922 Auguste Perret, the pioneer of reinforced-concrete construction, proposed L'Avenue des Maisons-Tours (the Avenue of Tower-Houses), which seemed to contemplate the undoing of Haussmann's Paris. Perret wanted to build 100 concrete residential skyscrapers between 150 and 200 m (492 – 656 ft) tall, along a road that is today the Périphérique freeway, and that would have been nearly four times as wide. He proposed another 200 such towers for a lush avenue stretching west from Place de la Porte Maillot to Croix de Noailles, passing through the present-day site of La Défense. Unlike his pupil Le Corbusier, who proposed levelling 240 hectares (593 acres) of the historic Marais, Perret did not propose to destroy the city in order to save it. While abandoning Haussmann's boulevards of unbroken facades, he was nonetheless interested in extending the city, connecting his suburbs via the Avenue de Neuilly and Avenue des Champs-Élysées to the core of Paris. His objective was far more radical than Corbusier's Plan Voisin; he wanted the towers to keep Paris – which, the writer Émile Zola said, was 'life itself' – pulsating in a new modern place.

Like Corbusier's city makeover, however, Perret was seeding an idea without a real backer. Later in life, however, Perret repudiated his utopian vision: 'When I was young, I sang the praises of the tower house. I have since changed my mind. When you stay on the 12th or 15th floor, you feel at first exalted, then overwhelmed with loneliness. One is bored to death. Man needs to maintain contact with the ground.'

TÊTE DÉFENSE
IM Pei
Paris (FR), 1970

In 1970 the French developer Jean-Claude Aaron, then in the process of building Paris's controversial Tour Montparnasse, asked IM Pei to design a 70–80-storey skyscraper on a prominent site in La Défense, the city's modern commercial district. It would be Europe's tallest, at least ten storeys taller than Montparnasse.

Pei agreed, but when he visited the site he realized that the tower would appear to viewers looking west as a blocky appendage to the Arc de Triomphe – visible straight down the Avenue des Champs-Élysées. Pei recommended that Aaron relocate the tower to the head of the avenue, and proposed a twin-towered building linked by catenary curves, like a giant U, so that the view through the Arc de Triomphe would remain unobstructed. 'The axis must be closed, yet remain open,' he explained. 'The combination must be there, otherwise you have no

space; it leaks out all over the place, just goes on and on.' Pei called his building a 'Diapason', a grand burst of harmony.

As Pei refined his design, many others submitted concepts for the so-called Tête Défense, including the French architect Émile Aillaud, who offered two concave mirrored buildings, reflecting La Défense while leaving a gap for views of Paris. Such dreams were dashed in 1982, when President François Mitterrand called for a *concours* that was won by the Danish architect Johan Otto von Spreckelsen; his

blocky Grande Arche de La Défense was completed in 1989. Perhaps inspired by Aillaud, Pei would design the mirrored, concave EDF Tower (now Tour Légende) at La Défense in 2001.

NÉCROPOLE DE NICE
GRAU
Nice (FR), 1982

GRAU's Necropolis – literally, city of the dead – was conceived with 'the "magic" and the symbolism of its geometries' as the starting and ending points of the design. The notion was to build a burial ground with no sense of historical memory or place. The city of the dead would be just … a city of the dead.

The idea was to construct a continuous building, 1 km (just over ½ mile) long, 15 m (50 ft) high, built into a sloping, sandy palisade near the banks of the Val River, west of Nice, and following the curve of the river valley. Directly behind the wall were four semicircular columbarium towers, a plaza composed of irregular stars for outdoor graves, and a pyramid standing in a reflecting pool, and dedicated to the three faiths: Catholic, Jewish and Islamic. In the woods at the far end of the bend in the road was an ossuary and cinerarium – for the bones and ashes of the dead – sketched as abstract representations of the Star of David, the Crucifix, and the Crescent and Star. The cemetery was self-referential, a set of pure forms (cylinder, pyramid and star), and the notion was to create a sequence of repetitive experiences that could be experienced only within its walls, rendering it an 'unreal' city.

GRAU said that the monumental cemetery was meant to be a unitary whole – and 'urban form' – not a collection of objects. Unfortunately, only the concrete lattice entrance and one of the star-shaped graveyards were built. The rest remains a polemic on oblivion and the form it might take.

MUSLIM CENTRE
Aires Mateus
Bordeaux (FR), 2014

The Muslim Centre in the southwestern French city of Bordeaux had all the hallmarks of Aires Mateus's work: crisp geometry, glowing white walls, voids and subtractions. But the Lisbon architects abandoned their lingua franca of straight lines and cubist forms, which they always manage to make weightless, and adopted two kissing, sinuous surfaces to create what they described as 'a whole without parts'.

The 12,000 sq. m (129,000 sq. ft) centre overlooked the Garonne River, and was divided into three distinct layers. The bottom, which acted as a plinth, had shops and stairways leading to the mosque. The upper floor, with patios open to the sky and a restaurant with a panoramic view, contained classrooms, meeting rooms and a library. These two formed a kind of sandwich, described by the architects as 'the mundane'. The 'sacred', they said, was the void between the two, intended to hold more than 4,000 worshippers. The floor and ceiling were like topographical projections, sculpted surfaces that touched at key points to define 'rooms' beneath the single span. The colour, amplitude and luminosity of light – from obscure to refulgent – mediated by the shading effects of the fluid interior forms, affirmed the sense of sacred space. Movement within the structure, which remained open on all four sides, was undetermined, reflecting the unmediated relationship of Muslims to their faith.

Tareq Oubrou, the mosque's progressive imam, had the city's backing, but there would be no groundbreaking until dykes on the Garonne were reinforced and Oubrou raised €24 million. He never did.

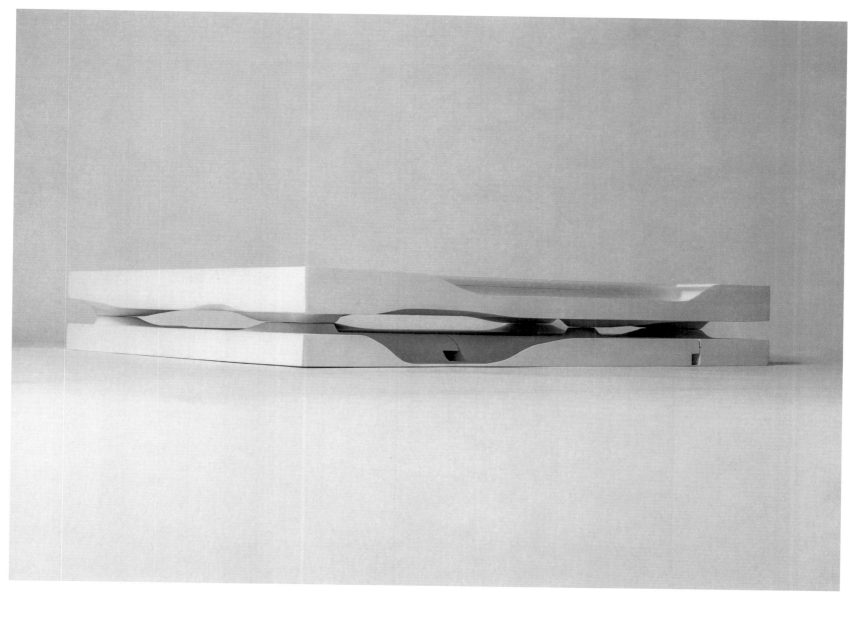

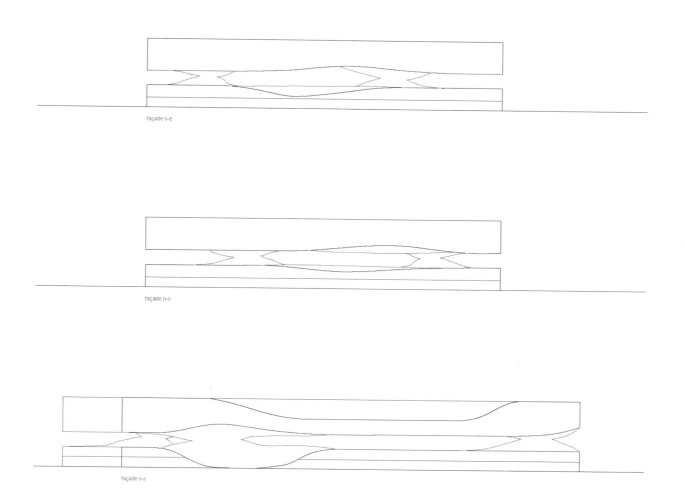

façade s-e

façade n-o

façade o-s

A BRIDGE FOR EUROPE
Gaetano Pesce
Strasbourg (FR), 1989

The Italian iconoclast Gaetano Pesce has spent decades thumbing his nose at grisaille blocks of Modernism and postmodern pastiche, both of which made his eyes sting and his taste buds smart. He set out to upend the bland, the routine, the sedate, splashing Candyland colours and gooey resins on to things like spaghetti armchairs, lozenge-bedecked tennis shoes and heart-shaped lamps skewered by Cupid's arrow. He unabashedly uncaged design.

So, when Strasbourg cast off fifty years of conservative rule, electing the Socialist Catherine Trautmann mayor in 1989, Pesce brought forth 'a bridge for Europe', meant to span the Rhine and thus unite France and Germany. Also called the 'European Union Bridge', since Strasbourg was the seat of the European Parliament, it was actually twelve connecting bridges that, viewed from above, formed a huge 'S' for Strasbourg.

A dozen artificial islands supported a national pavilion for each of the member states of the European Economic Union (Holland's, for instance, had working greenhouses growing fruit and vegetables, while France's was in the shape of its heavy-lift space vehicle, the Ariane rocket); in between, canals formed the outlines of the frontiers, producing a large map of Europe. This being Pesce, each of the twelve sections of road was in a different lollypop colour.

As with all bridges, Pesce's drew two sides together – in this case a continent, too – but his utopian dream was dismissed as a 'beautiful political failure … a crazy project [for] the representation of an ideal Europe'. It was idealism, indeed, that killed the bridge.

SKYLIGHT SPORT CENTRE
Josep Miàs
Port d'Envalira (AD), 2015

The highest paved road in the Pyrenees winds through the pass known as the Port d'Envalira, in Andorra, nearly 2,500 m (8,200 ft) above sea level. The Tour de France has made the climb famous, as has skiing in the nearby mountains. For centuries the pass was nothing more than a mule path – a smuggler's route – and until the first decade of the twentieth century there was just a tiny shepherd's hut on the site of what is now the closest town, El Pas de la Casa.

By the 1950s Envalira had taken on new importance. The French government wanted to build an advanced telecommunications tower, which opened in 1964. The Radio Sud building, 86 m (282 ft) tall, was decommissioned in 1981, but the pinnacle of the mountain grew into a skier's paradise. In 2015 the principality of Andorra held an ideas competition for a high-altitude, high-performance cycling and winter sports centre that would double as a threshold to the landmark radio tower. Mias's practice, MIAS Architects, won with a set of four sleek turtle-back pavilions arched like the limestone outcroppings smoothed by glaciers. Each concrete roof canopy was punctured by a skylight conforming to the curvature of the carapace. At ground level, a long window followed the contours of the rugged landscape, taking on the form of an epicanthic fold. These elongated glass-walled eyes were all that was visible of the 9,000 sq. m (96,875 sq. ft) structures dug into the snowdrifts of the alpine-white mountain pass. The buildings, the architects said, should be 'understood as new topography that joins the actual landscape'. In January 2022, however, construction began on a completely different sports centre.

FRANCE, ANDORRA

ECHEVARRIA
Ricardo Bofill
Bilbao (ES), 1977

Long before Bilbao was revived through a raft of urban projects in the 1990s (symbolized most notably by the Guggenheim Bilbao), the struggling city worked to reverse its fortunes through new architecture while also – somewhat paradoxically – attempting to maintain its industrial legacy. In 1976 the Echevarria steel company, a dominant figure in the city's economy and politics, hired the Barcelona architect Ricardo Bofill to design a new residential development on the site of its factory in the city's Errekalde district. Bofill was no stranger to reusing old industrial buildings, having developed his own office, La Fábrica (1973), inside the bones of an old cement factory on the outskirts of Barcelona. 'I have a weakness for towns undergoing transformation that do not want to remain anchored in the past,' he once said. Inspired by the scale and design of the factory's cavernous halls, the mixed-income housing development, which Bofill called a 'garden city', contained tall, hulking residential towers, schools and public facilities. The towers, resembling medieval castle walls, edged a classically inspired, publicly accessible central park, complete with fountains, topiary, hedge mazes, flower gardens and statuary.

The city council claimed the company never filed its paperwork for the project, and the development became bogged down in lawsuits. By 1987 the city had bought the land, and held a competition that drew such schemes as a zoo, a cable car and an enormous auditorium. None went forward, and the city eventually built a public park on the site.

WINE DOME
Mansilla + Tuñón Architects
Valbuena de Duero (ES), 2010

In 2008 the government of the region of Castilla y León, in northwestern Spain, announced that it would commit €1 billion over the next ten years to a programme called 'Cúpulas del Duero', 'Domes of the Duero'. Five buildings would be located along the Duero River Valley, emblems of the area's history, culture, agricultural heritage and commitment to sustainable development. Mansilla + Tuñón Architects was awarded two of the structures: the Energy Dome; and the Wine Dome, a visitor centre devoted to viticulture.

While the Energy Dome was tied up in endless lawsuits but was eventually constructed, if only partially, the Wine Dome remained a paper proposition. The architects used the term 'isotropy' – uniformity in all directions – to describe the winery shed. The vineyards along the banks of the Duero, Emilio Tuñón said, are planted in 'obsessive repetition'. They are also utterly horizontal. So, too, the building, whose gridiron of concrete troughs and beams resembled a painting by the American artist Sol LeWitt: perfectly parallel lines intersecting other sets of perfectly parallel lines.

The Dome was 86 m (282 ft) square, with an internal courtyard created by subtracting a square from the roof grid. The purloined piece was a gazebo by the river. The building was sunk to a level lower than the vineyards, allowing it to dissolve into the rows and rows of grapes. Tuñón commented that the landscape was, in reality, an artificial abstraction, and the Dome was just an extension of that fact. A shaky economy led the local government to divert the €15 million it had allocated for the Dome, halting the project.

LA CIUDAD EN EL ESPACIO
Ricardo Bofill
Madrid (ES), 1968

Of all Ricardo Bofill's imaginative housing ideas, none was as outright utopian as his vision for 'The City in Space' of 1968. First launched as a theoretical exercise (and book), the vivid concept morphed into a real project just a year later, when Madrid's Ministry of Housing – led by Bofill family ally Vicente Mortes – gave Bofill's studio a plot for the project in the city's Moratalaz district.

The goal was to create a neighbourhood-scale housing project from a conglomeration of overlapping, modular components that could grow and morph over time in response to changing demands. The base structure took the form of a fractal three-axis grid of concrete and steel blocks, which could be customized and expanded in virtually any way. Half of the space on each floor was reserved for communal use, circulation and gardens, forming highly social 'streets' and 'squares' in the air. Inspired by (and in turn inspiring) such in-progress Bofill housing projects as Barrio Gaudí in Reus, northeastern Spain, and Walden-7 in Barcelona, Bofill's vision instilled the urban planning principles of great historic cities into a single mega-project.

The undertaking was killed when a new city regime, fearful of 'subversive' urban ideas, was installed. Carlos Arias Navarro, an opponent of the project, became Minister of the Interior, and Mortes was relieved of his position. But Bofill's dreams of urban transformation would come true in future projects, many times over. The poet José Agustín Goytisolo contributed an essay to a book about Bofill's firm, *Hacia una Formalización de la Ciudad en el Espacio* (1968), in which he notes: 'Everything was going to change because in dreams/ Impossible things happen easily.'

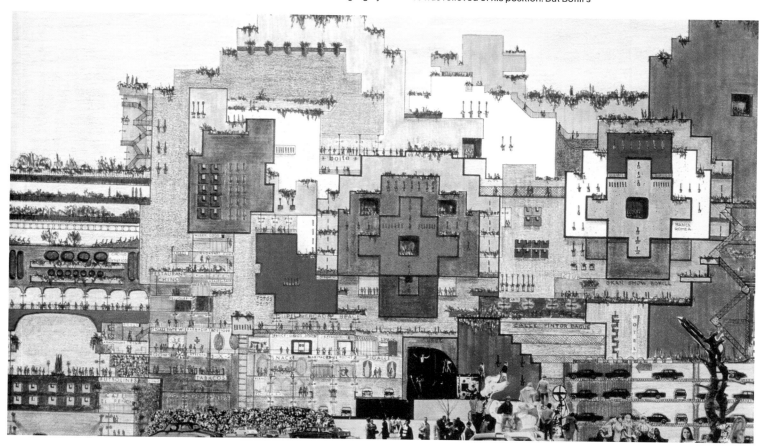

TELEFÓNICA TOWER
Alberto Campo Baeza
Madrid (ES), 2000

In 1999 Alberto Campo Baeza was awarded second place in a competition to build Ciudad Telefónica, on the northern outskirts of Madrid. Madrid's *El País* newspaper described the 271,000 sq. m (2.9 million sq. ft), 54 billion peseta ($334 million) 'Telephone City', with room for 10,000 employees, as 'pharaonic'.

But Baeza's single square tower 350 m (1,148 ft) tall defied the implied complexity and multiplicity of a sprawling corporate campus. The architect from Valladolid, Spain – who, ironically, didn't watch television and didn't own a mobile phone ('that happy device', as he called it), presented Juan Villalonga, the director of Spain's telecommunications giant, Telefónica, with a concise, controlled and tightly contained tower wrapped in non-reflective, corrugated stainless steel. Rising above a stone podium, four bolt-upright legs held six horizontal openframe girders or Vierendeel trusses, spaced twelve floors apart. From this rigid framework Baeza hung six modules, each with office buildings in a push-pull relationship to the upright nucleus. Some of the buildings would extend as much as 9 m (30 ft) beyond the perimeter of the square supports, while others would sit the same distance within. The result was a chequerboard of patios, eaves and floating buildings arranged in a genuinely vertical city. Baeza's tower, which would have been Madrid's tallest, lost to a low-slung, coruscating, serpentine design by Antonio and Carlos Lamela. The corporate accountants at Telefónica, however, backed away from the winner, skipped Baeza, and brought in third-place Rafael de La-Hoz to complete his glazed fortress, with four watchtowers guarding the perimeter; it became the largest glassed-in complex in Europe.

OUR LADY OF GUADALUPE
Enrique de la Mora y Palomar
Madrid (ES), 1960

After his design for a parabolic library at the Instituto Tecnológico in Monterrey was dropped, Enrique de la Mora y Palomar spent many years seeking a way to make concrete into a diaphanous shroud, like a delicate fabric draped over supporting columns. He designed and built at least eight projects using hyperbolic-parabo-loids, each time applying the experience gained from previous designs and further exploring the possibilities of the form.

For this church in Madrid, de la Mora produced a design with eight continuous tent structures, barely pinned to the raised stone plaza on which it rested – an essay in visual lightness with a cloak-like mantle that looked as if the wind had blown it open. The centrepiece among these thin-shell parabolas was the towering nave, its octagonal interior clamshell-shaped walls standing on four concrete pillars. From a dis-tance, one could imagine that de la Mora had in mind eight *mantillas* (the veils worn by Cath-olic women worshippers) gathered into a single, wafting scalloped lace cloth.

The concept of small parabolas encircling one soaring canopy began on paper, only to be erased. By 1965, when Our Lady of Guadalupe was finally built, the hyperbolic waves of de la Mora's early design had given way to more or less flattened butterfly wings, with the high nave poking out above. The church, exquisite in its own right, was nonetheless nicknamed 'El Sombrero Mexicano', for its obvious resem-blance to the pointed, protruding crown of the hat worn by the Mexican revolutionary Zapata.

GERMAN TENNIS CLUB
Carl Fieger
Barcelona (ES), 1926

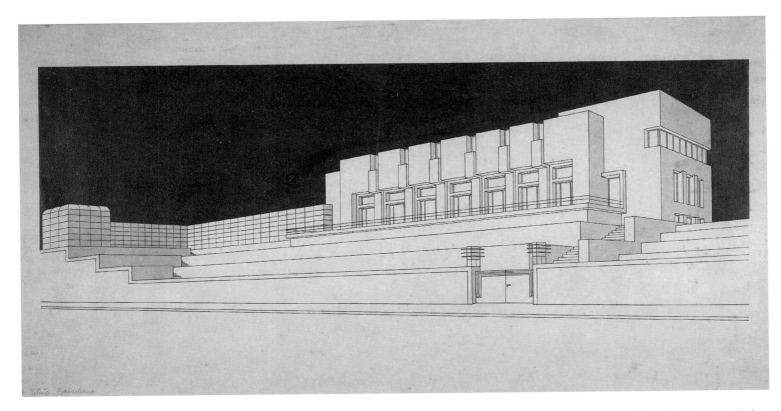

The name Walter Gropius is synonymous with Bauhaus, but camera-shy Carl Fieger was the quiet visionary who helped to create the avant-garde school in Dessau; Gropius could not draw, while Fieger could. His designs remain the definitive expression of the school's legendary buildings. And, while a few cognoscenti know Fieger's name, fewer understand the critical role he played. This was not just at the Bauhaus, but as an early innovator in his own right, from his 'round house' (1924), built from a standardized kit of parts, to his prefabricated house – the first in the German Democratic Republic – in 1953. Fieger's tennis club is believed to have been designed for the Barcelona International Expo-sition in 1929. The two-storey clubhouse, with tennis courts and a bowling alley, was a terraced complex on a slope directly above the sea. The facade is a powerful, moulded concrete surface, animated by the dynamic interplay of projecting window frames, imposing lintels, deeply incised windows and crisp, Mondrian-like patches of colour – red, white, blue-grey, black – ensuring that this is not a stolid box. A slender glass ar-cade extends from one corner of the clubhouse, becoming a modified L shape ending in a square glass pavilion. This steel-and-glass annex is an adaptation of the workshop wing of the Bauhaus building, which was completed around the same time as the Barcelona club, and in whose design Fieger played a key part.

Fieger's tennis club was largely forgotten, like much else of his work. Had it been built, it would probably still have been overshadowed by Ludwig Mies van der Rohe's German Pavilion, which was recognized almost instantly as an indisputable emblem of Modernism.

HÔTEL À MINORQUE
Pascal Hausermann
Minorca (ES), 1966

One of the pre-eminent bubble architects of the 1960s, Pascal Hausermann began experimenting with cell structures moulded from concrete, and later from polyester and polyurethane, to liberate architecture from a framework of rules in favour of free expression. With his confrères Chanéac (Jean-Louis Rey) and Antti Lovag, he founded the 'Habitat Evolutif'. Hausermann sought a thoroughly flexible building form that would evolve 'with the life it contains. It takes on the individuality of the spirit that inhabits it.' A house, he said, is no longer a straitjacket, a prison. He perfected a concrete veil system whereby shotcrete-encased self-supporting frames of chicken wire and steel reinforcing rods that could be twisted into a variety of shapes. Most of them resembled some type of bivalve.

Hausermann's hotel on the Mediterranean island of Minorca consisted of several layers of cells, resembling clams sunbathing on a rocky shore. Actually, these guest rooms were raised on splayed, telescoping steel legs. Large oval windows facing the sea reinforced the impression of a colony of living creatures that had crawled out of the sea. At the centre of the group was a large, glass-enclosed restaurant, its roof dipping in a sequence of hyperbolic curves pivoting around a central chimney that projected upwards like an outsized barnacle. The restaurant, too, was supported on massive steel legs. Down the slope stood the long swimming pool, with oyster-shaped windows in the deep end to allow bathers to take in the view. In common with many of Hausermann's mid-1960s commissions, the project seems to have died for lack of money.

PRAÇA MARTIM MONIZ
Tomás Taveira
Lisbon (PT), 1981

Tomás Taveira was one of Portugal's early adopters of postmodernism. Beginning in the early 1970s, he sketched a Pop art view of Lisbon, discarding the form-function dialectic in favour of orchestrating a psychological experience of the city based on the shapes and, he wrote, smells of its streets.

The neighbourhood around the large Praça Martim Moniz (Martim Moniz Square), at the centre of the city, dates from the Christian reconquest of Lisbon in 1147. By 1981, many of the ancient, narrow blocks had been razed, obliterating the identity of the area and leaving a *tabula rasa* awaiting a Modernist resurrection. But Taveira thought otherwise. His plan for Martim Moniz Square plundered the symbols of the city's living past in a sequence of towers poking up through a high podium, a clutch of scalloped pavilions sandwiched against the ramparts below the hill of São Jorge, and blocks of gable-roofed housing surrounding the square and marching up the hilly streets behind it. Although his orderly layout is a clear departure from the meandering streets of nearby Alfama and Mouraria – neighbourhoods that once comprised the Moorish core of Lisbon – Taveira's buildings and their relationship to the squares, large and small, that he conceived echoed the intimacy and inhabited feeling of those places. His houses, built above arcades, were pastel-coloured – further echoing old Lisbon – and were composed of abstract geometries using the characteristic azulejo tiles to evoke yet again the sensation of the city, without mimicking it. Taveira's proposal was rejected by the city authorities. But, in common with the decades'-worth of plans that preceded it, his competitor's plan was not built either.

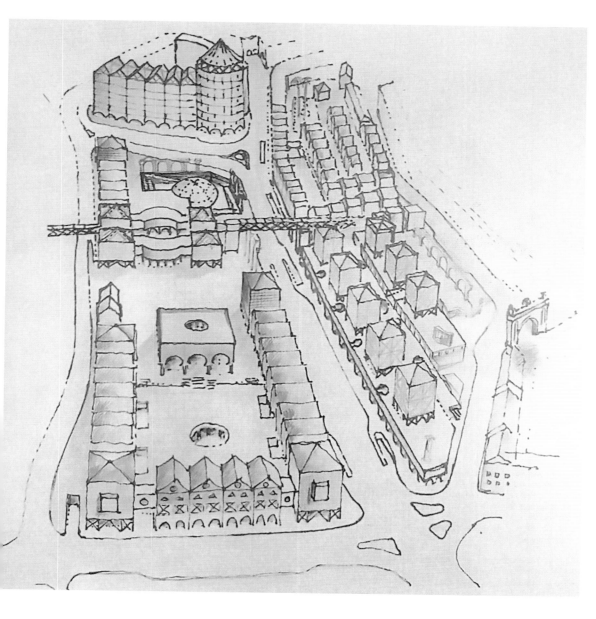

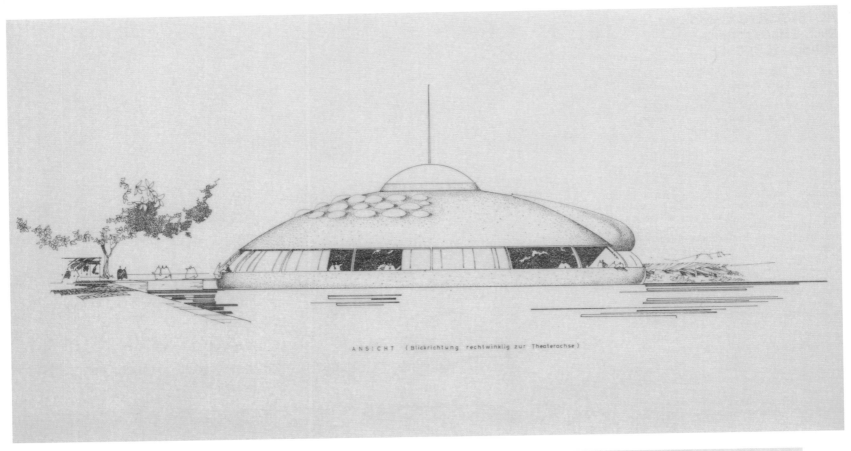

ANSICHT (Blickrichtung rechtwinklig zur Theaterachse)

THEATRE-BOAT
Justus Dahinden
Zurich (CH), 1970

The visionary Swiss architect Justus Dahinden was a critic of orthodox Modernism, veering in his work from pure functionalism into the realms of human spirit, sensation and sociality. Employing advanced technology, he dedicated his expressive designs to enhancing well-being, civic discourse and other utopian building ide-

als, in typologies ranging from housing prototypes to entire cities. He got quite a lot built, such as the pyramid-shaped Ferrohouse (1970) in Zurich, the spherical Mityana Cathedral in Uganda (1964) and the comically postmodern Library for the Technical University of Vienna (1987), with its square stone slabs and gigantic owl column.

In his home town, Zurich, Dahinden sketched out a 'theatre-boat' on the lake, a flying saucer-like, water-borne cultural centre that he named 'Drops on the Water'. It was one of sev-

eral concepts – including a metallic superstructure supported by pontoons, a 'floating island' deployed by tugboat, and a mysterious glowing dome – submitted to the city's Committee for a Floating Cultural Centre on Lake Zurich, and eventually made into an impressive book. Steering around the breathtaking lake to create changing performance environments, the facility had a stage with a sliding floor, making it suitable for theatre, music, civic events and even church services. Its intimate 'total theatre' design would unite actor and viewer, while in

the adjacent restaurant a continuous band of glazing and barnacle-shaped skylights would envelop visitors in the natural surroundings. The command centre was above the stage, in a domed space topped by a large antenna. But none of the book's proposals came to fruition, a function of local uneasiness with development, and the inability of the varied communities around the lake to come to consensus.

7132 HOTEL AND ARRIVAL
Morphosis
Vals (CH), 2015

From the time Peter Zumthor's Therme Vals opened in an out-of-the-way hamlet in Switzerland's Graubünden canton in 1996, the spa was a Mecca for design pilgrims. The labyrinth of naturally heated pools, walled in by compressed stone and concrete, was described as sensuous, quiescent, elemental, transcendent. When the people of Vals decided to sell their publicly owned landmark, Zumthor (who had been awarded the Pritzker Prize in 2009 in large part because of the baths) tried to buy them, but lost to the local developer Remo Stoffel. Stoffel, an architecture buff, launched a competition for a luxury hotel next door, then defied his own jurors and hired another Pritzker laureate, Thom Mayne, to add frisson to Zumthor's legendary reticence.

Mayne's firm, Morphosis, unveiled a mirror-clad 380 m (1,247 ft) tower (the height of the Empire State Building), which the firm described as 'transparent and slim' and 'a minimalist act' that 'reiterates the site and offers to the viewer a mirrored, refracted perspective of the landscape'. 'As in all our work,' Morphosis continued, 'the connection to site becomes paramount.' Slender as an aspen, the shiny six-sided irregular polygon would have been the tallest building in Europe. There would be only 107 guest rooms: the cheapest at 1,000 Swiss francs (£920) a night, the penthouse going for an eye-popping 25,000 Swiss francs (£23,000).

The skyscraper was dismissed as Luftschloss, a castle in the air. But Stoffel had the last laugh. He launched House of Architects, seven rooms at the spa designed by four of the world's biggest globetrotting architects: Tadao Ando, Kengo Kuma, Mayne and Zumthor himself.

APPARTEMENTS DE VACANCES MERUGNOUD
André Gaillard
Crans (CH), 1968

In the late 1950s the Swiss architect André Gaillard travelled the globe looking for ideal places to build resorts. He bought beaches in Haiti, land on the Mediterranean in Catalonia, Spain, and slopes in the village of Vercorin, in the Swiss Alps. And, although most of his work was in Geneva, his heart seemed to lie elsewhere, in the spectacular mountains overlooking the Rhône, where, an avid skier, he searched for the perfect spot for a resort. He found one, the untouched heights of Aminona, and for twenty years worked as architect-promoter of the new alpine site. There, he undertook twenty-three enormous prefabricated concrete and wood towers with inverted butterfly roofs, but only three of them were completed, since people just weren't buying the non-chalet design.

Gaillard didn't stop at Aminona, however; he set his sights on nearby Crans, an alpine village across the ridge from Aminona. For it he proposed a spectacular twenty-five-storey apartment building, a cross between a timber-framed chalet and a steel-framed skyscraper. The result was a hybrid fir tree that managed to allow the Alps to be breathtaking while still making a powerful impression of its own.

Although Gaillard's visions for the Alps remained central to his architecture, he provided almost no commentary on his work, leaving the draw-

ings to speak for themselves. Why the Crans apartments failed is not documented. It probably didn't help when Gaillard's bankers went bust, and the hostility of locals to his essentially urban ideas may have delivered the *coup de grâce*.

FESTSPIELHAUS
Hans Poelzig
Salzburg (AT), 1922

Hans Poelzig, arguably Germany's most exuberant Expressionist architect, found a perfect client in the legendary theatre director Max Reinhardt, who in 1919 hired him to redesign Berlin's Schauspielhaus (playhouse), resulting in a grandiose, ornately detailed concoction aptly nicknamed the 'stalactite cave'. In 1920 the two men reconnected to dream up a gargantuan Festspielhaus (festival theatre) for Reinhardt's new Salzburg Festival, in Hellbrunn Palace Park on the southern edge of the city. The location, which was set 'apart from the urban everyday hustle and bustle', as Reinhardt noted, would allow people to 'make a pilgrimage in the summer rest days, freed from their worries and efforts'.

Designed to combine several structures (including theatres, workshops, rehearsal halls, terraces and a restaurant) and merge with the hilly topography of its site, the mountain-like, cone-pyramid building, superimposed with circular arcades and rounded arches, resembled a fattened Tower of Babel or a nightmarish wedding cake. The elliptical main auditorium, evoking a towering grotto, was resplendent with rhythmic detailing and supported by concrete bows. Poelzig, who saw his work as an extension of the German Baroque, took inspiration from the area's Baroque-era Hellbrunn Palace and the Hellbrunn Stone Theatre, a former quarry transformed in the sixteenth century into a dramatic venue.

Runaway inflation and a lack of international financial help forced the architect to scale back his plans, and eventually doomed the project. The palace's stables served temporarily as a festival venue. In the 1950s the renowned modernist architect Clemens Holzmeister partnered with Reinhardt to carry out the director's Grosses Festspielhaus, a comparatively minimalist design in Salzburg's old town; it was completed in 1960.

UNIVERSITY OF APPLIED ARTS
Wolfgang Tschapeller
Vienna (AT), 2012

Established in 1867 as the Imperial Royal Arts and Crafts School, the University of Applied Arts Vienna (also known as the Angewandte) is a European trendsetter. In 2012 the avant-garde Viennese architect Wolfgang Tschapeller

won a competition to expand and renovate its facilities.

Tschapeller's radical proposal involved demolishing a newer structure linking the Wörle-Schwanzer and Ferstel buildings, which blocked an internal courtyard and kept these two historic structures from standing on their own. In its place he proposed what he called 'The Broadway', a large, ebullient stair extending from the exposed columns and slabs of the Wörle-Schwanzer building behind a remarkable shifting, suspended curtain wall, filled with stu-

dio spaces, cantilevers, and varied conical, spherical and waving extrusions. The frenetic addition would be 'a marketplace for cross-disciplinary projects', Tschapeller noted, its transparency helping to showcase the students' concepts to the city. On its roof the architect proposed two large pneumatic structures, to signal special occasions.

But Tschapeller didn't fit the mould for the organizer of the project, the Federal Real Estate Company. In 2014 the company put out a new tender, awarding the project to the established

local firm Riepl Kaufmann Bammer, which created essentially the opposite of Tschapeller's plan: a restrained reinforced-concrete-and-glass box focusing its attention inwards. Another entrant, Coop Himmelb(l)au, sent out an email comparing Riepl Kaufmann Bammer's scheme to a 'prison courtyard', and asking, 'Does it necessarily have to be the worst project which will now be realized?'

AUSTRIA

SPORTS CENTRE FOR VIENNA
Pier Luigi Nervi
Vienna (AT), 1953

The Italian master engineer Pier Luigi Nervi's Palazzetto dello Sport in Rome is considered one of the Eternal City's great modern wonders. Built in 1957 for the 1960 Olympics, its intricate, ribbed concrete-shell dome, braced by flying buttresses, evokes a sense of awe similar to that of being inside the Pantheon.

Several years earlier Nervi, along with his son Antonio, had proposed a similar building for Vienna that is widely considered to be the Rome project's prototype. Dropped in like a spaceship near the historic centre of the Austrian capital, the arena was much larger than the Palazzetto, accommodating 8,400 spectators in a main hall as well as administration, support and smaller gymnasia along the periphery. But its ceiling, composed of corrugated precast ferrocement ribs, is virtually identical to that of the Rome project, supported by inclined struts of precast concrete and an edge ring beam. (A second roofing skin ensured insulation.) The advantages of this new system included lightness, strength, mesmerizing detail, facility in building, and the consistent diffusion of light and sound. Unlike in Rome, the arena's roof contained a band of glazing near the edge, allowing glowing natural light (and perhaps too much heat?) into the arena. While the main hall was accessed via ramps, four zigzagging external concrete staircases added another sculptural element to the ensemble.

The competition was won by the Austrian architect Roland Rainer. His canted Wiener Stadthalle remains a modern monument, as well as the country's largest indoor arena.

GAUHALLE FOR VIENNA
Franz Pöcher
Vienna (AT), 1938

The megalomaniacal dictator Adolf Hitler fancied himself a city-planning expert. Reams have been written about Germania, his grandiose vision of a renewed Berlin, overseen by the Reich's chief architect, Albert Speer. But thanks to research by the Austrian planner and urban historian Klaus Steiner, son of an SS officer, the world learned as recently as 2011 that Hitler was equally obsessed with refashioning Vienna, the capital of his home country, which he called 'a pearl to which I will give a proper setting'. Among other ideas for the metropolis – bombastic memorials, stadia, factories, palaces, plazas, administrative buildings, bridges and roads – the Führer planned to flatten Vienna's Jewish quarter and (similar to Germania) replace it with a long marching street, crossing the River Danube, a triumphal arch at one end and a gigantic domed building at the other: the Gauhalle, or regional hall. According to designs by Franz Pöcher, a protégé of Speer, the meeting space, 350 m (1,148 ft) tall, ringed by arched entryways, buttressed with curved ribs and topped by a massive Nazi eagle, would be fronted by a colonnaded plaza and framed by a sweeping reflecting pool, fed by the Danube Canal.

Pöcher's plans, which he submitted just after the *Anschluss* in 1938, marked the beginning of the city's redesign. (That was to be overseen by another Speer employee, Hanns Dustmann). But by 1942 Hitler, in part consumed by his schemes for Linz – which he envisioned as the 'German Budapest' – had lost enthusiasm for the plans for Vienna. In 1942 Speer ordered the stoppage of all 'construction contractors' on 'non-war related projects' in the city. The Nazi defeat in 1945 doomed the plans for good.

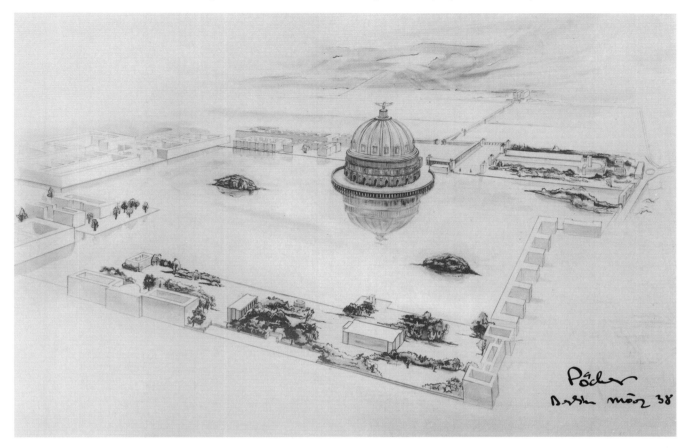

HIGH-RISE BUILDING FOR KARLSPLATZ
Leopold Bauer
Vienna (AT), 1933

The Viennese architect Leopold Bauer, a prominent student of the pioneering Modernist Otto Wagner, helped to shape the intricate, radical, geometric forms of the Vienna Secession. But by 1910 his style (and politics) had shifted dramatically to the right, veering towards the Classical and Baroque, a move that damaged his reputation with local critics and colleagues. In the early 1920s he used this language to envision cities filled with 'cathedrals of work', massively scaled offices and factories inspired to some degree by American skyscrapers.

In 1933, reportedly with the support of the authoritarian Austrian chancellor Engelbert Dollfuss, Bauer began designing a sixteen-storey reinforced-concrete-framed headquarters for the country's right-wing Christian Socialist government on Vienna's important town square, Karlsplatz, to celebrate the country's (temporary) economic resurgence 'in a way that is visible to the city of Vienna as well as to all foreigners who visit us'. After Dollfuss's assassination in 1934, the project was to become a memorial to his government, while providing thousands of direly needed construction jobs. The form of the glass-clad edifice combined Bauer's two most popular symbolic motifs: the three-tiered pyramid and the triumphal arch. At the pyramid's crown was a stained-glass-enclosed chapel topped with a large cross.

In 1935 the plan, like all Bauer's previous skyscraper proposals, failed. The economic and political situation was deteriorating rapidly (Germany would invade just three years later), and Bauer's notorious boastfulness and tall tales were making him increasingly unpopular in Vienna. His greatest successes came far from the capital, in his native Moravia, where he was able to complete a diverse array of houses, churches, factories, hospitals and, yes, offices.

MONTE CARLO PUBLIC PARK AND RESIDENCES
Emilio Ambasz
Monte Carlo (MC), 1998

The principality of Monaco, on the French Riviera, is the second-smallest and most densely populated country in the world, and one of the richest. Its millionaire residents are squeezed into just over 2 sq. km (less than one square mile) of land – a patch smaller than New York's Central Park.

In 1998 the monarch, Prince Rainier III, gave Emilio Ambasz the job of figuring out how to eke out a speck more land on which a park, hotels and apartments could be built. A plan existed to build an artificial peninsula on the coast, in water 80 m (262 ft) deep, but Ambasz had another idea: to remake the city's tiny harbour. He wanted to push the existing quay out towards the mouth of the port by building an earth-and-concrete dam in the waters of the shallow inlet. The face of the dam would trace a line that inverted the double-arch outline of the existing waterfront, giving the foreshortened port the same length of dockage as it previously had; after all, what would Monaco be without 90 m (295 ft) yachts moored in its front yard? Through Ambasz's plan Monte Carlo would grow by 10 hectares (25 acres). The project was arboreal, covered entirely in flora, following the architect's belief that buildings and nature are not separate.

The cost of the scheme, Ambasz says, would have been about €300m, about one-sixth of that of the offshore reclamation project. However, in 2005 Prince Rainier died, and his son Albert II decided not to proceed. Ambasz observed wryly, 'This was another one of my projects I lost because it was too cheap.'

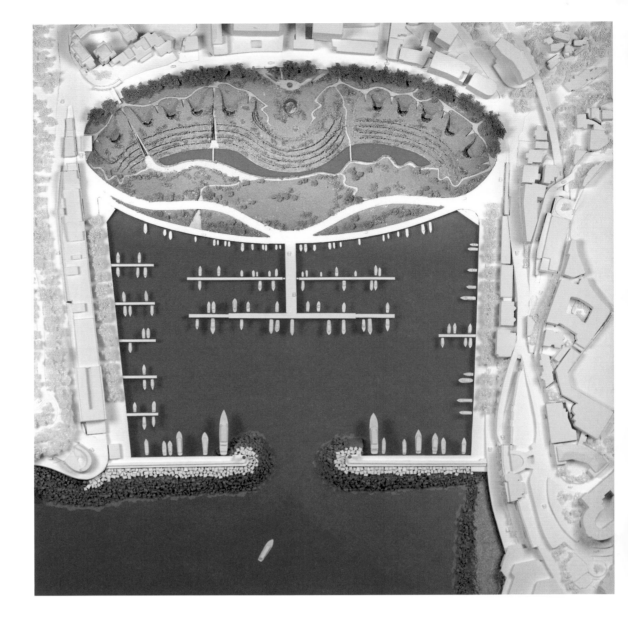

PALAZZO DEI CONGRESSI
Aldo Rossi
Milan (IT), 1982

For Aldo Rossi, architecture was a deeply personal journey with no definitive resolution. His work was rooted in the Milan of his childhood, which he described, in words and drawings, as 'a confusion of courtyards, suburban houses, roofs [and] gas storage drums'. The city – each city, for that matter, that he encountered on his life's pilgrimage – was his muse, alive with memory, shapes, shadows and the unpredictable enchantments of its occupants.

The Palazzo dei Congressi, a new conference centre in Rossi's home town, was intended to bring together fragments of Milan's architecture, roughly uniting the city's three great monuments: the Gothic Duomo, the Renaissance Revival Galleria Vittorio Emanuele II and neoclassical La Scala. The centre consisted of three halls, decreasing in size the higher they were on the site and connected along a roof-lit gallery that formed the backbone of the project. But it was Rossi's tower, with its pencil-point-sharp spire, that emphatically expressed his imaginative reconfiguration of familiar forms into an assemblage of new and old – without the cockeyed irony and cheap historical allusions of postmodernism. The apex of the cone was glass, and was to be lit at night in changing colours, a nocturnal landmark on the city skyline. Directly beneath the cone was a spherical chamber, an homage to the visionary eighteenth-century French architect Étienne-Louis Boullée, whom Rossi greatly admired.

The design of the Palazzo dei Congressi evolved through several unrealized iterations. The last, five years after the first, had a slender factory chimney – an image Rossi was to use frequently in his built projects, in reference to the collapse of industrial northern Italy.

STTS BUILDING
Piero Portaluppi
Milan (IT), 1926

The Milanese architect Piero Portaluppi has been described by his biographers as 'light-hearted and ironic'. He had been a cartoonist – which might explain his acerbic wit – but he was also a pragmatist. In his home town he designed more than one hundred buildings, from apartments to museums to a planetarium, as well as numerous hydroelectric power stations in the alpine valleys of Lombardy and Piedmont. Yet his pen seemed always to drift towards the satirical and sarcastic. In the 1920s he drew a skyscraper for New York for a make-believe company that he called SKNE, which, when pronounced in Italian would sound like 'scappane' – or 'run away!'

The STTS Building merged his impish tendencies with his earnest, inventive and decorative style. STTS was another imaginary company, but the proposal was in many ways a genuine reply to the rising tide of Rationalism sweeping through Fascist Italy. Portaluppi designed three different versions of an apartment building for Corso Sempione, a street once thought of as the Champs-Élysées of Milan. One had almost ridiculously useless triangular balconies projecting impossibly far from its face; the second, a mosaic of elongated hexagons; and the last (pictured) a crazy geometric maze extruded from its facade.

In each drawing, Portaluppi included a puckish figure – a well-dressed tramp carrying a suitcase and umbrella, with a white terrier tugging at its lead – whose posture of comic wonderment seems to ask, 'That's a building?' These proposals were, of course, dying for a client who never came along.

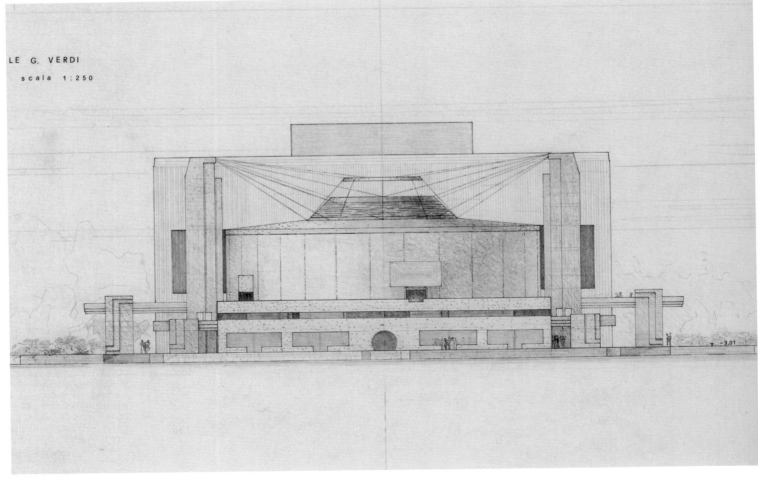

LE G. VERDI
scala 1:250

CIVIC THEATRE
Carlo Scarpa
Vicenza (IT), 1968

In 1968 the city of Vicenza invited three famed Italian architects – Franco Albini, Ignazio Gardella and Carlo Scarpa – to submit proposals for a new 1,250-seat theatre on the broad thoroughfare of Viale Roma. For his entry, Scarpa laid out a combination of grand foyer, open internal stairs and broad external terraces to make the building 'a lively place, even in the midst of everyday activity', as he put it.

The building's main component was a drumshaped auditorium (Scarpa likened it to a valve), edged by four immense columns. This would give the building 'a pretty lively plastic expressiveness', the understated architect noted, and support the theatre's roof by cables. The cable system facilitated a grand, radially ribbed circular rooflight, allowing the space to accommodate many activities outside theatre. To support diverse theatrical presentations, the stage could move horizontally via mechanical systems, which would become 'a show within the show'. The grand rectangular structure behind, containing the fly tower and support spaces, nodded to the city's renowned Palladian architecture.

Scarpa was disqualified for submitting a plan well over the allowable size and budget, but, as with so many competitions – particularly in Italy – nobody won; a combination of political timidity and public outcry doomed the endeavour. A subsequent competition in 1978, with entries from the likes of Oscar Niemeyer, also fell through. Finally, in 1987, the architect Gino Valle's project, clad with bands of red brick and white Vicenza stone, was chosen, but endless delays, including the bankruptcy of the construction firm, delayed its completion until 2007.

PALAZZO DEI CONGRESSI
Louis Kahn
Venice (IT), 1968

The American architect Louis Kahn first visited Venice on a Grand Tour in 1928, and immediately fell in love with it. He called the city, among other things, 'a pure miracle' and 'an architecture of joy'. After several trips – filled with unceasing wandering and sketching – Kahn built up a web of friends and professional colleagues that would eventually lead to his commission by the art historian and professor Giuseppe Mazzariol, director of the venerable Querini Stampalia Foundation, to design a Palazzo dei Congressi (Congress Hall) inside the Giardini della Biennale, site of the city's famous Biennale.

The Palazzo consisted of three structures, including a cube-shaped entrance hall and gallery building, connected by a network of public spaces. But after it shifted location, its primary form became – fittingly – a suspended concrete bridge structure over the canal near the Arsenale. The hammock-like building, supported by heavy piers at each end, had glazed flanks that would provide wide views to the entrance of the Grand Canal, and reveal the movement of people inside. It was topped with a series of domes as a tribute to the domes of the Basilica di San Marco.

While Kahn professed to have the utmost respect for Le Corbusier, who was then working on a hospital for Venice (one that was never built), the Swiss architect's plan was imposed on top of the city, while Kahn's grew out of his 'reverence' for it. Yet while Kahn would work with city officials for years, they eventually rejected the modern design out of concern for its ability to blend with the historical fabric.

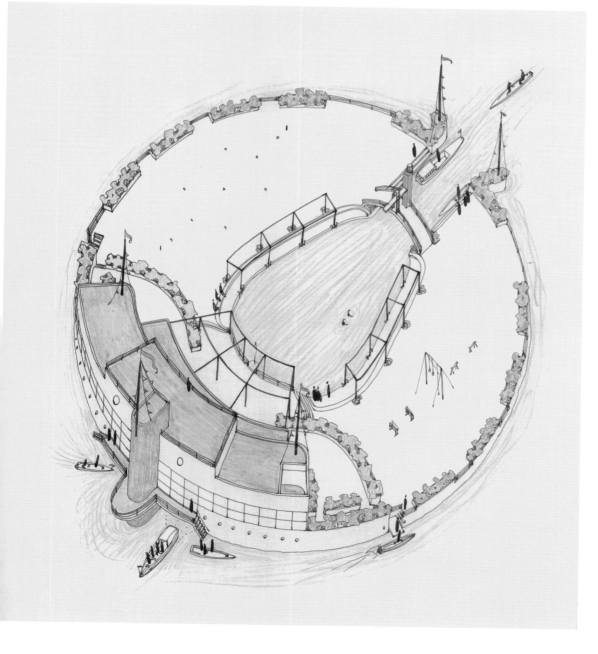

FLOATING ISLAND IN THE LAGOON FOR CHARLES DE BEISTEGUI
André Lurçat
Venice (IT), 1931

Neither the boat motif nor the floating motif of Lurçat's island in Venice was exactly novel in the architect's *oeuvre*. He was a founding member of the International Congresses of Modern Architecture, first held in 1928, but he nonetheless famously disagreed with his peers, saying that pure functionalism was '*misérabilisme*', which is loosely translated as 'the quality of enjoying being depressed'. In the late 1920s and early 30s Lurçat built the Hôtel Nord-Sud in Corsica and Villa Hefferlin in Ville-d'Avray, west of Paris, both of which, notes the historian Jean-Louis Cohen, resembled ships that had run aground. Lurçat had also proposed anchoring an aircraft carrier in the River Seine to serve as the city's airport.

Floating on a body of water was also the apogee of Lurçat's unsuccessful proposal (awarded in the end to Le Corbusier) for the aristocratic multimillionaire and self-proclaimed bohemian Charles de Beistegui's penthouse on Avenue des Champs-Élysées. Lurçat gave his patron a sequence of belvederes that culminated in an open-air pool with an unobstructed view of Paris. The residence was simply a *salon de fête*, a bachelor pad for surreal, upper-class parties. Two years later Lurçat pitched Beistegui a 'playful project' for a floating platform with a ship's stern and smokestack, lounges, an aubergine-shaped pool, swings, a sandy beach dotted with umbrellas, and a glassy residence, all fitting the bill of the earlier penthouse. It would have had spectacular views of the red-tiled roofs of Venice. But Beistegui didn't bite. In 1933 Lurçat completed his École Karl-Marx in the communist Paris suburb of Villejuif, and it was immediately hailed as 'the most beautiful school in France'.

PAGANINI THEATRE
Carlo Aymonino
Parma (IT), 1964

Carlo Aymonino, whose complex, often indefinable work centred on the intersection of city and politics, once said that the Paganini Theatre was the project he most regretted not completing. Aymonino, reacting to the sterile and deadening block apartments that were springing up in the ruins of post-World War II Italy, sought to re-create urban experiences expressing memory and the ineffable spirit of place.

The Reinach Theatre, later renamed the Paganini, in the historic centre of Parma had been bombed into oblivion during the war, leaving behind fragmentary walls at the corners of the Palazzo della Pilotta. Aymonino inserted his theatre into the rectangular void, extracting the pure forms of adjacent buildings and courtyards to give his new facade a series of shapes that reflected the internal volumes. His building maintains the formal order of the Pilotta's porch base, piano nobile and attic, recasting in concrete abstractions of the pillars, arches and flat lintels of the Renaissance building.

Aymonino lifted the entire building to maintain the ground-level pathways leading to the internal court of the palace, leaving the walkways of the old town centre unbroken. Inside, he carved out a matrix of cylindrical and prismatic spaces and crossing paths, tying the building to these complex pedestrian routes. The theatre itself, while reminiscent of Hans Scharoun's Berlin Philharmonic (1963), preserved a piece of the Reinach's history: Aymonino proposed rotating seats that would allow the space to be configured for just about any type of performance, from opera to juggling. He lost the competition to Luigi Pellegrin's underground theatre, but nothing was ever built.

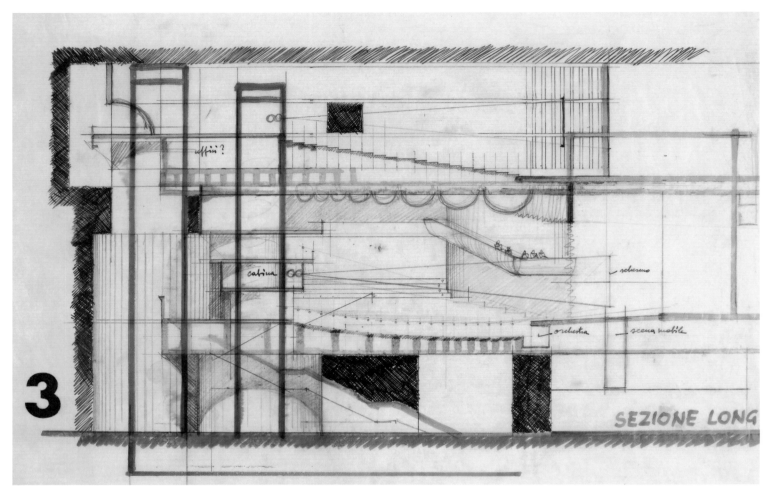

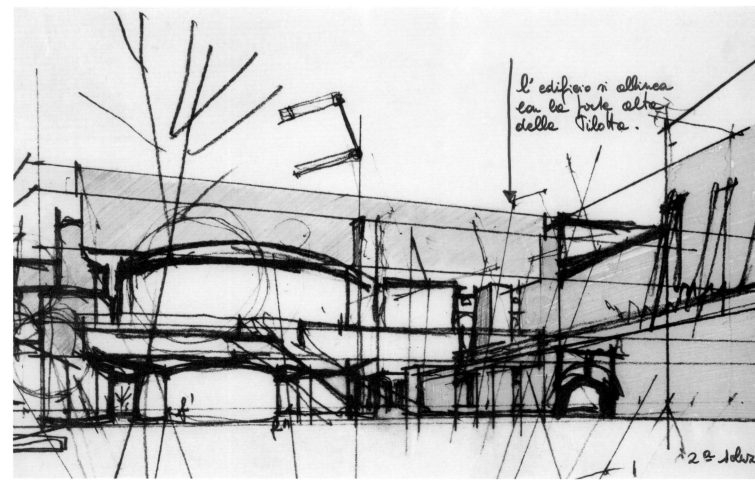

un sistema
combinato di
tre tipi di
percorsi

2ª soluzione - Carlo A

IL PORTO VECCHIO
John Portman
Genoa (IT), 1988

John Portman elevated the idea of hotel lobby from regal parlour to galactic extravaganza. For Genoa's anticipated celebration of the 500th anniversary of Christopher Columbus's departure from his home city into terra incognita, he turned his showmanship inside out.

Portman proposed installing a triangular island in the city's historic harbour, with a raised plaza shaded by a gridded sunscreen made of 'exploded' concrete columns, allowing strollers to walk through the quartered pillars supporting the canopy overhead – a nod to the medieval arcades of the city. There was also an undersea aquarium, with sail-shaped rooflights poking through the water's surface, like a flotilla moored in the marina. He intended to remove the highway cutting off the seashore from the row of twelfth-century buildings whose porticos once stood at the water's edge.

But the showstopper was a conical tower, sheathed in white Carrara marble, rising 257 m (843 ft) above the plaza. It would be the tallest tower in Europe. A ring of splayed columns at the base created a loggia opening onto a signature Portman touch: a bank of lifts to speed people to the observation deck thirty-three floors above the boats bobbing in the harbour.

The pencil-point tower was meant to 'give Genoa a visual identity, like the Eiffel Tower does to Paris or the Sydney Opera House does to Australia', Portman said when the project was unveiled. His plan was welcomed by some local press, but harshly dismissed by others as 'retrograde', and never won official approval. A different harbour aquarium, by Renzo Piano, opened in time for the Columbus quincentenary.

MUSEU DO MÁRMORE
Lina Bo Bardi
Monte Altissimo, Carrara
(IT), 1963

Lina Bo Bardi's Museu do Mármore (Marble Museum) is among the least documented of her many unbuilt works. The drawings show the architect's desire, as the architect Jane Hall has observed, to 'act like an archaeologist, observing and revealing what is already visible but not necessarily appreciated'. The crystalline, homogeneous marble of Monte Altissimo, in Italy's Apuan Alps, was discovered in 1517 by Michelangelo, who proclaimed it the finest in the world – better than the celebrated marble of nearby Carrara. On a visit to Milan, Bo Bardi quickly sketched three parallel stone-and-glass museum volumes clinging to the treacherous, sugary-white slopes of the quarry. The planar buildings shared the three-dimensional geometry of the slices cut into the twenty-million-year-old stone: flat walls, square edges, seamed lines. The long sheds were like vestibules guiding visitors through a sequence of views opening on to the quarries, the invincible, pure marble mountain, the water pouring from the alpine heights, the beech trees covering the jagged peaks. Bo Bardi projected a bridge across a ravine, leading to a wild garden planted with five enormous blocks – more references to the quarried marble forms.

The plan was stopped when the Brazilian military seized power in 1964, ousting the democratically elected president João Goulart; the junta soon shuttered Solar do Unhão, Bo Bardi's workers' museum in Salvador, in the northeastern province of Bahia. Taking up the battles of her adopted home, the Italian native despaired that back in Tuscany her design for the marble museum would be misinterpreted, especially, as she commented, 'in a country like Italy, still accustomed to judging architecturally in formal terms rather than content'. No further explanation is known for the project's demise.

FIAT NOVOLI
Aldo Loris Rossi
Novoli, Florence (IT), 1987

The name of the Neapolitan architect Aldo Loris Rossi could easily be confused with that of the famous Milanese postmodernist Aldo Rossi, but never his work. Loris Rossi was a utopian and subversive whose cues came from futurism, expressionism, ecology and Frank Lloyd Wright's organic architecture – amalgamated into indescribable concrete forms too frequently pigeonholed as Brutalism. His motto was 'break the boxes', which is precisely what he did.

Rossi was one of a group of architects recruited by Bruno Zevi – among them Richard Rogers, Leonardo Ricci, Ralph Erskine and Gunnar Birkerts – to build a business and residential centre on the site of an abandoned Fiat car factory and surrounding farmland in Novoli, less than 3.2 km (2 miles) from the dome of Filippo Brunelleschi's Cathedral of Santa Maria del Fiore in the heart of Renaissance Florence. Rossi's office structure, like the other proposed buildings, flanked a central park laid out by the landscape architect Lawrence Halprin, who orientated the project by slicing a pedestrian walkway diagonally through the old Roman road. Rossi's tower was irregular, asymmetrical, complex: a symphony of saucers, helical staircases, horizontal and vertical glass cylinders, wafer-thin, transparent offices, spires and tombstone-like slabs of concrete. The shapes and dimensions all flowed from the purposes of the interior spaces, and were, in Rossi's words, 'metropolitan fragments', which he defined as 'multifunctional spatial organisms'.

If nothing else, the building achieved one of Rossi's chief ambitions. The 'right to aesthetic quality', he wrote, 'is a requirement … at least equal to other human rights'. As the architect Giovanni Bartolozzi wrote, after a change of municipal administration, the whole project stopped and 'was thrown into the mud'.

PROGETTO DI SISTEMAZIONE DEL LITORALE DI CASTELFUSANO
Adalberto Libera
Rome (IT), 1933

In 1925 Mussolini proclaimed, 'The Third Rome will expand over other hills along the banks of the Sacred River up to the shores of the Tyrrhenian Sea.' The idea of connecting Rome to the sea was, in some ways, as old as the sea itself. The newest impetus came when the government purchased the pine forest of Castelfusano and launched a public competition to develop the Roman littoral. The location was believed to be near the site of Pliny the Younger's villa at Laurentum; for centuries architects had sketched versions of the first-century villa Pliny described.

Adalberto Libera, who will forever be associated with Mussolini's use of Rationalist architecture as imperial propaganda – his antiseptic geometry in near-perfect harmony with Il Duce's muscular image – presented an almost mystical vision for a new coastline. Using the ancient technique of tempera on wood, he painted six luminous white towers, raised on slender legs, guarding the endless quay like marble centurions. A pier, seemingly extending from infinity, bisects the waterfront, as the dark pine trees form an impenetrable line.

With his almost unbearable horizontality, repetitive monumentality and hazy wash, Libera conjures somewhere eternal, yet eternally modern. He lost the competition, which in any case amounted to nothing. Three years later a new plan was announced for La via imperiale, the 'imperial road', a bridgehead to urban development of the Tyrrhenian seaside, as part of a Universal Exposition for 1941. World War II put an end to these grandiose notions, but the idea of Rome-to-the-Sea has never died.

MOLE LITTORIA
Mario Palanti
Rome (IT), 1924

In 1924 the Milan-born, Buenos Aires expat Mario Palanti, already a devout follower of the Italian fascist leader Benito Mussolini, sent Il Duce a set of drawings entitled 'L'Eternale', which the architect described as a 'grandiose galleria–teatro–hôtel of vast proportions'. It had 4,500 rooms, 100 huge halls, a massive theatre, a concert hall, facilities for Olympic athletes, a hotel and a new parliament.

At eighty-eight storeys high, Palanti's skyscraper – twice the height of St Peter's – would be the world's tallest building, towering 350 m (1,148 ft) above Rome. At the pinnacle was a star-gazing observatory, telephone and telegraph stations, a carillon, and a lighthouse beaming its signal to the city's seven hills. The enormous, vaguely gothic, vaguely baroque tower immediately appealed to Mussolini's inflated self-regard as a political genius on the global stage. Here was a monument worthy of the fascist revolution, and the newly – and fraudulently – elected prime minister pledged that he would get it built.

Palanti had a knack for dramatic, atmospheric drawing, for imagery that packed a romantic, patriotic wallop. But a skyscraper in the heart of Rome would be a catastrophe, critics cried, a monstrous edifice dwarfing the grandeur of the ancient city. Mussolini lost his enthusiasm for Palanti's skyscraper, announcing in December 1925 his grand scheme to cleanse Rome of its medieval clutter, widen its boulevards and make it 'shine triumphantly for all peoples of the earth: gigantic, orderly, powerful as it was at the time of Emperor Augustus'. That grandiose dream, like Palanti's, would never be realized.

ARCHAEOLOGICAL MUSEUM AT SANTA MARIA IN COSMEDIN
Alessandro Anselmi
Rome (IT), 1983

The site next to the Basilica of Santa Maria in Cosmedin (recognized worldwide for its marble 'mouth of truth' mask, into which tourists have long nervously deposited their hands), adjacent to the Circus Maximus, the Palatine Hill and the River Tiber, was an ideal place for an archaeological museum. The project was proposed to city leaders by the avant-garde architect Alessandro Anselmi of the legendary urban and architectural studio GRAU (Gruppo Romano Architetti Urbanisti). Extending from the church into the river itself, the plan embodied the group's leap into unsentimental contextualism during the 1980s: exploring the area's matchless history while diving into the future.

In common with much of GRAU's work, this was a new type of building altogether: a kind of promenade/terrace/canopy/museum extending along a classical axis. Described by the writer Isabelle Auricoste as a 'rethinking of modernity in the light of archaeology' (and 'a big arrow pointing towards the Isola Tiberina'), its level, wavy promenades led to the triangular lookout, its reflection in the river completing a monumental silhouette. Several of the building's components alluded to the remarkable fragments of memory that have accumulated in its vicinity. Its long form harked back both to the tall campanile of the basilica and to the narrow valley between the Capitoline and Palatine hills, dominated by the Roman Forum, while the lookout nodded to the Portus Tiberinus, Rome's once great imperial port. As with so many modern proposals for the Eternal City's historic centre, this one never had a chance against Rome's sprawling, supremely powerful heritage-conservation apparatus.

SANCTA MARIA MATER ECCLESIAE
Luigi Moretti
Rome (IT), 1965

Luigi Moretti called his version of the Sancta Maria Mater Ecclesiae the *chiesa del concilio* (council church), because, he said, his almost impossibly indeterminate building was the embodiment of Pope John XXIII's Vatican II: a council held in 1962–5 as an attempt by the Catholic Church to face the modern world. Moretti was passionately, emotionally, yet also scientifically concerned with how humans experience the spatial qualities of buildings. His quest – modelled on the exuberant Baroque architecture of his native city, Rome – was to create contrapuntal spaces by manipulating light, form and movement. He called it 'parametric architecture', which in practice became decidedly maverick architecture.

The church of Sancta Maria – whose cornerstone had been blessed by the Pope – was meant to complete one edge of a state employees' housing project, where Moretti was architect in charge. He produced a distorted, contorted, anemone-like building, made of mounds and trumpet-arms, a temple built of converging and divergent ellipses that, Moretti said, had many 'abstract forms in an atmosphere of humanly sublime tensions'. One would enter through a sequence of compressed spaces, landing in the expansive sanctuary, large enough for 1,000 congregants. 'The interior space', Moretti wrote, 'will be elusive, formed by vaporous, continuous luminosity.' The light would enter from the opposing towers, whose mouths had tendrils, reinforcing the image of something biomorphic, and certainly not derived from historical church architecture.

The architect Adrian Sheppard, who worked with Moretti on the Watergate Development in Washington, DC, said that each of Moretti's buildings 'is a prototype … consumed by the invention of new forms'. The four massive housing blocks of the wider project were completed, but Moretti's church was scratched and a parish church was built 1.6 km (1 mile) away in 1985.

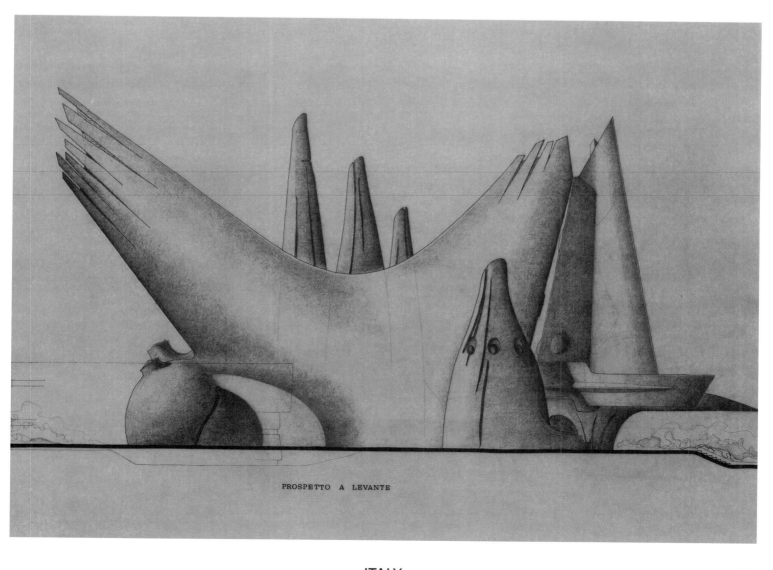

PROSPETTO A LEVANTE

PALAZZO DELL'ACQUA E DELLA LUCE
Pier Luigi Nervi
Rome (IT), 1940

In the late 1930s Benito Mussolini began planning for the 1942 Universal Exposition, colloquially known as E42, to mark the twentieth anniversary of his fascist regime coming to power. This complex of parks and gardens spread across 400 hectares (988 acres) south of Rome was supposed to launch the myth of a new imperial state, anchored by a colossal Arch of Empire, 240 m (787 ft) high and with a span of 600 m (1,969 ft), designed by Adalberto Libera and engineered by Pier Luigi Nervi. While doing the maths for the arch, Nervi also entered the competition for E42's palace of water and light, a temporary 'Historical Exhibition of Artificial Light' that, the competition stated, would include a grand fountain that would 'constitute an imaginative element of attraction, dazzling with light and water games'. Nervi designed a cubic helix, supported on three stilts and encircling a needle-thin lighthouse tower sitting in a basin of water. The open-ended spiral, which was clad in luminescent glass of the kind used for car headlights, culminated in a belvedere 'from which', he said, 'the view would have embraced everything' in the widespread exposition. Nervi's ribbon was taut and tense and eschewed any extraneous detail, expressing its own pithy geometry confidently.

The jury declined to award first prize to any of the sixteen entries, and instead asked Nervi to collaborate with two other architects on something 'more in the character of a grandiose fountain than that of a building'. Nervi declined the invitation – and, in any case, Italy's slide to defeat in World War II eclipsed further plans for E42.

MASTERPLAN FOR APRILIA
Adalberto Libera
Aprilia (IT), 1936

In the early 1930s the Fascist government of Benito Mussolini in Italy announced a plan to reclaim the Pontine Marshes, south of Rome, adding arable land and a series of new towns to this coastal region. A competition was held for Aprilia, one of the settlements, which called for a small town for 3,000 agricultural workers.

Adalberto Libera, who later designed the Palazzo dei Congressi in Rome (which is considered a monument to Italian Rationalist architecture), configured a rectangular town 720 m (2,362 ft) long by 400 m (1,312 ft) wide. On three sides he planted rows of trees to keep the winds of the Pontine from rushing through the town centre. The civic piazza was also framed on three sides by lines of trees. Each of the pillars of society – the church, the city hall and the civic theatre – has a tower, and each is represented as a perfectly distilled, logical version of itself. The

church, for instance, follows the outline of a Catholic basilica, but is without ornament or elaboration, to the point of appearing almost two-dimensional. It is the city hall, however – a cube with a long wing extending from its back – that makes this agricultural outpost into a vision of modernity. The brick facade is an unyielding repetition of deep-set windows with an andante tempo, as if to indicate that the pace of government is neither too fast nor too slow, weighty without being oppressive – or perhaps utterly unassailable and indifferent.

Most remarkable today is the way Aldo Rossi's cube-shaped red ossuary in Modena cemetery looks like a version of Libera's unbuilt centrepiece building.

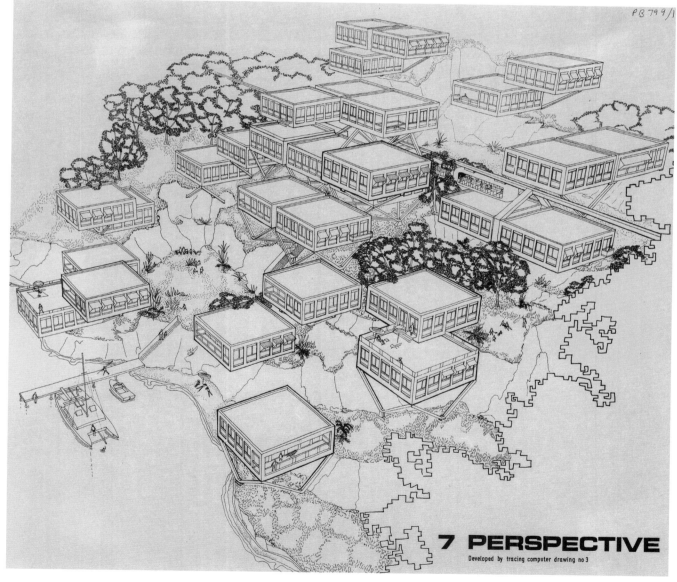

7 PERSPECTIVE
Developed by tracing computer drawing no 3

ISOLA DINO
Boyd Auger
Calabria (IT), 1968

Boyd Auger is not a name usually associated with CAD (computer-aided design) programs such as Rhino (one of Zaha Hadid's favourites) or CATIA (Frank Gehry's tool for drawing the Guggenheim Bilbao). But Auger was a pioneer who, literally, wrote the book on *The Architect and the Computer* (1972). In the late 1960s, in

collaboration with computer scientists, he designed one of the earliest computer-aided architectural design programs, later called the 'Basic Architectural Investigation and Design Program One', to improve the layout of housing developments, so that such amenities as daylight and privacy could be maximized.

All this sounds rather technocratic, but when combined with Auger's commitment to innovative structural design, the results could be stunning. When Gianni Agnelli, Italy's richest man and greatest industrial tycoon, purchased

the rocky island of Isola di Dino in the Tyrrhenian Sea, off the Calabrian coast, his firm asked Boyd to develop a scheme of 1,500 holiday homes and a hotel, for the steep limestone cliffs. Boyd's prefabricated dwellings were to be supported on space frames that would touch the ground at very few points. With the aid of his computer program, he designed an entirely random layout of concrete frames 9 m (30 ft) high with 7.5 m (25 ft) diagonals in alternate bays, allowing the modular homes to hang in the voids of the frames. Thanks to

the computer, not one house blocked the view or sunlight of another. A monorail would connect the houses. The project was cancelled, according to Auger, 'for financial reasons'.

ART MUSEUM STRONGOLI
Coop Himmelb(l)au
Strongoli (IT), 2009

From the moment the Guggenheim Bilbao opened in 1997, art museums were forced to think as much – and often more – about their buildings as about the art they contain. And architects have been co-opted into the zero-sum game of architecture supplanting art. Bold claims are glibly made, therefore, as in, 'the new Art Museum Strongoli is not only a place to experience art, but also [has] the potential to become one of the hippest destinations in southern Italy.'

This delusion – propounded by the Austrian architectural firm Coop Himmelb(l)au – wafted across the small hilltop town of Strongoli (population: 6,500) when the Milanese gallerist Carla Delia Piscitelli commissioned the museum. Perched atop Motta Grande, a plateau 1,500 m (5000 ft) high just above the town, the shimmering building was a ribbon of silvery steel flapping in an imaginary wind blowing over the lip of the escarpment. A cone-shaped structure was anchored to the summit, while a spiralling cantilever stretched out over the nothingness, seeming to defy the laws of gravity and engineering. It was bold, the heron's-beak silhouette only adding to the sense of a building aloft. Coop Himmelb(l)au said the curved skin and sculptural forms derived from the 'energy transforming parameters driven by wind and sun', which might have been true. But while the project circumnavigated the globe in news accounts, money was entirely lacking. The double entendre of the firm's name rang true: 'sky blue' and 'building in the sky' is what the proposition proved to be.

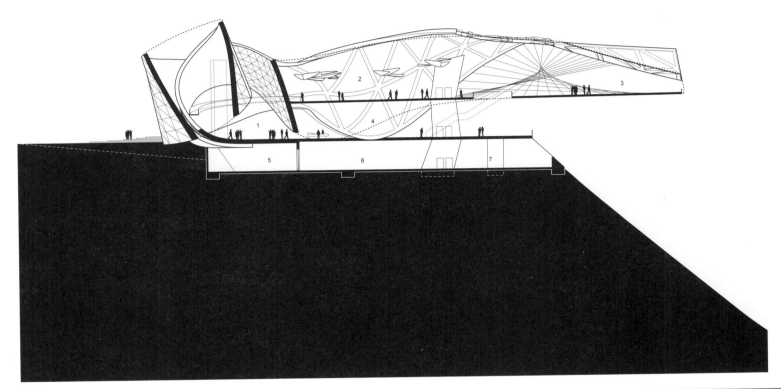

CIVIC THEATRE OF CAGLIARI
Maurizio Sacripanti
Cagliari (IT), 1964

Engaging in spatially experimental, kinetic architecture, the Roman architect Maurizio Sacripanti was so far ahead of his time that he barely managed to get any of his ideas built. In 1964 he entered a competition to reconstruct the Civic Theatre of Cagliari, the walled hillside capital of Sardinia. (The city's Teatro Politeama Regina Margherita of 1897 had been badly damaged during World War II.)

Cagliari's entry, 'Theatre in Motion', which took second prize, brought his cubist vision to the stage, presenting a machine-like playhouse filled with movable, telescoping prismatic modules, powered by hydraulics and programmed by computer punch cards, shaping the stalls, stage, floor, ceiling and more. The infinitely variable facility could accommodate any type of performance (or become the performance itself, as a moving, projecting cybernetic experience), with space, acoustics, lighting and stage configurations adjustable on demand. Theatre seats could face in any direction and be raised or lowered to any height. The building had a reinforced-concrete base and a ceiling formed by an enormous space frame, its myriad trusses supporting the moving blocks.

The competition winner (by a vote of six to five) was the team made up of Luciano Galmozzi, Pierfrancesco Ginoulhiac and Teresa Ginoulhiac Arslan. Owing to initial disagreements about the winning scheme, Sacripanti's plan was briefly considered, but eventually rejected. Construction was delayed until 1971, and completion was not until 1993. In 1976 Sacripanti won a competition to design a theatre in Forlì, near Ravenna, its stage including a similar system of movable pistons; but that project failed too.

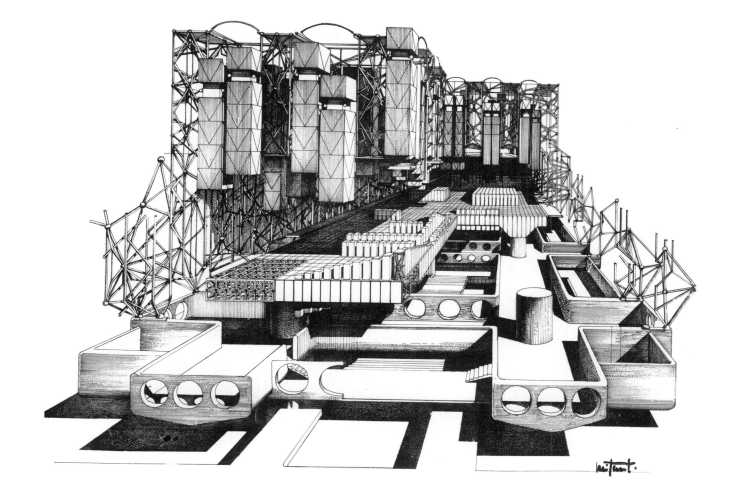

Europe
East

RU [4]

EE [2]

PL [7]

CZ [3]

HU [2]

SI [1]   HR [2]   RS [1]

BA [1]

XK [1]   TR [3]

MK [1]

AL [1]

GR [3]

ATLAS OF NEVER BUILT ARCHITECTURE

OBSERVATION AND WATER TOWER
Mart Port
Tallinn (EE), 1962

After the death in 1953 of the dictator Joseph Stalin, who had long demanded that all buildings in the Soviet Union and its republics reflect his preference for historicist monumentalism, Soviet architects went on a search for a more expressive, contemporary approach. The timing couldn't have been better; radical architecture of the 1960s was coming into its own worldwide, and Stalin's successor, Nikita Khrushchev, was incrementally improving relations with the West, leading to a degree of cross-pollination in many disciplines.

The Estonian architect Mart Port, later one of the country's most famous designers, submitted a suitably futuristic competition proposal for a lookout and water tower for Tallinn. Located in Mustamäe, a residential area edged with tree-covered hills southwest of the historic core, it was meant to become a forward-looking symbol for the city. Perhaps influenced by a nearby ski-jumping tower (which still stands), the hilltop structure was perched on reinforced-concrete legs, from which were suspended via concrete slabs a glass-enclosed, concave-roofed lookout and, below that, a truncated, barrel-shaped water tower. Antennae above suggest the building might have also served as a communications centre.

Port's rendering reveals a common graphic technique of the time: colourful ink drawing supplemented by wide strokes of dark felt-tip pen. In the depiction, residents look up at the engineering marvel, some of them appearing to cheer. No tower was built on the site, and Tallinn would have to wait until 1980 for its iconic spire: David Baziladze and Juri Sinis's television tower, made of stacked reinforced-concrete rings, which still looms 314 m (1,030 ft) over the city.

esivaade 1:10

EUROPE EAST

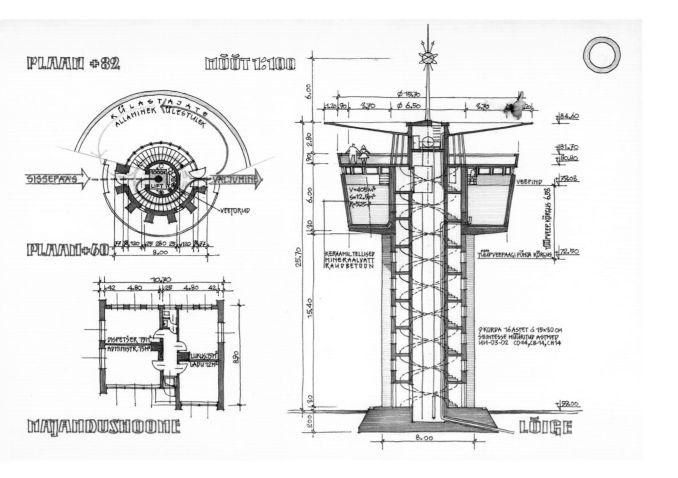

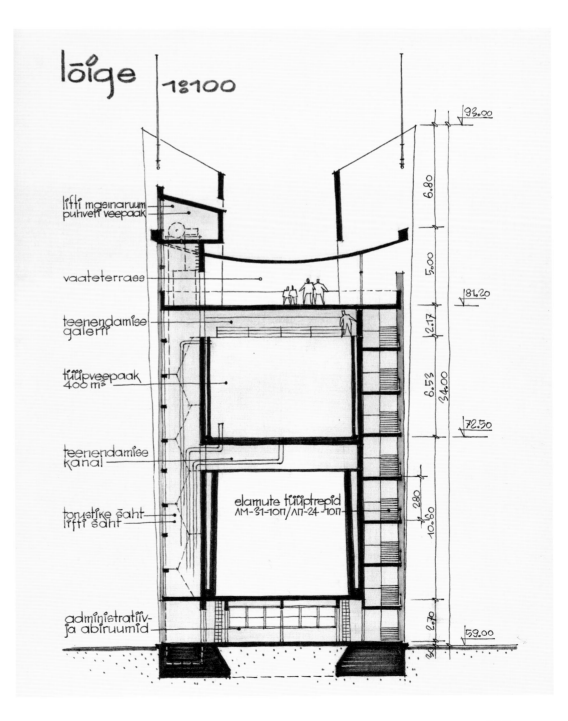

WATER TOWER RESTAURANT
Indrek Erm
Otepää (EE), 1991

In former Soviet republics such as Estonia, where the yoke of totalitarian control finally came loose in the early 1990s, architects who had toiled in relative anonymity were starting to get a taste of freedom and self-expression. In tiny, picturesque Otepää, in the south of the country, the young architect Indrek Erm was commissioned to design an ambitious new water tower at the highest point of the town, edged by a tall pine forest. Mayor Jaanus Raidal requested that it contain a café on top – a calm place to take in views of the town.

Erm's drawing, made in ink, chalk and pencil, depicts a structure that merges a massive concrete core with streamlined glass and steel flanks, lending the building a sense of both solidity and modernity, and allowing the forest to obscure its bulkier portions. The two cylindrical water tanks stand side by side in the centre, atop heavy pillars, while the slimmer edges contain a glass passenger lift, a service lift and stairs.

The idea was doomed when a new administration took over the town. Erm (who subsequently became a partner at Tallinn-based Arhitektibüroo Emil Urbel) notes that the technology of water towers was probably already outdated by the time the plan came around. The mayor, he says, wanted to employ public funds creatively to make both a new tourist attraction and a 'monument to himself'. Erm adds: 'Yes, we already had free elections, but the value of public money was still understood in a Soviet way.'

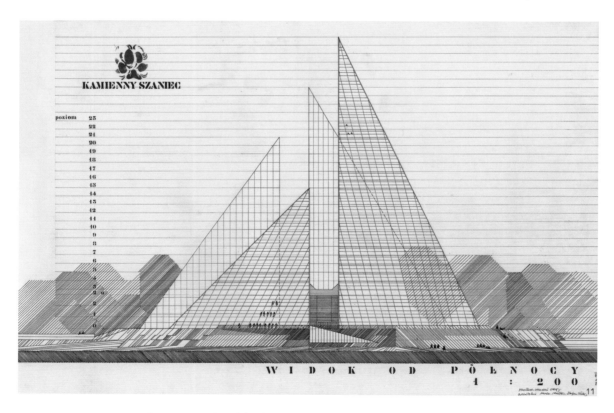

HOTEL AND RECREATION CENTRE OF THE CENTRAL COMMITTEE OF THE POLISH UNITED WORKERS' PARTY
Stefan Müller, Maria Müller
Kołobrzeg (PL), 1978

The architect, town planner and theoretician Stefan Müller spent much of his professional career on the reconstruction of the destroyed Polish city of Wrocław (formerly Breslau, Germany), as well as the smaller towns of Lower Silesia, working with his wife, Maria. Stefan Müller was no polemical historicist; in Wrocław he was working in a city with a Gothic heritage that, nevertheless, had intact works by two Expressionist giants, Hans Poelzig and Erich Mendelsohn.

The Müllers' entry to the competition for a hotel, sanitorium and resort in the Baltic Sea town of Kołobrzeg appears, at first sight, startlingly out of context. Situated in a park along the remnant of a stone rampart, the glassy, multi-storey building was composed of four pyramids attached to one another on three lower levels. The Müllers called the project the 'Stone Lair', after the ancient sea wall; the idea was that the pyramids would be visible from along the coast and from the sea, giving the appearance of a sailing ship at anchor. The pyramids were arranged in a pinwheel, and the three-sided shards were as assertively sharp as any of the work Daniel Libeskind would produce two or more decades later. Walkways emerged from gaps between the buildings, one extending as a long jetty into the sea, the others connecting to wooden boardwalks. Inside, steel I-beams and trapezoidal salons projected into the void of the central atrium.

Every conceivable amenity was in the plan, from apartments, clubs, cocktail lounges and a physiotherapy clinic, to an indoor swimming pool, newsstand and gymnasium – all behind the floating glass skin that enclosed the structures themselves. But no guest was able to enjoy the facilities; no resort centre was ever built on the Kołobrzeg waterfront.

PRZEKRÓJ A-A
1:200

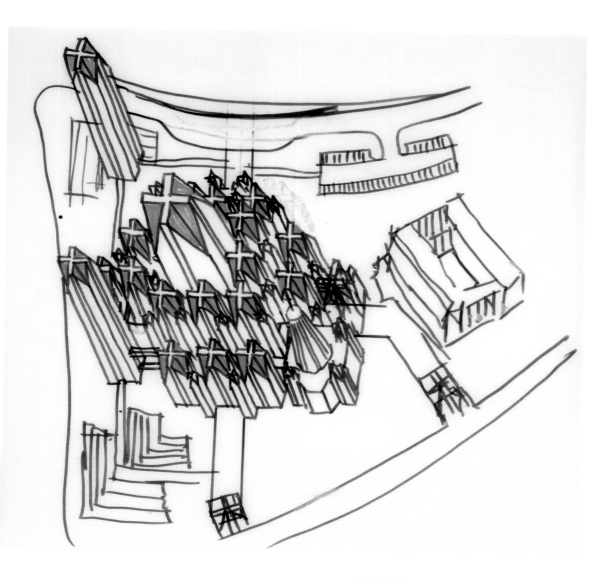

CHURCH OF THE BLESSED VIRGIN MARY, QUEEN OF POLAND
Witold Jerzy Molicki,
Maria Molicka
Gorzów Wielkopolski (PL),
1986

The prolific Polish architect Witold Jerzy Molicki won just about every (dramatic-sounding) architectural honour his country offered, from the Knight's Cross of the Order of Polonia Restituta to the Golden Badge of Merit for the Ministry of Construction. In 1986 he and his wife, Maria Molicka, also an important architect, entered a competition to design a new Catholic cathedral for Gorzów Wielkopolski, a town of just over 100,000 inhabitants in western Poland, near the German border.

Known as the Church of the Blessed Virgin Mary, Queen of Poland, the planned structure already had a complex history. In the late 1970s the parish had attempted to build a cathedral to celebrate the election to the papacy of Cardinal Karol Józef Wojtyła, Pope John Paul II. But, seeking to diminish the Church's power, communist officials had set aside for the building land in a basin that regularly flooded, and the project was soon abandoned as unfeasible. For the second iteration, a house for at least 5,000 faithful on a new site, the pair sketched a colourful, spectacularly elaborate building shaped from every variety, extrusion and axis of the symbol of the cross that one could imagine, creating a structure that, ironically, resembled a house of cards. Some versions of the scheme included a cone-shaped roof section; others installed a separate campanile. Most would contain chapels of various sizes, a large gallery, and an underground crypt.

In the end, the competition was doomed. The site again turned out to be very challenging, and a new structure was considered impossible in the context of the diocese's (and the country's) grim economic conditions.

EXTENSION OF THE ZACHETA ART GALLERY
Oskar Hansen
Warsaw (PL), 1958

The visionary Polish artist and architect Oskar Hansen was a pioneer of 'Open Form', the notion that buildings could evolve over time to meet the needs of their occupants. 'The idea is to harmoniously integrate Earth's biological life forms with the space of human activity,' he explained. In response to a call by the Polish Ministry of Culture, Hansen (along with the artists/architects Lech Tomaszewski and Stanisław Zamecznik) proposed an extension to Warsaw's Zacheta Art Gallery, an imposing neo-Baroque building dating from 1900. The team proposed inserting behind the existing structure a cubic glass-and-steel volume that could be shifted in virtually any way, somewhat like a Rubik's Cube. Connected to the ground through four corner pillars (with the entrance stair in the centre), the ground floor was completely open. The main volume, enveloped by a three-dimensional metal grid, consisted of interior partitions that could be shifted both vertically and horizontally. Ceiling heights could be adjusted from 3–15 m (10–49 ft), and stairs and bridges were also movable.

Hansen saw his system as applicable to any form of art, 'respecting the recipient's individuality' and creating 'a spatial atmosphere conducive to reflection, thus opposing the art of a dominant object in space – the cult of dogmatic dictates'. Polish bureaucrats weren't looking for revolutionary schemes, however, and the entry, which the writer Tomasz Fudala called 'one of the most radical designs in twentieth-century Polish architecture', never went any further.

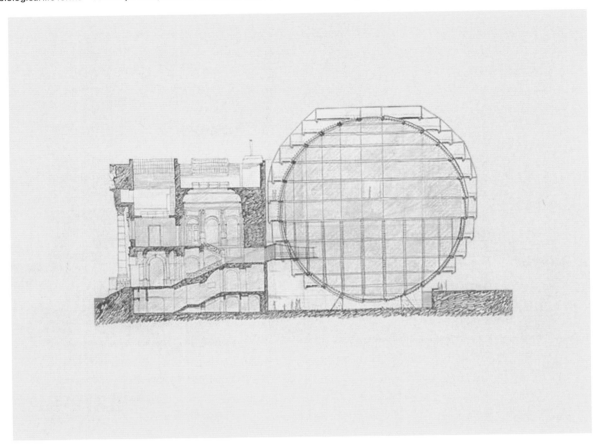

WITKA WATER SPORTS CENTRE
Maria Molicka
Niedów (PL), 1976

When a hydroelectric dam was built on the Witka River in 1962, the village of Niedów virtually disappeared beneath the newly created lake. In 1966 a campsite and a motel opened on a stretch of land sloping down to the water with a small beach, a boathouse with paddleboats and kayaks. Almost overnight, the reservoir became popular – leading, a decade later, to a competition for a building to transform this modest, home-grown summer getaway spot in southwestern Poland, near the German and Czech borders, into a destination.

In the shadow of the eighteenth-century Silesian Baroque Church of Our Lady of the Angels, its red mansard roofs and copper-clad bell tower watching over the village and its fifteen remaining residents, Maria Molicka proposed a ship-like, five-storey structure in concrete, tapering on all sides, with an expansive rooftop deck running the length of the building. Each guest room had a partitioned balcony facing the reservoir, and the centre stretched along a waterfront with jetties, boat slipways and a viewing stand, presumably for fans of water sports.

In the chronology of Molicka's works, the project is labelled 'Competition … First Prize', but there are no published accounts of it. The architect Joanna Majczyk speculates that Molicka won an in-house competition for the municipal design office in Wrocław (the regional capital), but that there was no money for 'non-housing developments'. Such designs were termed *półkownicy* in Polish, a play on words meaning something destined for the bookshelf, never to leave the office and be implemented. The beach was eventually sold to a private landholder and fenced off from the public, Molicka's design long since shelved.

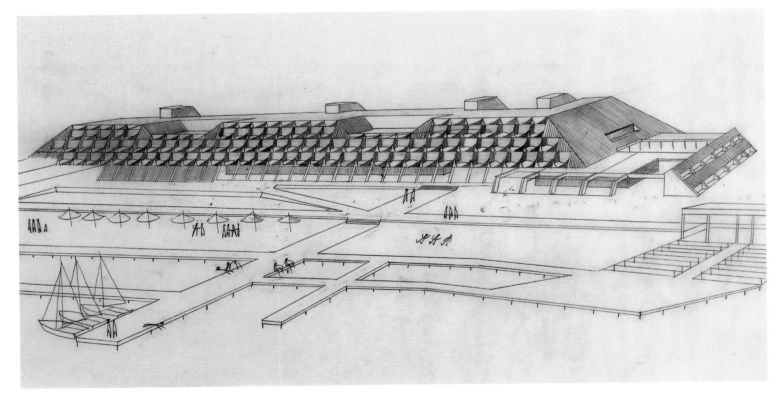

ST JACOB'S CHURCH
Jacek Burzyński and Wiktor Jackiewicz
Częstochowa (PL), 1957

Following the official rejection of Socialist Realism in 1956, Polish architecture experienced a rupture, as if the space-time continuum had torn open and Stakhanovite muscularity was swapped for the spatial and visual freedom of thin-shell reinforced-concrete structures. Such was the case with the winning competition entry by Jacek Burzyński and Wiktor Jackiewicz for a new St Jacob's church in the Catholic pilgrimage city of Częstochowa, south-central Poland. Burzyński and Jackiewicz's church consisted of a quartet of parabolic shells. The largest was the nave, an elongated arch terminating in a semi-circular, sloping apse, its ceiling 24.5 m (80 ft) high. The baptistry was of nearly equal height, while the shorter narthex – the entry – was partially enclosed in a floor-to-ceiling stained-glass window, with a concrete cross extruded from its face. Last, a leggy parabola 35.5 m (116 ft) high stood on the shell of the nave, its rectangular columns expressed on the interior as an east-facing, almost non-denominational clerestory. In an earlier version of their design, the architects sketched a pointier parabolic nave with an elongated opening at the base.

In September 1959 the teaching of religion was banned in most schools in Częstochowa. This was followed by an official edict proclaiming that brick, cement and steel could not be dedicated to religious purposes and had to be spent on public housing, schools and government buildings instead.

CHURCH OF CHRIST THE KING
Dominikus Böhm
Gliwice (PL), 1929

Gliwice's Church of Christ the King, designed by the Austrian architect Karl Mayr in 1934, is one of the city's more unusual sites. With its towering, square yellow-brick facade, tapering dramatically along its flanks and embedded with repeating cruciform patterns and portholes, the basilica looks like something the postmodernist architect Robert Venturi would have dreamed up in the 1980s.

Responding to an inflow of German residents in the 1920s, the commission for the church – directed by parish priest Father Bruno Pattas – was originally given in 1929 to the architect Dominikus Böhm, the designer of numerous holy structures in his native country of Germany. Böhm's two proposals attempted both to create a civic centrepiece (justified because the build-ing was at a major road axis) and to bring the ancient structures of Byzantium into the future. The first scheme envisaged a colossal oval building topped by an expansive dome, sur-rounded by a ring of tall, prismatic chapels, relating in scale and material to neighbouring buildings. Inside, deep ribs led the eye towards a glowing oculus. Two towering side-by-side campaniles rose in front, serving as striking beacons, visible throughout the city. The sec-ond iteration, scaled back significantly, featured a cross-shaped sanctuary accompanied by a monumental rectangular bell tower, set with small arches and large square openings.

The Archdiocese of Wrocław rejected both plans, and in 1934 it brought in Mayr, who lived and worked in Gliwice from 1930 to 1938. Less than two years later, in November 1935, the church was consecrated.

AUSCHWITZ-BIRKENAU MEMORIAL COMPETITION
Oskar Hansen
Oświęcim (PL), 1957

1.2 million people – nine out of ten of them Jewish – perished at Auschwitz, the largest Nazi extermination camp. A competition for a memorial was announced on 2 June 1956 by an organization of survivors dedicated to keep-ing alive the memory of those who died there. More than 685 sculptors and architects from thirty-six countries submitted a total of 465 de-signs. None from among this mountainous out-pouring was deemed totally satisfactory, but the proposal the judges were inclined to favour was conceived by the Polish architect Oskar Hansen. He devised 'The Road', a path 60 m (197 ft) wide and 1,000 m (3,280 ft) long, laid with granite cobbles, cutting diagonally across the entire camp. The line severed the orderly grid of bar-racks and transgressed the *Judenrampe*. One would travel the road without visual cues, direct references to suffering and sacrifice, or figurative memorials. At its end, 'The Road' became a wide stairway leading out of the camp, 'towards life'. Hansen wrote, 'The road is the site for sponta-neous gestures. If one should wish to leave a note with a name, or a figure of an angel, one could do it by the road.' In short, it was left en-tirely to the visitor to interpret or feel the mean-ing of the death camps. 'The Road' was a neutral platform. Rather than imposing a memorial, it permitted the camp to become one.

To Auschwitz survivors, 'The Road' was too ab-stract, too theoretical, too contingent; it didn't evoke suffering. It withheld meaning. It robbed the victims, living and dead, of their memories of anguish and pain. Their voices, impossible to ignore, silenced the proposal. A decade after the competition opened, a monument was fi-nally dedicated, elevating the extermination of Communist and Socialist political prisoners above the slaughter of Jews. The monument had become a palimpsest, writing the Soviet fight against fascism over the Nazi genocide.

CZECH NATIONAL LIBRARY
Jan Kaplický
Prague (CZ), 2007

Perhaps growing up in Prague, not far from Adolf Loos's Villa Müller, and being surrounded by his parents' collection of avant-garde books and magazines and toying with Froebel blocks and a Merkur metal construction set, it was inevitable that the Czech Jan Kaplický would name his one-man think tank Future Systems.

The future was his dream world, cars and sex his obsessions. He admired Bertrand Goldberg, the maestro of circular design, and the aviator-poet Antoine de Saint-Exupéry.
Exiled after the failure of the Prague Spring in 1968, Kaplický fled to London, where he worked with Denys Lasdun, Richard Rogers and Norman Foster. This was merely prologue, however, and he catapulted to fame in 1999 with his remarkable white blob, Lord's Cricket Ground Media Centre in St John's Wood, north London, the world's first all-aluminium, semi-monocoque

building. His Selfridge's department store in Birmingham, clad in 15,000 anodized aluminium discs mounted on a blue background, cemented his reputation for blazing past Modernism straight into a free-flowing, biomorphic future.
Future Systems won the competition for the Czech National Library with a 40,000 sq. m (430,000 sq. ft) structure that was promptly, and aptly, nicknamed the 'Octopus'. The building was clad in champagne-tinted anodized-aluminium tiles of shifting hues, from caramel at the base to wheat at the crown. Polka-dot

windows exposed the mauve interior to natural light, while an automated storage system could retrieve any one of ten million volumes in five minutes. The former Czech president Václav Havel's support of the proposal may have made it politically toxic, and when Kaplický died in 2009, he was still ensnared in talks with the Czech authorities about the library's fate.

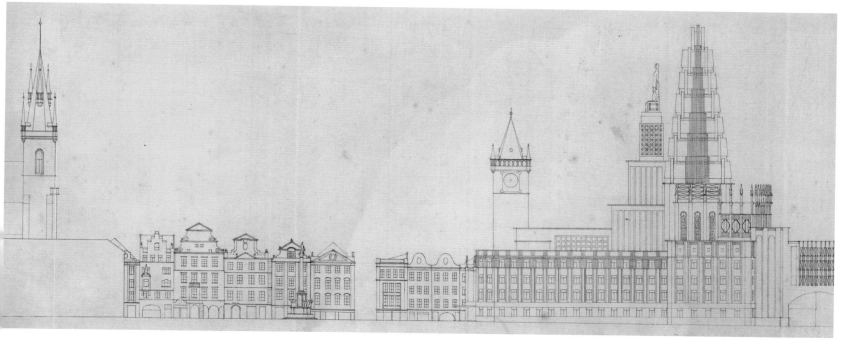

PRAGUE TOWN HALL
Josef Gočár
Prague (CZ), 1909

Prague's Old Town Hall stands as a potent symbol of the city: an impressive Gothic tower fronting Old Town Square, topped with cone-shaped turrets and fronted with a unique astronomical clock known as the Orloj. On close to ten occasions the city has announced competitions to improve and expand it, and the

designs dreamed up for each round endure as a timeline of visionary Czech architecture. In 1909 the influential Czech architect Josef Gočár, whose work boasted a superb sense of artistry and innovation thanks to close collaborations with artists and engineers, responded to the latest call for entries. His proposal, which would be erected on an adjacent site containing a jumbled block of houses, would unify the street wall into what he called a 'grouped mass'. It also attempted to give primacy to the State, not the Church, in the minds of locals.

Gočár created a sort of civic cathedral, its mass forming the most memorable of steeples (seen to the right of the drawing above). Behind a stone-panelled, stripped classicist base with a wide-columned portico rose three progressively larger and more unusual towers, each stepping down in unique formation. The result was a layered, ziggurat or wedding-cake silhouette, which one critic described as 'Wagnerian Modernism'. Visitors would enter via a wide-columned portico, followed by a tall vestibule, a light-filled reception hall and chambers

for the city council. Above this would be municipal offices, grouped on several floors by function. The design prefigured the Expressionist, Constructivist and early Modernist buildings that would soon proliferate in Europe. Gočár did not win the competition, and eventually all entries were foiled by the outbreak of World War I.

TRADE UNIONS RECREATION CENTRE
Věra Machoninová and Vladimír Machonin
Prague (CZ), 1967

Leaders of a generation of adventurous mid-century engineer-architects that emerged in the Eastern Bloc after the demise of Socialist Realism, Věra Machoninová and Vladimír Machonin combined the creative (Věra) and the managerial (Vladimír) to become a local powerhouse, building many of Prague's best-known Brutalist structures. In 1967 they entered a competition for the central recreation house of the Revolutionary Trade Movement (ROH), a building that was, despite its name, largely an exclusive hotel for communist functionaries. On a site near Prague Castle, the centre typifies the couple's adeptness with both bulky masses and intricate detailing. The essayist Ondřej Beneš describes how their proposal for the first phase of the competition was subtle, encompassing a cube-like massing of three distinct volumes enveloping a large central atrium. Their second-phase proposition, however, was anything but; it consisted of a stair-like structure, situated in blocks stepping up and fanning out from a truncated pyramidal base containing a cinema and large interior atrium. The radical form was intended to enhance the building's views and ventilation, as well as its relation to the hilly site.

The couple won the competition's highest honour, but no first prize was awarded. The 'Hotel Pyramid' design (by another couple, Neda Cajthamlová and Miloslav Cajthaml) selected in a subsequent competition was far less inventive. Instead of structural experiment, we simply get floor plates diminishing on either side as the building rises.

BUDAPEST CITY HALL
Erick van Egeraat
Budapest (HU), 2008

In 2005 a competition was held to put a new city hall on a plot of land in the centre of the Hungarian capital. The seeds for the task had been sown as far back as the eighteenth century, when the Viennese architect Anton Erhard Martinelli's baroque Invalidus Palace was only partially completed. The building stopped well short of Károly Körút, the major thoroughfare running past the seat of local government, and a shabby park and car park occupied the space between buildings and road.

The City Hall Forum, as the project was known, was awarded to the Dutch architect Erick van Egeraat in the spring of the following year. Van Egeraat proposed completing Martinelli's idea for four enclosed quadrangles by adding an L-shaped office building whose main facade shifted gradually from solid to a gateway held aloft on concrete pillars that looked like the boughs and trunks of massive maples. This main entrance leads to the Town Hall Square, a public plaza bounded by the new white city hall, the red-brick baroque palace and the neoclassical mid-nineteenth-century Lutheran church on Deák Square, to which the architect proposed to add a 65 m (213 ft) tower. Van Egeraat's concept was a porous structure that promoted the idea of Hungarian democracy, of civic space and public space merging into one.

The country's 'Two-Thirds Revolution' in 2010 put a stop to the City Hall Forum. The newly elected mayor of Budapest, István Tarlós, replaced the 'spectacular building' with what he proclaimed would be a 'much more useful ... public park'. A decade later, in 2021 (under a new mayor), the city announced a new competition to renew City Hall Park.

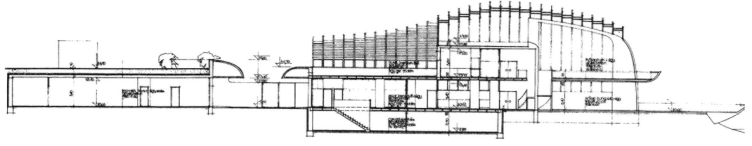

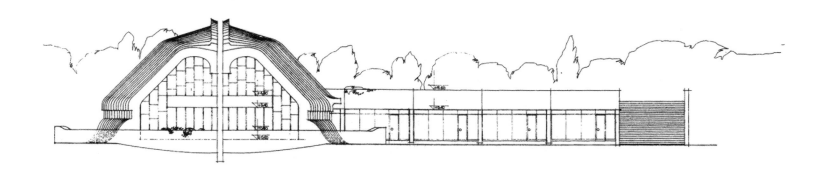

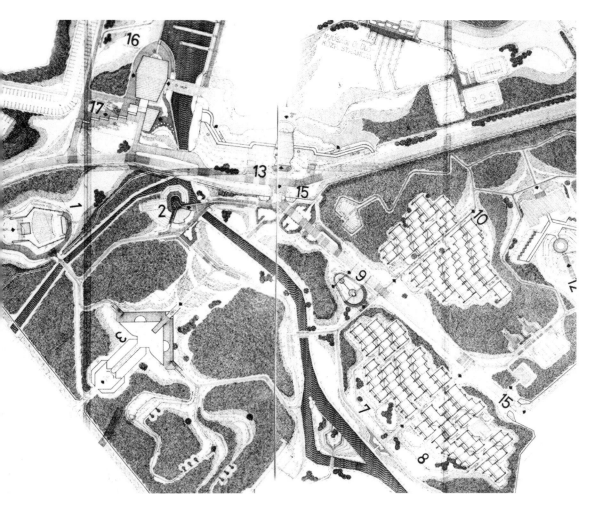

YOUTH CENTRE
Imre Makovecz
Velence (HU), 1973

It's a shame that more people outside his native country are not familiar with the work of the twentieth-century Hungarian architect Imre Makovecz. This anti-authoritarian firebrand focused his considerable training and talent not on the orthodoxy of his day, but on deftly merging modern architecture with taut natural forms and vibrant folk patterns. The designer, who was ardently religious, considered his buildings to be 'alive', suffused with divinity. 'Architects must take this step, the spiritualization of nature,' he said. 'It will not suffice to think that an empty white square, on the other side of nothingness, is the home of spirituality.'

By 1990 Makovecz had completed hundreds of buildings, founded the Hungarian Academy of Arts and won the Kossuth Prize, the country's most prestigious cultural award. One of his many unrealized designs was for a youth centre in Velence, a small town on a picturesque lake of the same name, 50 km (31 miles) southwest of Budapest.

Perched beside the water, the facility, linked by bridges, walkways and heavy vegetation, included an entertainment centre, restaurant, shops, outdoor cinema, lodging, and a hotel. All of its buildings, he said, were inspired by the structure of the human face and skull. 'My architecture is humanized architecture,' he noted. But it's clear that the architect took into account other parts of the body, as described in relation to his Church of St. Michael's Struggle, in Budapest: '[they] conjure up the interior of the chest, the lungs, and the heart, the place of breathing, of the soul, the place from which the soul begins its journey.'

SLOVENIAN PARLIAMENT
Jože Plečnik
Ljubljana (SI), 1947

Slovenia's pre-eminent architect, Jože Plečnik, acted as a bridge between history and modernity, uniting classical scale and monumentality with modern abstraction, colour and detailing. He trained under the famed Austrian architect Otto Wagner and went on to design many of Ljubljana's most notable buildings and land-scapes, including the National and University Library, Congress Square and the so-called Triple Bridge. In 1947, just after Marshal Josip Broz Tito's communist forces liberated Slovenia (and all of Yugoslavia) from German occupation, Ferdo Kozak, head of the Slovenian Assembly, asked Plečnik to devise a new Slovenian Parliament.

Plečnik sketched an acropolis-like hilltop scheme on the very site of the city's twelfth-century castle, highlighted by an octagonal structure atop a monumental stair. The assembly rejected that plan and called for a competition for a site in the city's Tivoli Park. Plečnik's new entry, called the 'Cathedral of Freedom', was fronted by a colonnaded base 50 m (164 ft) wide, surrounding a cylindrical building topped with a giant, twisting, cone-shaped cupola, spanning the assembly beneath and rising 120 m (394 ft) into the air.

It's not clear why Plečnik's scheme wasn't chosen, but many believe it was too grand and expensive for a country still recovering from a devastating war. The competition winner was the functionalist architect Vinko Glanz, and construction began on his much more modest scheme in 1954; it opened in 1959. Nevertheless, Plečnik's proposal, not Glanz's, has become a national symbol, appearing on the first stamp issued by Slovenia after independence in 1991 and later becoming the image on Slovenia's ten-cent coins.

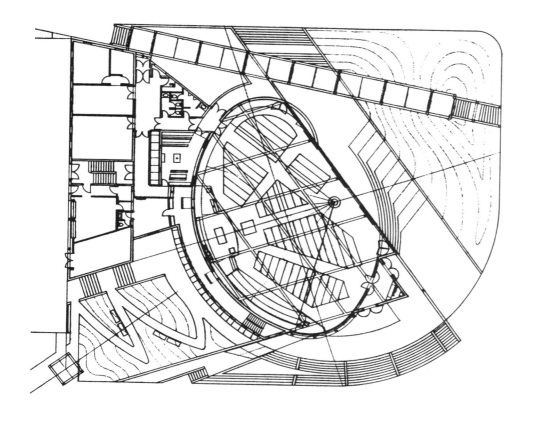

CHURCH OF ST JOHN THE EVANGELIST
Velimir Neidhardt
Zagreb (HR), 1991

One of Yugoslavia's (and later Croatia's) most prolific modern architects is Velimir Neidhardt. Born in 1943, just before Yugoslavia broke from the Soviet sphere of influence, he has designed dozens of architecture and urban planning projects, including Zagreb's National and University Library and Zagreb Airport.

In 1991 Neidhardt entered a competition to create the Church of St John the Evangelist in New Zagreb, a residential area south of the historic centre consisting largely of blank, socialist-era apartments and tower blocks. To adapt to this context while adding the necessary differentiation, he proposed a structure of monumental appearance, built of heavy blocks of Roman travertine laid out in a semicircle, sliced on an incline. The curved form would create a sanctuary in which pews fanned out from the pulpit, behind which light entered through an expanse of glass, filtered by bulky, raked louvres. Layered spaces spilled outside via a stepped landing and elevated walkway, framed by stone arches, hovering over a sunken landscape. The ensemble – uniquely vibrant in a sea of bleak uniformity – constituted a much-needed gathering space for Zagreb.

Velimir Neidhardt, who integrated technology into much of his work, embedded the structure with video equipment to project scenes complementary to each mass onto an arched wall as though holy frescos and paintings were coming to life. The architect believes the church regarded this strategy as 'too futuristic', or perhaps lacking in divine spirituality, and his proposal failed to win.

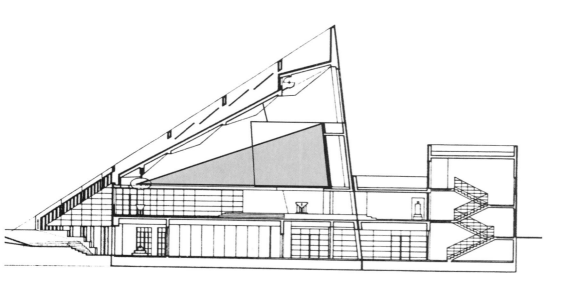

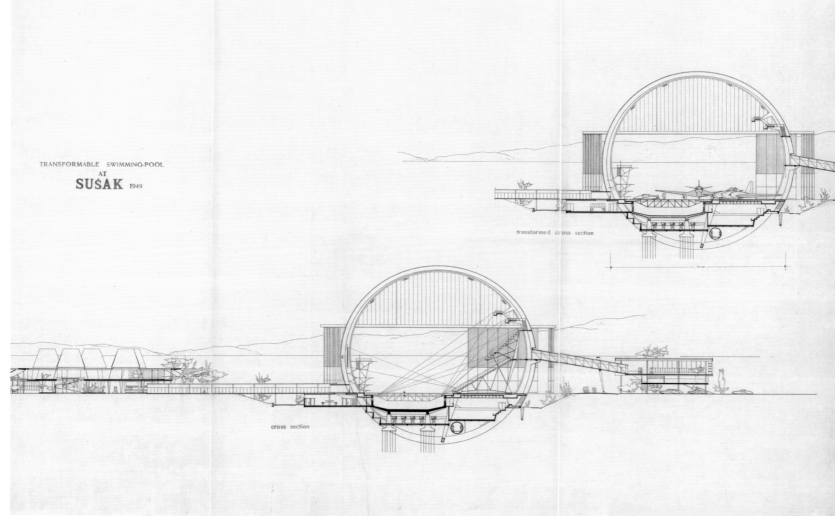

TRANSFORMABLE SWIMMING-POOL
AT
SUŠAK 1949

transformed cross section

cross section

MULTI-USE SWIMMING POOL
Vladimir Turina
Sušak, Rijeka (HR), 1949

The Croatian Modernist Vladimir Turina, practising in the rigid world of socialist Yugoslavia, specialized in technically advanced structures that were also human-scaled and distinctive. He preferred to call his works 'devices', not

'machines'. In 1949, as part of Yugoslavia's entry into the Universal Sport Exhibition, a world's fair held in Stockholm, Turina drafted a plan for a multi-use swimming pool in Rijeka, a quaint Croatian town overlooking Kvarner Bay in the northern Adriatic Sea.

Located on the coast in Sušak, a new neighbourhood filled with Soviet-style high-rises in eastern Rijeka, the swimming complex, covered by a transparent circular shell, consisted of two pools placed lengthwise atop a natural rock base. Lucky swimmers could view both the sea

and the hills while in motion, and the shell could move on iron rails to cover one pool or the other, depending on the weather. The floors of the pools could be lifted via hydraulics, turning the building into a tube-topped exhibition pavilion, or even an aeroplane hangar if necessary. 'New contents and new forms are sought in architectural thought,' said Turina. 'We wanted to show that new and contemporary forms of expression do not require extravagance in formal design.' Yugoslavia never hosted a Summer Olympics (although it did host the Sarajevo Winter

Games in 1984), and the plan never got beyond the drawing board. Furthermore, the plastic needed to realize it were not advanced enough at the time, as Turina expert Boris Maga noted in an interview in 1997: 'While today this could be brilliantly designed to that end, in that era no one could do it.'

BETON HALA WATERFRONT CENTRE
Sou Fujimoto
Belgrade (RS), 2012

Sou Fujimoto called this project in Belgrade the 'Floating Cloud'. Beton Hala, which translates as 'concrete hall,' is a popular area containing a vast row of 1930s warehouses on a stretch of promenade lining the Sava River. Situated below the ramparts of the Belgrade Fortress – the city's most important historical monument – and sliced through by a network of public transport routes and busy streets, the warehouses form a low, flat-roofed building that occupies a slim site sloping towards the river. Fujimoto's idea was to build a tangle of spiralling ramps that would form a canopy for a public plaza on top of these old warehouses.

Fujimoto's work has been described as 'an architecture of creative becomings', and to call Beton Hala Waterfront Center a building is both right and wrong. It is more like a whirlwind or galaxy of concrete ribbons with no beginning and no end. Eleven ramps trail from the spinning centre, becoming, among other things, a viaduct on toothpick-thin legs, connecting the spiral to the Belgrade Fortress and Kalemegdan Park up the hill; a glassed-in causeway flying out over the river; a curving walkway dipping into the water; a walkway landing on the embankment roadway; and another sweeping to meet the landscaped roof of the old warehouses. The ramps could be seen as either the building unravelling or the building gathering strips of matter to become itself. Fujimoto said: 'The architecture itself is not so strong, but it is an indicator of movement.' After three years the city dropped the project in order to focus on a development a little upriver, centred on a skyscraper that will be the tallest between Vienna and Istanbul.

211

BORO AND RAMIZ
YOUTH CENTRE
Marko Mušič
Pristina (XK), 1970

At the age of twenty-nine, Marko Mušič had already established himself as an insurgent, willing to test the spatial and structural limits of concrete by breaking free of the formalist Brutalist language. His answer to the competition for the Boro and Ramiz Youth Centre in Pristina (then the most youthful city in Yugoslavia, with half its population under the age of twenty-five) was a low-lying, sculptural concrete building, washed in white mortar, and made of more than a dozen undulating concrete girders of differing heights and lengths.

A scattered set of similar forms knitted together into a striking mass, the building had a restless, dynamic, agitated quality, which, Mušič said, was intended to reflect the 'enthusiasm, diversity, strength and impulses of young people'. Glass strips followed the rising and descending planes of the crook-necked girders, shedding an ambient glow over the interior spaces and resulting in a changing quality of light throughout the day and with the seasons. The massive spans also allowed fluid spaces, Mušič told the jury. 'They can easily disintegrate,' he said, adapting to an 'imaginative, inventive, uniquely sensitive [future] reality.'

The Boro and Ramiz centre – which was named after two fallen World War II heroes – became the victim of a kind of bureaucratic disappearance. Mušič himself had been awarded second prize, but the winners, whose entry was a towering Metabolic structure of glass composed within a steel rhomboid framework, never heard another word about breaking ground. As if the competition had never happened, in 1974 another was held. Its winning entry was built.

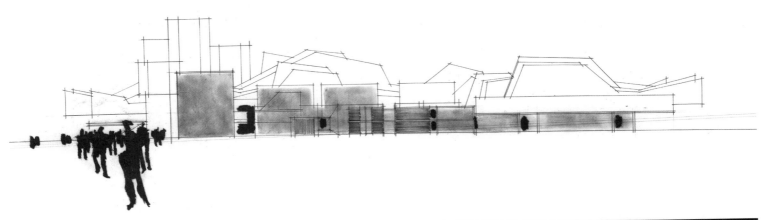

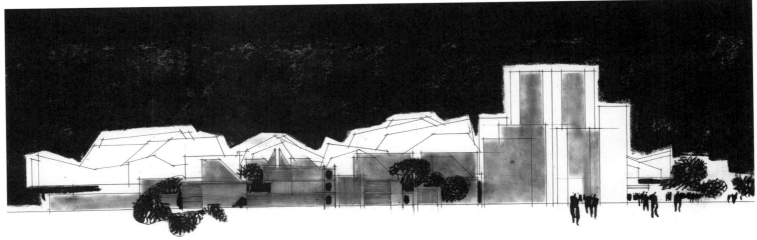

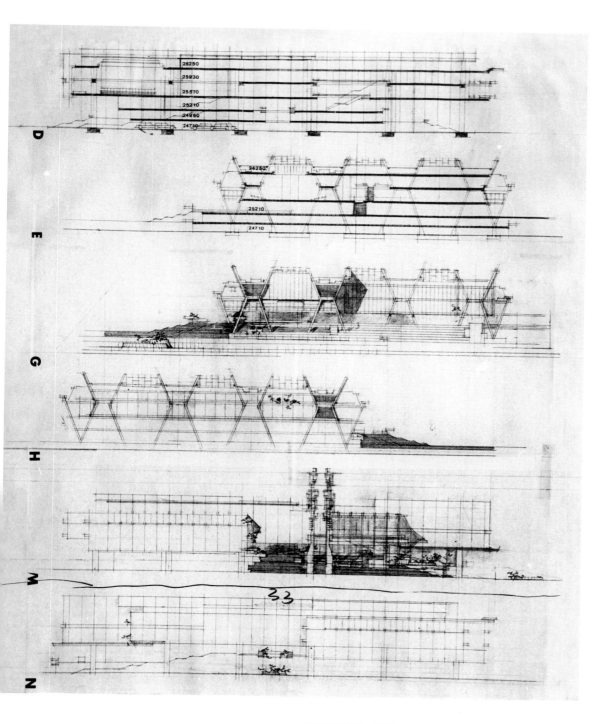

SKOPJE TOWN HALL
Edvard Ravnikar
Skopje (MK), 1966

On 26 July 1963 an immense earthquake killed more than a thousand people and destroyed 80 per cent of Skopje, the fast-growing political and cultural centre of Macedonia, then a federated state within Yugoslavia. Over the next two years the city, collaborating with the government of Yugoslavia and the United Nations, launched a masterplan competition to rebuild Skopje into a 'world city'. Participants included significant international architects and planners, such as Kenzo Tange (Japan), Maurice Rotival (United States) and Jo van den Broek (the Netherlands), as well as top Yugoslav architects, including the Slovenian architect and one-time student of Jože Plečnik, Edvard Ravnikar, who had almost single-handedly established his country's modern architectural infrastructure, promoting education, launching competitions and designing Republic Square (then Revolution Square), the centrepiece of Ljubljana.

While Ravnikar lost to Tange (who presented a linear 'city wall' of elevated Brutalist megastructures and later paired up with the Yugoslav architects Radovan Miščević and Fedor Wenzler to carry it out) on the masterplan, in 1966 he won a competition to build one of the project's focal points: Skopje Town Hall. The long, sculptural edifice, approached laterally via wide steps, was indicative of the architect's vibrant merger of functionalism, contextualism and lyricism, expressed through bold geometry and visible structure. Hovering above a raised public space on thick columns, the bridge-like building – a machine for governing, if there ever was one – featured panel-clad bays repeating horizontally along its length and partially revealed its futuristic, hexagonal steel structure. But, while international funding poured in for a university campus, cultural centre, transportation centre and federal government offices, nothing materialized for the town hall, nor would it for decades to come.

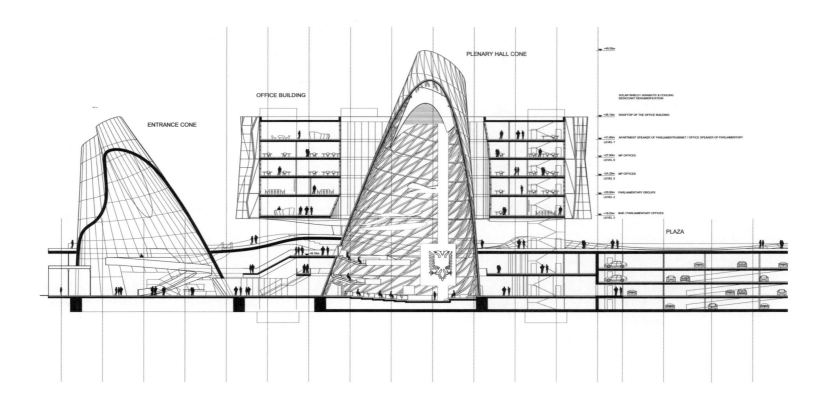

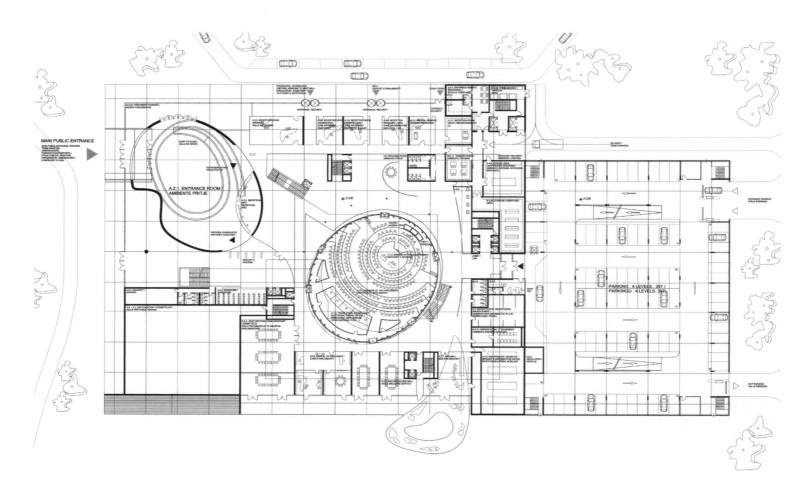

OPEN PARLIAMENT OF ALBANIA
Coop Himmelb(l)au
Tirana (AL), 2011

Sic transit gloria mundi – which is to say, earthly glories are short-lived – could easily be the motto embossed on the stationery of any architect who pronounces their own parliament design for a new regime the symbol of 'transparency of democracy'. Wolf Prix, the cigar-puffing, aphorism-spouting, self-styled 'radical' head of Coop Himmelb(l)au, said just that about his parliament for the Albanian capital, Tirana, and within two weeks found himself embroiled in a parliamentary dispute questioning whether the design competition he'd won was as transparent as the glass building he'd proposed. The nation's socialist opposition claimed that the jury was rigged, after the outcome was predicted before a formal award was made.

Prix's design, it seems, was stillborn. His concept – which required demolishing the tomb of Albania's late dictator, Enver Hoxha, a huge pyramid encrusted with Carrara marble – was a five-storey reinforced-concrete office block floating 7 m (23 ft) above a public plaza and pierced by a pair of leaning cones. The taller cone, housing the parliament, was encased in glass and shot up 50 m (164 ft) through the middle of the public plaza, representing transparency and the subordination of electoral government in one stroke. The office complex, in typical Himmelb(l)au fashion, was wrapped in a skin of perforated steel, the punctures configured according to the movement of the sun. From the landscaped roof of the office building the public could peer in from outside, looking down on their representatives in action.

The proposal became ensnared in the accusations over a fixed competition, efforts to save Hoxha's pharaonic crypt, and an Albanian government too broke to pay wages and pensions to its employees. In the end, no new parliament was built.

DEI ADMINISTRATIVE CENTRE
Tombazis & Associates
Architects
Athens (GR), 1972

When Tombazis & Associates won the competition for the DEI Administrative Centre, the Athens architectural practice was under the sway of Japanese Metabolism – a monumental style that, in the strange convergence of military dictatorships and architecture, suited the ruling Greek junta's self-conception as all-powerful and indestructible. Tombazis, who had trained with the great humanist Constantinos Doxiadis, didn't share the generals' world view; he was interested in finding ways to make Athens modern.

The enormous centre was planned for Faliro, a suburb of Athens, where the government would demolish the surrounding neighbourhood as well as the existing facilities of the Public Power Service – the national energy-producing company – and build a consolidated headquarters. Height restrictions, which had helped to preserve the area as a historical hub of Greek architecture, would be lifted.

Tombazis' design had no fixed centre, no core. It was a structure made of wings affixed to wings, in keeping with the Metabolist aim of allowing buildings to grow by accretion, cell by cell, like living organisms. The concrete building consisted of a grid of round towers 98 m (322 ft) high, with rectangular floor units slid in like trays in a bakery rack. It almost looked as if these units could be pulled in and out or cranked up and down at will. Certainly, they could have been placed and sized to suit the needs of their occupants. In practical terms, this meant there would be voids everywhere, permitting the building to be open in unexpected ways. The competition fell into chaos after uninvited architects cried foul, others withdrew, and the jury imploded.

CHURCH OF THE EVANGELISTRIA
Nikolaos Mitsakis,
Kyriakos Panagiotakos
Tinos (GR), 1930

The picturesque, mountainous island of Tinos in Greece's Cyclades Islands, about 20 minutes by ferry from Mykonos, is most of all a religious destination. Thousands of people come every year to visit the hilltop church of the Virgin Mary Megalochari, also known as the Church of the Evangelistria, a nineteenth-century monastery complex that is the most popular pilgrimage location in Greece thanks to its miraculous seventh-century icon depicting the Virgin.

In 1930 the church, supported by the Greek State, launched a competition for a new building capable of accommodating at least 6,000 worshippers. The next year well-known Modernist architects Nikolaos Mitsakis and Kyriakos Panagiotakos won with a reinforced-concrete structure that skilfully merged vernacular and modern forms and functions. The three-aisled basilica was covered with a 'turtle-shaped' dome, cut with a horizontal band of windows, lightening the structure and allowing beams of natural light inside. Opposite the front facade was a large sunken plaza, while administrative buildings and cells for both pilgrims and monks stepped down the sloping site, a solution that echoed much Greek hillside housing. Small openings and arcades throughout likewise nodded to local village planning. A monolithic, square-edged bell tower – a resolutely modern beacon – rose dramatically atop one side. After some back and forth, and even a court case, the committee overseeing the competition supported the plan. But the design was never implemented, largely owing to the global Depression and Greece's profound debt crisis.

Takis Zenetos has been described as one of the most innovative post-war Greek architects. In common with his contemporaries Yona Friedman in France and Michael Webb of Archigram in England, he was a proponent of an ideal future of suspended cities. For nearly two decades he pursued his notion of urbanisme électronique, an architecture that would translate the magic of cybernetics into daily forms of living. In the process, he rejected Modernism for 'a definite boundary between interior and exterior, thus making handsome boxes'.

Commissioned by Crete's regional development agency between 1964 and 1967, Zenetos worked on his design to make the tiny fishing village of Agia Galini into an urban centre of 6,000 inhabitants. His ambition, he said, was 'a structural system of building which is responsive to the natural environment and the topography of the area'. Agia Galini is practically etched into the rugged coastline of layered, tilted and folded limestone. Zenetos took those slabs as both a building material and a shape, transforming the two eastern hills of the village into horizontal buildings heaped, like the massive layered rocks, into a new – if exaggerated – form. The scale, too, was an enlarged projection of the wild, untouched shoreline, while the jagged, thin edges of the stepped platforms amplified the broken faces of the rock. In its simplicity, Zenetos's proposition was the existing village building writ large, yet facing the future.

Having presented his ideas for the village, Zenetos predicted that 'the most likely scenario is that this will stay at the proposal stage.' As it did.

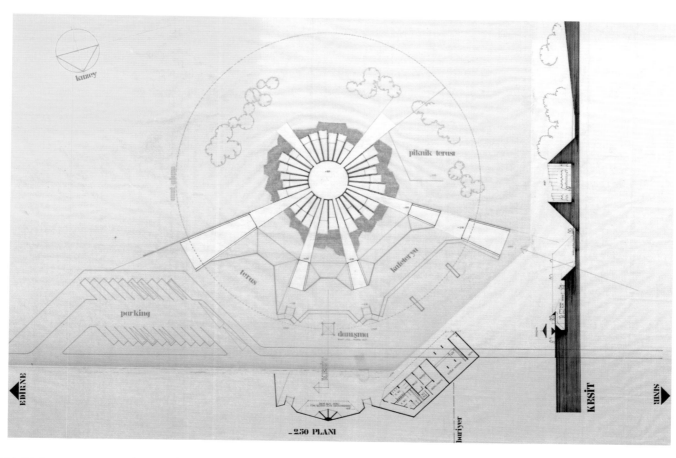

WORKERS' MONUMENT
Erkal Güngören
Edirne (TR), 1974

Erkal Güngören was perhaps best known for his monument Atatürk, His Mother and Women's Rights in Constitution Square, Izmir, overlooking the Aegean Sea. Güngören believed that architecture shorn of direct historical references and endowed with sculptural qualities could advance egalitarianism. At Edirne, he was interested in finding a way to make a monument, he said, that would 'not be a "monument"'. His Workers' Monument for this small city in the northwest of Turkey, just 5 km (3 miles) from the border with Greece, would be an 'organic … unprogrammed' space, he wrote, determining neither the visitor's 'psychological nor physical environment'.

The monument was a large circle of three concentric tiers forming a crater in the ground. Six separate tapering paths, representing the Six Arrows (Republicanism, Populism, Nationalism, Laicism, Statism and Revolutionalism) of Kemalism, the Turkish Republic's founding ideology, led to a truncated cone composed of massive concrete wedges roughly 7.6 m (25 ft) high. A bas-relief lining the interior at eye level depicted the 'sustained power' of hard labour.

The monument was buried so that it could not be understood from the outside, or at first encounter. From the terrace, on the outer ring, the visitor could see the conical mound beckoning, but there was no prescribed route down. The way in was a winding one, leading first down and then up again to the entrance of the tumulus-like cone. Güngören hoped the sequential experience would assuage any sense of being crushed under the structure's concrete weightiness. Turkey's invasion of the island of Cyprus in 1974 collapsed the monument.

DAS HAUS DER FREUNDSCHAFT
Hans Poelzig
Istanbul (TR), 1916

At the height – or perhaps nadir – of World War I, the influential German Modernist architecture association Deutscher Werkbund held an invited competition for the design of 'Dostluk Yurdu' in Istanbul, the 'friendship house' that would mark the alliance between Germany and Turkey. Peter Behrens, Walter Gropius, Theodor Fischer, Bruno Taut, Hans Poelzig and German Bestelmeyer were among those who submitted drawings for the huge complex, which was to contain spaces for concerts and exhibitions, a library and a café, and student quarters. The entries were, for the most part, interpretations of familiar styles – Renaissance, Islamic, Baroque – recast through the lens of industrialism.

While Bestelmeyer's neo-Palladian box, built to classical proportions, won the competition, it was Poelzig's that upstaged them all. The architectural historian Kenneth Frampton later described Poelzig's design as an early example of 'horizontal megaform': a massive, symmetrical building of five terraces climbing a hillside, dominating the city's skyline. His proposal was immediately compared to the Hanging Gardens of Babylon, and aptly so, since cascading roof gardens covered each level in flowering and ornamental shrubs. In his towering, narrow windows – with vaguely Moorish arches – Poelzig seemed to have adopted the carved wooden latticework and stained glass found in the screened, ventilating *mashrabiya* oriels of the Islamic world. Still, this was a thoroughly modern structure: one layer piled on top of another, punctuated by interminably rational and repetitive arcades and exterior staircases, almost a template for the reproduction of itself. There was German money and Turkish land set aside for the project. With the defeat of the Central Powers in World War I, however, the concept for Das Haus der Freundschaft imploded.

KOCATEPE MOSQUE
Vedat Dalokay,
Nejat Tekelioğlu
Ankara (TR), 1957

The Kocatepe Mosque, which today dominates the skyline of Ankara, was originally conceived not just as a very different building, but as an illustration of the forward-looking inclinations of the then-ruling party in Turkey's capital city. Announced in 1957 in an election campaign booklet, 'Towards Great Ankara', Vedat Dalokay and Nejat Tekelioğlu's scheme was a thin-shell concrete shroud that touched the ground at four corners, each flanked by minarets, sharp and skinny as missiles, stripped of the traditional balconies, galleries and spiral staircases. The prayer hall was essentially a tent, open on all sides, as if someone had driven stakes into the ground, holding the fabric tight and forming four parabolic entryways. The design was decidedly abstract, although the arches and dome echoed those of the country's most important mosque, Hagia Sophia in Istanbul.

Dalokay's mosque, which the government dubbed 'the greatest mosque of the republican era', was slated for a hilltop in Yenişehir (the recently built 'new city') not far from Anıtkabir, the mausoleum of Atatürk, the founder of modern Turkey. The mosque, in short, was shot through with political significance. Ground was broken and the foundations poured, then the project – which had never been especially popular – was withdrawn. According to Kishwar Rizvi, a historian at Yale School of Architecture, the official excuse was that the concrete shell structure was unsafe. A competition held in 1967 led instead to the completion twenty years later of a carbon copy of the sixteenth-century Ottoman Şehzade Mosque in Fatih, Istanbul. Kocatepe Mosque stands today on top of a supermarket, a monument to the marriage of conservative politics and religious orthodoxy.

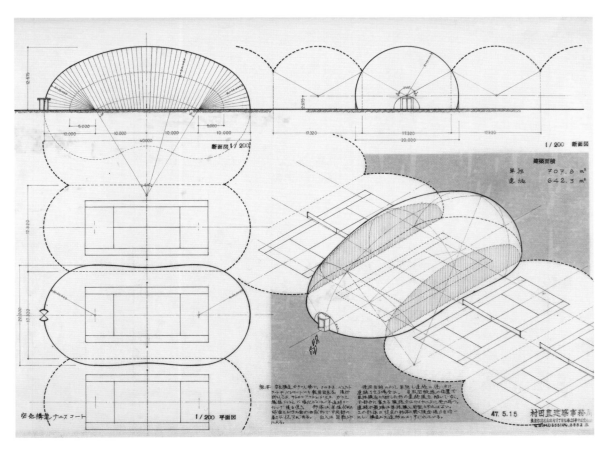

SOVIET YOUTH SPORTS FACILITY
Yutaka Murata
Moscow (RU), 1972

Yutaka Murata, who established his own firm in 1934, is best remembered for one of his final endeavours: the inflatable Fuji Group Pavilion at the 1970 Osaka Expo, consisting of sixteen interconnected, bright orange inflatable arched tubes rising like sea-monster tentacles from a giant circular foundation. His colleague Arata Isozaki called Murata – who worked on surreal plans for pneumatic structures for homes, schools, museums, playgrounds, transit stations and even Disneyland – 'an engineer who dreams'. That kind of uninhibited imagination helped to inform Murata's plans for the Soviet Youth Sports Facility, a series of interconnected pneumatic domes and partial spheres enclosed by a much larger pneumatic envelope, reinforced by tension cables. The plan – which could be mass-produced throughout the Soviet Union's massive sphere of influence – was part of an elevated athletic apparatus that considered sports success to be a key catalyst for advancing the communist movement. (The USSR, for instance, led the medal count in six of the eight Summer Olympics it competed in.)

The facility's clear, single-membrane outer envelope, partitioned by 'tetron mesh' screens, allowed outdoor activities, such as running and ice skating, to be carried out 'in light clothing', while the inner shells (of lower tensile strength, since they would not be subject to external weather) contained, among other offerings, a bowling alley, a gymnasium, tennis courts, a swimming pool, a botanic garden, sauna baths, cafés and a restaurant. As with many of Murata's inflatable plans, this one never came to fruition, although why it failed is not documented.

CRYSTAL ISLAND
Foster + Partners
Moscow (RU), 2007

The pioneering British architectural firm Foster + Partners has never been afraid to take on mega-scale projects for clients with big pockets (but sometimes questionable human-rights records). One of the practice's many incomplete proposals for Vladimir Putin's Russia is Crystal Island, a tent-like 'major urban destination' 450 m (1,476 ft) tall that would be the largest single building in the world. Edging the Moscow River on the Nagatino Peninsula, about 7.5 km (5 miles) south of the Kremlin, the 2.5 million sq. m (26.9 million sq. ft) mixed-use project would become its own neighbourhood, containing hotels, apartments, offices, shops, theatres, schools, exhibition spaces and public viewing areas, with parks at the periphery. Spiralling upwards in two directions to create a diagrid frame, the structure – resembling a flower, a spinning top, or perhaps a board-game piece – was filled with terraced winter gardens and clad in a second skin of breathable ETFE (ethylene tetrafluoroethylene) forming a buffer against the city's harsh summers and freezing winters. Vertical louvres provided additional sun protection and privacy, while embedded solar panels and wind turbines helped to power the complex. The building's spiralling form continued seamlessly into the outer park.

Proposed by the oil and real-estate magnate Shalva Chigirinsky in the frenzy of speculation just before the Great Recession of 2008–09, the project gained approval from the Moscow Public and Architectural Council. But the downturn doomed it, along with several more Russian towers of Babel, including Foster and Chigirinsky's more than 600 m (1969 ft) tall Russia Tower.

EUROPE EAST

PALACE OF THE SOVIETS
Moisei Ginzburg
Moscow (RU), 1934

Certain architectural competitions become defining landmarks of their age. A prime example is the contest for the Palace of the Soviets – a gargantuan political base (complete with congress halls and administrative facilities) for a radically new ruling power – which drew the world's attention and became a worldwide symbol for the so-called triumph of socialism. Eventually planned for the site of the soon-to-be-demolished Cathedral of Christ the Saviour, the palace's widely publicized 'All-Union Open Competition' of 1931 drew 272 designs, mostly from decidedly modern architects around the world including Walter Gropius and Le Corbusier. Many of the key members of the Russian avant-garde participated, including Vladimir Tatlin, Alexander Vesnin and Ivan Leonidov. Moisei Ginzburg, creator of the noted experimental, collective housing estate Narkomfin in Moscow, produced a masterpiece of Constructivist vision: a grand, glass-clad dome, its lofty lower spaces opened up via bridge-like supports. Set with a spiral ramp and internal terraces, the building's stepped storeys curved up towards a massive crowning rooflight. Despite a wealth of radical ideas – a more backward-facing scheme took the prize. Three entrants, Boris Iofan, Vladimir Shchuko and Vladimir Gelfreikh, were in 1933 merged into a single team that produced an architectural wedding cake 415 m (1,362 ft) tall, stacking neoclassical form upon neoclassical form, all faced in heavy granite. Stalin and his stripped-down, bombastic historical architecture, it seemed, had triumphed over the avant-garde and the utopian. Yet in the end neither prevailed. When World War II broke out, construction of the tower halted. Parts of the foundation were disassembled and used for anti-tank obstacles. Plans resumed after the war but never gained traction, and an outdoor pool was eventually built on the site of the destroyed cathedral.

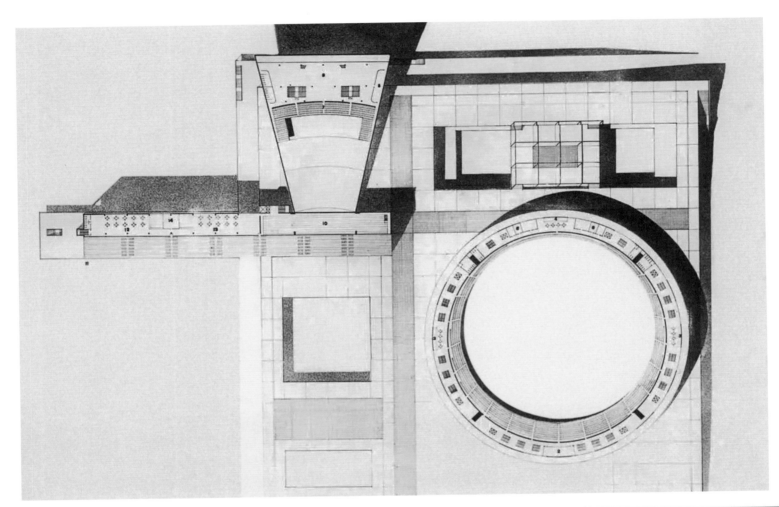

PERM MUSEUM
Valerio Olgiati
Perm (RU), 2008

The Swiss architect Valerio Olgiati hardly ever builds anything. But he is legendary, if largely unknown outside the cognoscenti, for the twenty-five or so buildings he has completed. From his office in the idyllic Alpine hamlet of Flims, 130 km (81 miles) from Zurich, and his brooding, monotone concrete home, Villa Além, in rural Portugal, Olgiati produces works of silent purity and palpable presence. His designs are stripped of nods to history, context or social consciousness, since he believes there is no such thing as objective truth or shared consciousness. He invented the term 'non-referential architecture' to explain his approach, which he says concerns only the experience of space, newness, construction, contradiction, order and sensory making.

Olgiati's museum in Perm, a Russian city at the easternmost edge of Europe, embodied all these qualities. A stack of eight differently sized boxes, made entirely of swan-feather-white concrete, rising on the banks of the Kama River. Each floor was clad in a screen of massive scalloped concrete shingles so that, seen from afar, the building looked like a pile of Christmas gifts wrapped in a custom-made, obsessively precise, glossy paper. As expected of Olgiati, the building had a way of holding its own defiant ground. The architect said of his work, 'I build for myself, because I am the benchmark. This is not arrogance. How else would I measure something?' He shared first and second prize in the competition, but the project stalled.

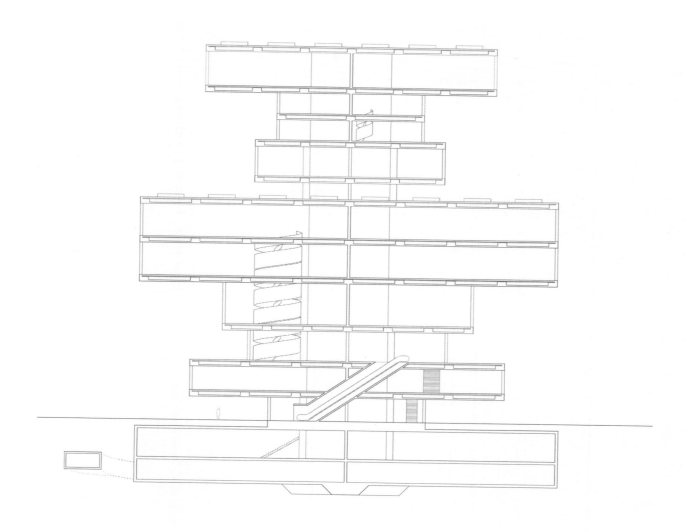

Middle
East

LB [1]

IR [5]

IQ [5]

IL [8]

KW [1]

BH [1]

QA [2]

AE [5]

SA [2]

ATLAS OF NEVER BUILT ARCHITECTURE

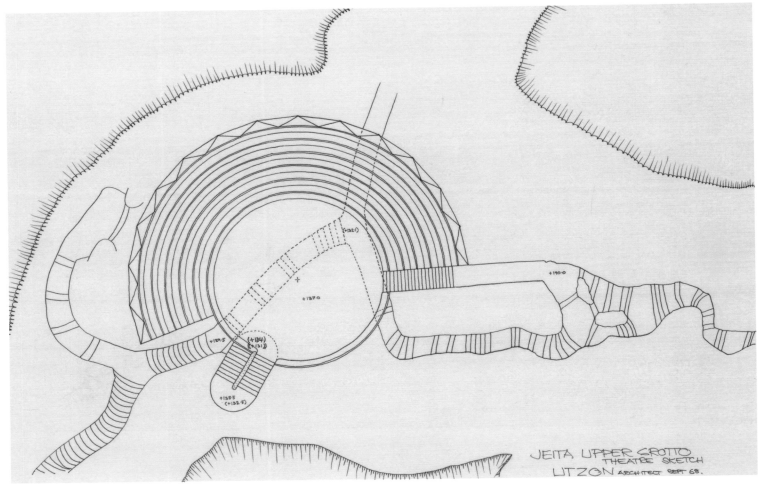

JEITA UPPER GROTTO
THEATRE SKETCH
UTZON ARCHITECT SEPT 68.

JEITA GROTTO THEATRE
Jørn Utzon
Jeita (LB), 1968

Jeita Grotto, in the valley of Nahr el-Kalb, about 20 km (12 miles) northeast of Beirut, has been described as a 'setting for Dante's Hell, amorphous and incredibly sinister'. The perpetual slow drip of water through limestone has pro-

duced a labyrinth filled with columns, draperies, mushrooms, chambers 12 m (39 ft) high, and the world's largest-known stalactite.

In 1968, after a concrete tunnel was built allowing public access to the upper caves, Jørn Utzon was asked to design a concert stage for this underworld. Aware that he couldn't touch any of nature's inimitable and fragile wonders, he conceived a prefabricated steel cage that would be made of modules built outside and carried inside, one by one, for assembly. The wiry spider's web followed the contours of the lime-

stone walls and barely touched the ground, providing, Utzon said, 'protection and a geometrical form to underline the amorphous form of the room'.

The structure would have been illuminated by specks of red, orange, yellow and whitish-grey light. The audience would enter along a darkened path, beckoned by the campfire-like glow of light in the distance. Once they were seated, the theatre would darken to black, then the semicircular stage would be flooded in white light; the audience would remain shrouded in dark-

ness. When the performance ended, the cave would be brightly lit, revealing the eerie formations of a strange world, and triggering an atavistic memory of when caves were humans' only refuge and formed the podium for the first storytelling. Although Jeita Grotto opened to visitors in 1969, internal political strife in Lebanon halted the plan for the theatre in 1970.

NETANYA CITY HALL
Zvi Hecker, Alfred Neumann, Eldar Sharon
Netanya (IL), 1963

Named after the department-store mogul Nathan Straus (co-owner of Abraham & Straus and RH Macy's), who helped to finance its inception, Netanya is a white-sand Mediterranean resort city – sometimes called the 'Israeli Riviera' – wedged between Tel Aviv and Haifa. Among the interesting things to see there, the mundanely blocky, nondescript City Hall is not one of them.

Things could have been remarkably different had a futuristic competition scheme by the structuralist architects Zvi Hecker, Alfred Neumann and Eldar Sharon come to fruition. Their triangular building, framing a large internal courtyard and set in a geometric plaza, epitomized the trio's keen focus on a new building block that would upend the plodding restrictions of the square and the rectangle: the polyhedron. With its angled faces, variability and ability to self-support, the geometry, often arranged in relentlessly fractalized patterns, would help create an integrated, dynamic architecture based on structural honesty, prefabricated efficiency and climatic protection. At Netanya, truncated tetrahedral blocks formed a superstructure resembling an intergalactic battleship, offset with hexagonal panel walls and triangular window openings. Such geometric complexity, turning structure into ornament, would, the architects noted, 'continue a Mediterranean tradition that has been largely ignored until now in modern architecture'.

The competition yielded no winner, but the three men did build the City Hall of nearby Bat Yam, just south of Tel Aviv – a complex, colourful, geometric tour de force, if not exhaustingly so. The critic Robin Middleton called it 'violently triangulated'. Nonetheless, it stands as a treasured landmark to an intensely visionary time.

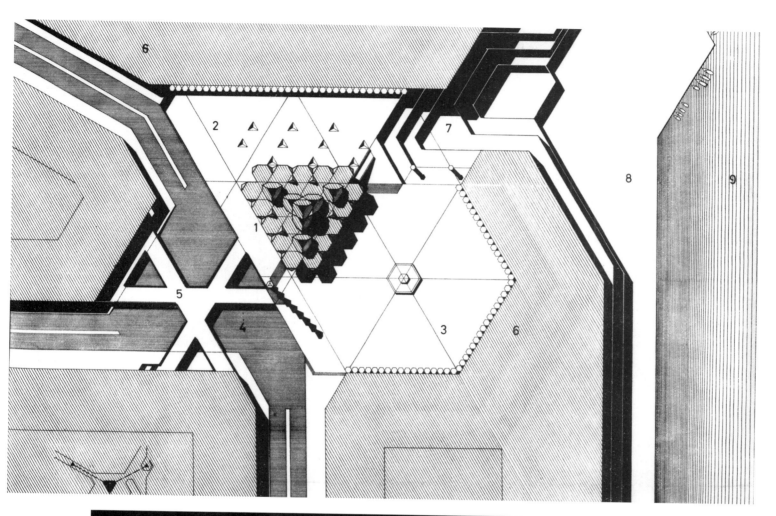

TEL AVIV ARCADES
Studio Precht
Tel Aviv (IL), 2018

When PENDA (now Studio Precht) received the commission to design a condo tower in Ramat Gan, the firm said that the thousands of Bauhaus-inspired buildings in nearby Tel Aviv fuelled its imagination. The thirty-two-storey tessellated tower it proposed was a chequerboard of stacked terraces made of brick-clad, three-dimensional prefabricated concrete parts. Each level consisted of arched openings set well back beneath canopies whose strict geometry of planar surfaces and igloo curves made the facade seem to vibrate. It looked like a ziggurat without the successively receding layers. The repetitive lines and curves were a direct reference to the Modernist works of the German-Jewish refugees who had settled in the area, and to the hand-laid silica brickwork of Jaffa, Tel Aviv's old Arab quarter.

Ramat Gan gets blisteringly hot, but the architect conceived a building that would not do what a typical glass structure would: consume megawatts for air conditioning. The terraces were shades, umbrellas poised against the Mediterranean's burning sunlight, allowing natural cooling for the interiors. Every room had its own terrace so that life could be lived inside and out, public and private. In a sense, the terraces became a vertical plaza that, like any public space in a sweltering climate, offered respite, the chance of casual encounters and visual delight. The architect Chris Precht said, 'A glass tower is the formal illustration of an island without a connection. It's unsustainable in southern regions, it's a bad neighbour as it heats up its surroundings and lacks a sense of identity.'

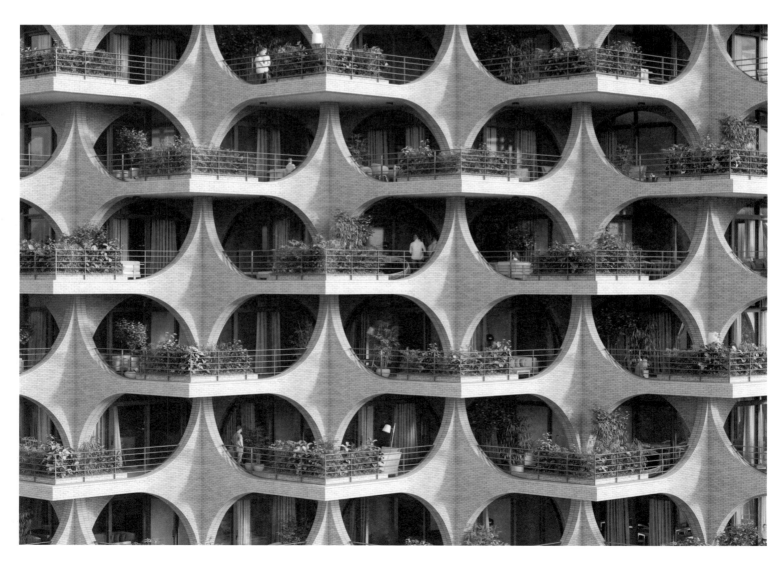

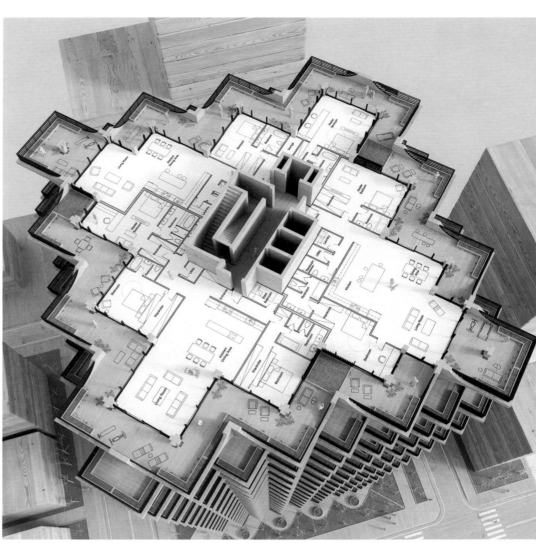

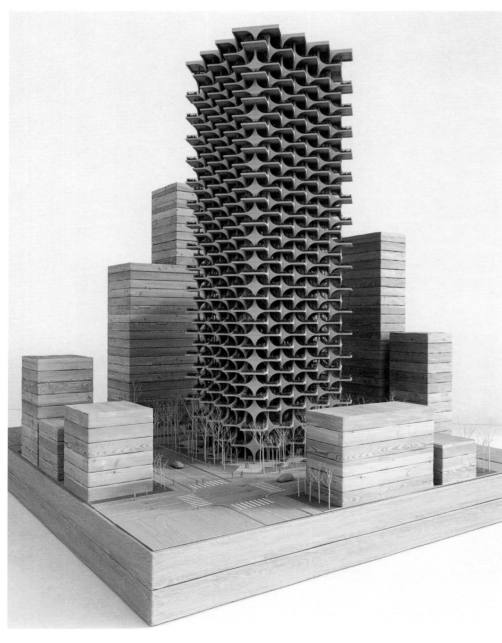

MIDDLE EAST

ANDROMEDA HILL RESIDENTIAL DEVELOPMENT
Mordechai Ben-Horin
Tel Aviv (IL), 1990

The 1980s was an era of expanding wealth in Israel, as well as an epoch of architectural expansionism, when both ancient streets and 1930s Modernist neighbourhoods were being rehabilitated while suburbs were springing up. Andromeda Hill was a project in Jaffa, a port city on the eastern shore of the Mediterranean, which was intended to lure wealthy overseas investors into buying apartments in a pricey new development – part of a longer-term strategy of pushing Palestinians out of their once thriving cultural and commercial city. Named after Andromeda rock, an outcropping in Jaffa harbour where, according to Greek myth, Andromeda was chained as a sacrifice to appease the sea god Poseidon, Mordechai Ben-Horin's stack of concrete boxes was a neo-Brutalist mega-structure that incongruously gave the visual impression of an old Ottoman hillside fortress. It appeared as if Ben-Horin – best known for his sweeping, Guggenheim Museum-like Asia House and his barnacle-encrusted Dizengoff Tower, both in neighbouring Tel Aviv – had collected the rubble of dozens and dozens of Jaffa's bulldozed sandstone homes and compressed them into a huge pyramidal pile.
The concept was throbbing with mad energy, and must have caused the developer to wince.

A few years later Andromeda Hill, completely redesigned by another architect to suit a more polite, bourgeois palate, was being hocked as part of a million-dollar sales campaign for Israeli exiles living in New York. The newly built complex didn't sell, however, and for another decade it was reported in the Israeli press as a financial albatross.

REINHARDT MUSICAL THEATER CENTER
Nadler Nadler Bixon Gil
Tel Aviv (IL), 1970

Sometimes an idea conceived in purity dissipates amid the squabbles of politics and patronage. Nadler Nadler Bixon Gil's competition entry for the Reinhardt Musical Theater Center, represented a design shift for a firm that had played an outsized role in the birth of Israeli civic architecture. By the mid-1950s, they had shed Bauhaus for Brutalism, but their 1970 theatre, on the public plaza in the centre of Tel Aviv where the Palace of Justice and Museum of Art had recently been built, now dismantled a concrete monolith by turning it into a sequence of repeated, bare concrete components.
The project was composed of prefabricated modules 6.8 m (22 ft) wide. Clusters of these modules grew to differing heights, signalling three theatres: one large, one small, one experimental. The modules, like slabs of hewed stone, were anchored firmly to the plaza as if they had been quarried on the spot. The walls climbed in sloped stages, at pitches unique to each theatre, like columnar-jointed rock, unified yet distinct. Nadler Nadler's departure into a stratified Brutalism was, however, consigned to the footnotes of a controversy that erupted after Salo Hershman's winning entry was embroiled in accusations of a rigged jury. The Israeli Supreme Court ruled otherwise, but the Reinhardt was swept away in the whirlwind. In 1973 the Finnish architect Alvar Aalto was asked to design another theatre adjacent to the site, but he died before producing any sketches.

HEBREW UNIVERSITY
Richard Neutra
Jerusalem (IL), 1923

Most acclaimed for his work in Southern California, the Vienna-born architect Richard Neutra created designs for locales around the globe, from Cuba to Pakistan. Shortly after moving to the United States, the Jewish architect – who had worked under the renowned architect Erich Mendelsohn on a proposed commercial centre in Haifa, Israel (then Palestine) – was approached by an international Zionist committee that included Albert Einstein and Rabbi Mordecai Kaplan (founder of the Reconstructionist branch of Judaism). They wanted him to design a library for the new Hebrew University in Jerusalem, which was then rising on Mount Scopus, in the northeast of the city, on a site with panoramic views of the city and the Temple Mount. The project was led by Professor Heinrich Loewe, a leading German library expert.

Neutra's design, revealing the Streamline Moderne influence of Mendelsohn, consisted of a low, horizontal central entrance framed by two long wings of progressively increasing height. Long roof eaves helped to shade outdoor terraces. Inside, the service area on the first floor was flanked by a two-storey layer of reading rooms and a three-storey layer of offices and book stacks.

While the committee praised Neutra's proposal, they eventually selected a domed, neo-Romanesque design with many arched windows and heavy masonry walls by the German-Israeli architects Fritz Kornberg and Benjamin Chaikin and the Christian Zionist Patrick Geddes, who had designed one of the university's several masterplans and worked on other buildings on the campus. Neutra never did work on the campus, but in 1935 his mentor Mendelsohn completed the university's Hadassah Medical Center, which is still considered one of the best hospital buildings in Israel.

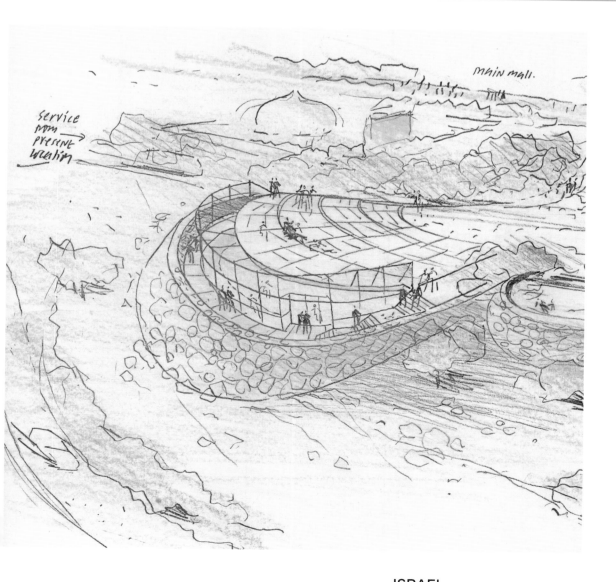

SACKLER GALLERY
Norman Foster
Jerusalem (IL), 1988

Founded in 1965, the Israel Museum in Jerusalem was designed by Alfred Mansfeld and Dora Gad as a Modernist white acropolis sitting in the Judaean Hills, overlooking the Valley of the Cross, and near the Knesset – the national parliament – and Hebrew University. Mansfeld devised a matrix of tall and low modular units, influenced by the Bauhaus, each roughly 11 sq. m (120 sq. ft), which could grow organically, like a village.

The museum did grow, more like Topsy, and in 1986 plans were launched to add space and improve the clarity of the complex. Norman Foster's Sackler Gallery was part of this effort to add a smooth sense of flow through a set of buildings that had no central focus. The gallery was to be inserted underground, beneath the Isamu Noguchi-designed sculpture garden, a raw plateau of sand and rocks upon which sat defiantly modern sculptures. Eight square galleries, ranging in size from 150 to 900 sq. m (1,615–9,688 sq. ft), would be built beneath the rocky berms Noguchi had piled on the western promontory of the site. Visitors would enter via a sloping, glass-enclosed ramp that followed the crescent-shaped sweeps down into the earth. Foster noted on a sketch that the ramp 'could be an exciting event' even when the gallery was closed.

In 1991 the museum became cash-strapped and the plan stalled. By the end of the decade, the monumental $50 million gateway by James Ingo Freed of Pei Cobb Freed had been commissioned, but that too collapsed after Mansfeld helped to torpedo the semi-circular, flat-topped structure. Finally, in 2010, the museum opened a $100 million expansion designed by the minimalist architect James Carpenter.

HURVA SYNAGOGUE
Louis Kahn
Jerusalem (IL), 1967

Following Israel's capture of Jerusalem during the Six-Day War of June 1967, Louis Kahn was asked to redesign Hurva temple, the most important synagogue in Jerusalem, which had been destroyed decades before – and not for the first time (*hurva* means 'ruin' in Hebrew). Of his new Hurva, Kahn would say, 'The outside of the building belongs to the sun, the interior belongs to the shadows.'

Kahn designed a many-layered synagogue with a perimeter of sixteen stoic piers tapered like the stolid sloping stones of Karnak, Egypt, which had fascinated him since he had sketched them in 1951. Hurva's pylons would be made of the same Jerusalem stone as the sacred Western Wall of the city. Inside, four massive concrete towers bore upside-down concrete pyramids, which, Kahn said, 'unfold like leaves of a tree'. At the centre was the *bima*, an intimate sanctuary for reading the Torah. Neither the stone pylons, the concrete towers nor the ceiling pieces ever quite touched. The building was ruins surrounding ruins, the stone and concrete adding the weight of eternity. Within, one void after another was alternately filled with refulgent and sombre light, suffused through the gaps in walls and ceiling.

The proposal sparked a nationwide debate centred on whether the old Hurva should be rebuilt as a living museum or Kahn's constructed as a new symbol of the continued presence of Judaism in Jerusalem. Israel's prime minister put the project on hold, but Kahn kept redrawing the design until his death in 1974. Over succeeding decades, the debate – which has looped in other architects – has carried on, but no new temple has ever been built.

Creator of the stirring Miami Beach Holocaust Memorial (1990), the Florida architect, sculptor, painter and photographer Kenneth Treister designed buildings that merge intricate craft and sculpture, vernacular vocabulary and advanced construction technology, such as sprayed concrete and lengthy cantilevers. A major influence was Frank Lloyd Wright, with whom Treister developed an unbuilt fraternity house while still a student at the University of Florida.

An ardent supporter of Israel, in 1985 Treister proposed the Israel Center for Design Excellence, also known as 'Tel Or', a village-like arts colony ascending a ridge along the Judaean Hills around Jerusalem, for creatives in such fields as architecture, landscape architecture, interior design, fine arts, industrial design, writing and the decorative arts. 'We're not painters or architects, we're all one,' said Treister, who saw the community as a sort of Israeli Bauhaus, celebrating the unity of the arts and integrating them into industry and society. His evocative drawings depict the complex climbing from a partially embedded community centre to a circular central park edged by courtyard houses, up to a domed conference centre floating over a stone base, its series of angled roofs stretching out to the valley below. Behind it were the art studios, clustered by discipline into groups of four around open social spaces. Their patinated copper roofs resembled tree leaves. Treister's proposal – in theory drawing world-class artists from around the world – gained favour among the government, which promised the architect a site and aid with funding. But when the Soviet leader Mikhail Gorbachev opened the borders of the USSR in the late 1980s to allow persecuted Jewish people to emigrate to Israel, the leadership's focus quickly shifted. 'They were trying to house hundreds of thousands,' said Treister. 'They were no longer interested in a village for 300.'

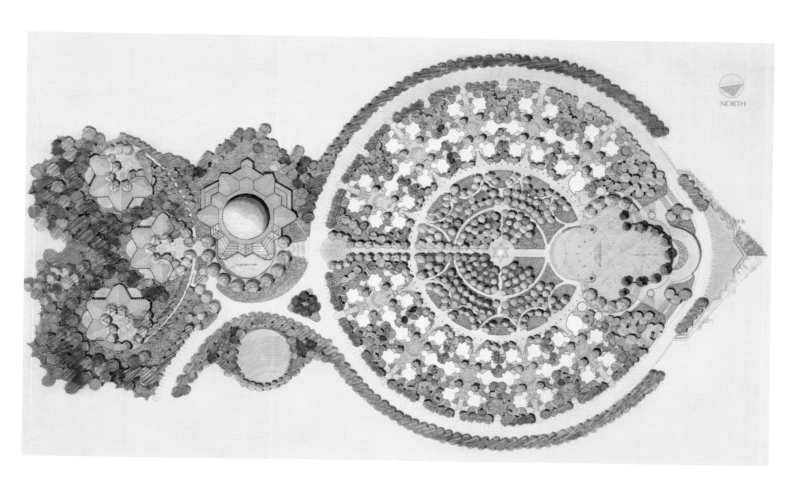

MIDDLE EAST

ISRAEL

LUNAR COMPLEX
Habibeh Madjdabadi
Loshan (IR), 2017

The work of Habibeh Madjdabadi, one of Iran's talented young architects, balances local culture and geography with advanced technology and global ideas. The approach is illustrated well by her Lunar Complex – named for its evocation of a lunar landscape – on the dusty Qazvin-Rasht Freeway in the heart of the hot, arid Iranian plateau. Commissioned by a local businessman who had inherited the site, the structure was to contain a fuel station, a marketplace, toilets and short-term accommodation.

Echoing the curved dunes and sandy hues of the region (not to mention some of its desert animals), the sinuous, bumpy building was clad in a pigmented concrete resembling *kahgel*, a conglomerate of clay and straw commonly employed in the region. Its intricately stepped, climbable roof followed tradition in a place where roofs become a sort of public plaza, with people using them to walk from one house to another. Its large entrance canopy, casting deep shadows, responded to the harsh environment, as did the replacement of large windows with small perforations and nozzle-shaped rooflights, which would project changing shadows onto the building surface. 'Most of the time we design shadows rather than light,' noted Madjdabadi. Rooflights were arranged linearly, illuminating individual market stalls in the manner of the oculus-like rooflights of nearby bazaars. The building would be air-conditioned, but, as Madjdabadi put it, 'the problem is not entirely handled by engineers. Architecture has to do its part, creating optimum conditions for reducing energy consumption and providing a sense of comfort for travellers crossing the desert.' According to the architect, the client had overestimated his financial abilities, so the project was shelved.

BUBBLE SYSTEM
Justus Dahinden
Moghan, Kashmar (IR), 1975

The long tradition of architects experimenting with pneumatic formwork construction – bubble houses built around an inflatable/deflatable membrane – dates at least from the work of the Los Angeles architect Wallace Neff, who in the first half of the twentieth century built some 1,200 structures using his patented 'airform' technique. The Israeli architect Haim Heifetz tried to improve on Neff's dome structures in the 1960s and 70s, as did the Italian Dante Bini at the same time with his 'Binishells'.
Justus Dahinden, the Zurich-based architect who had searched for pragmatic and constructible ways to put human foibles at the core of his work, was brought to Moghan, Iran, to build an entirely new city. For this flat, arid location, devoid even of trees, he devised a modular system of bubble houses. Taking his cue from the arch – the 'dominant Islamic architectural element' – he devised a settlement of mainly single-storey houses, with small private courtyards, arranged into compact residential areas. A dense network of footpaths, which did not cross roads with cars, put any place in the new village within an eight-minute walk of the central bazaar. The concrete domes were cross-ventilated, using the age-old system of two-storey air catchers to funnel cool breezes in through distinctive, quarter-moon towers.
The earthquake-resistant bubbles could be built inexpensively using local labour from clay specially treated to resist erosion. One had only to inflate the plastic membrane with compressed air. By connecting tubes to the domes, a wide variety of different floor plans could be made. One prototype was built, but when the Islamic Republic ousted the Shah in 1979, the project was cancelled.

NATIONAL PARLIAMENT OF IRAN
René Sarger, Mohsen Foroughi, Heydar Ghiai, Claude Parent, André Bloc
Tehran (IR), 1962

One of the great unheralded buildings of Paris is the Maison de l'Iran, a futuristic compilation of floating cubes and spiral stairs within the Cité International de Paris. It originally offered student housing, and is now the home of the Avicenna Foundation. The building's design team included École des Beaux-Arts-trained Iranian architects Mohsen Foroughi and Heydar Ghiai, along with the French architect Claude Parent, the sculptor André Bloc and the engineer René Sarger.
Almost concurrently, the same designers teamed up to work on a much more high-profile proposal: the national parliament of Iran.

The well-connected and -regarded Foroughi was a natural to lead the project. Son of former Prime Minister Mohammad-Ali Foroughi and dean of the faculty of architecture at the Tehran School of Fine Arts, he had designed Iran's senate building with Ghiai and Bloc in 1955, as well as the masterplan for the University of Tehran. His team's initial studies, published in the French journal *L'Architecture d'Aujourd'hui*, revealed a futuristic structure indicative of the forward-looking direction prescribed by Shah Mohammad Reza Pahlavi. The complex was topped by a steel

trussed double dome resting on Y-shaped columns reinforced with a system of cables, creating an advanced self-tensioning system. Under the dome, the building focused on a sunken assembly hall organized by a ribbed seating system and tiered presentation platforms.
Shah Pahlavi never managed to build his parliament, however. While the existing pyramidal parliament building was later designed by Amirali Sardar-Afkhami in 1976, it wouldn't be constructed until after Pahlavi was overthrown during the Islamic Revolution in 1979.

PAHLAVI NATIONAL LIBRARY
Arieh Sharon
Tehran (IR), 1976

Envisioned as one of the world's largest, most prestigious libraries – and as a tool to help transform an emboldened Iran into a more modern and literate place – the Pahlavi National Library was the dream of Shah Mohammad Reza Pahlavi and his cultural counsellor, Shojâ'eddin Shafâ. The scheme would help to highlight a new $3 billion urban centre in northern Tehran, known as Shahestân Pahlavi, the masterplan of which (also not built) was at the time the subject of duelling proposals by the firm Llewelyn Davies and a team led by Louis Kahn and Kenzo Tange.

In 1976 an international competition was launched for the library, soliciting designs that would blend modernity and tradition. More than 3,000 entries came from 87 countries, by architects as varied as Wallace Harrison, Gaetano Pesce, and Alison and Peter Smithson. One of the most fascinating schemes was that of one of the founding fathers of Israeli Modernism, Arieh Sharon, who proposed a machine-like megastructure, floating several storeys above ground and thus unlocking public spaces both above and below. The building's diagonally cross-braced exoskeleton facilitated lofty interior spaces, extensive glazing and copious natural light. An 'interior street' 200 m (656 ft) long connected eight separate library blocks (four on each side), while books would be distributed via paternoster lifts in the structural piers rising from the basement.

The winner of the competition was to be announced, along with an exhibition, on 16 March 1978. But by January the Islamic Revolution had broken out, and the project – like the Shah's regime – came to an abrupt end.

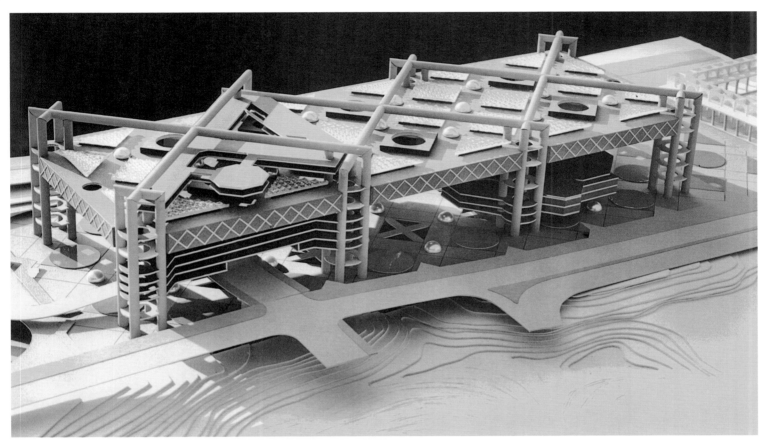

MODERN ART MUSEUM
Alvar Aalto
Shiraz (IR), 1969

About a decade before the Islamic Revolution upended Iranian society, Alvar Aalto, already in his seventies, visited Shiraz at the suggestion of Queen Farah Pahlavi (née Diba), the glamorous and brilliant wife of Mohammad Reza Pahlavi, Iran's last shah. Diba, who had studied architecture in Paris, wanted Aalto to design a hilltop museum for modern art near the university campus of this ancient, garden-filled city. During his stay Aalto began sketching a plan that showcased his customary sensitivity to landscape, local vernacular and formal rhythm. In a nod to the site's long, stepped terraces and nearby sculpted ruins, he formed a group of narrow, interconnected structures, stacked and slightly angled from one another, flanked by a walled sculpture garden and a public park. He called it 'an accumulation of rising terrace forms'. Inside the museum, wedge-shaped, open-plan spaces, including a columned main hall, reflected the stepped form of the exterior, creating a serrated, mountain-like profile. Nature was brought into the galleries via indirect sunlight, which permeated through decorative rooflights and large clerestories and was reflected from curved surfaces.

Despite some frustration over the pace of progress, Aalto laboured on working drawings until his death in 1976. When the revolution overthrew the shah three years later it put a definitive end to the project. Aalto designed a total of fifteen museums, only three of which were ever built. Among his other misses was the Baghdad Art Museum (1957), with deep roof overhangs and a durable facade designed to counter that city's harsh conditions.

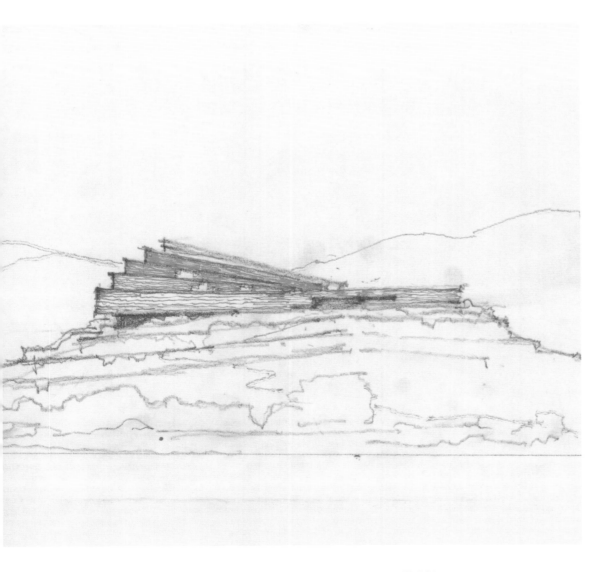

CEREMONIAL PARADE GROUND
Makiya Associates
Tikrit (IQ), 1984

Trained in England (at the universities of Liverpool and Cambridge) and a passionate advocate of incorporating early Islamic motifs into modern work, Mohamed Makiya became one of the favoured architects of the Iraqi dictator

Saddam Hussein, who during that decade envisioned grand plans around the country, from palaces to mosques to river-front redevelopments. In 1984 Makiya Associates began designing a ceremonial parade ground in Saddam's home town of Tikrit, a small city on the River Tigris about 170 km (106 miles) north of Baghdad. (The firm had just two years earlier been named a finalist for the contest to design Saddam's Baghdad State Mosque.)

The site, at the edge of the town, was 1 km (just over ½ mile) square and incorporated space

for military parades, sporting events and cultural happenings. As per Makiya's signature, the enclosing walls evoked the gates of such ancient Mesopotamian cities as Babylon, with heavy buttresses, long arcades (*riwaqs*), arched openings and decorative brickwork. Scattered around the site would be imposing pavilions, triumphal arches, grandstands and *allées* of trees. 'It was huge!' Makiya noted in an interview with *Bidoun*, a publication promoting the art and culture of the Middle East. 'He [Saddam] wanted it the way he had in Baghdad with the

swords! So the army could promenade through it like they do in Red Square. I ignored this request. I designed a complex for it – for festivals, for the feast, not for the tanks.'

The financial costs of the gruelling Iran–Iraq War (1980–88) made it impossible for Saddam to pursue many of his grand projects, however. By 1986 this one had been set aside.

FINE ARTS MUSEUM OF BAGHDAD
Alvar Aalto
Baghdad (IQ), 1957

Among the list of celebrated Modernist architects invited by the Iraqi Development Board to help design the future Baghdad in the mid-1950s – including Le Corbusier, Walter Gropius, Gio Ponti, Josep Lluís Sert and Frank Lloyd Wright

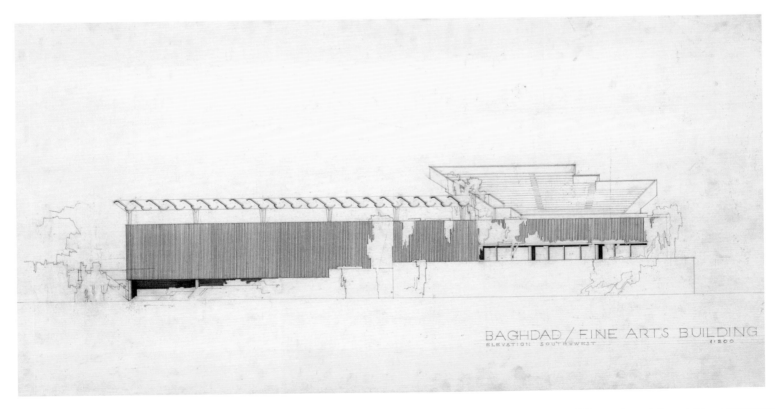

– was the Finnish master Alvar Aalto. Aalto was at one point set to design the civic centre's general post office and museum of fine arts, but neither was built. The three-storey museum was intended to house a vast collection of paintings, sculptures and decorative arts spanning many epochs (including the rich collection of the Armenian oil magnate Calouste Gulbenkian, founder of the Iraq Petroleum Company). Aalto's International Style design projected simple, forward-looking sophistication and was well protected from the city's harsh weather.

'A certain simplicity is possible here, a simplicity that does not habitually exist in the European climate,' the architect noted. Outside, the square structure, shaded with dramatically deep canopies, was clad in dark blue ceramic tiles – evoking the coloured, glazed bricks of ancient Babylonian city gates – and framed by wedge-shaped columns. Inside, five asymmetrical, interlocking galleries, linked by a diagonal walkway, were arranged echelon-style, while a tooth-like system of cane-shaped rooflights provided soft, indirect natural lighting. On the

roof was a brise-soleil-topped sculpture garden containing a fanning amphitheatre, sloping with the roofline of the building.

It was the 14 July Revolution of 1958 that stopped Aalto's Baghdad projects from advancing. The architect received a letter from the new government indicating that the museum had not been abandoned, but nothing happened after that. He never built anything in the Middle East, or indeed anywhere else outside the Western world.

STATE MOSQUE OF BAGHDAD
Venturi, Rauch & Scott Brown
Baghdad (IQ), 1982

The State Mosque of Baghdad began as an invited competition summoned into existence by the ruthless Iraqi president Saddam Hussein. Seven architects submitted designs for what was touted as the world's largest mosque – large enough to accommodate 30,000 worshippers.

Venturi, Rauch and Scott Brown (VRSB)'s entry took conventional imagery and distorted it. Their mosque adopted the Islamic hypostyle form, in which the prayer hall is made of row upon row of columns supporting arches that seem to multiply to infinity. With the aid of Ove Arup's engineered trusses 70 m (230 ft) long, the endless arcades were lifted high overhead, liberating a great, open space below. The exterior walls were elaborately decorated, inscribed with calligraphy and layers of Islamic geometric designs, and topped by a crenellated parapet. In keeping with the Iraqi dictator's anti-Shi'a faith, the unprecedented faceted blue dome, which advertised the mosque across the city, was placed off-centre, over the worship courtyard or *sahn*. From beneath, the dome appeared to be an immense tree, its spreading limbs shading the people beneath.

Despite intending to be 'at once modern and familiar', VRSB's mosque didn't wow the regime.

Still, as an exercise in state-sponsored glorification, the competition served its purpose. It spread a contagion of mosque-building one-upmanship that is still ongoing. It sparked a race to design mosques with taller minarets, larger domes and more elaborate interiors. As for the State Mosque of Baghdad, in 1989 – round one having fizzled out – Saddam Hussein convened a new competition. The winning design was sidelined by the Gulf War in 1990, and was successively reactivated and cancelled until Saddam was toppled in December 2003.

IRAQI PARLIAMENT BUILDING
HNNA
Baghdad (IQ), 2013

Nothing, it seems, comes easily in Baghdad. The competition to design a new $1 billion building for the Iraqi Council of Representatives was overflowing with drama and, eventually, failure. The project's anonymous jury, assembled by the Royal Institute of British Architects, chose as the winning entry – besting more than 130 proposals – the relatively low-profile UK firm Assemblage (now HNNA), then led by Australian Peter Besley and English architect Hannah Corlett.

Their design centred on including the public and creating a work of urban design rather than an architectural object. Most of the 20-hectare (49-acre) complex was formed as a pattern of indoor and outdoor streets and courtyards, connecting an arrangement of buildings with varying functions. Within this ensemble, the key landmark was the Council of Representatives, a circular structure (a symbol of convergence and stability, noted the architects) encircling the semicircular Great Hall and Council Chamber, edged with a monumental *brise-soleil*, whose large fins allowed glimpses in and out. Between the spaces was a huge entrance foyer, dramatized by raking rooflights.

But within months of the jury's decision, rumours swirled that the Iraqi authorities were in discussion with the third-place entrant, the object-specialist starchitect (and native of Baghdad) Zaha Hadid to design the structure. By 2014 Hadid had reportedly signed on. She died in 2016, however, and the plans were marred by a hail of Isis-fuelled violence, internal political upheaval, and a need for more pressing infrastructure. Today the site stands empty, and the council still meets in Baghdad's Conference Palace, a Brutalist structure designed in 1983 by the Finnish architect Kaija Siren.

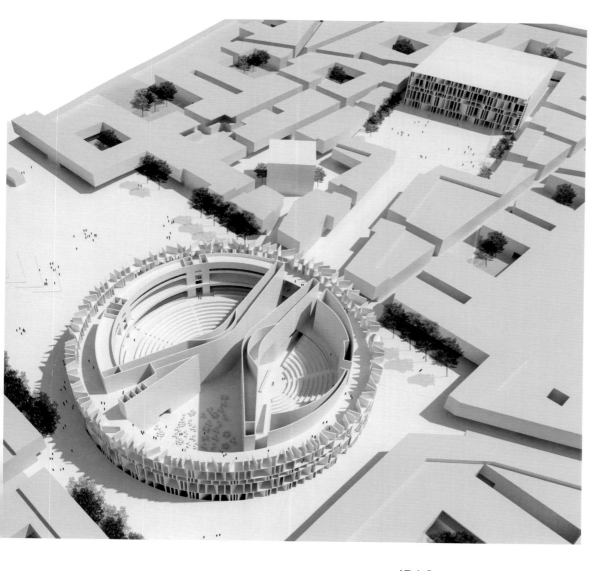

PLAN FOR GREATER BAGHDAD
Frank Lloyd Wright
Baghdad (IQ), 1957

In May 1957 Frank Lloyd Wright boarded a plane in the baking sun of Phoenix, Arizona, heading for another sweltering locale: Baghdad, Iraq. Wright, a long-standing lover of Arab design and culture, had been invited by the country's Cultural Commission to design a new opera house. According to Wright scholar Bruce Brooks Pfeiffer, on their descent into the airport Wright noticed a long, thin island in the Tigris River. Upon meeting King Faisal II, he argued that this would be preferable to any busy downtown site. 'The island, Mr Wright, is yours,' replied the King. Wright's opera was to be part of a broader plan developed by British designers Anthony Minoprio, Hugh Spencely and Peter Macfarlane that included cultural spaces, offices, athletic facilities, government buildings and a university complex, by such renowned architects as Le Corbusier, Alvar Aalto, Willem Dudok, Gio Ponti and Walter Gropius.

Wright enlarged his plans wantonly as he worked. Virtually every element – the opera as well as a civic auditorium, a planetarium, art museums, a grand bazaar, a monument to the legendary eighth-century Abbasid caliph Harun al-Rashid, mounded earthworks, gardens, fountains and tiered highways – shared the curving language of caliph-era Baghdad when it was surrounded by concentric circular walls and known as the 'Round City'. The centrepiece Crescent Opera, marked by a tall minaret-like spire and an arch of sculpted medallions, was topped with an intricate cone-shaped dome, engulfed by a garden and reflecting pool, and edged with a spiral ramp evocative of an ancient ziggurat. Following the coup of July 1958, the king was brutally murdered and the plan quickly rejected by the military leadership.

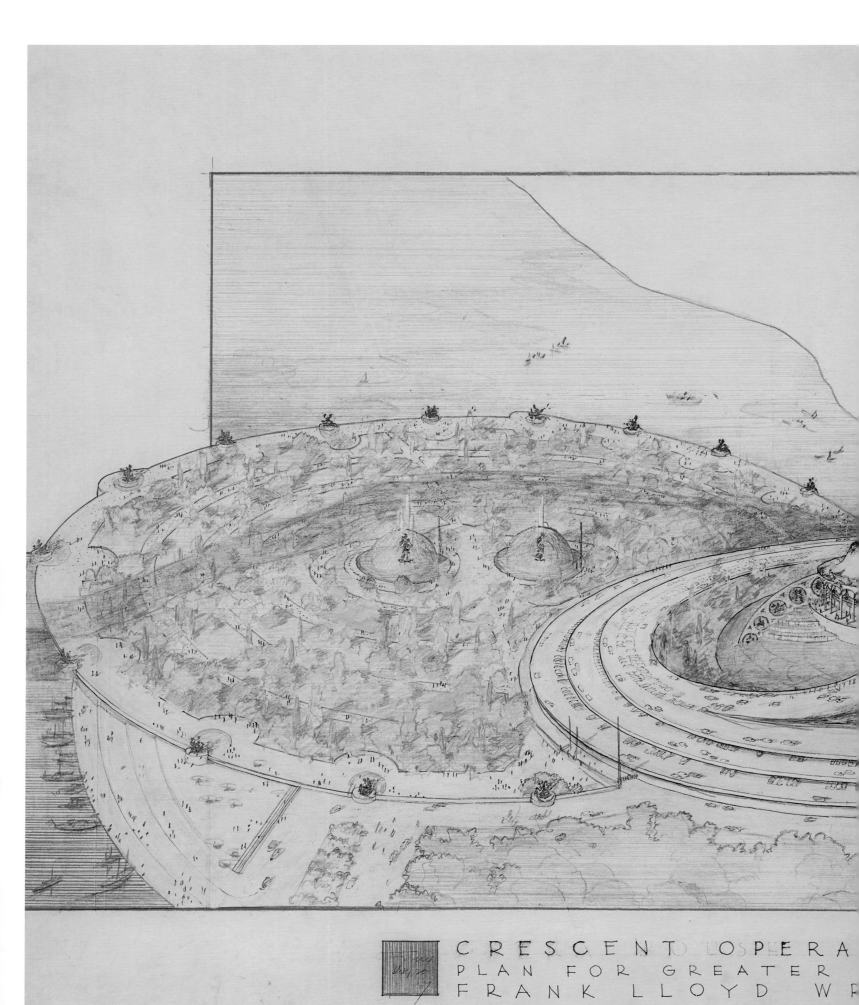

CRESCENT OPERA
PLAN FOR GREATER
FRANK LLOYD WR

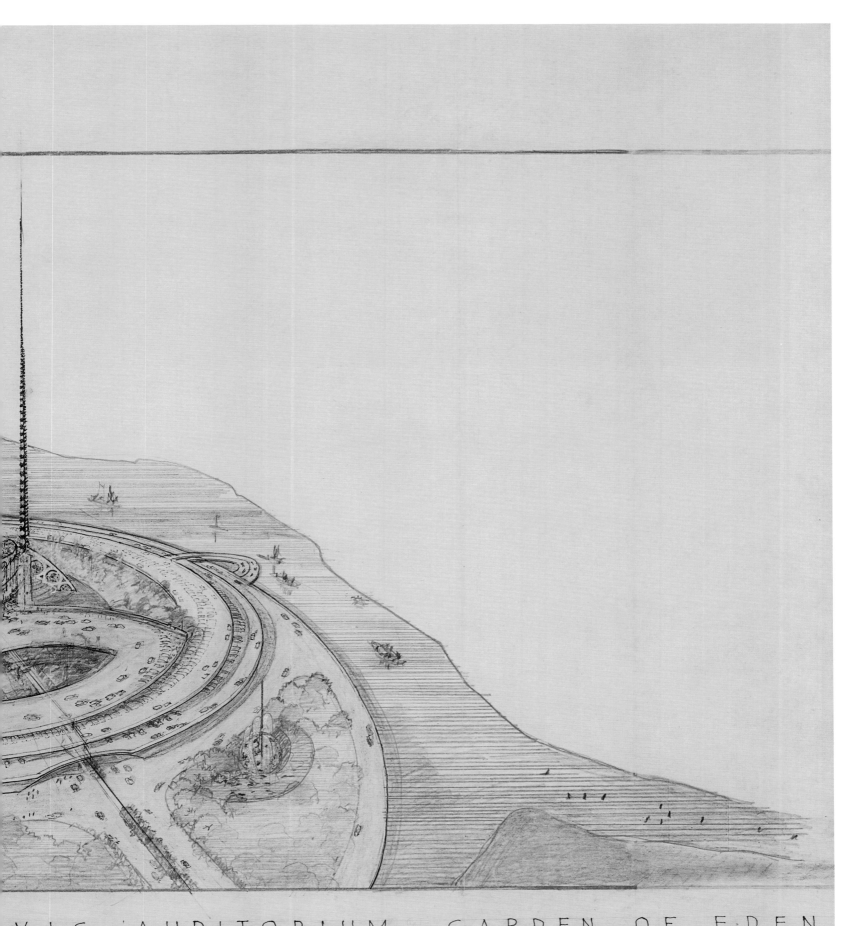

VIC AUDITORIUM.   GARDEN   OF   E·DEN

HDAD

T   ARCHITECT

KUWAIT SPORTS CENTRE
Pier Luigi Nervi
Kuwait City (KW), 1969

In 1968 Kuwait's emir, Sheikh Sabah Al-Salim Al-Sabah, invited four Western architects to conceive a sports centre in anticipation of the plan to host the Pan Arab Games in 1974. Kenzo Tange (Japan) and Frei Otto (Germany) paired up; Pier Luigi Nervi (Italy), Felix Candela (Mexico) and Lloyd, Morgan & Jones (United Kingdom) went solo.

The stadium was key; it was meant to seat 40,000, with the possibility of accommodating another 20,000. Tange and Otto proposed a steel cable-net roof extending a shroud over the stadium seats. Candela's thin-shell concrete scheme was a little like a geodesic dome, in which he had inscribed 'Arabic' features. Lloyd, Morgan & Jones's dome was similar to the firm's recently completed Astrodome (1965) in Houston, then the world's largest domed stadium. Nervi defied expectations: instead of a reinforced-concrete ribbed roof of the kind that had made him world-famous, he offered a concrete stadium covered by a freestanding transparent dome. A space frame made of aluminium tubes covered in a clear plastic, this 'Triodetic Dome', as Nervi called it, would have been supported on sixty-four inclined buttresses. At 256 m (840 ft) in diameter, it would have been almost double the diameter of the Astrodome. Comparisons with Richard Buckminster Fuller's 'Dome over Manhattan' were unavoidable, and led to speculation that Nervi wasn't necessarily interested in winning the competition – which, indeed, he lost to Tange and Otto – but rather wanted to position his firm as a leader in the use of new materials and technology. The Games were cancelled when the Arab–Israeli War broke out in 1973, and with that, the project ended.

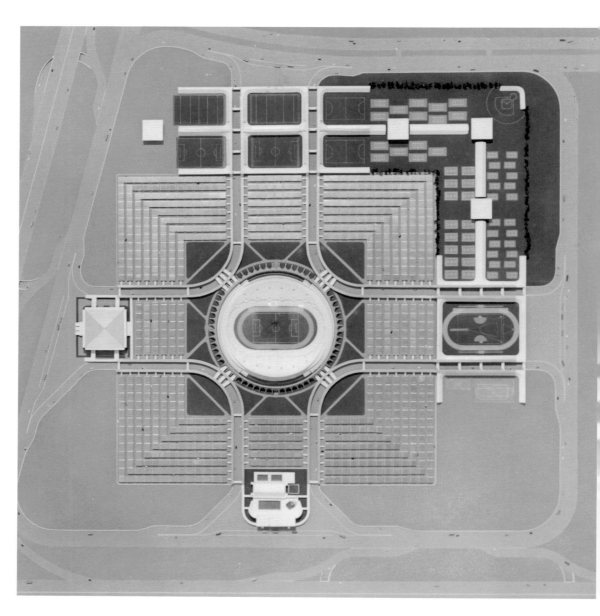

ARRIYADH SCIENCE COMPLEX
Douglas Cardinal
Riyadh (SA), 1988

The Canadian architect Douglas Cardinal's flowing, emotional architecture draws on his Indigenous background (he has Blackfoot ancestry), nature-based and human-centred philosophy and contextual approach. His most recognized buildings include the Smithsonian National Museum of the American Indian in Washington, DC, and the Canadian Museum of History in Ottawa, but he has both built and imagined a voluminous body of work.

In the mid-1980s Cardinal collaborated with the construction company SaudConsult to win an international competition for a science centre in Riyadh. He spent months in Saudi Arabia developing the design and was especially moved by the region's ancient culture, mud-brick architecture and vast desert, with its blazing blanket of stars at night. The resulting complex, for a site on the periphery of Riyadh (and linked to the city via a space-age monorail), felt like its wild surroundings; its reddish sandstone structures would take shape like dunes and rock formations, and its curving envelope wrapped around a central oasis, filled with water and dotted with fig, date and palm trees.

Hovering over the oasis – and accessed via a neck-like funicular – was a spherical omnimax-planetarium emulating the glowing desert moon. 'I was totally mesmerized by the land and the culture,' says Cardinal, who took further inspiration from the Koran's vivid descriptions of the landscape. The project was championed by by His Royal Highness Prince Sultan bin Salman Al Saud, who had flown a mission on the US space shuttle in 1985, but over time the project – which was one of Cardinal's favourites – simply disappeared.

SAUDI AIR DEFENCE HEADQUARTERS
Arthur Erickson
Riyadh (SA), 1978

As tension in the Middle East increased in the 1960s, the Saudi-Arabian military spun off its Air Defence as a stand-alone ministry. It followed that the division would need its own headquarters, and Arthur Erickson, who had already been working in the kingdom, won the competition held in 1978.

Erickson was interested in modernizing Saudi-Arabian architecture while nodding to the thick-walled, introverted desert forms that had emerged in the region's harsh climate. His low-lying pyramid was open at two ends, allowing light and air to filter in, and the remaining wings with offices hung like mirrored glass prisms, as the architect called them. A central core was carved from the lower storeys of the building, sheltering an inner garden in the Islamic tradition. A five-storey stepped concrete roof shielded the mirrored office cubes, which would reflect the oasis of date palms surrounding the pyramid. Erickson said, 'I was inspired by a royal divan at the head of a garden in Shiraz; it had faceted mirrors in its great vault that scattered the cypresses and pools into myriad reflections.' The use of simple geometry, he felt, would intensify the play of desert light and shadow. Many strains of Islamic architecture ran through the seemingly modern structure, from the notion of a sheltered cave faceted with mirrors, borrowed from Iran's Divan style, to hanging cubes recalling muqarnas, the ornamental vaulting found on buildings throughout the Middle East.

The project was administered by the US Army Corps of Engineers. Perhaps unsurprisingly, the Canadian architect was sidelined in favour of a venerable American firm that completed the headquarters.

BAHRAIN NATIONAL CULTURAL CENTRE
Sir Basil Spence
Manama (BH), 1976

The Brutalist architect Sir Basil Spence – arguably Scotland's greatest and most visionary designer since Charles Rennie Mackintosh – is best remembered for his folding brick Coventry Cathedral (1962) in England and his layered, cone-shaped Beehive wing for the New Zealand Parliament Buildings in Wellington. Amazingly, few of his audacious designs went unbuilt, despite plenty of controversy, but his final design, a competition entry in 1976 for the Bahrain National Cultural Centre (the first major facility of its kind in the Persian Gulf, containing a library, congress hall, and spaces for performing), lost out to a proposal by the Finnish architect Timo Penttilä – which was also never built. Spence died in November of that year at his country home in the Suffolk village of Yaxley. In that idyllic location he had sketched out dozens of drawings, creating a sort of Brutalist Bedouin village, with a stepped concrete landscape of hills, bluffs and city walls, topped with varied, interconnected concrete domes reminiscent variously of tents, mushrooms, umbrellas and funnels. A centrepiece structure resembled a chunky spaceship, supported by flying buttresses and anchored with parabolic concrete canopies. Translucent stone apertures would allow glowing light to show through from the inside.

Numerous international architects and jurors were invited to participate in the competition, which was chaired by the long-standing dean of MIT Architecture School Lawrence B Anderson. Anderson noted that the doomed undertaking couldn't include any local architects because 'there weren't any.' He alluded to friction between Penttilä and the authorities, but the autocratic government never revealed why the winning project didn't go ahead.

GOVERNMENT CENTRE
James Stirling
Doha (QA), 1976

Like other oil-rich Gulf states, Qatar found itself swimming in petrodollars after the oil embargo of 1973. In 1976 the government launched a design competition for a massive civic centre along an artificial 7.5 km (4.7 mile) corniche on Doha Bay, that would give Qatar the patina of modernity on a par with the West. The invited architects were to design a government centre for all eleven ministries (each run by a member of the Qatari royal family). Four architects competed: Kenzo Tange, James Stirling, the American firm the Architects Collaborative and the German architect Günter Behnisch.

Stirling laid a row of ten horseshoe-shaped buildings in a razor-straight line overlooking the bay (the last building, for the Ministry of Justice, was placed on a triangular park beyond). The eleven-storey buildings became successively smaller to reflect the size of the individual ministries. Each had a peristyle garden, an Arabic entrance arch and a multi-storey clerestory that was the minister's penthouse. An elevated inter-ministry tram would run through a mall – spanned by the concrete buildings – looking like a section lifted from London's Underground network. Stirling's neatly defined buildings were inscribed with repetitive *brise-soleils* that provided a visual refrain uniting the long string of structures. He also sketched a palm-lined public promenade that attempted a democratic gesture in a thoroughly autocratic fiefdom.

The emir of Qatar, Sheikh Khalifa bin Hamad Al Thani, alone picked the winner, Tange, whose megastructure depicted a bureaucracy as a single, impenetrable entity. Squabbles among the ruling family led to various sheikhs building their own ministries independent of the envisioned complex, short-circuiting the plan. Stirling lost, but in the end so did the putative winner.

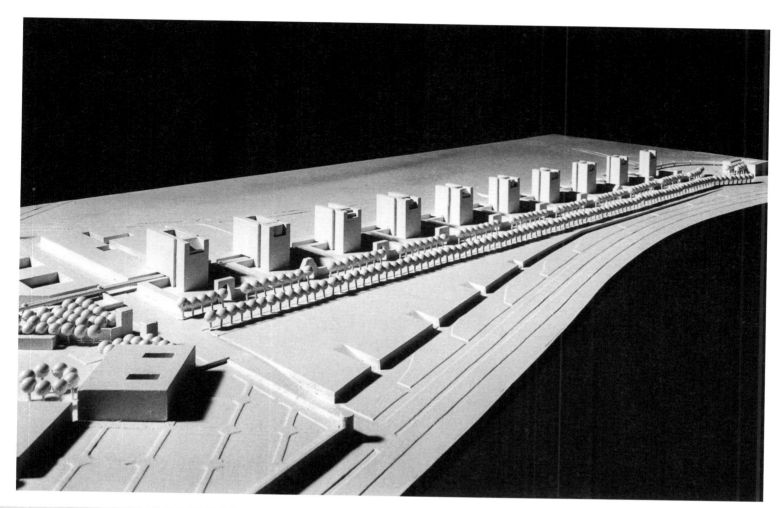

QATAR NATIONAL LIBRARY
Arata Isozaki
Doha (QA), 2002

Precious few of the behemoth visions of Japan's Metabolist architects – who fused architectural megastructures with concepts of biological growth – came to fruition. One of the movement's latest incarnations came in 2002, when Arata Isozaki was commissioned by the Emir of Qatar to design the Qatar National Library in Doha.

Much of the design drew on the architect's 'City in the Air' concept from the 1960s, in which tree-like buildings were set on a series of trunk-like columns, exploring new zones for development and radically fusing architecture and urban infrastructure. 'I showed [the Emir] my book,' the architect said in an interview. 'Looking through it, he stopped at the City in the Air project from 1962 and said, "Oh, this is very interesting!" I said, "It's a project from my student days. Impossible to realize. Just a dream." But the Emir said, "No, I want this."'

Perched near the top of three columns, each 120 m (394 ft) tall, the glass-clad library fanned dramatically outwards, its cantilevered platforms widening as the building rose. At its base was a wide podium containing museums of contemporary art, science and natural history. Construction commenced in 2005, but the Emir soon halted it, never revealing why; he eventually let the project die. OMA would build a very different version of the library in 2018. Still, in 2011 Isozaki built the Qatar Convention Centre, also a revival of one of his Metabolist schemes

(that one for a railway station in Florence). Supporting its thin, wide roof are tube-like columns that resemble intertwined trees.

UAE TEMPORARY MUSEUM
Shigeru Ban
Abu Dhabi (AE), 2009

Shigeru Ban has carved a niche for himself as the king of temporary pavilions, creating wood, cardboard and fabric structures around the world to aid with disaster relief, host art exhibitions and music events, and even serve as schools and churches. In 2009 he entered an invited competition to improve Khalifa Park, a facility of 500,000 sq. m (5,382,000 sq. ft) adjacent to the enormous Sheikh Zayed Grand Mosque and designed as an escape from the ever-growing metropolis.

Containing a variety of dispersed venues – including a library, maritime museum, gardens, a splash park and a military parade ground – the park posed one chief problem: how to get people to each venue in the city's extreme heat. In response, Ban proposed a temporary (or perhaps permanent?) series of shaded, partially air-conditioned paper tube-framed colonnades along the park's main axis, connecting the scattered facilities and lined with greenery, water, and large and small courtyards. Further nods to the local vernacular included rooftop domes, tall arched gateways, and the possibility of a large cone-shaped structure to help mark the green space.

Ban's plan was not selected, and in the end very few changes were made to the park. John Galloway, another entrant to the competition, noted later that 'they ultimately didn't do anything, and it looks the same right now as it did when I walked the site a decade ago.' However, in 2014 Ban did get to build a paper-tube structure in the city: an infinitely smaller pavilion for the Abu Dhabi Art Fair.

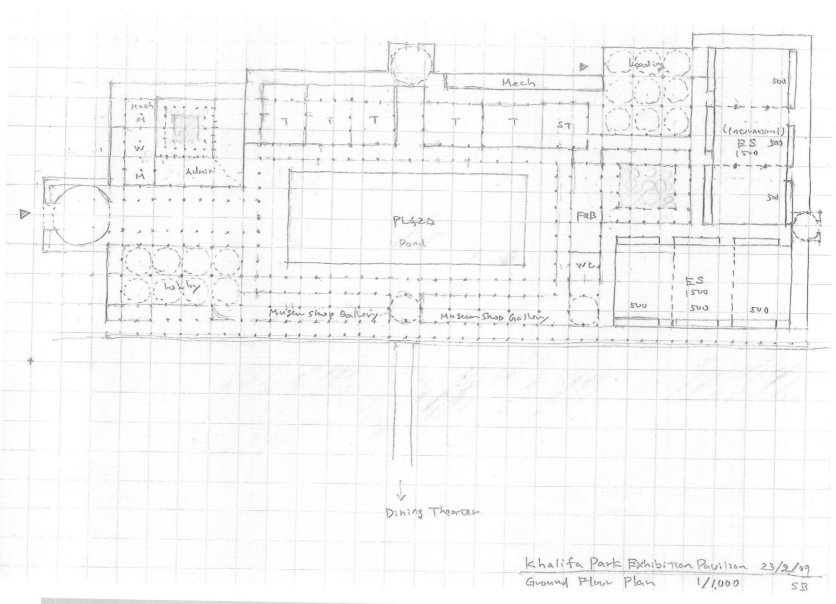

UAE PARLIAMENT
EYRC
Abu Dhabi (AE), 2011

When one thinks of the United Arab Emirates, the word 'parliament' does not spring to mind. But shortly after the turn of the millennium the Emirates began searching for a location to convene its new Federal National Council, a quasi-parliamentary body (indirectly elected by the small percentage of Emirati citizens who have voting rights) in Abu Dhabi. From a competition list that included such giants as Zaha Hadid and Norman Foster, the small California firm Ehrlich Architects (later EYRC) took the prize.

Designed to symbolize, as Steven Ehrlich put it, 'a harmonious balance of Islamic heritage and global modern aspirations', the 120,773 sq. m (1.3 million sq. ft) complex abutting Corniche Road on the Persian Gulf would be topped by a filigreed canopy (evocative of local *mashrabiya* screens), under which lay a circular assembly hall surrounded by offices, meeting halls and a visitors' centre. The assembly hall was topped by a dome 100 m (328 ft) in diameter, inspired by a five-petalled desert flower and supported by deep concrete ribs with intricate Islamic patterning, coloured glass, and an oculus through which light would filter. The peripheral buildings, resting on a podium, were terraced to suggest the region's sculpted dunes, and clad in light-coloured stone to evoke local mud-brick architecture.

As with many unbuilt dreams in autocratic countries, the true reason for the project's cancellation was never revealed. But work stoppe[d] suddenly after the Arab Spring uprisings [of] 2010, suggesting that the UAE was not ready [to] promote any sort of representative governme[nt] however limited.

MINA FISH MARKET
Tabanlıoğlu Architects
Abu Dhabi (AE), 2018

Stretching several miles from the city's breakwater to the Mina Zayed port, Abu Dhabi's waterfront, known as the Corniche, is the historic heart of the city and arguably its most popular leisure spot. Tucked between the Corniche's beaches, parks, malls and embassies are a few old marketplaces specializing in such staples as vegetables, dates, teas, spices and fish.

In 2018 the Istanbul-based practice Tabanlıoğlu Architects was invited by the Abu Dhabi developer Modon Properties to design a modern variation at the port: the 10,000 sq. m (107,600 sq. ft) Mina Fish Market. The firm's designs included a masterplan to reinvigorate several local souks and revitalize the area with new hotels, retail and leisure in a landscape of alleys, arcades, patios, courtyards, pedestrian streets and linear parks. The market's vaulted canopies, made of glass-reinforced concrete, recalled the wavy outlines of traditional market tents, not to mention the choppy Persian Gulf nearby. Under the canopies, glazed spaces, accented with fishing nets and bulbous lighting evocative of buoys and fishing lures, would be topped by varied ceilings – of wood, plaster, stone and glass – while the market's centre contained an open courtyard.

Modon and Abu Dhabi's Department of Municipalities and Transport eventually dropped the firm's design and took over the project. In 2022 they opened the new market, with a far less ambitious concept and little masterplanning around it. Containing more than 100 stalls, the building is a tinted glass box shaded by slats of wood and steel and fronted by arched plaster arcades. No architect or masterplan is named in official releases.

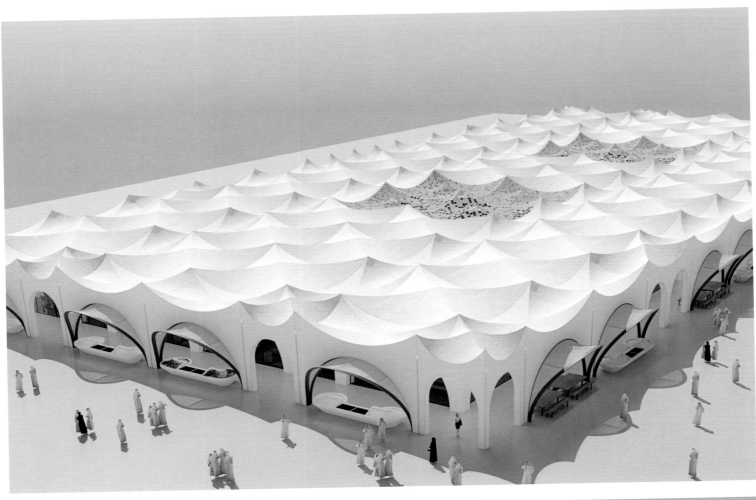

DUBAI SOLAR INNOVATION CENTER
Antoine Predock
Dubai (AE), 2012

The architect Antoine Predock of Albuquerque, New Mexico, has long juggled the futuristic and the prehistoric, incorporating advanced applications (particularly related to sustainability) while blurring the line between architecture and landscape. His competition entry for the Dubai Energy and Water Authority's Solar Innovation Center, showcasing solar technology and acting as the centrepiece of the Emirate's new Mohammed bin Rashid Al Maktoum Solar Park, was partially embedded into arcing dunes, staying cool via the Earth's thermal mass.

The 'village', consisting of varied structures separated by paths and greenery, was covered by a light, tent-like roof, embedded with solar collectors of cell-thin film. The air pocket between the undulating roof and the amorphous solar collectors would create another natural source of cooling. New Mexico is a great training ground for creating eco-friendly designs in a harsh environment, Predock told Engineering.com in November 2018. 'You're kind of self-taught in terms of what you can get away with and [what] you can't in that kind of climate,' he said. Inside, interactive paths unfurled along gently descending ramps. At the end of the exhibition sequence visitors would ascend the spherical 'sun' of the IMAX theatre to experience views in all directions. Next to that structure a large, cone-shaped structure expelled warm air from the complex via the 'chimney effect' which exploits the rising of hot air in order to cool interior spaces.

The competition was won by Kettle Collective, founded by former RMJM chief Tony Kettle. The ziggurat-like building 88 m (289 ft) tall, inspired by traditional Islamic geometry and covered with thousands of integrated solar panels, was completed in 2021.

DUBAI OPERA HOUSE
Zaha Hadid
Dubai (AE), 2007

As early as 2005 word leaked that the UK-based starchitect Zaha Hadid might be designing the most 'Zaha' of projects at the peak of a global building boom: the $100 million Dubai Opera House. By 2007 it was official, and designs began circulating for what would become the Persian Gulf's first opera house, on an island in Dubai Creek, the historic focus of trade in a city that had long embraced the economic engines of oil and real estate.

Containing a 2,500-seat opera house, an 800-seat 'theatre', an art gallery, a performing arts school and a themed hotel, the complex surged out of the ground as a flowing built landscape inspired by the local dunes and mountains. It was anchored by a grand foyer and culminated in varied peaks, textured with abstract Islamic motifs, housing each element of the programme.

By 2009 the global property meltdown had killed the endeavour, along with hundreds more speculative proposals in the overheated Emirates, including works by Jean Nouvel, Snøhetta and OMA, and even a hotel for Donald Trump at the base of Palm Jumeirah. The opera's developer, Sama Dubai (which was later rescued by a massive government bail out) nixed virtually every project in its pipeline. Other Hadid spectacles in the UAE disintegrated as well, including a torquing performing-arts centre on Saadiyat Island in Abu Dhabi.

Once the financial dust had settled, Dubai did get its opera house: a far less elaborate design sketched by Atkins architects and engineers and developed by Emaar Properties. It opened in 2016, the year Hadid passed away.

Africa

MA [1]

DZ [2]

EG [5]

BF [1]

GH [1]

KE [1]

RW [1]

CD [1]

TZ [3]

MZ [1]

ZA [2]

ATLAS OF NEVER BUILT ARCHITECTURE

263

ATLANTROPA TOWER
Peter Behrens
Strait of Gibraltar, 1928

From 1928 until his death in 1952, the German architect and engineer Herman Sörgel diligently promoted his idea of a supercontinent called Atlantropa. If two gigantic dams were built across the Strait of Gibraltar and the Dardanelles Strait, the waters of the Mediterranean would slowly sink, and 576,000 sq. km (222,400 sq. miles) of new arable land would emerge. A huge network of hydroelectric plants, sufficient to power all of Europe, would be built, along with bridges and tunnels across the shrunken sea. What were then the Belgian Congo and French Cameroon would disappear beneath a vast lake; the Chari River would reverse flow to become a navigable waterway to the Mediterranean; fresh water would irrigate the Sahara Desert. Europe's teeming population would have a new continent to inhabit. Such a version of Manifest Destiny – with all its assumptions about African inferiority – did not worry Sörgel or many of his contemporaries. He assembled support from renowned architects including Erich Mendelsohn and Ludwig Mies van der Rohe. But it was Peter Behrens's design for the skyscrapers that would guard the canal locks that captured the true power of the technological sublime. Behrens caught the spirit of Sörgel's not-so-impossible idea – his 400 m (1,300 ft) tower stood ramrod stiff, a pure rectangular form reduced to its thinnest possible profile, emblematic of the mastery and economy of modern materials over the natural world. Adolf Hitler, deeming Atlantropa too 'pacifist' eventually barred Sörgel from publishing another word about it, and although it was resumed after World War II, it became more science fiction than believable proposition.

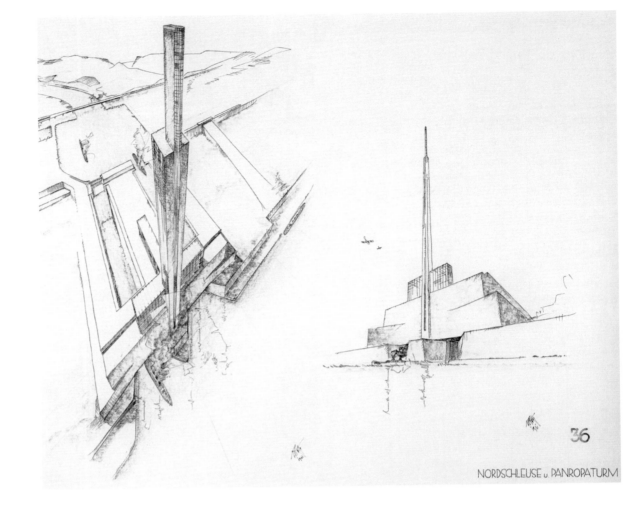

NORDSCHLEUSE u. PANROPATURM

AL NOOR TOWER
Valode & Pistre
Casablanca (MA), 2014

Not surprisingly, when the Saudi businessman Sheikh Tarek bin Laden (Osama bin Laden's half-brother) announced that he was going to build three skyscrapers in Africa, the news flashed around the world. The sheikh's idea was to create a triad of towers, one in East Africa, one in West Africa, and one in South Africa. The Dubai-based billionaire developer planned the first, Al Noor (The Light), for Casablanca, Morocco, where he already had considerable investments, and the Parisian architect Valode & Pistre won the assignment for the $1.5 billion behemoth, which would have been the tallest building on the continent. The height of 540 m (1,770 ft) was an analogue for Africa's 54 countries, and its 114 floors the number of chapters in the Koran.

The building consisted of two arcs converging on a strip of glass forming a high atrium in the shape of two hands held out in prayer. Exposed, missile-shaped elevators sped to the top in a manner reminiscent of the futuristic American hotels of John Portman. On the outside, the building looked like a great white kaftan, hood raised, embroidered with black windows in an abstract pattern that read as a mysterious scroll, but which were in fact intended as a representation of Africa's 1,500-plus languages. To many the 'hood' at the summit, with its glowing faux diamond illuminating the night sky, looked like Sauron's dark fortress in JRR Tolkien's *The Lord of the Rings*. However, buildings taller than the 210 m (690 ft) minaret of the Hassan II Mosque are forbidden in Casablanca and the city planners would not yield to the sheikh's plan.

AFRICA

OBUS E OFFICE TOWER
Le Corbusier
Algiers (DZ), 1938

The Modernist titan Le Corbusier developed several mega-scale masterplans for cities around the world, from Paris to Rio de Janeiro to Casablanca. Not all came to fruition, but the scorched-earth ideas they encouraged very much did. This was particularly true in the colonial world, where his concepts served as a kind of roadmap to tear out culture, urban fabric and history in favour of a modern utopia ruled by science and order.

Over the course of more than a decade, Corbusier proposed plan after plan for Algiers, an obsession that began with his objection to a strictly ordered masterplan proposed in 1931 by the French colonial government. Breaking from the rationality of his own past proposals, he put forward a sinuous scheme that he called Plan Obus (French for both shell and, not coincidentally, bombshell), the most spectacular (and destructive) elements of which included a giant bridge stretching over the city's bustling Casbah quarter and an elevated highway containing fourteen residential levels beneath it. The plan also called for a new business district on the Cape of Algiers, focusing on a lozenge-shaped office tower (strikingly similar in form to the Pan Am Building in New York, designed by Pietro Belluschi and Walter Gropius two decades later). The tower was faced by a gridded brise-soleil, a guard against the African sun and a vague reference to traditional Islamic *mashrabiya* window screens. At the top was a hotel and restaurant, while the base contained a parking garage and linked to other parts of the district, much of it embedded under a large new road. In June 1942 Corbusier's plan was rejected unanimously by the local council. Their statement included: 'It is not desirable to attempt such a random experiment on such a considerable perimeter.'

HAMMAM SALAHINE THERMAL BATHS
André Ravéreau
Salahine (DZ), 1965

In 1949, while travelling in the M'zab Valley, Algeria, the Limoges-born architect André Ravéreau was seduced by the northern Sahara architecture of Ghardaïa Province. From that journey, he later wrote, he intuited 'a balance that we call aesthetic', with the presence of a rigour that he liked in Auguste Perret, his teacher at the École des Beaux-Arts in Paris, and 'the exhilarating forms of Le Corbusier'. A decade later Ravéreau settled in Ghardaïa, hoping to learn from vernacular architecture the intimate mastery of building by doing without succumbing to imitation. By the mid-1960s he had developed his own desert idiom.

At Hammam Salahine, the Algerian Ministry of Tourism asked Ravéreau to sketch a spa. The baths were in a palm grove on a slightly sloping oasis. The idea was to gravity-feed source water to the spa, so the architect partially buried the building, turning the below-ground spaces into a kind of thermal catacomb. He relieved this compression with sequences of ceramic parabolic barrel vaults, gently arching roofs, a pyramid, and two enormous cupolas with anemone-vents, inspired in part by the work of the eccentric Spanish architect Antonio Gaudí. The cupolas covered the thermal baths and were shaped and behaved a bit like tagines, trapping vapour and, ingeniously, draining the condensation to irrigate the oasis. At the tips of the vents, enamelled ceramic pots would shimmer in the sunlight. The baths, then, coaxed complexity from simplicity, and defied any aesthetic orthodoxy.

Despite Ravéreau then being Algeria's chief architect of historic monuments, the tourism ministry rescinded his commission. Years later a spa was built, borrowing Ravéreau's barrel vaults, but nothing else.

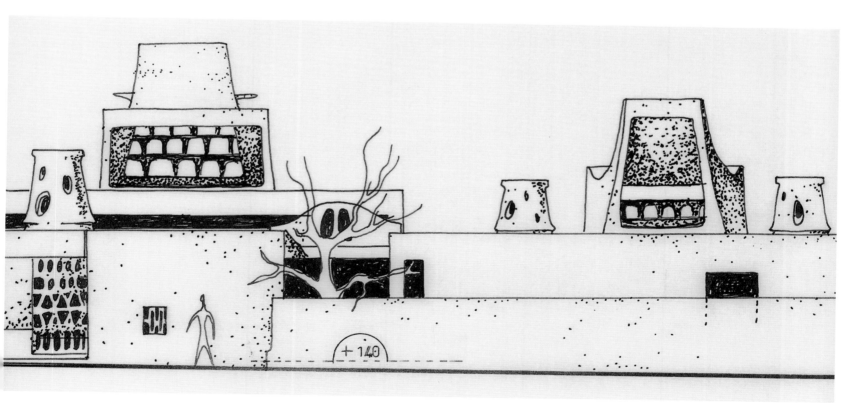

MAADI 2000 SKYSCRAPER
Riad Architecture
Cairo (EG), 1982

One of Egypt's longest-running architecture offices, Riad Architecture was established in 1934 by the famed Cairo architect Mahmoud Riad, who began his career working for Shreve, Lamb & Harmon on the Empire State Building in New York, and worked on the Arab League Headquarters, the Nile Hilton and the USSR Embassy, among other iconic structures in Cairo, as well as planning Nasr City, a new district east of the capital. By 2023 Riad was in its third generation of leadership, led by the founder's grandson Mahmoud MM Riad.

In the 1980s the firm began designs for the Maadi 2000 Skyscraper, also known as the Nile Golden Tower, a residential skyscraper along the fabled but underused Nile waterfront in one of Cairo's wealthiest neighbourhoods. The building, perched on a short concrete podium, would have risen 150 m (492 ft) above the city, making it the tallest residential tower in Egypt at the time. Because of the extremely deep site, Riad created a series of boomerang-shaped apartments with staggered edges, ensuring views to the Nile from both bedrooms and living rooms. That shape, along with a facade formed from a combination of glass and concrete render, gave the building intricate frontages.

But the scheme's developer, Hoda Abdel Moneim (nicknamed the 'Iron Lady'), founder of the developer Hedico, had oversold the size of the tower to potential investors, and in fact zoning permitted only half the height that she was touting. Such methods put her in the bad graces of the authoritarian government, which charged her with crimes including forgery and embezzlement; she fled the country in the late 1980s.

CAIRO SCIENCE CITY
Weston Williamson
+ Partners
Cairo (EG), 2016

The spirit that the Cairo Science City was meant to embody was summarized by the project's sponsor, the Library of Alexandria, as: 'The domains have blurred.' Science and the inquiry into nature and nature's ways can no longer be categorized neatly; complexity and chaos are lodestones of knowledge.

Not surprisingly, Weston Williamson's response to the brief was a building that, in essence, wasn't really a building. The practice's 125,000 sq. m (1.3 million sq. ft) Science City, in 6th of October City (named to commemorate the day in 1973 when the Egyptian Army crossed the Suez Canal to dislodge the Israelis temporarily from the Sinai Peninsula), was a village beneath a canopy of white mushroom columns covering a mound rising from the desert. The mush-

rooms – which provided shade, shape and intrigue – were the first encounter with complexity. Beneath this forest of discs was a round, high mound incised by stripes divided by arbour-like furrows cut into the barren sand dunes. Within these stripes were a dense collection of rooms, byways, gardens, labs and halls – as well as the Alexandrian Library. All would be criss-crossed by narrow, landscaped open-air streets designed to become mini microclimates, as in most traditional North African towns.

Overall, the architect said, there would be 'no strict definition between private and public spaces … The complex is designed to function as though it were a Petri dish, a place where disparate elements are brought close together to enable a reaction.' The metaphor fitted. Standing guard over the site was an observatory, tilted almost at the angle one might set a telescope to gaze into the Milky Way.

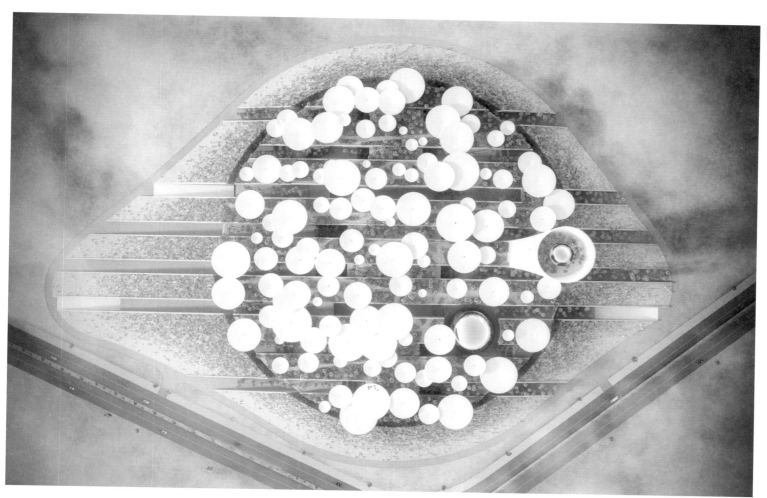

STONE TOWERS
Zaha Hadid
Cairo (EG), 2009

The Iraqi-born British architect Zaha Hadid made intense, and intensively curvaceous, buildings. Where there were straight lines in her work, they invariably morphed into swoops and swirls. Her Stone Towers, for the upscale suburb of Katameya, New Cairo, did all that on a decidedly Brobdingnagian scale.

Eighteen double-slab buildings, spread over a 17 hectare (42 acre) plaza – which Hadid called the 'Delta' – along with a five-star hotel, added up to 1,430 residential units and more than 2.8 million sq. m (30 million sq. ft) of office space. A sequence of glass slabs, nine north of the plaza, nine south, lined up in apparently endless repetition, giving the impression of a single object viewed in a hall of mirrors. Halfway up the east and west facades of the north towers, the buildings bent, like an egret's neck, swooping out and up to shade the glass curtain wall. The facades of the south towers curved, too, more like snakes' heads reaching out of water. Elsewhere, curved precast facades perforated with narrow dashes were intended to mimic the play of shadow and sunlight on ancient Egyptian stonework. Gaps between the rows of buildings provided landscaped alleys. Hadid called the undulating facades a series of 'ripples' and 'ribbons' that avoided 'the monolithic repetition of static building masses ... Each building follows a similar set of rules, yet is entirely unique.' A decade later Rooya Group, which had commissioned Hadid, stopped touting the project, instead promoting a pseudo-Mediterranean development for the site.

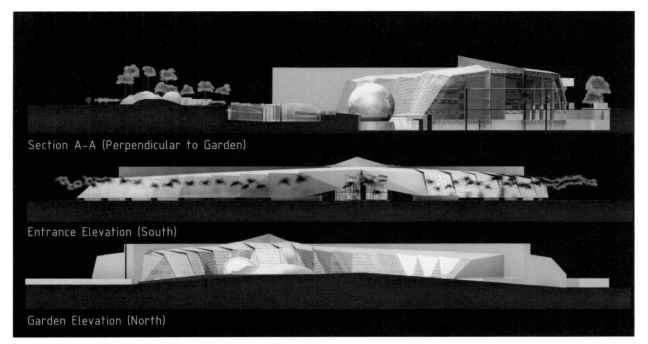

Section A-A (Perpendicular to Garden)

Entrance Elevation (South)

Garden Elevation (North)

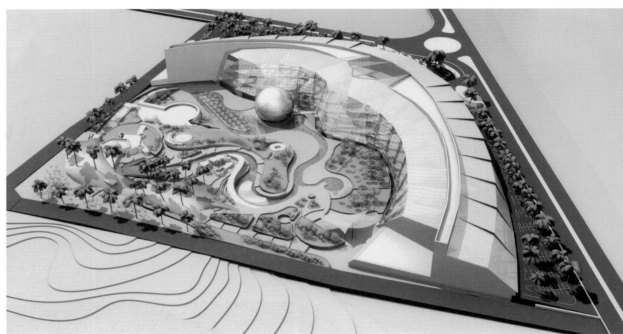

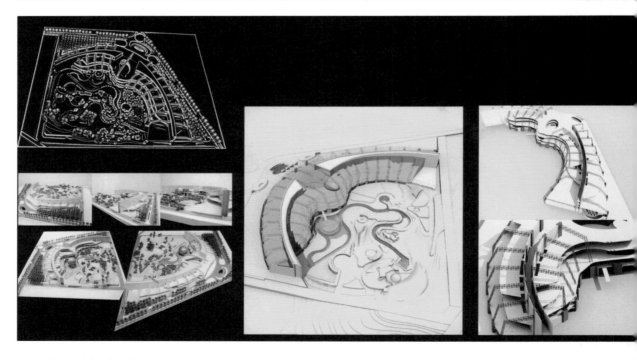

TECHNOLOGY MUSEUM
Gamal Bakry
Cairo (EG), 2001

Born in Port Said, an Egyptian city at the northern mouth of the Suez Canal, on the Mediterranean, Gamal Bakry grew up at a crossroads of European and Egyptian architecture. Not surprisingly, the Aga Khan Award-winner rejected all orthodoxy, looking for an architecture, as he said, that 'does not grow without roots that extend in earth [nor] without branches and leaves staring into the sky'. He achieved celebrity in 1971 with the Villa Badran, the irregular geometry and curving lines of which, inspired by the mud architecture of rural Egypt, informed all his later buildings in subtle ways.

Bakry won the competition for a science museum in 6th October City, near Giza, with a sloping, four-storey crescent fixed firmly to the ground. The skin of the building was a series of pyramidal planes cascading, like weathered limestone scales, to represent the periodic leaps in scientific discovery throughout history. The tilted pieces allowed indirect sunlight to filter into the galleries below. The outer rim of the crescent touched the ground, presenting a solid face to deflect the intense desert sunlight; the north-facing, cooler inner rim was a continuous window opening onto an exterior exhibition plaza. Another low, long, covered concourse, mirroring the arc of the museum, would have provided a place for hanging out and observing the crowds. The building would have been entered or exited via sweeping ramps, gestures of hospitality that would have seemed to beckon democratically in their gentle repose. The project became ensnared in the corruption of Hosni Mubarak's regime, and was dropped.

LUXOR HILTON
Mahmoud Riad
Luxor (EG), 1964

At the onset of the Cold War, the hotelier Conrad Hilton set out 'to show the countries most exposed to Communism the other side of the coin'. The Middle East was prime turf, and Egypt high on the list. The country's president, Gamal Abdel Nasser, had taken control of the Suez Canal, made deals with the Soviets, and was pursuing pan-Arab unity couched in anti-imperialist rhetoric.

The Nile Hilton, designed by corporate-friendly architect Welton Becket, arrived in Cairo in 1959. Sleek and antiseptic, it was outfitted to make any CIA agent feel right at home, with golf course-green lawns, championship tennis courts, icy air conditioning and direct phone lines to the United States, served up with hamburgers and milkshakes. And, although Nasser invited the Yugoslavian president, Josip Broz Tito, to the ribbon-cutting, the firm wanted more. Hilton turned to Mahmoud Riad, the local Cairo architect for Becket's building, to produce three more Hiltons: the Alexandria, Aswan and Luxor.

For the Luxor hotel, Riad cross-linked the ancient dynastic architecture of the site – Luxor is near two Pharaonic monuments: the temples of Karnak and Luxor – with the Modernism of the Nile Hilton. The podium combined the gently sloping, smooth stone walls of Luxor Temple with the rhythmic columns of Karnak. The tidy five-storey rectangular box containing the hotel rooms was raised above, held aloft on thin piles and incised with ribbon windows. Rising through the middle of these forms holding hands across time is a pylon, as if Karnak Temple itself were pushing up through the sandy desert floor. The Six-Day War of June 1967, in which Israel routed the Egyptian army, halted the new hotel just as construction was about to begin.

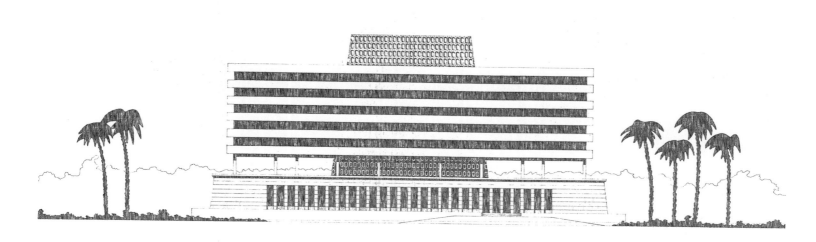

BURKINA FASO
NATIONAL ASSEMBLY
Francis Kéré
Ouagadougou (BF), 2015

In 2014 President Blaise Compaoré of Burkina Faso stepped down as a result of violent protests against his plans to manipulate the constitution to remain in office after twenty-seven years, but not before protestors had set the National Assembly ablaze. Many celebrated Compaoré's resignation as a revolution from dictatorial rule, and Burkina Faso-born Francis Kéré, who was approached by a group of activists, intellectuals, musicians, artists and politicians, aimed to capture that hopeful, democratic spirit in his design for the building's replacement. The striking stone-clad structure was intended to draw people in while also catalysing development in the capital city. It took the form of a monumental stepped pyramid, offering public gathering spaces including terraced vegetable gardens planted to echo the landscape of every region of the country. 'It's important for [the people] to see the capital differently, to be able to appreciate it,' said Kéré. 'I want the building to become the most ... permanently public space in Burkina Faso.' Below the pyramid were the main assembly hall and support functions, as well as a large, shaded space sheltered by the pyramid's steps and lattice structure, serving as an open civic plaza. The remainder of the site was to be planted with native trees, filled with seating and gathering spaces, and activated with shops, exhibition spaces, and shaded bicycle and car parking. The charred former parliament nearby would remain as a ruin, a memorial to those who died in the conflict.

The plot that had been proposed for the new building became problematic, however. Officials suggested a site outside the city, but Kéré refused, and the project quietly disappeared.

BURKINA FASO

276   AFRICA

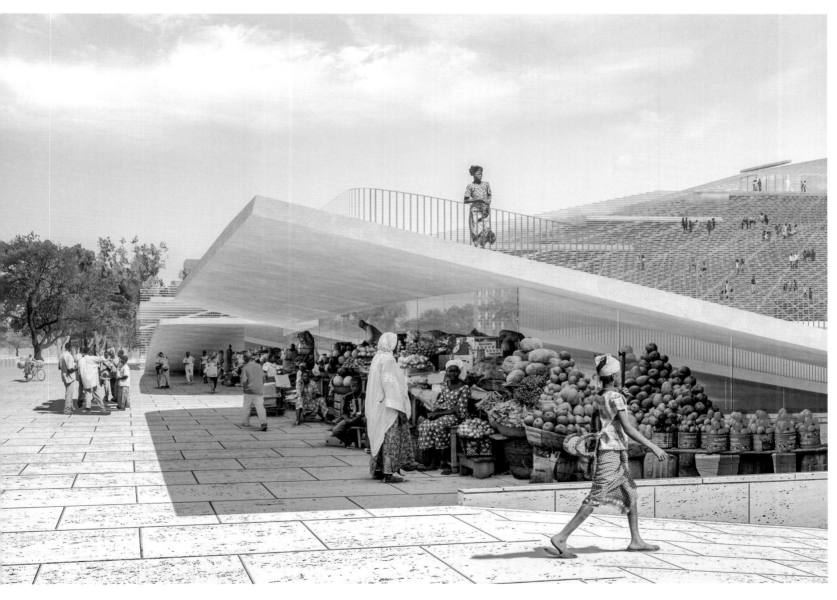

KWAME NKRUMAH PRESIDENTIAL LIBRARY
Mario Cucinella Architects
Akosombo (GH), 2013

Built in honour of the political figure who led Ghana to independence in 1957, the Kwame Nkrumah Presidential Library was instigated by Samia Nkrumah, his daughter, who now leads her father's Convention People's Party. The elder Nkrumah, who long promoted the goal of a united Africa, free of colonial influence, was overthrown by a military coup in 1966 and died in 1972.

The site of his library, designed by the Italian architect Mario Cucinella, was about a two-hour drive north of Accra, on the edge of Lake Volta, the largest artificial lake in the world by surface area. (Its dam, instigated by Kwame Nkrumah, provides much of the country's electricity.) Arranged on six levels and stacked like a wedding cake to enhance shading, the circular building was orientated around an inner void, ringed by ramps and balconies and traversed by walkways, creating diverse, flexible spaces, unique viewpoints and lively interaction. 'It's a place for study, but it's also a place for meeting and exchanging ideas,' said Cucinella.

Containing first-floor laboratories, workshops and exhibition spaces and upper-floor reading rooms, book stacks and special collections, the building was topped by a panoramic restaurant and roof terrace and featured a 300-seat basement auditorium. Curved and slatted wood salvaged from Lake Volta would clad portions of the exterior. Sustainability was a priority: photovoltaic panels on the roof provided renewable energy, reflective outer surfaces reduced heat, and a system of natural ventilation cooled the building, with colder air from the basement rising through the building and exiting near the crown. Despite tireless effort, Samia Nkrumah was unable to raise the funds to make her dream a reality.

GHANA

NATIONAL BANK OF ZAIRE
Eugène Palumbo
Kinshasa (CD), 1978

In 1967, two years after seizing power in Congo (today the Democratic Republic of the Congo), Mobutu Sese Seko announced his policy of *recours à l'authenticité* (return to authenticity), intended to eliminate all traces of Belgian colonialism in Congo by drawing on 'our real image as Africans'. He renamed the country Zaire, required every citizen to assume an Africanized first and last name, dress in traditionally inspired clothing and cook local cuisine, and, unsurprisingly, forced into exile all foreign experts and entrepreneurs. The Italian-born and -trained architect Eugène Palumbo, who had been working for UNESCO on schools in the country, escaped this fate because his associate, the Congolese architect Fernand Tala N'Gai, was closely connected to the newly ascendant elite. Palumbo held out for nearly a decade under Mobutu's rule, designing several emblematic public buildings. These include the unexecuted extension of the National Bank of Zaire, a monumental Internationalist work completed in 1960 by the Belgian architect Georges Ricquier. Palumbo didn't exactly adhere to Mobutu's concept of home-grown architecture, drawing inspiration instead from the sweeps and curves of contemporary Brazilian architecture. Formed as a section of a circle, like a scallop shell, the new bank offices, vaults and cashiers' salon had a cast ceiling hung from boomerang-shaped structural concrete beams converging at the rear. A floating mezzanine, accessed via an open circular stairway, balanced on a mushroom-shaped pier. Cobalt-blue tiles along the base, as well as the open arches formed by the beams, added even more octane to the dramatic structure. One of many buildings that Mobutu dreamed would hoist Zaire onto the world stage, Palumbo's bank remained on paper.

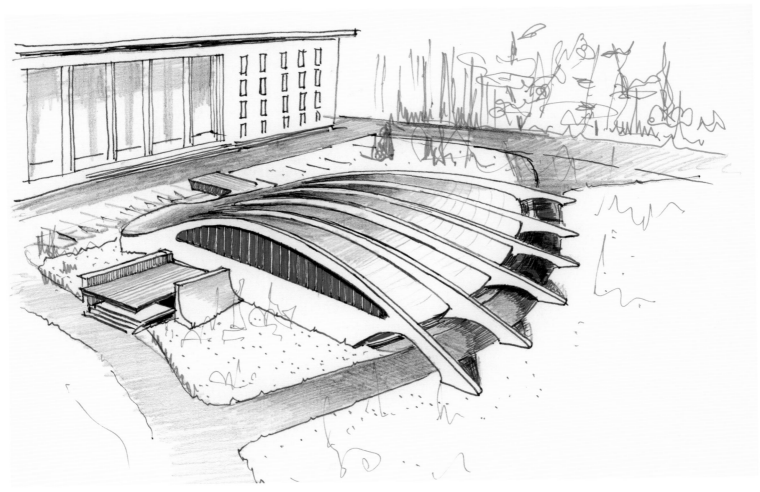

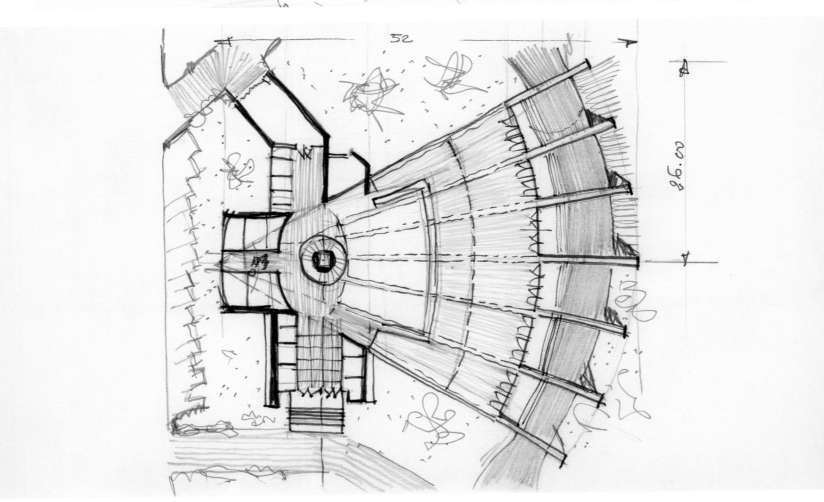

NGAREN: THE MUSEUM OF HUMANKIND
Daniel Libeskind
Rift Valley (KE), 2019

When Richard Leakey, the Kenyan palaeoanthropologist who discovered the most complete skeleton of an early human, announced his plan to build a museum dedicated to the exploration of more than two million years of human history and the origins of the universe, he declared, 'I want to show, from the beginning, what happened to this block of rock which got thrown into space and ultimately developed atmospheres, water, and how out of all that life began.' He intended Ngaren: The Museum of Humankind to be more than a place to show the fossils discovered in the Rift Valley, the cradle of humankind; he said it should be a call to action. Ngaren, which would sit at the edge of a cliff overlooking the Rift, was where humans would come face to face with the reality that we, in common with all other species on Earth, are mortal.

Daniel Libeskind, who knows a thing or two about building museums that speak to the limits of humankind, proposed a design drawn from 1.8-million-year-old hand axes, which early humans fashioned out of flint and chert. The museum looked like a pair of upright cupped stones with sharp, sheared faces, much like the tools discovered in the valley below. To one side was a mound, another rock, perhaps waiting to be shaped. Against the backdrop of the wide, eternal valley, the museum appeared ancient: stone was speaking for human ingenuity and hubris. After Leakey died in January 2022, the location of the proposed museum was changed, and Libeskind's design was deemed unsuitable for the new site.

DRONEPORT
Norman Foster
Various (RW), 2016

Since about 2009 the novelist and war reporter Jonathan Ledgard has been buttonholing politicians, bankers, bureaucrats and anyone else with power in an attempt to solve the riddle of how to build a sustainable, equitable future. By 2013 he had hit upon the idea of 'droneports', simple, locally built structures to enable drones to deliver vitally needed blood and refrigerated medicines to remote African villages. Ledgard approached Norman Foster, the architect best known for building skyscrapers and corporate headquarters at the epicentre of the planet-destroying free market – but also an avid aviator, glider pilot and environmentalist. Ledgard reportedly said to him: 'Norman, you've built the biggest airport in the world. Come and build the smallest.'

A prototype droneport was unveiled at the Venice Biennale in 2016, an elegant, inexpensive vaulted dome 'the weight of an elephant, and touching the ground just as lightly', Foster said. It could be built using a minimal kit of parts, unloaded from a small storage crate. The permeable structures could be constructed easily using a hand-operated brick press, from local clay and rocks. Strong enough to survive the extremes of rainy seasons and dry, droneports could be linked in multiples. In Foster's renderings, they became a clinic, post office, marketplace, and garage for making and fixing drones. Ledgard and Foster hoped that each would be the sole property of the local community, its ultimate appearance a reflection of the people who built it. The government of Rwanda committed a site, but the very regime that refused to build roads to make lifesaving medicines and blood available to its rural citizens did not follow through.

AFRICA

THE DRONEPORT
The vault - a timeless form   6·50 ↑   built over temporary prefab formers

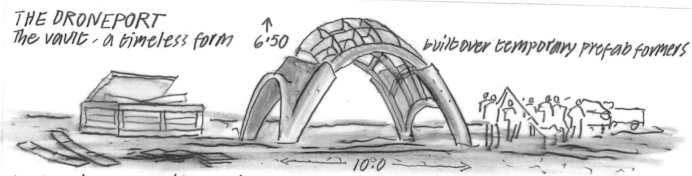

←   10·0   →

local earth + New additives = high strength elements. Assembled by the local community

modules are combined to produce the droneport - a civic structure - of the eaves
and the landscape - a social hub - clinic - post office - market

The Norman Foster Foundation brings together engineers and students from ETH
Zurich - Cambridge UK - MIT - University of Madrid - to explore the possibility
of erecting a test module at the 2016 Venice Biennale. Funding permitting!

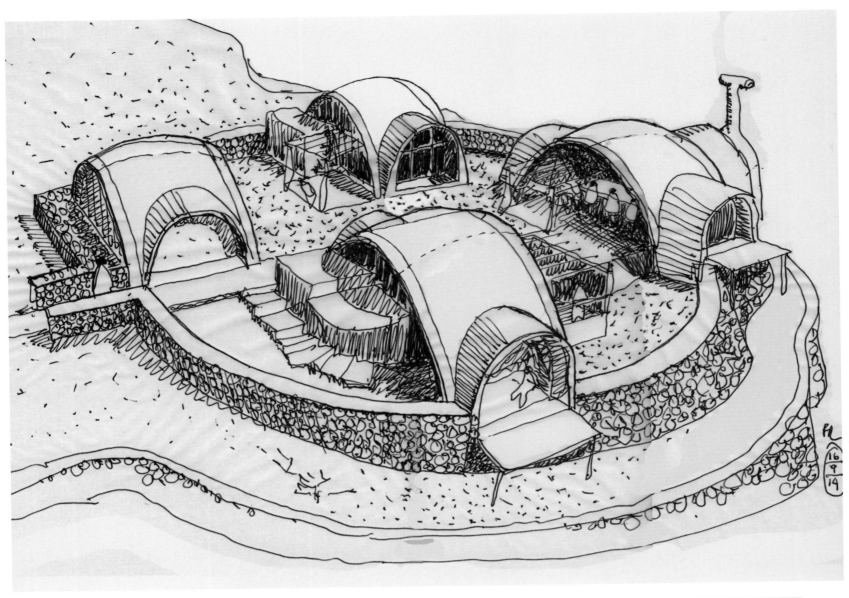

LAETOLI HOMINID FOOTPRINT MUSEUM
Peter Rich Architects
Ngorongoro Conservation Area (TZ), 2014

In 1978 the palaeontologists Mary Leakey and Paul Abell discovered the oldest known footprints of early humans – a trackway left by three hominids 3.6 million years ago – while walking through wet volcanic ash in the Great Rift Valley at Laetoli, Tanzania. They took castings, then buried the 27 m long (89 ft) track under a mantle of soil and lava rocks. There it stood, untouched, until 2014, when Tanzania's stewards of what had by then become a World Heritage Site commissioned Peter Rich to build a museum that would allow the footprints to be uncovered and viewed.

Rich, a South African, had spent decades personally exploring sub-Saharan African concepts of design, space-making and building, and his Mapungubwe Interpretation Centre of 2009 had brought him global awards and attention. At Laetoli he proposed several groups of buildings clad entirely in stone, lined internally in richly yet simply patterned brick. The structures – containing an amphitheatre, a museum, a children's biodiversity school, a science compound and an archive of archaeology – were comprised of sequences of vaults, domes, arches and cairns and separated by patios and passageways. Some of the structures were lifted off the ground like sheds, while others were anchored like tents. The stones were red and black and buff, organized in swirling spirals and random conglomerates, turning Rich's buildings into mounds rising like natural outcroppings from the Ngorongoro grasslands and ravines. Tanzanian officials hoped to find upwards of $200 million, but couldn't. UNESCO, meanwhile, worried about tourists and poachers ruining the site, slowed the project until it stalled indefinitely.

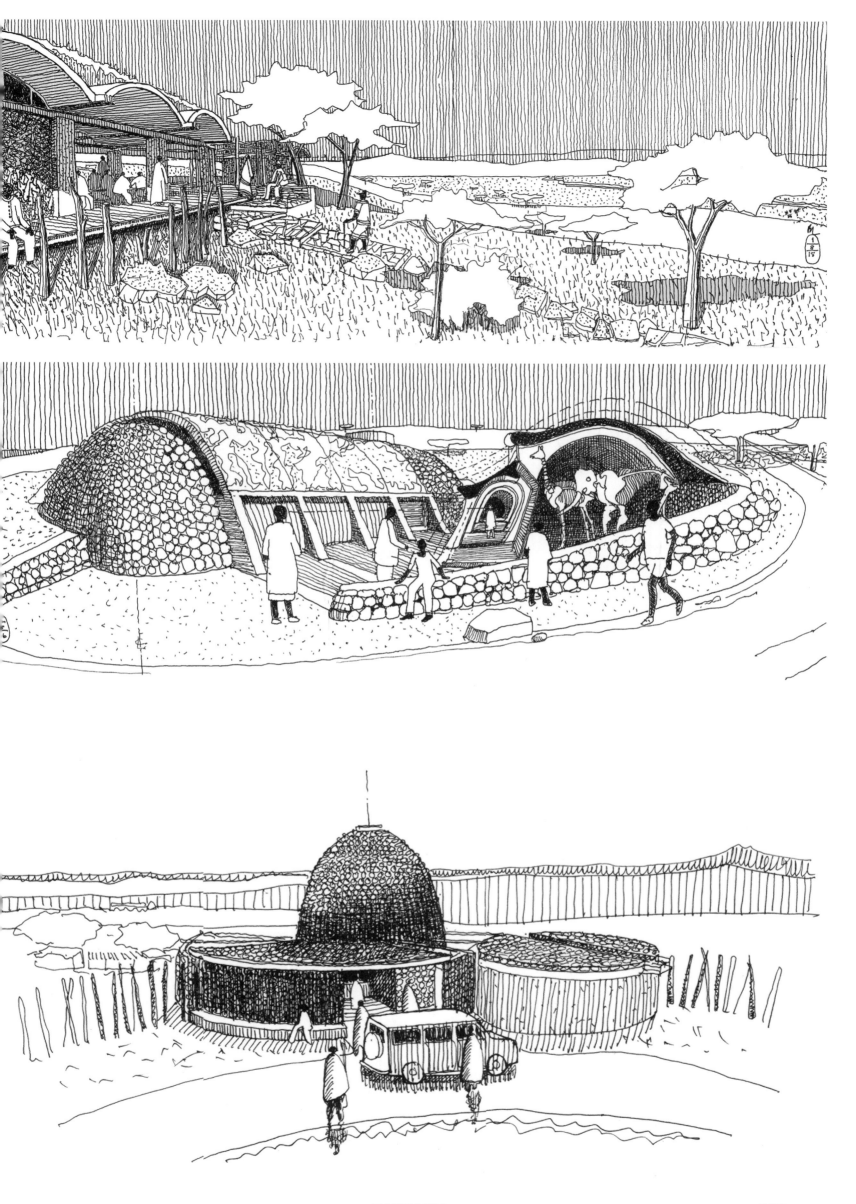

ÉGLISE POUR TANGANYIKA
Oscar Nitzchke
(TZ), 1955

Oscar Nitzchke is far more famous and influential for what he didn't build than for what he did. His Maison de la Publicité of 1934 is a paper masterpiece, a kinetic structure composed of neon letters, illuminated signage, posters and projection screens, that was the progenitor of the Centre Pompidou in Paris, a little over forty years later, and an unsurpassed benchmark of the Modernist dream of building as propaganda machine. His Palais de la Découverte (1938), in collaboration with Paul Nelson and Frantz Jourdain, is another prescient drawing – aborted by the Nazi invasion of Paris – testing the possibility of suspending a massive roof by cables from a leaning, ovoid concrete shell. The Église pour Tanganyika (Church for Tanganyika) is little developed beyond the splendid rendering and a few sketches on a single sheet of lined, yellow notepad paper. The church is a sort of reprise of Corbusier's Ronchamp Chapel, completed that same year, with a twist. The colour elevation appears to be playing the curved, vaulted surfaces of the concrete towers against the incised curtain wall of what might be anodized aluminium columns, supporting the swayback roof – like the roof at Ronchamp. As with so much of Nitzchke's work, there is nothing much to go by other than the drawing itself. We are left to imagine and, frankly, to delight in the playful human qualities he demonstrates: the simple rail holding the bell; the deep shadows cast by the window surrounds; the diminutive cross perched, like a songbird, at the pinnacle of the highest tower. The drawing makes you believe this place already exists. Which, one suspects, it did, for Nitzchke.

NEW TANU NATIONAL HEADQUARTERS
Kishō Kurokawa
Dar es Salaam (TZ), 1972

One of the founders of the Metabolist movement, the Japanese architect Kishō Kurokawa exported its ideas around the world, to Europe, the United States, the Middle East and elsewhere in Asia. In 1972 he won a competition to design the headquarters of the Tanganyika African National Union (TANU), which had been the principal political party in the struggle for sovereignty in what is now Tanzania.

The building, designed for the harsh conditions of Dar es Salaam (then the country's capital), contained not only the ruling party's headquarters but also the national assembly and a cultural centre. Employing Kurokawa's *kairō*, or covered corridor system, the raised structure's long, low profile would shade surrounding streets, augment the scale of the whole neighbourhood, and allow breezes through its length, while its mountain-like, reinforced-concrete 'urban roof' arched over an enclosed public plaza, providing visitors with protection from the harsh sunlight. Its large structural beams also shaded space inside the building, while roof monitors and wide ventilation slots brought in natural ventilation. Not long after Kurokawa won the competition, the government voted to move the nation's capital to Dodoma, in the centre of the country. Leaders held a new competition to masterplan the city and its capitol, which was won by the Canadian firm Project Planning Associates. The creation of the new capital was anticipated to take about ten years, but at the time of writing it has taken more than forty, and it is still far from complete. A new assembly designed by the Kenyan architect James Kimathi was finally finished in 2006.

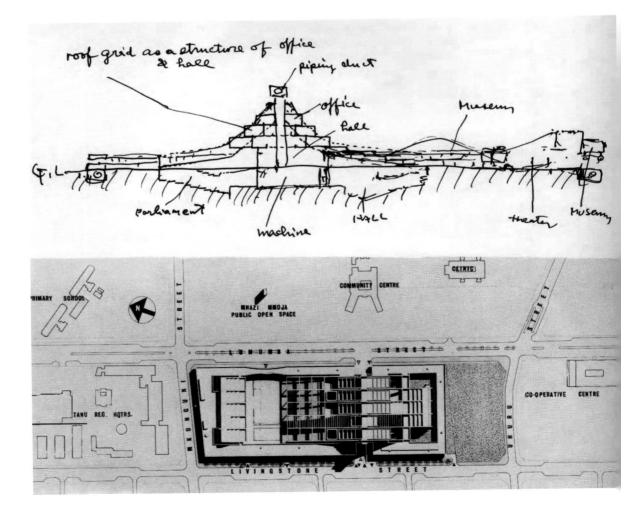

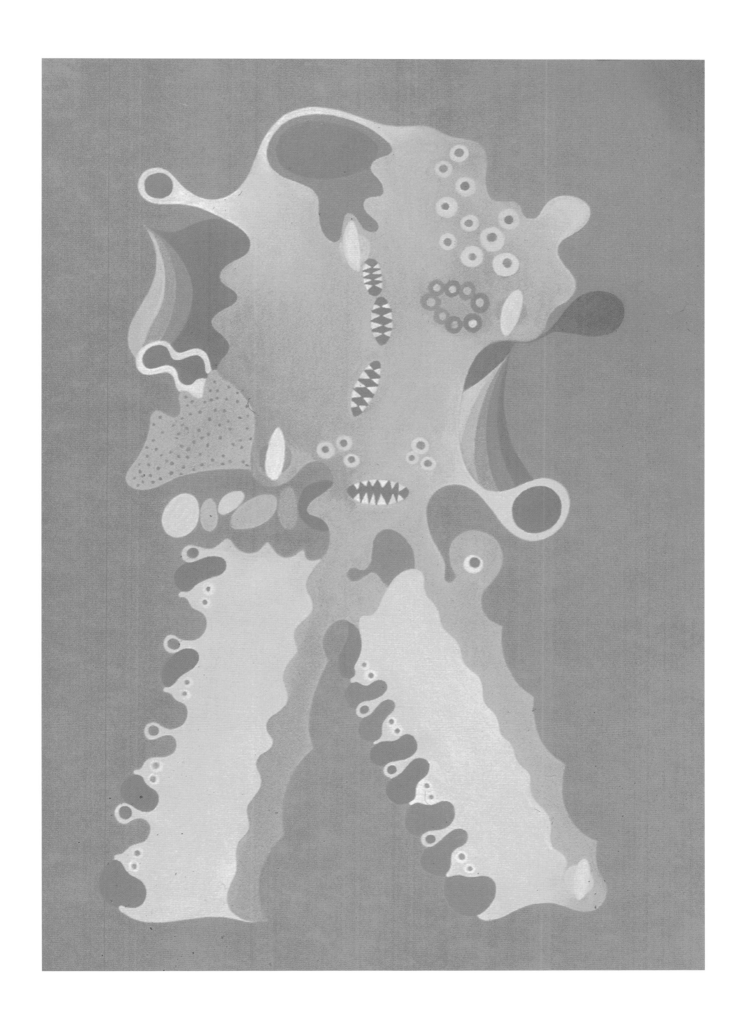

HOTEL SÃO MARTINHO DO BILENE
Pancho Guedes
Bilene (MZ), 1955

The Lisbon-born Mozambiquan architect Pancho Guedes was described in *L'Architecture d'Aujo- rd'hui* in 1962 as 'a solitary figure who works in virtually non-existent milieu yet has managed to surround himself in an almost mystical aura'.

That aura arose from his *Stiloguedes*, a term he coined to describe the buildings he was de- signing in Mozambique's capital, Lourenço Marques (now Maputo). He said that his 'quite purposely strange buildings', contorted, decorated, full of spikes and parts that hung down and even appeared to fall off, had 'the quality of apparitions'.

At Bilene, Guedes proposed to cast concrete directly onto the immense white sand dunes of Uembje Lagoon to make a series of inflated and deflated rooms that, like the bubbling foam of

the surf, receded from the beach through the interior of the building. The roof took the shape of the dunes, and a stream flowed through the lounge. Once the concrete had cured, the sand would be excavated, leaving behind self- supporting arched forms, like tortoise shells. He likened these organic forms to the rounded mud enclosures built by the Indigenous people of southern African, known as *kraal*.

Guedes had travelled to Bilene with a group of friends and a travel agency, who wanted to build a hotel on the spectacular lagoon. He designed

the plans in one night, he said, 'without stopping'. But the clients baulked. They didn't have the money, and they lacked the courage to see such a radical proposition through. Guedes produced another proposal using straw, blocks made from local sand, and materials requisitioned from the forestry service, but it too was declined.

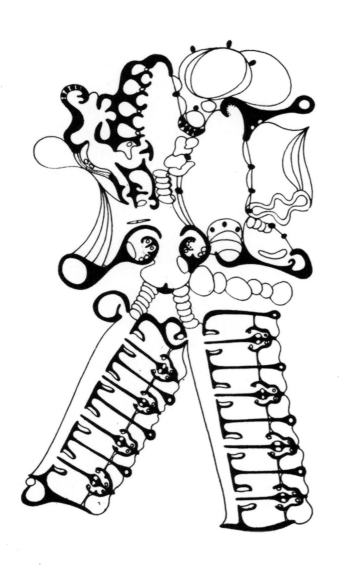

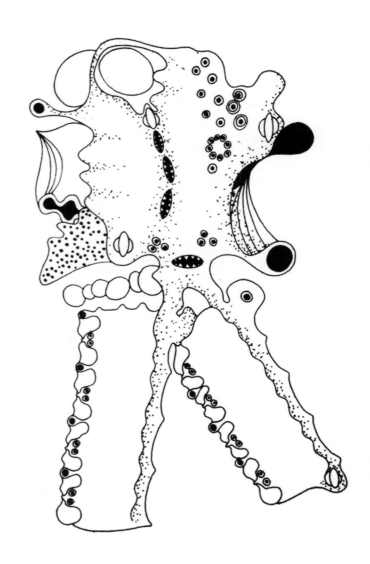

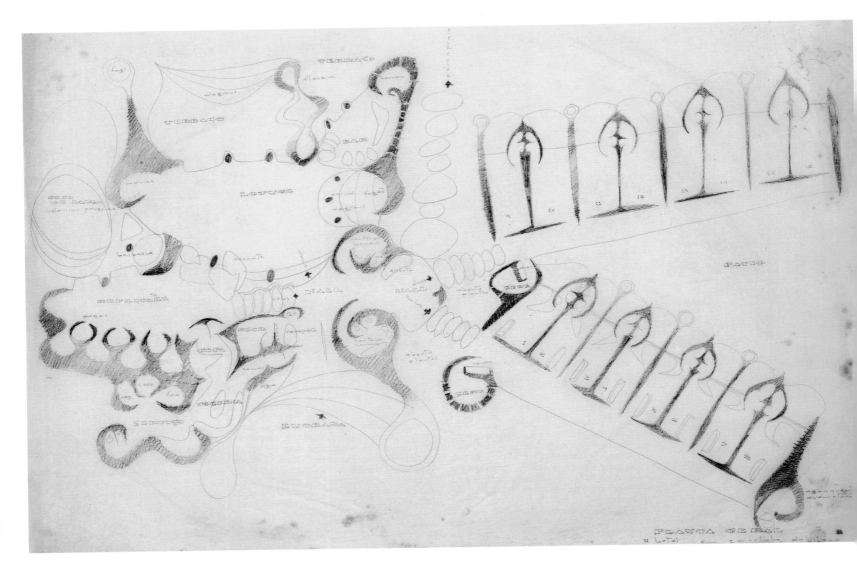

AFRICA

MOZAMBIQUE

MINISTRY OF TRANSPORT
Norman Eaton
Pretoria (ZA), 1944

The South African architect Marguerite Pienaar has written that in the mid-1940s, while much of the rest of the world was at war, a cadre of this isolated sub-Saharan nation's architects were 'profoundly influenced by Brazilian modernity'. Norman Eaton was among the foremost. In 1944 he was commissioned to design a build-ing for the Ministry of Transport, a massive civic structure to house a thousand office workers, immediately south of Pretoria City Hall. A year later he was on a boat destined for the Americas, his early sketches of the ministry in hand, hoping to absorb all he could on the frontier of the new.

Eaton met Frank Lloyd Wright and Ludwig Mies van der Rohe, but his personal encounter with Oscar Niemeyer, and especially his experience of the Ministry of Education building in Rio de Janeiro, was deeply affecting. Niemeyer's Edu-cation Ministry was, Eaton wrote in his diary, 'great, free, open planning on a brilliantly imag-inative scale. An excellent solution of [the] sun protection problem.' The Brazilian influence on the South African Ministry of Transport is easy to spot. Its six undulating roof gardens and swimming pool, adjustable brise-soleils guarding the offices from the intense sunlight, towering, light-filtering pierced screens at either end of the public plaza, and vertical fins on an egg-crate grid translated freely from the language of Brazil's Modernists.

Unfortunately, Eaton's building exceeded th[e] height limit for buildings in the city, and whe[n] costs escalated, the project became the stu[ff] of electoral politics. Local officials were angr[y] at Eaton, and his bosses in national governmen[t] wouldn't defend his work. He was dismisse[d] after four years, his ministry building done i[n] by political expediency.

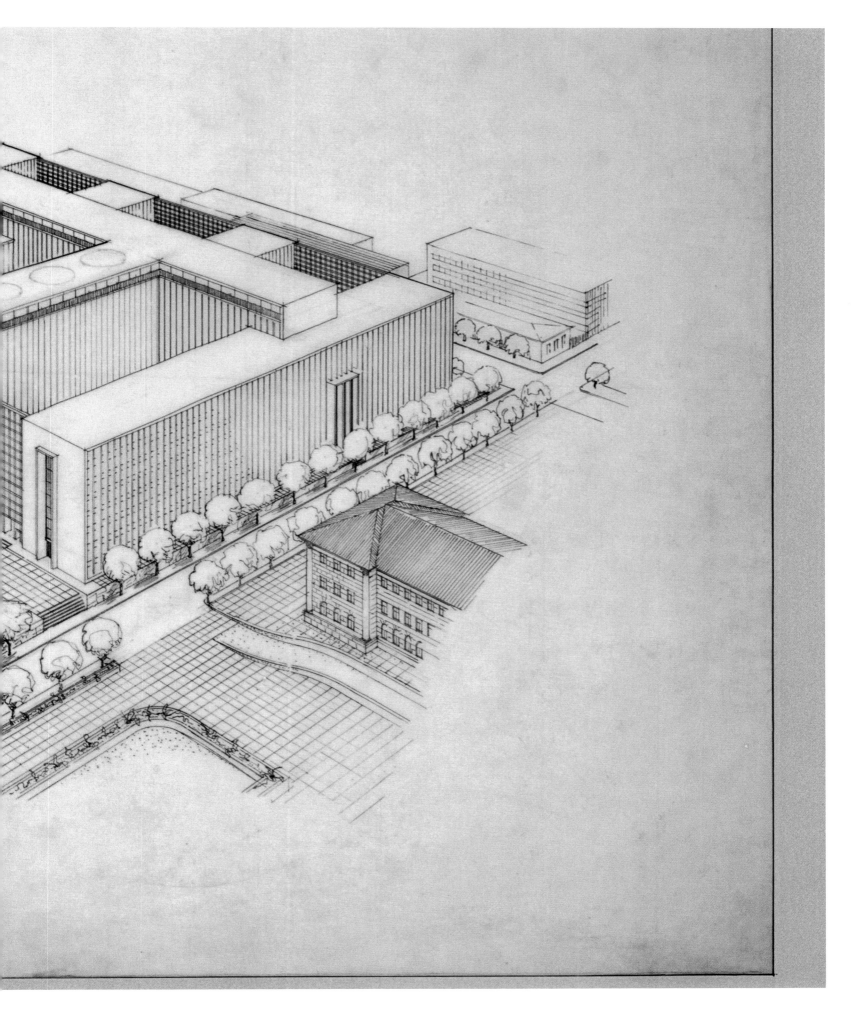

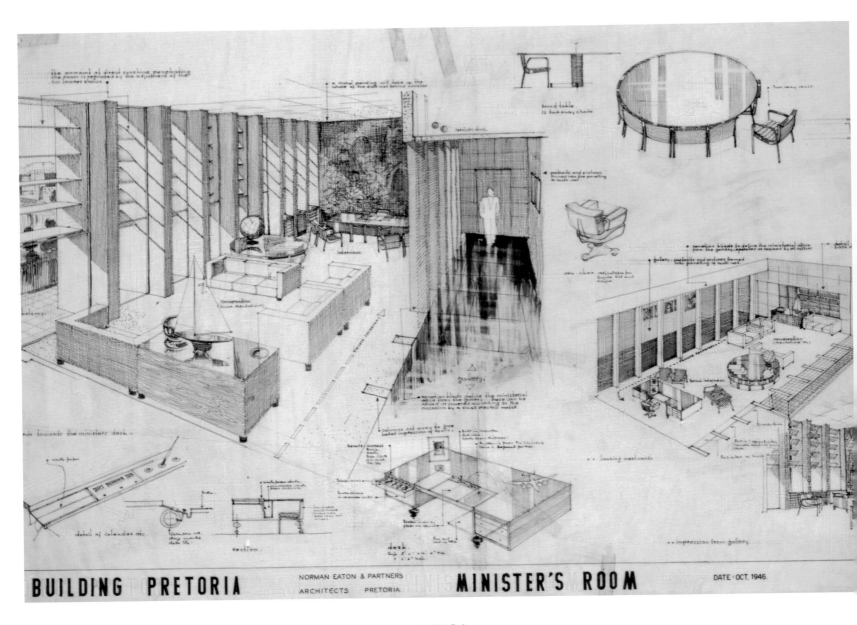

BUILDING PRETORIA NORMAN EATON & PARTNERS **MINISTER'S ROOM** DATE: OCT. 1946.
ARCHITECTS PRETORIA

AFRICA

PRODUCTIVE (RE)PUBLIC
SHELTERS
Jo Noero
Cape Town (ZA), 2013

Much of the emphasis when it comes to tackling global warming and carbon emissions by globetrotting architects and their academic acolytes is on complex systems that require massive inputs of cold, hard capital. Essentially, the climate crisis is treated as a technological problem that can be overcome with expensive technological answers. When the Cape Town architect Jo Noero was asked by the MAXXI museum in Rome to look at 'Post-Oil Architecture', his response was, first, that 'the free market mechanism of the global economy is unsustainable, unfair and unjust.' South Africa, which emerged from apartheid in 1994, was one of the worst countries in the world for the disparity between rich and poor, with a third of its population living on less than $3.20 a day.

Noero understood that there would be no infusion of capital to confer energy independence – and a zero carbon footprint – on the average South African shanty town. He proposed a simple, tree-like biogas-producing structure that could be installed easily even in small spaces, and would be both a shading device and a mini-farm, growing food and harvesting water while generating gaseous fuels (mostly methane) through the fermentation of organic matter. Noero explained that, rather than planting trees, 'the application of these machines would offer up new spatial realms at both a household and community scale.' The system had the added benefit of being entirely off the grid. The energy it produced would be distributed among nearby residents, who would control their own energy production and consumption. But even such an inexpensive and self-sustaining project as Noero's could find no backing in an impoverished sub-Saharan country.

Asia

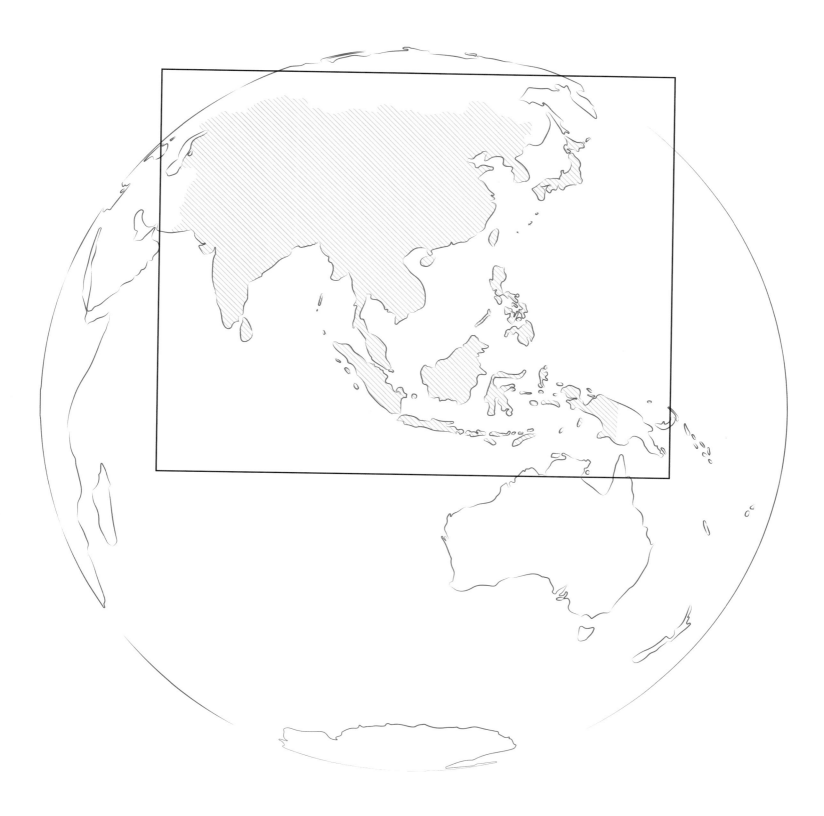

KZ [1]

AF [1]

PK [2]

CN [6]

KR [2]

JP [8]

IN [8]

LK [1]

TH [1]

PH [2]

ID [2]

ATLAS OF NEVER BUILT ARCHITECTURE

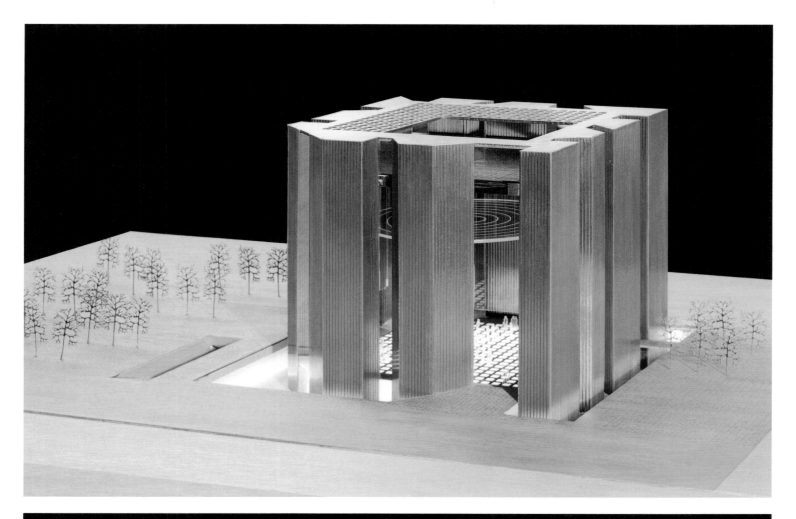

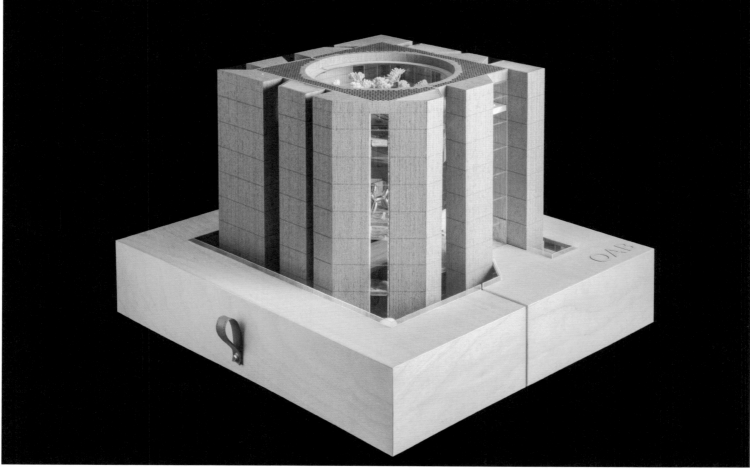

MUSEUM OF MODERN ART
Office of Architecture in Barcelona
Almaty (KZ), 2016

Almaty, Kazakhstan's former capital, lies in the shadow of the snow-capped Trans-Ili Alatau mountains, on the Silk Road, the ancient route that linked East to West, Asia to Europe. The country declared its independence only in December 1997, so it was no surprise that its largest city would look west to project an image of modernity. The idea of a museum of modern art began with the Kazakh oligarch Serzhan Zhumashov, chairman of the multimillion-dollar construction company Capital Partners. As one Kazakh newspaper boasted when it was announced, a private consortium would build 'one of the most famous museums of modern art in the world'.

That is where Carlos Ferrater, founder of the Office of Architecture in Barcelona, entered the fray. The museum was conceived as the gateway to the city's centrally located botanic garden (also designed by Ferrater). His vision was pure geometry: the circle in the square. A huge cylindrical space was surrounded by coppery windowless towers, neatly completing a cube. Slashes between the towers allowed light to pour into the central space. A rooftop garden sat below the parapet, completing the illusion of a square prism. Most of the galleries were buried underground, while the central space was very nearly a void, soaring, cathedral-like, and silent.

Whether Ferrater's concept could have polished Kazakhstan's image is anyone's guess. The kleptocracy was flush with petrodollars and billionaires, so the money was there, but the design was dropped. On 20 September 202? Almaty's mayor unveiled a new design for the museum by the global firm Chapman Taylor.

KAZAKHSTAN

AFGHANISTAN HOTELS
Marcel Breuer
Kabul (AF), 1973

As part of a larger strategy to promote tourism and economic growth, in 1973 Afghanistan's Ministry of Tourism signed an agreement with the renowned Modernist architect Marcel Breuer to design at least two new hotels in the capital, Kabul, and in the central city of Bamyan. Breuer would tackle the conceptual design while the German firm Walter Brune + Partner would produce the working drawings and supervise construction. (Breuer had visited the country a year earlier on behalf of the World Bank – helping to secure funds for the endeavour – and had suffered a nearly fatal heart attack.)

In his plans Breuer stressed the need to produce structures that melded the vernacular architecture of Afghanistan with Modernist principles. While his proposals still relied largely on the modular precast-concrete building techniques for which he was known – one was six storeys tall and had a rather fortress-like presence – several designs exhibited local characteristics, 'in sympathy', as Breuer put it, with the area's predominant mud-brick construction. Varied ideas showcased textured stone cladding, curvilinear plans following the topography of the site, communal courtyards, clustered rooms and even round concrete yurt-like structures. Foreshadowing the demise of the project, Breuer's assistant Robert Gatje wrote in his notes that the team from the World Bank was 'overwhelmed with the difficulties of getting anything done over there and seem almost surprised that we are interested in what is not, after all, a terribly "big" project'. Indeed, the hotels never proceeded further than the design phase, made impossible to execute by the country's unceasing political instability.

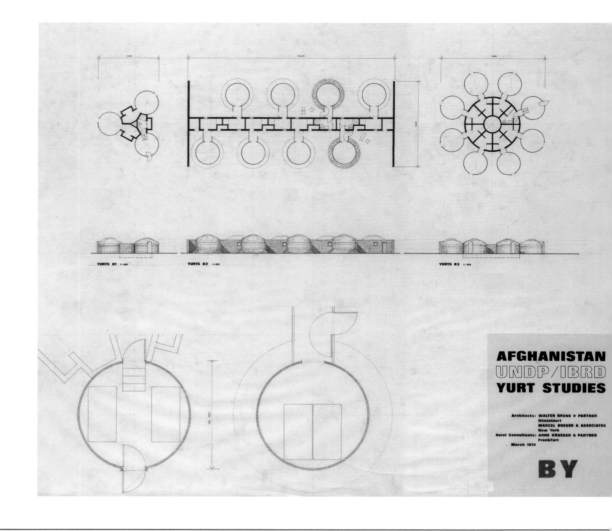

PAKISTAN NATIONAL ASSEMBLY
Arne Jacobsen, Louis Kahn
Islamabad (PK), 1963

Islamabad ('City of Islam') became Pakistan's capital in 1963. Unlike the nation's former hub, Karachi, and most of its heaving cities, this one was planned on a virgin site under the direction of the Greek planner Constantinos Doxiadis. Twenty-six major architects, including Walter Gropius, Minoru Yamasaki, Kenzo Tange, Marcel Breuer, Gio Ponti and Sven Markelius, were considered for key civic buildings. Under the guidance of Sir Robert Matthew, president of the Royal Institute of British Architects and the International Union of Architects, the country zeroed in on Tange, who designed the Supreme Court; Ponti, who produced the Secretariat; and Edward Durell Stone, who landed the National Assembly and Presidential Palace.

The Assembly commission had, however, been awarded initially to the Danish architect Arne Jacobsen, one of the first designers to bring Modernism to Scandinavia. His rectangular, three-storey structure, clad inside and out with white marble and topped by a hanging metal roof, surrounded a courtyard, a public restaurant and a 350-seat circular assembly hall (with a public gallery for 300–400 spectators). A mosque was embedded underneath, with offices above, a 'hanging garden' outside, and anodized-aluminium *brise-soleils* shading the facades. Pakistan's Capital Development Authority (CDA) asked Jacobsen to adjust his plan to incorporate Islamic motifs explicitly, including arches, domes and a 'dominating' mosque nearby in place of the underground facility. But Jacobsen – a Modernist purist – refused to adorn his concept. 'I do not find it possible to attach Islamic or other religious factors to one's architecture,' he wrote. The CDA immediately turned to Louis Kahn, who developed a 'President's Estate' of civic buildings and monuments – weighty blocks composed of squares, circles, triangles and domes carved into a sculpted landscape around a central square – that included the Assembl Presidential Palace and Supreme Court. Bu his ambitious scheme was terminated in 196 following confrontations over design and bud get. Once again, the CDA demanded explic Islamic references and even grander expres sions of power. They finally found a more suit able, and pliable, architect in Stone, whos merging of classical organization, tradition ornament and grand modern form met all the requirements. Kahn, meanwhile, designed th National Assembly for Dhaka, Bangladesh – bu it was not completed until 1982, eight years afte his death.

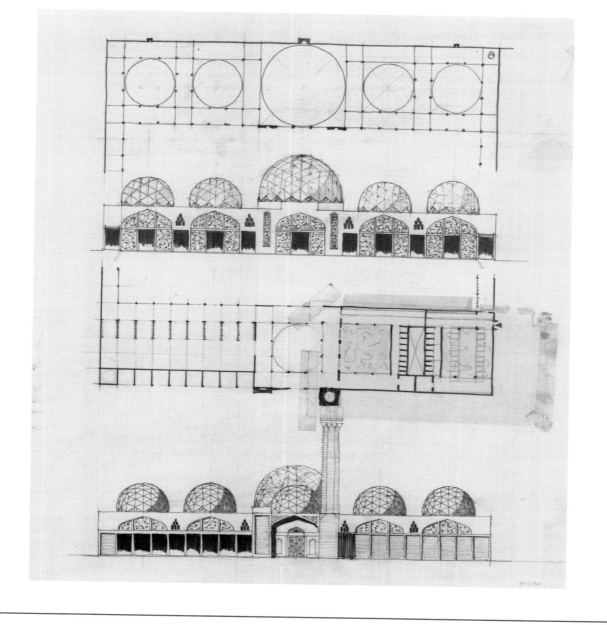

PUNJAB MOSQUE
Hassan Fathy
Punjab (PK), 1957

The Egyptian Hassan Fathy spent his life battling homogenizing Western Modernism, fighting for vernacular traditionalism, whose cultural authenticity, for Fathy, derived from the Islamic world. He was seen as a lonely guru, his work shunned and marginalized in Egypt. His best-known undertaking, the partially built New Gourna Village, is a troubled masterpiece representing his core conviction: that architecture must be indigenous, rooted in local place and culture, using local materials, labour and construction techniques.

In 1957 Constantinos Doxiadis, the lead architect of Islamabad, the new capital of Pakistan, invited Fathy to work with him in Greece. It was during this time that Fathy sketched the Punjab Mosque. The mosque was much more than 'quaint rustic scenes; domes, vaults, and arches; courtyards; mudbrick', as one critic characterized Fathy's sketches. In his proposal, Fathy attempted to amalgamate modern and idiomatic. By placing a plastic-covered geodesic dome over the central prayer hall and a fan-folded, corrugated-metal roof – a 'wind-catcher' designed to let cool air wash into the mosque – he was not attempting a new orthodoxy; he was rather looking to employ innovative, ultra-light structures to support a traditional aesthetic. He aimed at a design that 'has a symbolic value in tradition', where 'space, shape, decorative motifs, color, light, and even acoustics, are traditional.' Yet an uneasy tension resulted. In one drawing there appear to be sixteen small geodesic domes, along with a large, central one, sitting atop walls etched with stone arabesques. The Pakistan government initiated the design, but why the project never proceeded remains murky. It may be that when Fathy left Doxiadis's office in 1961, the relationship with Pakistan ended, too.

ORIGINAL PLAN FOR CHANDIGARH
Matthew Nowicki
Chandigarh (IN), 1950

The name of Chandigarh, the capital city of the states of Punjab and Haryana, is nearly synonymous with that of Charles-Édouard Jeanneret, more famously known as Le Corbusier. But it almost wasn't: Matthew Nowicki, a Polish architect who immigrated to America after World War II, was the original chief designer of the city. He had been recruited by the New York architect and urban planner Albert Mayer, hired by the newly independent Indian government to create a state capital from scratch.

Nowicki's assignment was to design everything from a parliament, high courts, office buildings and a university, to schools, markets and swathes of housing. Over the summer of 1950 he sketched endlessly, proposing a monumental capitol complex, resembling a walled city, roughly 300×120 m (1,000×400 ft), from which emerged a trio of parabolic arches shrouding the legislature. The roof of the largest hall was formed by six parabolic structural ribs; at one end it was glazed with highly decorative small squares filled with swirls, spirals, diamonds and squares of coloured glass. Light streaming through the immense window would have illuminated the speaker's dais, expressing faith in a government conducted fully in sunlight, not shadow.

Nowicki drew a city to human scale. Even the superblock housing, developed with Mayer, was low-lying and stretched along tree-like pathways, deliberately avoiding the long, linear facades and monumental urban plazas advocated by Le Corbusier. Nowicki's were expressive structural forms, in which he hoped to capture, he said, the Indian 'way of life'. On 31 August 1950 he was on a plane that crashed in the Egyptian desert. No one survived. Indian officials handed the Chandigarh project to Le Corbusier, and Nowicki's version was blotted from history.

NATIONAL WAR MUSEUM
Sameep Padora
+ Associates
Delhi (IN), 2017

In 2017 India's ministry of defence announced the winners of competitions to design a National War Memorial and National War Museum at Princess Park, in the centre of Delhi's government district. The memorial, designed by the architect Yogesh Chandrahasan, opened in 2019. But the museum, won by Mumbai-based Sameep Padora + Associates (sP+a) – chosen over 200 entries, including those by Zaha Hadid Architects and Studio Libeskind – never materialized. Lifted off the ground on wide arches, sP+a's fractured, eroded sandstone-clad design was meant to contrast with the heavy, opaque national monuments nearby, and touched the ground at only eleven points, helping to protect the park's trees beneath it. It was intended to lead visitors through a physical timeline of the country's armed forces. Sculpted and glazed openings, piercing the meandering galleries from below, connected displays – such as artefacts and uniforms – to the outdoors.

According to widespread reports, however, the competition was quickly bogged down in bickering and back-stabbing. The runner-up, Gurgaon-based Aakar Design Consultants, claimed that sP+a's proposal was structurally faulty and visually misleading and had plagiarized various international projects. The matter was referred to new government committees, while such groups as the Delhi Urban Art Commission, the Heritage Conservation Committee and the Central Vista committee lodged complaints about the winning entry's scale and fit within the neighbourhood. In 2020 the *Hindustan Times* reported that the Ministry of Housing and Urban Affairs had shortlisted new architects for the project, but at the time of writing no firm had been named the winner.

GREATER NOIDA HOUSING
FXCollaborative
Noida (IN), 2008

New Okhla Industrial Development Authority, more commonly known by its acronym as Noida, is a planned city nearly 30 km (20 miles) from Delhi, in the northern Indian state of Uttar Pradesh. The town was established in 1976, grafted to the rich, loamy soil of the Yamuna River basin. Today, as its moniker implies, the new city is pockmarked with industrial parks and apartment towers.

FXCollaborative (then called FXFOWLE Architects) was handed a 19 hectare (47 acre) site on which 1,700 apartments were to be planted. The firm transformed a massive development into an assignment fine-tuned to the Loo, the powerful, hot, dust-filled summer winds that gust from the west. These dry winds and intense heat have given rise to a traditional architecture of natural ventilation: balconies, verandas, courtyards and through-and-through rooms.

At Greater Noida Housing, however, the architects were designing towers ranging from seven to forty-three storeys, not single- or two-storey homes. Accordingly, they conceived apartment buildings that were as much void as enclosed space. This was done by raising pairs of sheer walls clad in terracotta – in red hues common to the region – and stretching wafer-thin floor plates between the flat pillars. Apartments could run front to back, side to side, open to breezes and sunlight. If an enclosure were omitted or the walls stepped back, deep terraces, gardens and gateways could emerge, making the buildings porous and visually exciting. The firm also arranged the buildings north–south, putting the taller ones at the northern edge of the site to allow air and sunlight to reach the lower structures to the south. The Great Recession, it seems, swallowed the proposition, which never resurfaced.

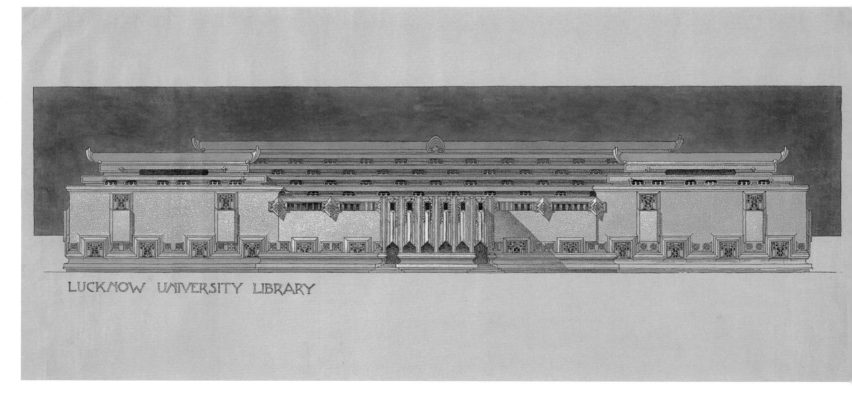

LUCKNOW UNIVERSITY LIBRARY

LUCKNOW UNIVERSITY LIBRARY
Walter Burley Griffin
Lucknow (IN), 1935

Walter Burley Griffin arrived in the northern Indian city of Lucknow expecting to stay three months, enough time to complete his drawings for a commission to design the university library there; in the end he stayed until his death fifteen months later. He had made 46 preliminary sketches at his home, Castlecrag, outside Sydney, having dismissed an earlier set of plans for the colonial university, drawn by the British architectural luminary Edwin Lutyens, as 'pure Roman' – by which he meant captivated by history and full of imperial pretensions. In Lucknow, Griffin (an employee of Frank Lloyd Wright) found the city's ancient architecture 'exquisite', and wrote to his wife and collaborator, Marion Mahony Griffin, that he had 'a hunch that much of my architectural predilections must have come from Indian experience [in a previous life]'.

The library project, underwritten by the Raja of Mahmudabad, was composed of 'bold, earth-pressing cubic masses', as Griffin's biographer Christopher Vernon put it. The upper tier was made of long, flat, slender terraced slabs, capped by an upturned roof, and the lower storey had the quality of a stone fortress – albeit one inscribed with elaborate, abstract geometric designs and decked with exuberant ornamental cartouches. Inside, Griffin carved the reading-room and display-hall ceilings into elongated, Mughal arches – pointed vaults with flat haunches rising from curved springers. The building looked and felt Indian, while being genuinely forward-looking.

Construction stalled under the constraints of the local colonial bureaucracy, and Griffin suffered a punctured gall bladder; five days later he died from peritonitis. With his wife he had designed fifty projects in Lucknow, but his library never rose above its foundations.

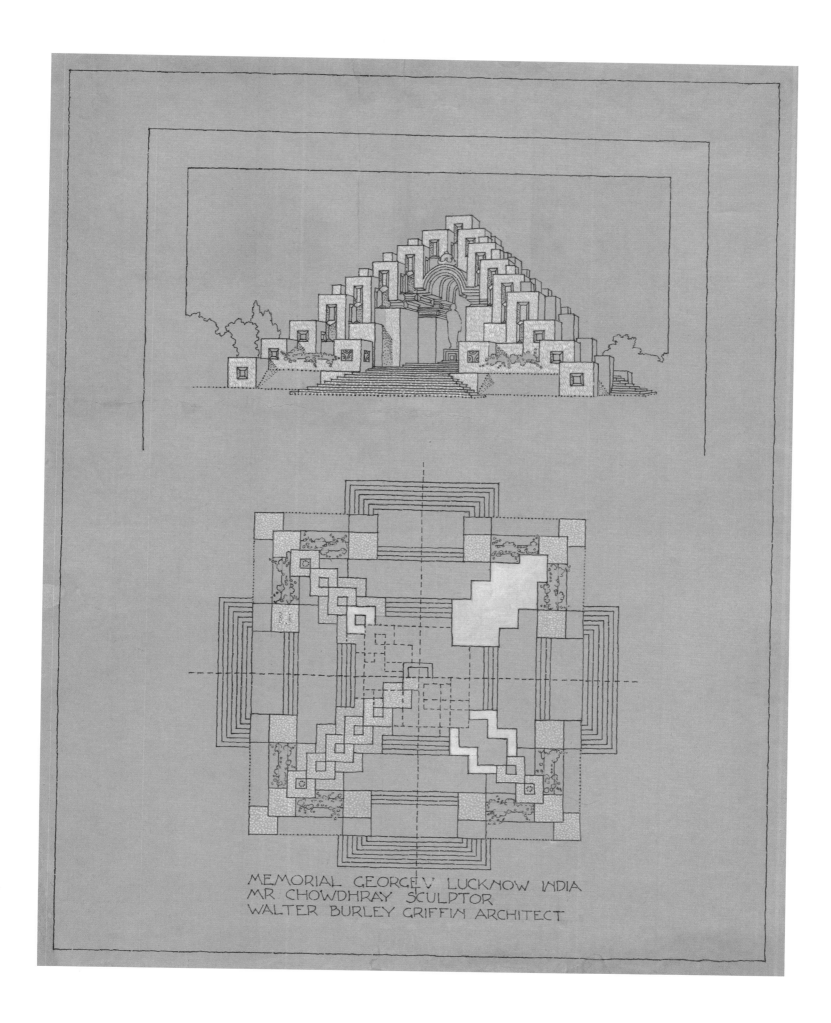

MEMORIAL GEORGE V LUCKNOW INDIA
MR CHOWDHRAY SCULPTOR
WALTER BURLEY GRIFFIN ARCHITECT

KING GEORGE V MEMORIAL
Walter Burley Griffin, Marion Mahony Griffin
Lucknow (IN), 1937

While working on the failed commission for the new library at the University of Lucknow (see opposite), the Griffins took on dozens of other undertakings throughout India, including private houses, gardens, housing projects and public buildings. 'I feel comfortable here and find endless source of interest in the environment of an ancient civilization,' Walter wrote to his father.

Perhaps their most unusual effort, also in Lucknow, was a civic memorial to King George V, who died in 1936. The specifics of the commission are not documented, but this was the Griffins' only work related to the British in India. Located on the street now known as Mahatma Gandhi Marg, the memorial rejected the historicist styles of most imperial monuments in favour of a pyramidal canopy of squared blocks marked with smaller squared recesses and softened at the base by lush planters. Visitors would enter via a cruciform grouping of broad, low stairs, leading to a statue 4 m (13 ft) high designed by the famed Indian sculptor DP Roy Choudhury. In many ways the piece recalls an Indian temple, and as such it constitutes an example of the Griffins' ability to integrate Indian architecture sympathetically into modern design (an approach they called 'localized modernism').

There is no record of why their proposal wasn't carried out, but Walter's death in the same year likely provides the reason. He died at Lucknow's (yes) King George's Hospital. Years later a sculpture of Mahatma Gandhi was placed on the site.

SHIVA MUSEUM
Sanjay Puri
Jaipur (IN), 2018

The Shiva Museum, intended to tell the history of the Hindu god known as 'the Creator', was to be built by the Rajasthan government's Amber Development and Management Authority on a small plot facing an existing temple. For this oddly shaped, compressed site, Sanjay Puri fashioned a pair of wedge-shaped buildings united under a single roof. Between them was a wide walkway, framing views of the neighbouring temple – which otherwise would have been completely blocked by the new museum.

The entire volume, which rose to the modest height of 21.6 m (71 ft), was made from pale yellow- and orangish-ochre sandstone, to be quarried locally. Courtyards were scooped out of the sides of the buildings to allow indirect sunlight to flood the passage between the wedges, and Puri used *jaali* walls – traditional perforated stone screens with calligraphy and geometric patterns – to absorb heat while allowing light to filter, like tiny stars, into the museum. The light made its way in through a roof that was a glazed space frame lined with more *jaali* blocks. The landscaped scoop-outs, the latticed stone and the thickened walls would keep the building cool in the hot desert climate, where temperatures can reach 35°C (95°F) for eight months of the year.

A sequence of interior bridges, made of projecting cubes of sandstone, led between the wedges and eventually to the rooftop terrace garden, which had an amphitheatre on one side and a solar array on the other. Officials had planned to build a music museum after the Shiva Museum was completed, but neither happened.

TAJ MAHAL PALACE HOTEL ADDITION
Achyut Kanvinde
Mumbai (IN), 1970

Master of a vernacular-inspired, Brutalist form of Modernism, Achyut Kanvinde and his firm Kanvinde, Rai & Chowdhury built many of the celebrated structures of post-colonial India. In 1970 the owner of Bombay's (now Mumbai's) legendary – and spectacularly ornate – Taj Mahal Palace hotel invited Kanvinde and two other major Indian architects, Ram Sharma and Raj Rewal, to submit alternatives to an existing scheme by the Los Angeles architect Welton Becket for an addition adjacent to the Taj, on the site of the old Green's Hotel (1890).

Kanvinde's scheme harmonized effectively with the Indo-Saracenic Revival Taj, featuring off-centre stone slabs, arched vaults, corbelled brackets and rounded upper bay windows, yet it remained breathtakingly modern thanks to its sculpted form, clustering and stepping outwards as it rose, like an etched, colossal bluff. The design provided the best possible sea views to all rooms, assisted with shading, and shaped lively and varied spaces.

None of the alternative schemes was chosen, and Becket's conventional design won by default, leading to speculation as to why the Indian firms were invited in the first place. But, as Becket's project went forward, Patell Batliwala & Associates (the Mumbai practice appointed to execute the conceptual plans) submitted its own scheme, which the client preferred. That firm's twenty-storey Taj Tower, completed in 1972, added Saracenic arched windows, recessed screens, granite and stucco panels, and a protruding, upward-thrusting square crown to what was a squat, conventional twenty-three-storey tower.

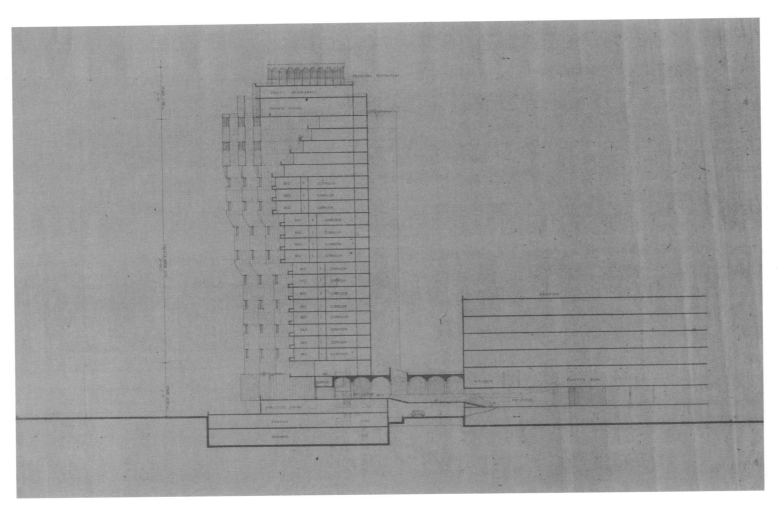

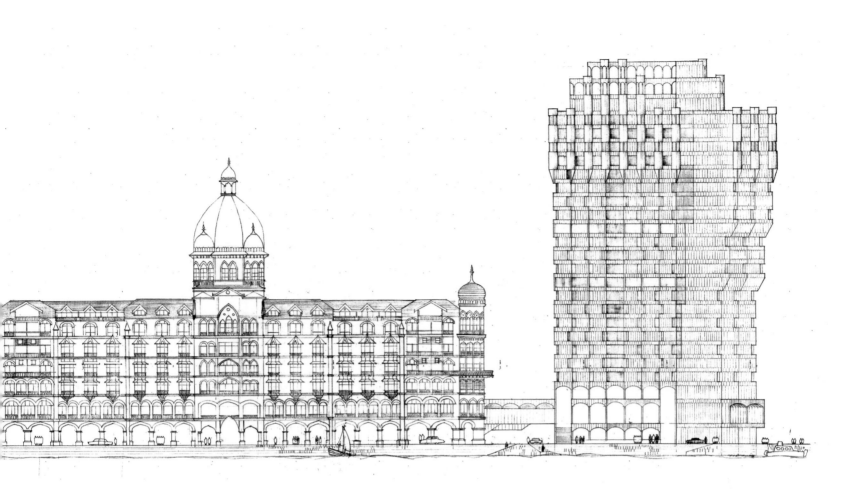

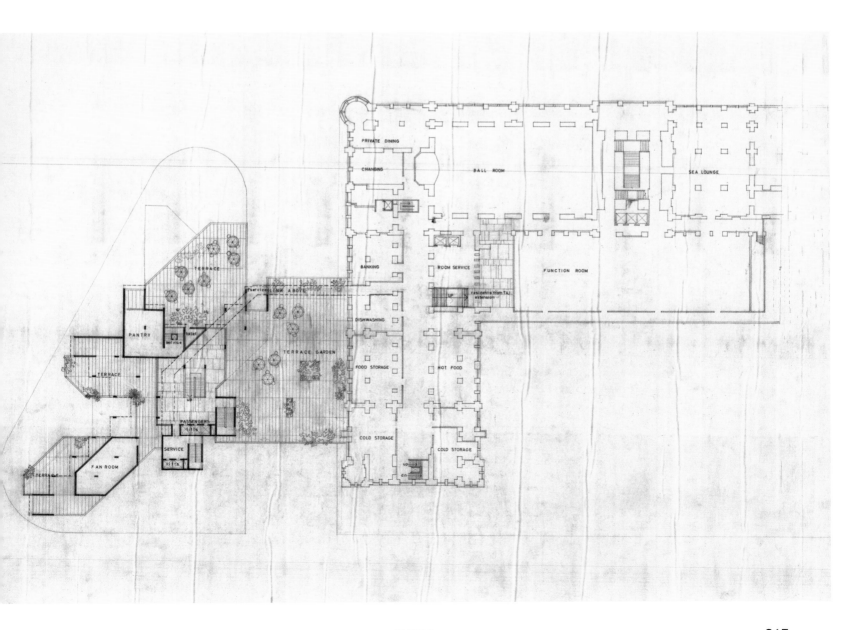

BOYCE HOUSES
Charles Correa
Pune (IN), 1962

The architect and urban planner Charles Correa, one of India's key post-Independence architects, merged the forward-looking principles and language of Modernism with traditional, time-tested Indian vernacular, responsive to both culture and climate. The launch of his firm in the 1950s coincided with India's first major push for large-scale development through state-controlled industry. He endeavoured to harness this force to improve the housing of everyday Indians, creating prototype after prototype, each embedded with his seven 'cardinal principles' for housing, the first of which was 'open-to-sky space'. Most of these experiments incorporated traditional Indian outdoor typologies, such as courtyards and terraces.

With Boyce Houses, on Ganeshkhind Road in Pune, a major city about 150 km (93 miles) southeast of Mumbai, Correa attempted to draw together the varied ideas from his prototypes into a cluster of townhouses. Employing reinforced-concrete frames with brick infill, Correa stacked assorted units one above the other in an interlocking pattern, forming double-height, garden-filled verandas, protecting the main living areas from searing sunlight and monsoon rains, enabling the prevailing east–west breezes (each apartment was essentially a breezeway) and generating abundant possible plans. As with most of his residential projects, Correa was careful not to over-programme these spaces: 'You start with a basic house, but you have to let people change it to their own needs,' he once said. He also designed active passageways between buildings, creating a vibrant and varied sense of community.

Correa never received the go-ahead from his clients, whom he identifies in his archives simply as 'Dr and Mrs Boyd'. However, the effort informed several more recent projects embracing lush, outsized buffer zones, both by Correa and by other architects around India.

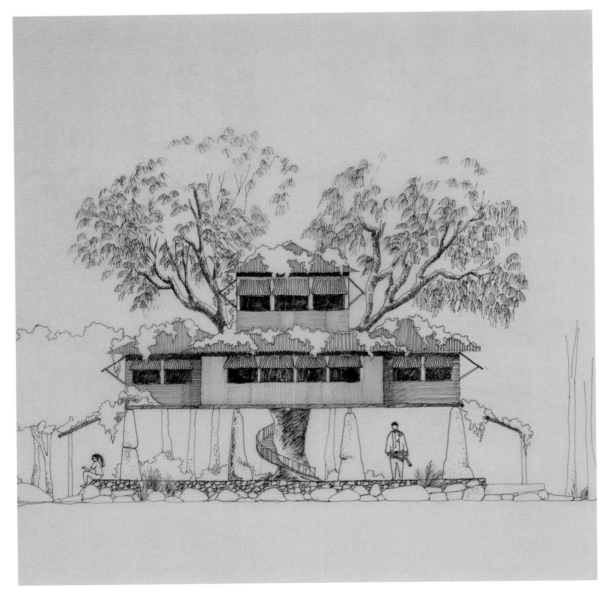

YALA BEACH HOTEL
Geoffrey Bawa
Yala National Park, (LK), 1968

Geoffrey Bawa was Sri Lanka's most influential architect, whose quiet, reserved manner (despite the fact he drove around in a Rolls-Royce) disguised a revolutionary. He invented a new architecture by ripping open the bungalows built by British colonizers in his native Colombo, the capital of what was then known as Ceylon. He invited in the sensory experiences of the tropical monsoon climate, lush landscape and ancient culture of the island nation, yet strongly adhered to Modernist ideas of open floor plans and 'indoor-outdoor' rooms.

The Yala Beach Hotel underscored Bawa's desire to stretch Modernism onto a vernacular canvas. The Yala National Park is an expansive forest preserve that skirts the Indian Ocean in the southeast of the country, with fine quartz sand dunes along the shore giving way to weathered granite outcrops. Bawa's hotel had three sets of cottages: rock, sand dune and tree house. The tree houses were cruciform, reached by a spiral staircase wrapped around the tree trunk; the rock houses had low bulwark walls with boulder-like, thatched roofs hoisted above; the sand-dune houses appeared to be carved into the sandy hillocks, with eyebrow windows and fanciful wind-catching chimneys popping up playfully like the snouts of exotic beasts. The buildings blended in yet stood out; they made themselves known – who could miss a two-bedroom, two-storey tree house? – but never felt as if they had parachuted in, like a colonizing army. Bawa's biomorphic and landform *casitas* were eternally confined to paper, however. The rocky bluffs and dunes at Yala remain undeveloped but for the odd tent-cabin encampment.

马家窑彩陶
博物馆

MAJIAYAO CERAMICS MUSEUM
Anna Heringer
Lintao (CN), 2014

The German architect Anna Heringer says: 'Architecture, like the landscape, like our own bodies, erodes over time. No material stays forever.' When she builds – after first sculpting her projects in clay (she eschews the architect's usual toolkit of pencils, paper, AutoCAD or Rhino) – she seeks to harmonize her plans with the specific nature of each place.

Thousands of years before the time of Christ, Lintao, in the north-central Chinese province of Gansu, was home to the Majiayao, a Neolithic culture that is now known mainly for its painted pottery. The Ceramics Museum was intended as a space for exhibiting the 3,000-year-old pottery of this culture, as well as contemporary pieces. Heringer decided to build using the same earth in which local farmers grow their crops to make clear the relationship between the fired ceramics and the museum's unfired clay walls. It also underlined the fact that the pottery had been protected for aeons within its earthen bed.

The rammed-earth building consisted of three layers: an outer wall with niches for the ancient ceramics; a second wall in the middle for contemporary pottery; and a third wall enclosing an inner courtyard, as in much traditional Chinese architecture. The building materials drew upon the earth: straw, mud, rock, terracotta, stone and wood. As an object, the museum looked as if it had been made by hand – which, indeed, it could have been. Like so many projects in twenty-first-century China, however, it simply never materialized.

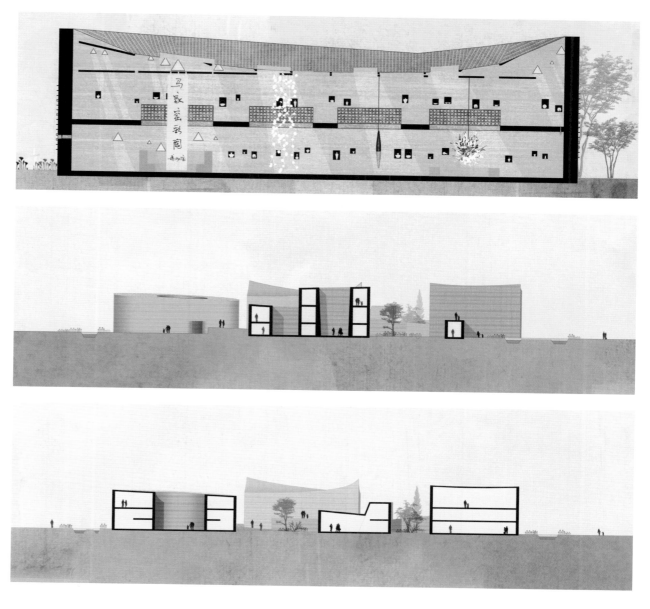

XU BEIHONG
MEMORIAL HALL
AQSO
Beijing (CN), 2010

The Xu Beihong Memorial Hall was a museum and research centre dedicated to Xu Beihong, the pioneering twentieth-century artist known for his ink-and-wash paintings of horses and birds, and his exploration of a style that reflected modern China. The scheme was intended to be built near Xi Hai in central Beijing, a tranquil lake where, appropriately, ducks – which appear in many of the artist's paintings – congregate. Seeking to interpret the shimmering colours and angular energy of the artist's work, AQSO proposed a copper-mesh skin for the public face of the building, tweaked and bent into a container of polygons. At a distance, the building appeared solid, but when experienced close up, it revealed itself as soft and diaphanous, an effect produced by overlapping the mesh in various patterns. AQSO saw this duality as a metaphor for the artist's paintings: deceptively simple, yet deeply complex. Inside, neutral spaces allowed the art to speak directly to the viewer. The interior, however, continued the notion of several interpretations by subtracting chunks from the uniform grid of concrete floor plates. The voids, falling in different places, made an atrium that leaned and twisted in a similar way to the exterior as if to remind visitors that one must approach art in a state of suspended disbelief.

Memorial Hall was commissioned by a quasi-official local design group as bait to raise money for the project. After submitting its proposal, AQSO never heard another word. Memorial Hall ended in silence.

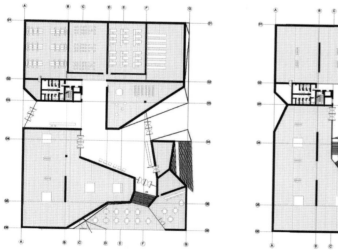

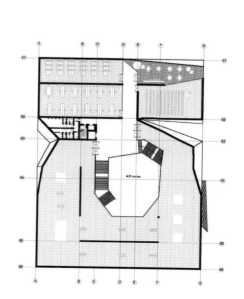

QINGDAO MUSEUM
Steven Holl
Qingdao (CN), 2013

The outline of Qingdao Museum began when Steven Holl sketched the city's Jiaozhou Bay Bridge, one of the longest spans in the world, then redrew it as a swirling bridge 22 m (72 ft) wide, covering the proposed site of a new cultural centre. At intervals along this 'light loop',

as he called it, were four cubes, large buildings that were to house four museums: modern, classical, public and performing arts. The buildings were hollowed out, producing light shafts in odd sizes, at odd angles. The light loop connected these Swiss-cheese structures, but also defined the public spaces: a great plaza in the crook of the elbow of the modern museum; a terrace scooped out, like a white concrete canyon, from the midriff of the classical museum; and small water gardens tucked just about everywhere else.

Typical of Holl's work, the complex floated in the manner of – what else? – a bridge. The ground spaces were thus free, and there would be no defined path, allowing the visitor to roam and to experience the buildings from beneath, as a single entity. The light loops would have two rows of galleries, which Holl compared in their elongated layout to the storytelling of ancient Chinese scroll paintings.

The facades were monochrome, some of sanded aluminium, others of stained concrete, but the undersides would be painted in the

rich polychrome colours of traditional Chinese buildings. These shades would bounce off the surfaces of the pools and at night produce a shimmering glow, like neon through fog, when the soffits would be washed with light.

The museum, intended as the pivot for a civic expansion of Qingdao, was abandoned in favour of massive housing projects.

HUA TUNG CHRISTIAN UNIVERSITY
Walter Gropius, IM Pei
Shanghai (CN), 1946

Although he had never been to China, in 1946 Walter Gropius (and his late-career firm the Architects Collaborative) received a commission from the United Board of Christian Colleges in China to design Hua Tung Christian

University, a new campus for 3,000 students on the site of the city's former Hongqiao airport. The facility would merge three existing Christian institutions: Hangchow (Hangzhou) University, Soochow (Suzhou) University and St John's. Since Gropius's knowledge of the country was cursory, he asked one of his former students at the Harvard Graduate School of Design to join him as an associate: IM Pei, who had grown up in the classical garden city of Suzhou and had shown promising ability to convert Chinese traditions into contemporary designs.

The masterplan, organized as an academic centre and three residential compounds, set out to update historical Chinese planning for the twentieth century. 'Avoiding outright imitation of the old style, it tends to express the ancient philosophy of the Chinese people and their love of nature,' said Gropius. The layout evoked a traditional Chinese garden, with a central artificial lake, covered connecting paths, and an open composition of rectangular courtyards. Within this armature the architects placed modular, steel-framed two- or three-storey buildings

that were intimate in scale, integrated with the landscape, and evocative of traditional Chinese wooden architecture.

The project came to an end early in 1949, when it became clear that communists would win the country's civil war. By the early 1950s the Communist Party had expelled all three institutions and all other Christian missionary agencies.

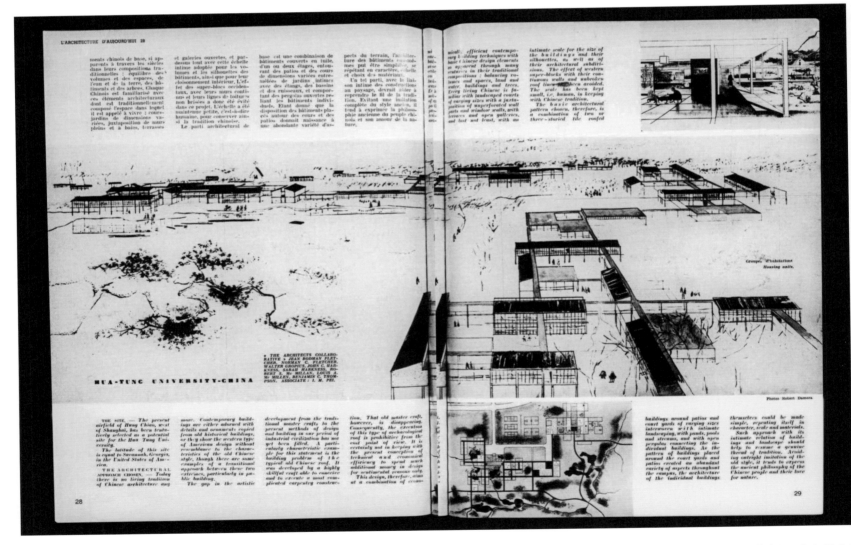

SINO TOWER
Paul Rudolph
Hong Kong (CN), 1989

Never able to realize his prefabricated, enve-
lope-busting visions for high-rises in North
America, Paul Rudolph executed a handful of
fascinating towers in Asia at the very end of his
career, including the Concourse and the Colonnade in Singapore, the Wisma Dharmala
Tower in Jakarta, and the Lippo Centre in Hong
Kong. His crowning achievement would have
been the Sino Tower, a mixed-use competition
design for the Sino Land Company set to be
the tallest tower in Southeast Asia. Evoking
the tiered silhouette of a Chinese pagoda, the
ninety-storey structure would have edged
Hong Kong's Victoria Harbour, about 1.6 km
(1 mile) from the city's Central District.
The structure climbed upwards from an open
A-frame base 46 m (150 ft) tall formed by eight
angled twin columns, allowing light and air
down to the street while leaving room for sky-
walks, a low commercial building and a suspended sky lobby. From there the exposed
columns would be engulfed first by a hotel, then
by offices. The floors were grouped in clusters
of ten, breaking down the building's massive
scale, differentiating its many sections, and
carving out space for services and mechanicals. Floors and terraces cantilevered from the
columns, while faceted windows slanted outwards, creating a cut-jewel profile and ensuring that the sun would not directly hit the glass,
yet would still create mesmerizing reflections.
At the apex, floors containing more support
spaces were clad in shimmering silver leaf.
None of the competition's entries was ever
implemented, relegating another bold Rudolph
idea to obscurity.

CHINA

LONG TAN PARK
MVRDV
Liuzhou (CN), 2004

The Dutch architect MVRDV's plan for 2,700 new houses in the industrial city of Liuzhou, near the UNESCO World Heritage Site South China Karst mountains, began with a tricky proposition. Could one build anything on the hills without permanently scarring the beauty of the limestone landscape, which tropical moisture had dissolved into countless ridges, towers, fissures and sinkholes? MVRDV answered with a provisional 'yes', provided the homes themselves became a bulwark against further erosion while in some manner mimicking the natural topography.

The site was a limestone quarry where five rock faces had been sheared off. MVRDV proposed cladding the slopes in clusters of boxy homes, with floors and walls of concrete mixed with local rock, helping them to blend into the mountains. Since the limestone varied in hardness, some of the structures would need to be built on columns, others attached by dowels, and still others carved like grottos into the stone. Wide stairs and terraces separated the houses, creating a skein of streets, giving the look and feel of an ancient Italian hilltop village. The houses themselves had a primal, almost atavistic character: simple, unadorned rectangular boxes with large picture windows, piled high on the vertiginous escarpments. MVRDV believed that present-day cliff dwellers would prefer the similar-but-separate containers, on a played-out quarry on the outskirts of one of the world's smoggiest cities, to what the firm called 'hotel' living. Like so many plans made during the boom years, the lofty-sounding proposition had its oxygen sucked away by a bigger project, the Italian architect Stefano Boeri's 30,000-unit Forest City masterplan, which took more than a decade to break ground.

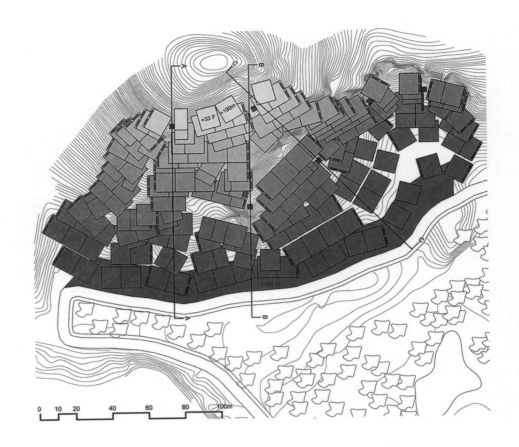

THEP THANI
John Portman
Bangkok (TH), 1982

During the run-up to the bicentennial celebration of the founding of Bangkok, John Portman designed Thep Thani, a mixed-use complex in the heart of the city's business and financial district. The early 1980s were hot for Bangkok real estate when Portman, the genius of dizzying, eye-shattering, soaring hotel atria, pitched his plan for office towers and a hotel, sitting on top of a public plaza enclosing a shopping mall. The idea was a modern riff on traditional Thai architecture. The two office towers rose from either side of the landscaped pedestrian plaza, their outward-facing sides stepping inwards in four-storey increments. Separated by the plaza 48 m (157 ft) wide, the pair of buildings looked like a single pyramid that had been sawn straight up the middle. The aperture framed the hotel, which was formed of two interlocking pyramids, an exaggerated, massively up-scaled motif taken from Bangkok's celebrated Wat Benchamabophit Dusitvanaram, a Buddhist temple with high, sharp gables and sequenced roofs.
The hotel's interior, following the contours of its sloping roof, consisted of balcony corridors that became smaller as the building climbed skywards, forming a sixteen-storey interior atrium. In classic Portman fashion, high-speed glass elevators would jet straight up the centre of the atrium, and bridges would connect passengers to the balconies leading to their rooms. A two-level skybridge – housing a restaurant – was to be suspended twenty-three storeys above the plaza, connecting the office buildings and turning the site into a huge gateway. Portman, who doubled as a developer, didn't win over the Thai authorities, and the gambit failed.

GATOT SUBROTO OFFICE BUILDING
Paul Rudolph
Jakarta (ID), 1990

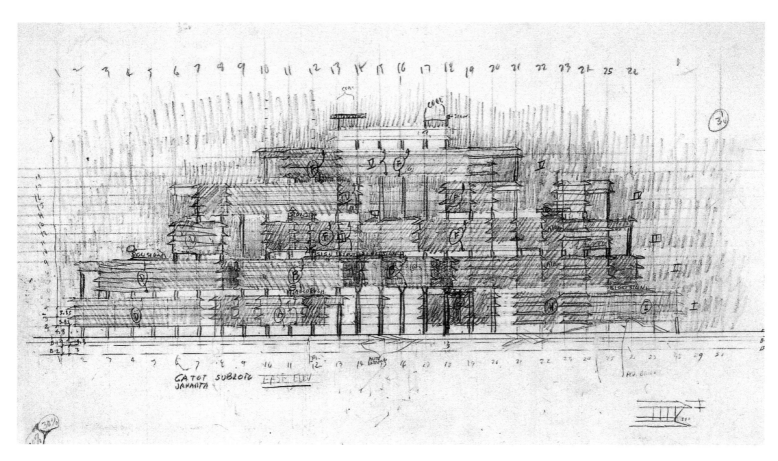

Paul Rudolph spent the final years of his career working predominantly in Asia, where visionary, well-heeled clients supported his extraordinary (and extraordinarily difficult) plans. A good example is Dharmala Group, a large Indonesian conglomerate specializing in import/export, finance and real estate, among other fields. In 1982 he designed the company's Jakarta headquarters, the Wisma Dharmala Building, a lively tower with deep overhangs shielding the lower floors, and an internal courtyard.
But Rudolph failed to realize a later project consisting of eight interconnected towers along the city's busy Jalan Gatot Subroto. Dharmala would occupy the main tower, while other structures – fitting together in all directions, like Tetris blocks – would be rented to office and residential tenants. Each block, lit from above via long, translucent skylights, would be separated from the next by an outdoor planted deck, giving the building an extraordinary amount of open space. 'I see it as purely a response to a climate and the feeling of an accommodating environment,' said Rudolph, who also planned a large pool at the base of the building.
As in Rudolph's other buildings for the company, large overhangs shielded glass walls, while tall, thin columns freed up volume (creating what he called a 'perforated wall') for open space and light. All were strategies, he noted, tha[t] might have been much harder to achieve in th[e] United States. 'They are freer. They are not s[o] stringent,' he said of Indonesia's building law[s] Nonetheless, the unusual scheme worried som[e] local planners and citizens, while Dharmala'[s] growing internal struggles inevitably killed it[s] ability to make the building happen.

PERURI 88
MVRDV
Jakarta (ID), 2012

MVRDV's answer to the longstanding problem of how to build cities in the sky was Peruri 88, designed for Jakarta, Indonesia's seaside capital city of ten million people. The eighty-eight-storey building was a cluster of concrete and glass boxes stacked Jenga-style, reminiscent of OMA's Interlace (2013) in Singapore. Some appeared on the brink of collapse; others were wedged in like Archimedean levers. These structures, built over a commercial complex, would rise to a height of forty-four storeys. One looked like a riff on Arquitectonica's Atlantis, in Miami (1982); another appeared to be a chunk pried from Ludwig Mies van der Rohe's Seagram Building in Manhattanm (1958). Rooftop parks sprouted from the massive blocks, which were stuffed with offices, townhouses, lofts, live/work spaces, cinemas, a wedding chapel and – Islam being the largest religion in Indonesia – a mosque. Two of the tottering structures had steep, sloping roofs with stutter-step seating for those brave enough to take in the views from the summit.

The assemblage was shot through with horizontal gaps, reinforcing the image of a city in the sky. But, for a visitor standing in the ground-level courtyard and peering up, the structure would have become like a carbon-fibre matrix. Inside the seven-storey mall, escalators as thin as kite strings climbed fifteen and twenty storeys, nonstop to their destinations. Out of one side of the pinwheel of structures, a slender, white luxury hotel climbed to 400 m (1,310 ft). Winy Maas, MVRDV's co-founder, said the project represented 'a modern icon literally raised from [Jakarta's] own city fabric'. But critics called it banal. Fifty-five skyscrapers were planned near the subway stop on Jakarta's new metro, among them Peruri 88.

326   ASIA

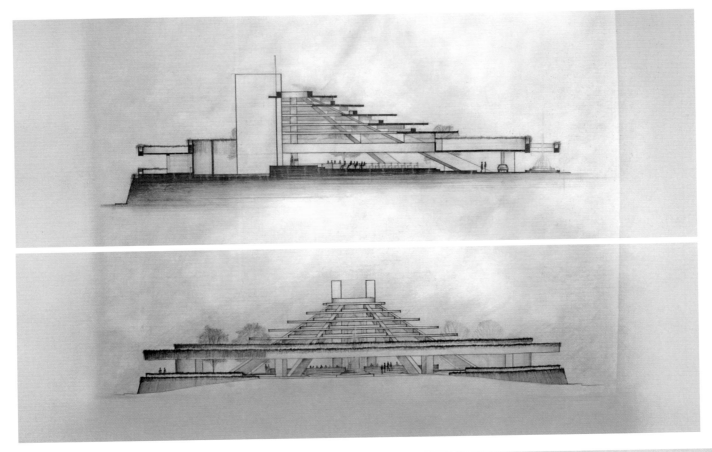

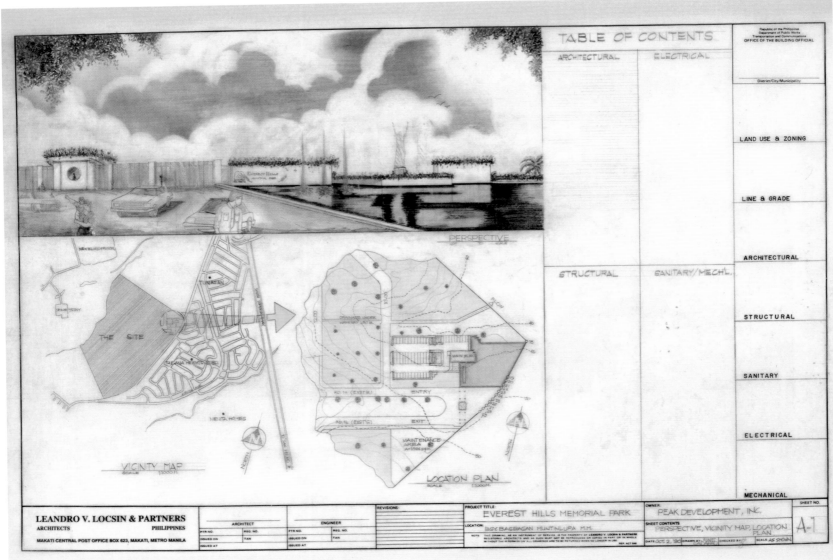

EVEREST HILLS MEMORIAL PARK
Leandro Locsin
Muntinlupa (PH), 1990

Breaking free from the United States after World War II, and needing to rebuild after merciless wartime destruction, the Philippines underwent an unprecedented period of planning and reconstruction in the second half of the twentieth century. Key to that undertaking was the systematic employment of reinforced concrete, and no architect in the country was as fluent in the use of this material as Leandro Locsin, whose sophisticated approach and vast knowledge of vernacular culture, climate and landscape made him arguably the Philippines' most important Modernist. One of his many local inspirations was the truncated pyramid, a form particularly common to Filipino homes that made its way into his art centres, schools, cemeteries, churches, monasteries and more.

In designing a hillside chapel for the private cemetery Everest Hills Memorial Park in Muntinlupa, a city on the southern edge of Manila, Locsin explored the form through a massive floating roof composed of stepping concrete slabs and angled glass planes. With an external diameter of 70 m (230 ft), it was the largest sacred space the architect would ever conceive, and it was set to be the park's focal point. Under the sizable crown – supported by angled peripheral beams, a textured reinforced-concrete base, and a central altar shooting upwards – was a circular chapel, along with crypts, niches and a peripheral walkway, separated by a wide pool punctuated by plants and trees that allowed freshly cooled air to enter. The complex project wasn't able to get off the ground before Locsin passed away in 1994, and it died with him.

MUSEUM OF INDIGENOUS KNOWLEDGE
Kengo Kuma
Manila (PH), 2014

The Museum of Indigenous Knowledge was launched by the Ginhawa Institute, a promoter of local Indigenous culture, and designed to exhibit Filipino artefacts and stories. It was a perfect example of the iconoclastic architect Kengo Kuma's concept of 'negative architecture', which placed environment at the forefront and cast the building in a supporting role.

Set on a corner site in the centre of Manila, the five-storey structure was hollowed out by a cave-like ravine, partially open to the sky, filled with tropical landscaping and clad with lush vegetation and craggy rocks, supported by a steel ring structural system. The rocky aesthetic, designed with specialists from zoos and amusement parks, was inspired by the museum's exhibits (some of which dated back to the Neolithic period) and by local landscapes, such as Callao Cave in Peñablanca and the Banaue rice terraces in the mountains of Luzon. 'We realized the richness of these Indigenous cultures and their crafts couldn't be understood in the asphalt and concrete context of a city like Manila. So we decided to bring a "piece" of landscape representative of all that diversity to the centre of the city,' said Kuma.

Decked areas contained a café and shop, while internal galleries both rose above the central court and were tucked into three levels underground. It was intended that Filipino craftspeople would contribute to the interior elements, such as woven pandan-mat cladding, a thatched ceiling above the entrance, an abacá rope feature wall in the lobby and Sama Dilaut pavilions on the roof. But the development teams supporting the foundation demanded a commercial high-rise component, altering the plan drastically, and Kuma's team decided to pull out of the project.

ROOF +20.20m

4F +13.90m

3F +09.90m

1F +03.30m

GF +00.00m

B1 -04.95m

B2 -08.25m

Section A   S=1:750

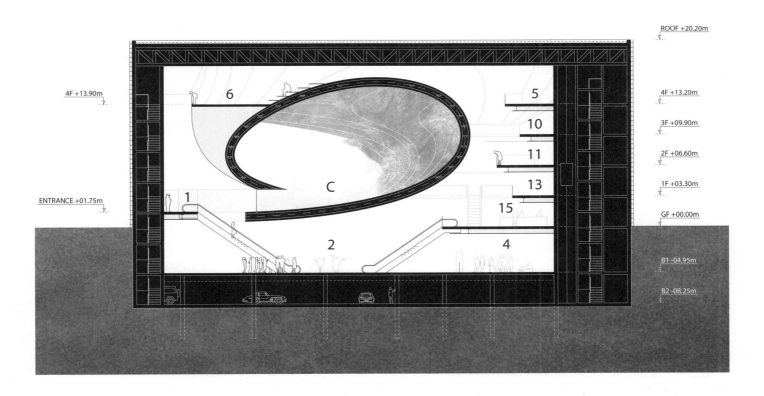

4F +13.90m

ENTRANCE +01.75m

ROOF +20.20m

4F +13.20m

3F +09.90m

2F +06.60m

1F +03.30m

GF +00.00m

B1 -04.95m

B2 -08.25m

Section B   S=1:750

SEOUL PERFORMING ART CENTER
Jean Nouvel
Seoul (KR), 2006

In 2006 Jean Nouvel won the competition for a performing arts centre on Nodeul Island, the artificial spit in the middle of the River Han, as it flows through Seoul. Nouvel looked at the flat-as-a-crêpe ellipse and concluded that the island was too unnatural to build on. He proposed first to remake Nodeul after 'the ideal image of the Korean landscape and Korean spirit', which would mean constructing an island of mountains, rocks, trees and a waterfall in the middle of the modern city.

In the midst of this deep landscape, Nouvel planned to tuck what he said would be 'a very mysterious architecture'. Peeping out of the trees and rocks would be two shimmering gold forms – the opera house and the concert hall – seductive, precious objects for city-dwellers. The opera house would be a redder shade of gold, the concert hall yellower. Inside, lighting would cast images for each music venue: the Greek musician and poet Orpheus for the opera house; a projection of trumpets for the concert hall. Jean Nouvel wanted to design an effect: every branch, every leaf, every rock would become a composition, leaving one with a vague impression of Bukhan Mountain, a granite crag at the northern periphery of Seoul, set in a rocky, uneven forest. This tapestry would create a trompe l'œil, suggesting that the island was bigger than it is, and that it shrouded a treasure. The design never progressed beyond this initial outline, however. Fifteen years later the island was opened as a music centre with cookie-cutter concrete buildings sitting on the barren reef.

THE CLOUD
MVRDV
Seoul (KR), 2011

MVRDV's residential towers known as The Cloud were doomed almost from the moment they were announced. They were to be built at the entrance to the Yongsan Dreamhub, an enormous proposed business complex in the South Korean capital, Seoul. MVRDV's plan looked deceptively simple: a pair of almost identical towers, one of fifty-four floors, the other sixty, standing on a plinth with public gardens below. The skyscrapers were perfect rectangular prisms, concise, controlled, cubistic stelae, until the twenty-seventh floor. Up there, halfway to the sky, the Cloud broke free. As in so much of MVRDV's work, the buildings became a city in the sky in the form of a bridge of lofts that seemed to sprout from the geometry of the concrete matrix cladding. The extrusion was, indeed, cloud-like, having the fluffy fullness of a cumulus.

But, almost as soon as renderings were released, an angry chorus cried, 'Shame!' Firefighters and families of survivors of al-Qaeda's attack on the Twin Towers in New York on 11 September 2001 exclaimed that the bridge looked just like the plume of smoke at the point of the planes' impact. The conspiracy-minded were quick to add that Daniel Libeskind, who had designed the original masterplan for the reconstruction of Ground Zero, had also furnished the masterplan for Yongsan Dreamhub. MVRDV received threatening emails, and the firm's plea that the design was based on such parameters as sunlight, outside space and quality of life for its inhabitants and the city-dwellers more generally went nowhere. The Cloud was eventually scrapped, and two years later, in 2013, the fiscally strapped hub was cancelled in its entirety.

ASIA

TEMPLE OF ATOMIC CATASTROPHES
Seiichi Shirai
Hiroshima (JP), 1954

Seiichi Shirai, who died in 1983, only weeks before he would have become Japan's first Pritzker Prize laureate, said of the Temple of Atomic Catastrophes that he had 'pursued an image of deep sadness, a lone building standing on a bleak plain … associated with memories of brutal violence, the idea of a desolate ruin'. The more deeply he contemplated 'this narrative mode of thinking', he said, the more he needed to shed 'biased concepts and stereotypes', which was no simple matter, given that his subject was the worst human-inflicted devastation – 130,000 dead in a single bomb blast – in a long history of humanity's inhumanity. Shirai wanted to design 'the eternal, collective symbol of hope rather than a metaphor defining the memory of tragedy'. He came up with a cylindrical memorial hall, 9 m (30 ft) in diameter, rising from a pool of clear water flowing so gently that not even a ripple could be seen by the naked eye. The black granite cylinder passed through a square volume, measuring 23 m (75 ft) on each side, hovering in space, its mirror image reflected on the water's surface – the Platonic ideal silent in its clarity and simplicity. Shirai wrote that he thought 'the most important thing was to obtain a formal purity that had never appeared before human eyes in the past.' Still, the allusion to a mushroom cloud was intentional.

Kenzo Tange's Hiroshima Peace Memorial Park was completed the year Shirai published his plans for the temple, which led to his building being dismissed as a political gesture. Years later it would be the basis of his Pritzker nomination.

HOTEL IZU
Tadao Ando
Shizuoka (JP), 1987

Tadao Ando, the self-taught former boxer who first came to prominence for his introspective concrete house in Sumiyoshi, Osaka, once said, 'I want to make space in which people are so quietly moved that they don't talk about it to others.' His work, he said, is intended to appeal to the senses, the way wind or light or freezing cold might do: imperceptible, weightless, empty.

In common with all his works, the Hotel Izu took form as a complex of large-scale, geometric concrete buildings that the architect intended to become an element of the topography. The hotel was set on a promontory above precipitous cliffs at the ocean's edge, in the shadow of Mt Fuji. Ando centred twin sets of four cubes rising from 30 m (100 ft) above sea level to 80 m (260 ft), with an observation deck, restaurant and theatre concentrated on the site. Each structure was built on a grid of 5.6 m (18 ft) squares and arranged on different levels, adopting the contours of the headland. Visitors would enter through a central gate at the top of the complex and follow a long wall past the café; the wall curved, leading to concrete trellis framing an artificial lake. Water from the lake spilled towards the sea, becoming a stepped cascade woven between the asymmetrical buildings. The hotel rooms themselves had views of the sea or of Mt Fuji. Through an approach that Ando described as 'using walls to defeat walls', the hotel was intended to become a sensory encounter with the lush, ever-changing landscape. The site where the resort was meant to be remains untouched to this day.

MOON TOWER
Shin Takamatsu
Osaka (JP), 1987

Few architects have lived up to the 'more is more' spirit of postmodernism in quite the same way as Shin Takamatsu, whose outrageously expressive buildings (many of them, somehow, built) take inspiration from the spiritual, cosmic, futuristic and industrial. 'I am an old-school architect,' he once said. 'Always dreaming of architecture as a monument or as something with a symbolic presence.'

In 1995 Takamatsu entered a competition to develop a centrepiece for Rinku Town, a new commercial development on reclaimed land adjacent to Kansai International Airport in the Osaka suburb of Izumisano. Takamatsu's Moon Tower, thirty-five storeys and 198.5 m (651 ft) tall, accommodating a 300-room hotel, shops, a large casino, and a museum of the work of the French visionary artist Gérard Di-Maccio, was topped by a shining, convex moon 90 m (295 ft) in diameter. The reinforced-concrete building emerged from a bulky, round base, rising five storeys above ground and five storeys below it. From there the tower's shaft was clad in glass with vertical textured lines and solid edges, evoking a sense of gravity. This dramatically offset the floating character of the shell-like 'moon', wedged between two 'jaws' containing the museum: a crystalline, mirrored hall showcasing Di-Maccio's masterpiece, the massive oil painting *Grande Toile* (1997), on the ceiling. Under the museum a hemispherical glass dome contained an otherworldly restaurant inspired by the artist's work.

In the end, the competition stalled and was never implemented. Rinku Town's focal point is now the fifty-six-storey Rinku Gate Tower Building (1996), by Nikken Sekkei. The Di-Maccio museum eventually opened in 2010 in the tiny town of Niikappu, in the far north of Japan.

ASIA

HELIX CITY
Kishō Kurokawa
Tokyo (JP), 1961

Kishō Kurokawa helped to instigate the Metabolist movement, a group of radical Japanese architects who discarded International Modernism in favour of buildings predicated on the reproductive cellular structures found in living things. Metabolists sought to build structures around a spine and outfitted them with prefab-ricated, replaceable components – like living cells – which could be changed when they had outlived their usefulness.

While working for his mentor Kenzo Tange on a redevelopment plan for Tokyo, Kurokawa proposed the megastructure Helix City, based on the twisted ladder of DNA discovered in 1953. Kurokawa's horizontal structure, erected 31 m (101 ft) above ground (at the time the maximum height permitted for new buildings in Tokyo), supported an entirely new, vertical city, with railways and cars running underground.

He devised two types of tower: 'bamboo' and 'tree'. 'Bamboo' was a hollow stalk with airports in the void, and residential cells adhering to the outer circumference. 'Tree', in contrast, had a trunk supporting radiating discs that diminished in diameter as they climbed skywards. It was as if someone had made a spiral sculpture from lollipop sticks. These 'branches' were terraced platforms for homes, schools and public offices. Every ten floors the spirals intersected, creating a network of criss-crossing passages.

Kurokawa's design, like those of his early colleagues, was a witty provocation but also serious, if far-fetched, proposition. Before h[e] abandoned his early approach, he did buil[d] an iconic Metabolist structure, Tokyo's Nakag[in] Capsule Tower, which has been likened to 10[?] prefabricated concrete washing machine[s] glued to a single shaft.

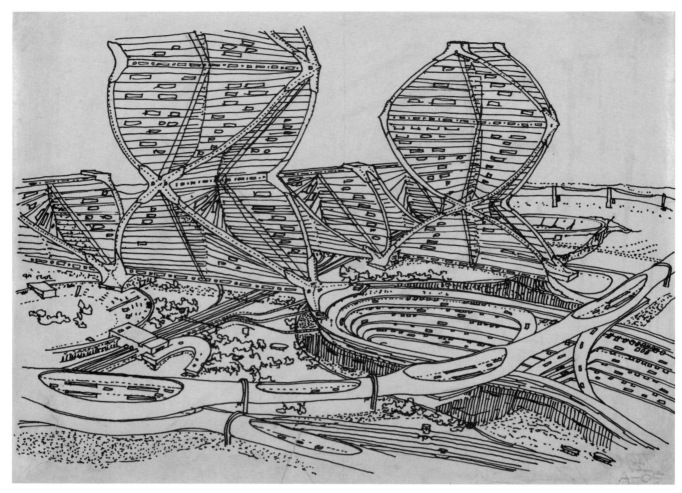

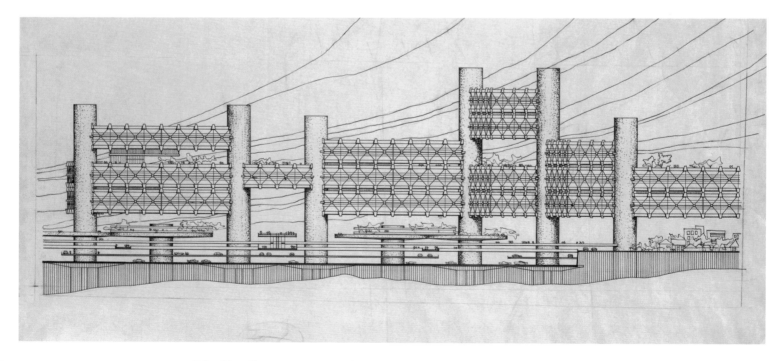

CITY IN THE AIR
Arata Isozaki
Tokyo (JP), 1960

In his essay 'Incubation Process', published in a special issue of the art magazine *Bijutsu Techo* in 1962, Arata Isozaki put forward his vision of future cities, which, he proclaimed, 'are destined to self-destruct/ Ruins are the style of our future cities/ Future cities are themselves ruins.' Isozaki had witnessed the atomic obliteration of Hiroshima: 'I grew up near ground zero. It was in complete ruins, and there was no architecture, no buildings and not even a city … So, my first experience of architecture was the void of architecture.'

At the time Isozaki proposed his City in the Air, Tokyo's planning regulations allowed a maximum building height of 31 m (102 ft). 'Tokyo is hopeless,' he wrote. 'I am leaving everything below 30 metres to others. If they think they can unravel the mess in this city, let them try. I will think about architecture and the city above 30 metres. An empty lot of 10 square metres [108 sq. ft] is all I need on the ground. I will erect a column there, and that column will be both a structural column and a channel for vertical circulation.'

Isozaki imagined massive tree trunks with huge megastructures branching in all directions above the city's clogged streets. Parks, pedestrian walkways and motorways linked the aerial clusters; the connecting limbs resembled *sashi-hijiki*, the traditional wooden brackets inserted directly into the pillars of Buddhist temples.

It was a relentlessly modern city, conceive[d] from the ashes of war, imbued with the apoc[-] alyptic imagery of a mushroom cloud. Perpet[-] ually influential, Isozaki's City in the Air attaine[d] a life truly in the air, but never on the ground.

TETRAHEDRON CITY
Richard Buckminster Fuller, Shoji Sadao
Tokyo (JP), 1968

Never one to run out of earth-changing ideas, Richard Buckminster Fuller was consumed with the tetrahedron, a four-sided triangular solid that he rightly called 'nature's building block' – one that could easily (and relatively cheaply) be applied to mass production. In early 1968 Fuller and his long-term collaborator Shoji Sadao developed the concept of Triton City. This prototype 'tetrahedronal floating city for 100,000 people' was composed of interconnected, expandable floating 'neighbourhood platforms' filled with tetrahedral modules surrounded by public gardens and terraces and supporting housing, schools, supermarkets, shops and services. 'Three-quarters of our planet Earth is covered with water, most of which may float organic cities,' explained Fuller in his book *Critical Path* (1981).

Later in 1968 Fuller was able to apply the concept to a commission by the Japanese media mogul Matsutarō Shōriki (owner of the conservative Japanese newspaper *Yomiuri Shimbun* and of the Yomiuri Giants baseball team) to design Tetrahedron City on the site of Yomiuri Land, a theme park owned by Shōriki on the still relatively undeveloped western edge of Tokyo. Supported by a 200-storey, open-truss aluminium frame and sitting atop hollow reinforced-concrete foundations 61 m (200 ft) deep, the crystalline structure would house a million people (roughly 300,000 families) in 'plug-in' terrace apartments of 186 sq. m (2,000 sq. ft) each. The behemoth, containing its own interior harbour, was designed eventually to float in Tokyo Bay, perhaps after having been floated down the nearby Tama River. As with virtually all Fuller's large-scale ideas, however, the plan was most likely unachievable. Shōriki's death in 1969 put an end to any attempt to realize it.

DENTSU CORPORATION HEADQUARTERS
Kenzo Tange
Tokyo (JP), 1964

Kenzo Tange was a pivotal figure in Metabolism, the post-war Japanese movement that amalgamated megastructures with notions of organic biological growth – resulting in dreamed-up cities that floated in Tokyo Bay and plug-in module towers that could spread ever wider, like forests of bamboo. His ideas, which he made public in his Tokyo Plan of 1960, caught the attention of Hideo Yoshida, the head of Dentsu, Japan's largest advertising company.

Yoshida's site, in the Tsukiji district, lay along a busy expressway, and Tange saw the location as a proving ground for his concept of a 'three-dimensional network' that could radiate from a single starting point. He created a complex made of enormous concrete cores supporting huge horizontal trusses, their frameworks connected by lattice bridges in the sky. Large voids between the trusses reinforced the impression of spaciousness and interconnection – as though all the parts were sleeved in and interchangeable. Employing this matrix to connect one megastructure to another, Tange said, would extend 'the core system right and left and forward and rearward ... [enabling] the building to conform to all kinds of future development'. The city would grow in an orderly, organic fashion.

'Mr Yoshida was so happy when he saw the proposal that he began talking of the likelihood of a similar kind of redevelopment for the entire Tsukiji district,' Tange recalled. Things fell apart, however, when Yoshida died as construction was about to begin. Tange's subsequent plan, which opened in 1967, was quietly corporate and decidedly not Metabolist.

COSMOS COMMERCIAL BUILDING
BOLLES+WILSON
Tokyo (JP), 1989

Peter Wilson had been designing innovative housing in Japan for about a decade when the Kyoto architect Shin Takamatsu sent him to meet Keitaro Nakamura, an urban prospector who owned a number of sites on Cosmos Street in Tokyo. Nakamura, who hoped to rename the street 'Architects' Street', believed a dash of proper 'architecture' would increase the value of his holdings. He gave Wilson the job of constructing a new building, with no instructions for its function: 'It's up to you,' he said. Wilson, whose designs emerged from the process of drawing, took the only clue he had of the developer's intentions – a newspaper cutting with a picture of Nakamura in the centre – and went to work. Since he couldn't read the newspaper, the voids between the words became the genesis of the building's facade. Cosmos Street, in effect, became *furoshiki*, a wrapping-paper package folded neatly at the corners; the packaging was as important as the contents. The structure, with its unknown use, was nonetheless practical. A central mast, in the form of a black ninja with splayed legs pinioned to the ground, kept the building aloft while allowing it to sway in an earthquake; the ground was folded upwards to hide the site behind; and the roof was a wavy pavilion to draw attention away from the water tanks of Tokyo's skyline.

Not long after Nakamura saw the drawings, he faxed Wilson saying he'd seen a video about Prince (now King) Charles's promotion of replica classical Georgian terraces in the United Kingdom, asking if Bolles+Wilson could adopt a similar design. They faxed back, 'No way,' and thus ended the newspaper-wrapper building.

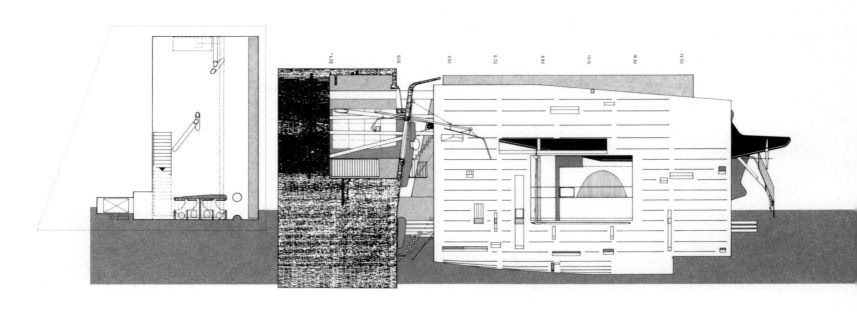

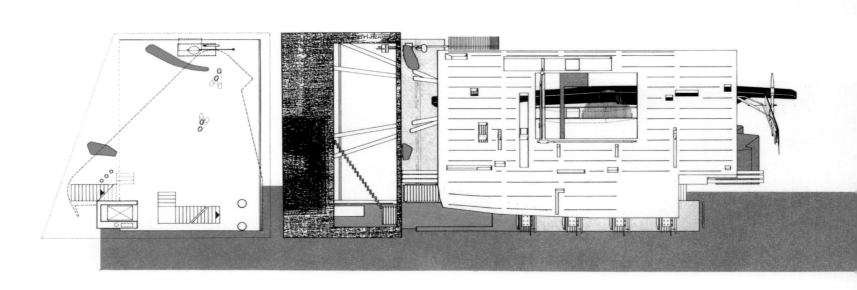

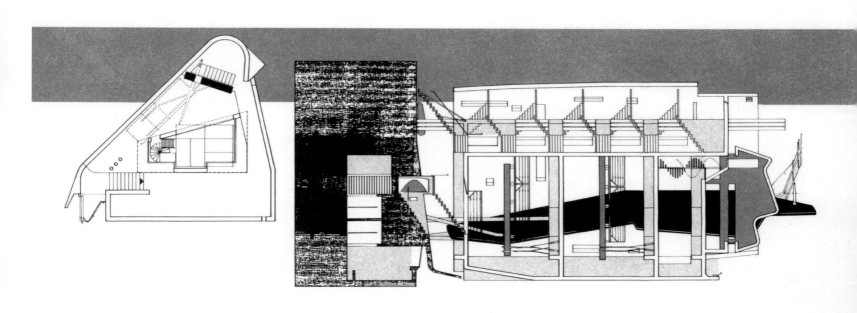

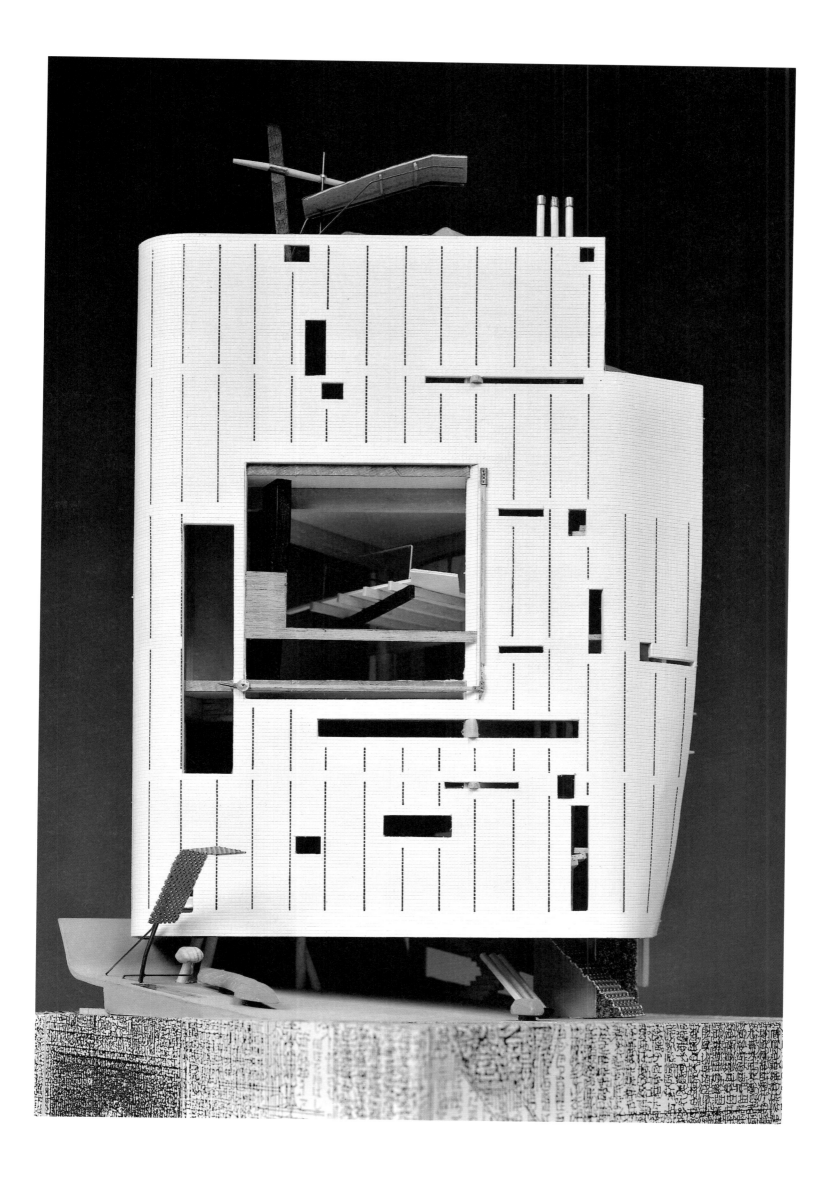

Australasia

AU [5]

NZ [2]

NO. 2 BOND STREET
John Andrews
Sydney, New South Wales
(AU), 1987

John Andrews, who passed away in 2022, was one of Australia's most feted late Modernist architects, having designed such local and international icons as the megastructure-as-campus Scarborough College in Toronto (1963), the stilted and stepped Harvard Graduate School of Design's Gund Hall (1972) and the Brutalist-meets-High-Tech King George Tower in Sydney (1976). In 1987 Andrews was commissioned by the Australian developer McNamara Group and its Japanese partners C Itoh and Shimizu to design a thirty-one-storey office tower in Sydney's central business district, adjacent to the Stock Exchange. A previous proposal had failed because it would have demolished historic buildings on George Street, including the neo-Renaissance George Patterson House (1892), and cast long shadows over adjacent Australia Square.

Andrews suggested two interconnected, polygonal-planned towers, the second elevated fifteen storeys on a large cylindrical column. 'They can complement each other and they don't have to fight,' he said in an interview with the Australian Institute of Architects of the new and historic buildings. The existing structures would be renovated as a hotel and shops.

While city officials approved the plan, its unusual design, as Andrews put it, 'scared the pants' off the developers. 'They couldn't imagine that the thing wouldn't fall over.' He added: 'It just slowly died … some silly thing went there in its place. It wasn't a sensible use of the site or anything else.' But while the developers tried, they never got permission to demolish George Patterson House. It still stands as the Establishment Hotel.

MINERALS AND MINING MUSEUM
Glenn Murcutt
Broken Hill, New South Wales (AU), 1987

Few architects achieve prominence the way Glenn Murcutt has by being a sole practitioner sitting alone at a drawing board, without aid of staff or a computer. Murcutt's buildings – all in Australia – have been described as touching the Earth lightly. He has been called an eco-architect, but that misinterprets his aim, which has been to design each of his buildings in response to the minute particulars of a given place.

The Minerals and Mining Museum was for a wide street in Broken Hill, a remote outback boomtown that existed solely because the surrounding desert contained some of the world's largest deposits of silver, zinc and lead. Addressing both the harsh climate and local history, Murcutt adapted the local rammed-earth building technique for a thermal 'blanket', and added a giant, hovering steel parasol roof for shade, stretched over a shed-like building recalling the immense ridge of mine tailings that had built up over a century. He used strategically positioned wind scoops to pull air through the building for natural cooling. The zigzagging red-earth walls – which embraced a decommissioned pit-head frame that was visible beneath the metal roof – would draw visitors along a dark linear path, broken by slits admitting bright flashes of sunlight, evoking the visceral sensation of a descent 2,000 m (6,562 ft) long into the bleak, occasionally lit mineshaft.

Economical, terse, spare, the building summarized Murcutt's deliberative, unimposing ethos. Soon after he completed his drawings, Broken Hill City Council scuttled the plan, citing cost. Locals, however, said the real reason was to make a political attack on the independent councillors who had commissioned the museum.

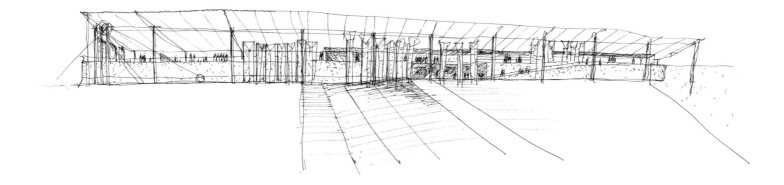

GROLLO TOWER
Harry Seidler
Melbourne, Victoria (AU), 1995

When the multimillionaire Melbourne property developer Bruno Grollo unveiled his plans for the world's tallest building – which would soar 0.5 km (1/3 mile) above the city's old docklands – few people were surprised that he had named the tower after himself. Still fewer were surprised that Harry Seidler, the tough, opinionated architect whose tall buildings practically owned Sydney's skyline, was the designer behind it. Seidler's design was big, brassy, colourful and eco-friendly. He described his 120-storey pyramid as 'essentially like three 40-storey buildings above each other, with sky lobbies serving as ground floors'. To support its enormous weight, diagonal exoskeletal bracing was attached to trapezoidal columns running the full height of the building. Windows with bronze-coloured photovoltaic-celled film offset the white columns and braces, while a tilted, solar energy-collecting apex crowned the structure, somehow transforming the silhouette into that of a praying mantis.

The building was massive, so overpoweringly bulky that it made the crowded skyline around it look like an emaciated backdrop to its hulking, domineering presence. The concept of a tall tower in 1995 was not popular, so the scheme did not progress. Two years later Grollo tried again and commissioned local Melbourne-based firm Denter Corker Marshall to design another tower on a different site in the Docklands. DCM's proposal was 137 storeys tall to Seidler's 120. By 1998, the State government supported the concept, however the idea was scrapped due to Grollo lacking sufficient funding. He was dragged into a failed tax fraud prosecution, then exported the DCM design to Dubai, where it was also not built.

60–64 CLARENDON STREET
Romberg & Boyd
Melbourne, Victoria
(AU), 1968

Robin Boyd achieved international fame as a critic as much as – perhaps more than – as an architect. An early champion of Kenzo Tange and the Japanese Metabolists, in a way he became a convert to Metabolism himself.

Boyd's residential towers for Clarendon Street in Southbank – one of his last works before his untimely death in 1971 – constituted an unabashed megastructure, reflecting what he considered the essence of Metabolism: 'a three-dimensional network of beam-buildings … proposed to levitate criss-cross, on service masts, leaving a continuous open cityscape below'. Following Tange's edict against furyu – 'meaningless prettiness' – Boyd banned all ornament in favour of a knock-out punch of

pure vertical and horizontal planes hovering in mid-air. In the first version, which was also called the Carnich Towers, Boyd devised, in Professor Philip Goad's apt description, 'trays of space … held aloft on angled concrete props that branch off trunk-like vertical slabs'. Later versions shifted these 'trays' onto single concrete masts, varying from seven to twenty-one storeys tall. In all Boyd's many iterations of the concept, the main living areas cantilevered from the cores, and large patios were carved from the spaces between floors.

Boyd's practice had been stuck in low gear for some years, and with these large-scale towers he was trying to break free of small residential projects. In his dramatic depiction, Boyd conceived an unobtainable future for Southbank. He may indeed have inadvertently eased the transformation of the factories and warehouses of east Melbourne into a concatenation of the 'visual idiocy' he so deplored. Ultimately, the concept failed to convince the developer, who sought out new architects; years later a bland tower was built on the site.

ROBIN BOYD'S SKETCH FOR
COMBINED PROJECT 60-64
CLARENDON ST. + CORNER SITE

STATE LIBRARY AND MUSEUM
Edmond and Corrigan
Melbourne, Victoria
(AU), 1985

Founded in 1854, the State Library Victoria – with its imposing neoclassical facade and luminous, domed main reading room – is Australia's oldest and busiest library and one of the first free public libraries in the world. By 1984 the facility was running out of space, and – hoping also to incorporate the Museum of Victoria – it invited nine architecture firms to submit designs that would allow it to retain its existing site and expand onto the site of the former Queen Victoria Hospital (which itself had needed to expand) next door. Of the proposals, easily the most intriguing came from provocateur Peter Corrigan and his firm (founded with his wife, Maggie Edmond) Edmond and Corrigan. Corrigan – who was also an industrious set designer, not to mention a noted student of architectural history – seemed to merge these passions with a design highlighted by a stepped pyramid containing new reading spaces and the library's stacks. The behemoth, set into a new public plaza, was cut at its centre with a long triangular window and topped by a pyramidal skylight, flooding light into a large atrium. The adjacent historic structure was reconfigured with oval reading rooms and a cone-enclosed spiral staircase.

Corrigan called his unique response a 'type of more magical proposition to engage in a more imaginative way'. In early 1986 the jury awarded the project to the Sydney-based firm Ancher Mortlock & Woolley. But that scheme went unrealized, too, when the government decided to sell the hospital site rather than develop it. The library chose to renovate its existing building, a project that took more than fifteen years to complete.

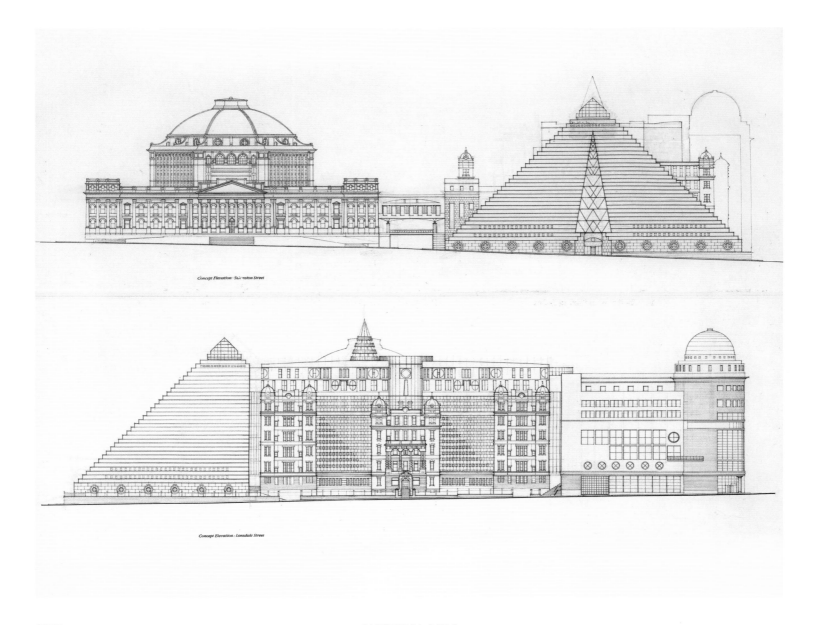

Concept Elevation · Swanston Street

Concept Elevation · Lonsdale Street

AUSTRALASIA

JAMES COOK MEMORIAL
Donald Miller
Gisborne (NZ), 1966

On 9 October 1769, when the English explorer James Cook piloted the ship Endeavour to the mouth of the Tūranganui River, where Gisborne, New Zealand, now stands, it became the first European vessel to land on the island since the Dutch seafarer Abel Tasman had reached its waters 127 years before. In 1966 the town of 30,000 inhabitants began to plan for the 200th anniversary of the sighting of land. The *Gisborne Photo News* remarked on 10 August 1966, 'Gisborne local bodies and citizens have been concerning themselves with the form of a memorial to mark the event. Obviously something must be done, and that something must be on a scale commensurate with the occasion.'

Enter Donald Miller, a 'local design consultant', who had worked on shopping centres, churches and garages, among other projects. A devotee of concrete steeples and inclined roofs, Miller proposed a tower 61 m (200 ft) high, surmounting Kaiti Hill, overlooking Cook's landing site. Radiating from the four corners of the base were eight halls, pairs of inverted Vs sleeved into one another. The tapering tower, which was bisected by a trio of unevenly spaced slabs, was capped by twin pylons projecting skywards. A lift would have taken visitors to the observation deck for commanding views.

Miller's soaring vision was too expensive, it seems. In 1969 a statue of Captain Cook was erected instead, but it was later discovered that this was an imposture – a bronze cast of a marble statue imported from Italy by Captain Cook Breweries in Auckland. It stood for fifty years, and was finally replaced in 2019.

89 DIXON STREET
Roger Walker
Wellington (NZ), 2004

As the global financial collapse of 2007 neared, gleeful investors kept on throwing out bold and outlandish proposals worldwide. A case in point is the flamboyant developer Terry Serepisos's NZ$60 million mixed-use building for Wellington, designed by the exuberantly eccentric postmodernist Roger Walker. (Walker's most famous project is Wellington's Park Mews, with its myriad pointed roofs, porthole windows and ever-shifting facade.)

Located on a stretch of Dixon Street that Serepisos called 'dark and dingy', the fourteen-storey speculative tower contained shops, offices and 100 apartments. With its canted glass walls, projecting fins, surreal turrets and cylindrical protrusions, the building looked like several structures jumbled together. Walker said he had in fact taken inspiration from the breadth of Wellington's eclectic houses. 'Many are assemblages of different forms and we're trying to do that with commercial buildings,' he told the *New Zealand Herald* in February 2004. 'This will be a real eye-catching but working building.' The interior was organized around a soaring atrium, and Serepisos predicted that the undertaking – which included the redevelopment of the historic Deka Building (which was eventually demolished in 2015) – would transform this section of Dixon Street 'into a really beautiful and people-friendly space'.

Eventually the familiar script of projects dashed by the crash played out. Meanwhile Serepisos, who bought Wellington's Phoenix football team in 2007, went on to star as the boss in the New Zealand production of 'The Apprentice' in 2010, and – after having accrued debts of more than NZ$200 million – was declared bankrupt by Wellington's High Court the following year.

Index

ATLAS OF NEVER BUILT ARCHITECTURE

PICTURE CREDITS

Phaidon Press Limited
2 Cooperage Yard
London E15 2OR

Phaidon Press Inc.
111 Broadway
New York, NY 10006

phaidon.com

First published 2024
© 2024 Phaidon Press Limited

ISBN 978 1 83866 653 8

A CIP catalogue record for this book is available from the British Library and the Library of Congress.

Commissioning Editor
Virginia McLeod

Executive Editor
Joe Pickard

Editorial Assistant
Phoebe Stephenson

Production Controller
Lily Rodgers

Design
SJG / Joost Grootens, Julie da Silva, Katla Taylor, Dimitri Jeannottat

Research Assistants
Eric Baldwin, Loup Calosci, Penelope Goldin, Clara Gross

Printed in China